Personal Finance For Dummies

Cheat Sheet

P9-CEV-177

20 Keys to Personal Financial Success

1. **Invest in yourself.** Invest in your education, your health, and in your relationships with family and friends. Having a lot of money isn't worth much if you don't have your health and people with whom to share your life.

2. **Take charge of your finances.** Procrastinating or postponing important financial decisions and plans is detrimental to your long-term financial health. Don't wait for a crisis or major life event to get your act together.

3. **Either manage your finances yourself or hire financial and tax advisors who charge a fee for their services and don't have conflicts of interest.** People who sell products and work on commission are salespeople, not advisors. Work in partnership with advisors. Never abdicate control.

4. **Never buy items on credit that depreciate.** Items that depreciate include cars, clothing, vacations, and so on. Use debt only to acquire financial assets that are likely to appreciate such as education, real estate, or a business.

5. **Use credit cards only for the convenience of making purchases without cash or check.** If you have a propensity to run up credit card debt, then get rid of your cards and use only cash, checks, and debit cards.

6. **Don't try to keep up with the Joneses by living beyond your means.** Many who engage in conspicuous consumption are borrowing against their future, and some end up in bankruptcy.

7. **Save and invest at least 5–10 percent of your income.** Preferably, you should invest in a tax-deferred retirement savings plan to reduce your taxes and to be financially independent in the future and/or have a secure retirement.

8. **Understand and utilize your employee benefits.**

9. **Never purchase a financial product on the basis of an advertisement or salesperson's solicitation.** Companies that conduct aggressive advertising or sell their products through salespeople and cold calling generally have the worst financial products and the highest commissions.

10. **Avoid financial products that carry high commissions and expenses.** These are disclosed in a prospectus for investments but are revealed only through your persistent questioning for insurance and other products. Most types of investments and insurance are available today without having to purchase them through a salesperson, which means without having to pay commission.

. . . For Dummies: #1 Computer Book Series for Beginners

Personal Finance For Dummies

Cheat Sheet

11. **Don't buy any financial product that you do not understand.** If it's too complex or the marketing pitch is not objective and informative, gather more information before making a decision.

12. **Invest the majority of your long-term money in ownership vehicles that have appreciation potential such as stocks, real estate, and your own business.**

13. **Avoid making emotionally-based financial decisions.** Investors who panicked and sold their stock holdings after the 1987 stock market crash, for example, missed a tremendous buying opportunity. Take your time making important financial decisions after a major life change such as divorce, job loss, or death in your family.

14. **Make investing decisions based upon your needs and the long-term fundamentals of what you are buying.** Ignore the predictive advice offered by financial "experts." Never make decisions based on news headlines. Nobody has a working crystal ball, and information about today's and yesterday's events is already reflected in investment prices now.

15. **Unless you have a terrific rent-control deal, own your home.** In the long run, owning is more cost-effective than renting. Don't buy until you can stay put for a number of years.

16. **Purchase broad insurance coverage to protect against financial catastrophes.** Eliminate insurance for small potential losses.

17. **Research before you buy products (financial and otherwise) or services, and/or make financial commitments.**

18. **If you're married or have a long-term partner, try to manage your finances in a comprehensive, joint fashion.** Set aside time periodically to discuss financial goals, issues, and concerns. Be accepting of your partner's "money personality."

19. **Read publications that have high quality standards and that aren't afraid to take a stand and recommend what is in your best interests.**

20. **Be patient.** Prioritize your financial goals and start working toward them. Focus on your accomplishments and learn from your mistakes.

For more information about IDG Books,
call 1-800-762-2974 or 415-312-0600

. . . For Dummies: #1 Computer Book Series for Beginners

Praise for Eric Tyson

"Eric Tyson is doing something important — namely, helping people at all income levels to take control of their financial futures. This book is a natural outgrowth of Tyson's vision that he has nurtured for years. Like Henry Ford, he wants to make something that was previously accessible only to the wealthy accessible to middle-income Americans. With Ford, it was automobiles; with Tyson, it is thoughtful financial planning. I am enthusiastic about his efforts and see this book as yet one more step down the path of turning his vision into practical reality."

> — James C. Collins, coauthor of *Beyond Leadership,* Lecturer in Business, Stanford Graduate School of Business

"This book provides easy-to-understand personal financial information and advice for those without great wealth or knowledge in this area. Practitioners like Eric Tyson, who care about the well being of middle-income people, are rare in today's society."

> — Joel Hyatt, founder, Hyatt Legal Services, one of the nation's largest general practice law firms providing personal legal services to families and individuals

"As small-business owners, we were busy and overwhelmed by all the insurance sales pitches we were getting from agents until we met Eric Tyson. He showed us how to get better coverage and save nearly $2,500 on our life and disability insurance policies alone. It was actually hard to believe — we thought there was some kind of catch!"

> — Nina Weisbord and Kyle Terres, retail picture-framing store owners, were interviewed on the KTVU Channel 2 television program "On the Money," a weekly S.F. Bay Area business program for consumers. Tom Vacar, business reporter for Channel 2, said "Tyson's advice was a godsend."

"Eric Tyson gives our readers personal finance information that they can act on — not simplistic advice. He writes for beginners as well as for those experienced in money matters, and is always on top of current issues, from mutual funds to dealing with personal debt to selecting the best insurance."

> — Katherine Rabin, Business Editor, *San Francisco Examiner*

"Eric Tyson provides a unique, much-needed service: giving financial advice without the conflict of interest inherent in selling products. The service was personal and tailored to my situation, and I became educated in the process of deciding what options to follow."

> — Lisa Baker, college administrator

"Eric Tyson has provided my family and my business with financial advice for the past five years, saving us thousands of dollars in taxes and insurance and significantly enhancing our investment returns without taking great risks. Equally important, he has helped my wife and me sort out our finances, develop a roadmap, and be in control. Eric conducts his business with integrity, clarity, and dedication."

— Dr. Peter Mazonson, M.D., health care consultant

"Using a well-conceived combination of theory and practice, Eric Tyson's personal finance course offers students a unique opportunity to learn how to effectively manage their own finances and plan for future financial security. His approach is refreshing, and his course has been immensely popular."

— Susan Wolf, Manager, Corporate Programs, University of California, Berkeley Extension

"*Personal Finance For Dummies* is well thought out, very easy to read, and provides useful information. Eric Tyson understands and speaks informatively about financial issues, a confusing and complex subject area."

— Bob Agnew, Program Director, KNBR radio

What graduates of Eric Tyson's personal finance course say

"When a friend literally dragged me to Eric Tyson's personal finance course at U.C. Berkeley, I was very skeptical. I told her to expect someone just plugging his own services. Eric proved me dead wrong. He had ethics, integrity, and a sense of humor. Far from seeking easy clients, he offered his students practical advice on how to manage their own financial affairs from start to finish. This is an essential life skill most of us never learn in school. Principled voices like Eric Tyson's — in classes and in books like this one — are badly needed."

— Matthew Soyster, creative director and marketing consultant

"One of the most practical classes I have ever taken. Eric is knowledgeable, realistic, and upbeat. He provided very substantial "take-it-with-you" material that you can use now."

— Annette F., manager

"The class was terrific! I only wish I had taken it 55 years ago!"

— Arthur H., retired

"Eric has a wonderful sense of humor that makes this dry subject quite palatable. He's a leader who helps the common man."

— Michael J., photographer

"I think the whole class was great. The real estate exercises were especially instructive. It highlighted many mistakes I had made and didn't realize and taught me what to watch out for."

— Julia R., Registered Nurse

"Everything was excellent! You make the most boring subjects interesting and always very amusing!"

— Nicholas D., consultant

"This class was down-to-earth, useful, and comprehensive. You provided a lot of everyday information, and your sense of humor is a big help in learning."

— Carrie M., technician

"Interesting, fun, and relevant. You're an excellent speaker."

— Nancy S., marketing assistant

"Well organized, easy to understand, friendly, and humorous! I like the way you answer people's questions — you're patient and help people feel less guilty and anxious about money."

— Rona R., teacher

"Eric's class was superb. I already have two friends ready to take it the next time it's offered!"

— Christine M., health care consultant

"Excellent presentation of an enormous amount of information. Eric understands the big picture and has a thorough understanding of the consequences of various financial moves."

— Lynnea K., realtor

"This was the best use of my time in a class with regard to my future (with the possible exception of the sex ed course I took in 7th grade!)."

— John P., engineer

What the press says about "... For Dummies" books

"More than a publishing phenomenon, 'Dummies' is a sign of the times."
— The *New York Times*

"... you won't go wrong buying them."
— Walter Mossberg, *Wall Street Journal,* on IDG's ... *For Dummies* books

"This is the best book ever written for a beginner."
— Clarence Peterson, *Chicago Tribune,* on *DOS For Dummies*

What readers say

"Contained all I needed to know as a novice — was easy reading and humorous."
— Wayne Toensmann, ParkerTown, New Jersey

"Wonderfully irreverent and very humorous."
— David C. Ritchart, Missoula, Montana

"Straightforward simple and understandable methods are used to present a complex subject to those without the background to have understood it any other way."
— Jim Goyette, Fresno, California

"It saved my sanity."
— D.M. King, Pensacola, Florida

"Understandability combined with humorous treatment of a dull subject."
— Wilton Webb, Golden, Colorado

™

References for the Rest of Us

COMPUTER BOOK SERIES FROM IDG

Are you intimidated and confused by computers? Do you find that traditional manuals are overloaded with technical details you'll never use? Do your friends and family always call you to fix simple problems on their PCs? Then the *". . . For Dummies"*™ computer book series from IDG is for you.

". . . For Dummies" books are written for those frustrated computer users who know they aren't really dumb but find that PC hardware, software, and indeed the unique vocabulary of computing make them feel helpless. *". . . For Dummies"* books use a lighthearted approach, a down-to-earth style, and even cartoons and humorous icons to diffuse computer novices' fears and build their confidence. Lighthearted but not lightweight, these books are a perfect survival guide to anyone forced to use a computer.

> *"I like my copy so much I told friends; now they bought copies."*
>
> **Irene C., Orwell, Ohio**

> *"Quick, concise, nontechnical, and humorous."*
>
> **Jay A., Elburn, IL**

> *"Thanks, I needed this book. Now I can sleep at night."*
>
> **Robin F., British Columbia, Canada**

Already, hundreds of thousands of satisfied readers agree. They have made *". . . For Dummies"* books the #1 introductory level computer book series and have written asking for more. So if you're looking for the most fun and easy way to learn about computers look to *". . . For Dummies"* books to give you a helping hand.

IDG BOOKS ®

PERSONAL FINANCE FOR DUMMIE$™

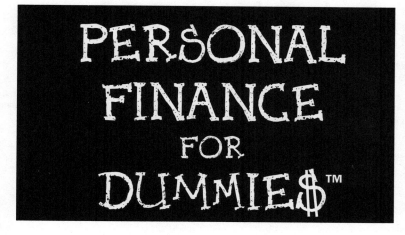

PERSONAL FINANCE FOR DUMMIE$™

by Eric Tyson

Foreword by Charles R. Schwab
Chairman and CEO
The Charles Schwab Corporation

IDG BOOKS

IDG Books Worldwide, Inc.
An International Data Group Company

San Mateo, California ◆ Indianapolis, Indiana ◆ Boston, Massachusetts

Personal Finance For Dummies

Published by
IDG Books Worldwide, Inc.
An International Data Group Company
155 Bovet Road, Suite 310
San Mateo, CA 94402

Library of Congress Catalog Card No.: 94-75042

ISBN: 1-56884-150-7

Printed in the United States of America

10 9 8 7 6 5 4 3 2

1D/QU/QY/ZU

Distributed in the United States by IDG Books Worldwide, Inc.

Distributed in Canada by Macmillan of Canada, a Division of Canada Publishing Corporation; by Computer and Technical Books in Miami, Florida, for South America and the Caribbean; by Longman Singapore in Singapore, Malaysia, Thailand, and Korea; by Toppan Co. Ltd. in Japan; by Asia Computerworld in Hong Kong; by Woodslane Pty. Ltd. in Australia and New Zealand; and by Transword Publishers Ltd. in the U.K. and Europe.

For general information on IDG Books in the U.S., including information on discounts and premiums, contact IDG Books at 800-762-2974 or 415-312-0650.

For information on where to purchase IDG Books outside the U.S., contact Christina Turner at 415-312-0633.

For information on translations, contact Marc Jeffrey Mikulich, Foreign Rights Manager, at IDG Books Worldwide; FAX NUMBER 415-358-1260.

For sales inquiries and special prices for bulk quantities, write to the address above or call IDG Books Worldwide at 415-312-0650.

 is a registered trademark of IDG Books Worldwide, Inc.

About the Author

Eric Tyson

Eric Tyson first became interested in money matters two decades ago. After his father was laid off during the 1973 recession and received some retirement money from Philco-Ford, Eric worked with his dad to make investing decisions with the money.

A couple of years later, Eric won his high school's Science Fair with a project on what influences the stock market. Dr. Martin Zweig, who provided some guidance, awarded Eric a one-year subscription to the *Zweig Forecast*, now a famous investment newsletter. Therefore, Eric's project must have led to Dr. Zweig's current fame. Of course, Eric's mom and dad share the credit with Martin for Eric's victory.

Despite being handicapped by a B.S. in Economics and Biology from Yale and an M.B.A. from Stanford, Eric remains a master at "keeping it simple."

After toiling away for a number of years as a management consultant to Fortune 500 financial-service firms, Eric finally figured out how to pursue his dream. He took his inside knowledge of the banking, investment, and insurance industries and committed himself to making personal financial management accessible to us all.

Today, Eric is a San Francisco-based personal financial counselor, writer, and lecturer. He has taught thousands of people from all income levels. So, he knows the financial concerns and questions of real folks just like you.

An accomplished freelance personal finance writer, Mr. Tyson writes a column for the Sunday *San Francisco Examiner,* the largest circulation paper in the S.F. Bay Area. He has been published and quoted in numerous local and national publications including the *New York Times, Forbes, Parenting, Business Week,* and Nolo Press's *Nolo News.*

His weekly radio program airs on the San Francisco radio station KNBR. Eric also teaches the Bay Area's most highly attended personal financial management course, at the University of California, Berkeley. So, if you needed an excuse to take a vacation in the Bay Area, now you have it!

IDG BOOKS About IDG Books Worldwide

Welcome to the world of IDG Books Worldwide.

IDG Books Worldwide, Inc., is a subsidiary of International Data Group, the world's largest publisher of business and computer-related information and the leading global provider of information services on information technology. IDG was founded over 25 years ago and now employs more than 5,700 people worldwide. IDG publishes over 195 publications in 62 countries (see listing below). Forty million people read one or more IDG publications each month.

Launched in 1990, IDG Books is today the fastest growing publisher of computer and business books in the United States. We are proud to have received 3 awards from the Computer Press Association in recognition of editorial excellence, and our best-selling *...For Dummies* series has over 7 million copies in print with translations in more than 20 languages. IDG Books, through a recent joint venture with IDG's Hi-Tech Beijing, became the first U.S. publisher to publish a computer book in The People's Republic of China. In record time, IDG Books has become the first choice for millions of readers around the world who want to learn how to better manage their businesses.

Our mission is simple: Every IDG book is designed to bring extra value and skill-building instruction to the reader. Our books are written by experts who understand and care about our readers. The knowledge base of our editorial staff comes from years of experience in publishing, education, and journalism — experience which we use to produce books for the 90's. In short, we care about books, so we attract the best people. We devote special attention to details such as audience, interior design, use of icons, and illustrations. And because we use an efficient process of authoring, editing, and desktop publishing our books electronically, we can spend more time ensuring superior content and spend less time on the technicalities of making books.

You can count on our commitment to deliver high quality books at competitive prices on topics customers want to read about. At IDG, we value quality, and we have been delivering quality for over 25 years. You'll find no better book on a subject than an IDG book.

John Kilcullen
President and CEO
IDG Books Worldwide, Inc.

IDG Books Worldwide, Inc. is a subsidiary of International Data Group. The officers are Patrick J. McGovern, Founder and Board Chairman; Walter Boyd, President. International Data Group's publications include: **ARGENTINA'S** Computerworld Argentina, Infoworld Argentina; **ASIA'S** Computerworld Hong Kong, PC World Hong Kong, Computerworld Southeast Asia, PC World Singapore, Computerworld Malaysia, PC World Malaysia; **AUSTRALIA'S** Computerworld Australia, Australian PC World, Australian Macworld, Network World, Mobile Business Australia, Reseller, IDG Sources; **AUSTRIA'S** Computerwelt Oesterreich, PC Test; **BRAZIL'S** Computerworld, Gamepro, Game Power, Mundo IBM, Mundo Unix, PC World, Super Game; **BELGIUM'S** Data News (CW) **BULGARIA'S** Computerworld Bulgaria, Ediworld, PC & Mac World Bulgaria, Network World Bulgaria; **CANADA'S** CIO Canada, Computerworld Canada, Graduate Computerworld, InfoCanada, Network World Canada; **CHILE'S** Computerworld Chile, Informatica; **COLOMBIA'S** Computerworld Colombia; **CZECH REPUBLIC'S** Computerworld, Elektronika, PC World; **DENMARK'S** CAD/CAM WORLD, Communications World, Computerworld Danmark, LOTUS World, Macintosh Produktkatalog, Macworld Danmark, PC World Danmark, PC World Produktguide, Windows World; **ECUADOR'S** PC World Ecuador; **EGYPT'S** Computerworld (CW) Middle East, PC World Middle East; **FINLAND'S** MikroPC, Tietoviikko, Tietoverkko; **FRANCE'S** Distributique, GOLDEN MAC, InfoPC, Languages & Systems, Le Guide du Monde Informatique, Le Monde Informatique, Telecoms & Reseaux; **GERMANY'S** Computerwoche, Computerwoche Focus, Computerwoche Extra, Computerwoche Karriere, Information Management, Macwelt, Netzwelt, PC Welt, PC Woche, Publish, Unit; **GREECE'S** Infoworld, PC Games; **HUNGARY'S** Computerworld SZT, PC World; **INDIA'S** Computers & Communications; **IRELAND'S** Computerscope; **ISRAEL'S** Computerworld Israel, PC World Israel; **ITALY'S** Computerworld Italia, Lotus Magazine, Macworld Italia, Networking Italia, PC Shopping Italy, PC World Italia; **JAPAN'S** Computerworld Today, Information Systems World, Macworld Japan, Nikkei Personal Computing, SunWorld Japan, Windows World; **KENYA'S** East African Computer News; **KOREA'S** Computerworld Korea, Macworld Korea, PC World Korea; **MEXICO'S** Compu Edicion, Compu Manufactura, Computacion/ Punto de Venta, Computerworld Mexico, MacWorld, Mundo Unix, PC World, Windows; **THE NETHERLANDS'** Computer! Totaal, Computable (CW), LAN Magazine, MacWorld, Totaal "Windows"; **NEW ZEALAND'S** Computer Listings, Computerworld New Zealand, New Zealand PC World; **NIGERIA'S** PC World Africa; **NORWAY'S** Computerworld Norge, C/World, Lotusworld Norge, Macworld Norge, Networld, PC World Ekspress, PC World Norge, PC World's Produktguide, Publish& Multimedia World, Student Data, Unix World, Windowsworld; IDG Direct Response; **PANAMA'S** PC World Panama; **PERU'S** Computerworld Peru, PC World; **PEOPLE'S REPUBLIC OF CHINA'S** China Computerworld, China Infoworld, PC World China, Electronics International, Electronic Product World, China Network World; IDG HIGH TECH BEIJING'S New Product World; IDG SHENZHEN'S Computer News Digest; **PHILIPPINES'** Computerworld Philippines, PC Digest (PCW); **POLAND'S** Computerworld Poland, PC World/Komputer; **PORTUGAL'S** Cerebro/PC World, Correio Informatico/ Computerworld, MacIn; **ROMANIA'S** Computerworld, PC World; **RUSSIA'S** Computerworld-Moscow, Mir - PC, Sety; **SLOVENIA'S** Monitor Magazine; **SOUTH AFRICA'S** Computer Mail (CIO),Computing S.A.,Network World S.A.; **SPAIN'S** Amiga World, Computerworld Espana, Communicaciones World, Macworld Espana, NeXTWORLD, Super Juegos Magazine (GamePro), PC World Espana, Publish, Sunworld; **SWEDEN'S** Attack, ComputerSweden, Corporate Computing, Lokala Natverk/LAN, Lotus World, MAC&PC, Macworld, Mikrodatorn, PC World, Publishing & Design (CAP), Datalngenjoren, Maxi Data,Windows World; **SWITZERLAND'S** Computerworld Schweiz, Macworld Schweiz, PC Katalog, PC & Workstation; **TAIWAN'S** Computerworld Taiwan, Global Computer Express, PC World Taiwan; **THAILAND'S** Thai Computerworld; **TURKEY'S** Computerworld Monitor, Macworld Turkiye, PC World Turkiye; **UKRAINE'S** Computerworld; **UNITED KINGDOM'S** Computing /Computerworld, Connexion/Network World, Lotus Magazine, Macworld, Open Computing/Sunworld; **UNITED STATES'** AmigaWorld, Cable in the Classroom, CD Review, CIO, Computerworld, Desktop Video World, DOS Resource Guide, Electronic Entertainment Magazine, Federal Computer Week, Federal Integrator, GamePro, IDG Books, Infoworld, Infoworld Direct, Laser Event, Macworld, Multimedia World, Network World, NeXTWORLD, PC Letter, PC World, PlayRight, Power PC World, Publish, SunWorld, SWATPro, Video Event; **VENEZUELA'S** Computerworld Venezuela,

Acknowledgements

There are many people I would like to thank personally (and some I will have to thank the next time I speak with them!), but space limitations preclude my ramblings.

First, I'd like to thank all of my financial counseling clients and students for having the self-confidence to learn more and ask for help. And for teaching me about their financial concerns and questions so that I could write in a way that helps more people.

Becoming self-employed was probably one of the hardest things I've ever done, and without the support and input of my good friends and mentors Peter Mazonson, Jim Collins, and my best friend and wife Judy Lee, I couldn't have accomplished what I have. I might not ever have mustered the insanity and desire for self-flagellation that comes with being a writer if it weren't for Judy turning me on (to writing).

I hold many people accountable for my perverse and maniacal interest in figuring out the financial services industry and money matters, but most of the blame falls on my loving parents, Charles and Paulina, who taught me most of what I know that's been of any use in the real world.

I'd also like to thank Maggie McCall, David Ish, Paul Kozak, Chris Treadway, Sally St. Lawrence, George Paolini, K.T. Rabin, Brenda Moore, Will Hearst III, Ray Brown, Susan Wolf, Rich Caramella, Jackie Lewis, Danny Schwager, Loralee Howard, Beth Greer, Steve Seligman, Bob Moon, Lisa Baker, Bob Agnew, Renn Vera, Maureen Taylor, Jerry Jacob, Robert Krum, and Duc Nguyen for believing in and supporting my writing and teaching.

Many thanks to all the people who provided insightful comments on this book including Mike van den Akker, Gretchen Morgenson, Craig Litman, Gerri Detweiler, Mark White, Alan Bush, Nancy Coolidge, and Chris Jensen.

And thanks to all the wonderful people at IDG books on the front line and behind the scenes, especially John Kilcullen, who had the vision, foresight, and courage to do this book, Janna Custer, Megg Bonar, Marian Bernstein, Tracy Barr, Diane Steele, Mary Bednarek, and David Solomon. I'd especially like to thank Corbin Collins, my project editor, and Judy Lee for other thoughtful suggestions and willingness to help me meet difficult deadlines.

(The publisher would like to give special thanks to Patrick J. McGovern, without whom this book would not have been possible.)

Credits

VP & Publisher
David Solomon

Managing Editor
Mary Bednarek

Acquisitions Editor
Janna Custer

Production Director
Beth Jenkins

Senior Editors
Sandra Blackthorn
Diane Graves Steele
Tracy L. Barr

Production Coordinator
Cindy L. Phipps

Associate Acquisitions Editor
Megg Bonar

Editorial Assistant
Darlene Cunningham

Associate Project Editor
Corbin Collins

Editors
Pam Mourouzis
Barbara L. Potter

Technical Reviewers
Alan Bush
Gerri Detweiler
Craig Litman
Gretchen Morgenson
Michael van den Akker
Mark White

Production Staff
Tony Augsburger
Valery Bourke
Chris Collins
Sherry Gomoll
Mary Breidenbach
Drew Moore
Kathie Schnorr
Gina Scott

Proofreader
Henry Lazarek

Indexer
Sharon Hilgenberg

Book Design
University Graphics

Cover Design
Kavish + Kavish

Contents at a Glance

Cartoons at a Glance

By Rich Tennant

page 398

page 7

page 339

page 49

page 379

page 331

Table of Contents

Foreword

*W*hen Eric Tyson asked me to write the foreword to this personal finance book, I gladly agreed. I've known Eric for several years and have read many of his fine articles on personal finance. We share a common interest in educating people about the importance of handling their money wisely.

This book is not a "get rich quick" or "doom and gloom" type of book. It's a no-nonsense, straightforward, easy-to-read personal finance book. I think it will point you in the right direction and help you sidestep many costly mistakes.

During more than three decades in the investments and securities business, I've had the opportunity to compare notes with thousands of successful investors. What continues to fascinate me is the tremendous diversity in approaches they've taken in building their wealth. What works for one person does not necessarily work for another. Some people defy conventional wisdom and still succeed. But everyone has to find his or her own method and comfort zone.

Clearly, there is no certain path to financial success. But common themes emerge that will greatly improve your chances of success. One is taking responsibility for your own affairs. With this book, you can easily learn enough about finances to start thinking for yourself. It's okay to get help, but ultimately, it's your money and your future.

Constructing your financial future is much like building a house. You keep at it, a brick at a time, a step at a time. The hard part isn't learning the intricacies of finance but acquiring self-knowledge and managing your emotions. Of course, it's also about thrift, patience, and persistence.

For most of us, especially those who haven't accumulated much in the way of assets, the first priority is spending less than we earn. Saving is not easily practiced. In our consumption-oriented society, setting aside money for the future requires extraordinary personal discipline. Most of the voices we hear are contending for our resources. *Spend* — that's the message we hear at every turn. But when you *save* money before frittering it away, the money can build into impressive amounts because of the power of compounding. Saving is the bedrock of personal finance. Start now. Stay with it. Enjoy the journey.

Charles R. Schwab
Chairman and CEO
The Charles Schwab Corporation
San Francisco, California
February 1994

Introduction

● ●

*W*elcome to *Personal Finance For Dummies*. For a number of years, I dreamed of writing a personal finance book that would be different. The book would clearly convey in plain English the most important concepts that you need to know in order to manage your personal finances. It would give specific answers to financial questions where it could, and where it couldn't give the answers, it would suggest the best resources to turn to.

More importantly, the book wouldn't break your toes if you dropped it on your foot. It wouldn't go on and on, delivering page after page of endless lists of pros and cons and every single service provider for each product. It would not be the financial version of *War and Peace*.

As fate would have it, my path crossed that of IDG Books (thankfully — I finally found computer books that made sense and that helped me with my problems). The . . . *For Dummies* approach is how I had conceived my personal finance book; I just didn't know it at the time!

Why You Need This Book

Many Americans are financially illiterate. If you are, it's probably not your fault. We simply don't teach how to manage personal finances in our schools — not in high school, not even in some of the best colleges and graduate schools. Most schools do not offer Personal Finance 101. They should. (Of course, if they *did,* I wouldn't be able to write fun and useful books like this — or maybe they would use this in the course!)

Personal finance and financial planning are not just about investing — far more than that is involved. Personal finance encompasses many areas besides investing, such as spending, taxes, saving, insurance, and planning for major goals like education, purchasing a home, and retirement. And because money is not an end in itself but part of your whole life, this book helps connect your financial goals and problems to the rest of your life.

Even if you understand the financial basics, thinking about your finances in a holistic way can be difficult. Sometimes you're too close to the situation to be objective. Like the organization of your desk or files (or *disorganization,* as the case may be), your finances may reflect the history of your life more than they reflect a comprehensive plan for your future.

You are a busy person. You want to know how to diagnose your situation quickly (and painlessly) and what you should do from there.

Unfortunately, after figuring out which financial strategies make sense for you, choosing specific financial products in the marketplace can be a nightmare. You have literally thousands of investment, insurance, and loan options to choose from. Talk about information overload!

You probably hear about most products through advertising that can be misleading if not downright false. Of course, some very ethical and useful firms advertise, but so do those that are more interested in converting your hard-earned income and savings into their profits. And they may not be here tomorrow when you need them.

You want to know the best places to go for your circumstances. That's why some people choose to hire someone like me as a financial counselor. As a result, *Personal Finance For Dummies* is filled with specific, tried-and-proven product recommendations.

There are some common financial problems and mistakes, and different people keep making those same mistakes *over and over*. This book, like a good friend, can whop you upside the head to keep you from falling into the same traps.

As a practicing financial planner, I know the dangers and pitfalls that await you when you seek "financial help." Every day, I see and hear about these problems. Although every profession has some bad apples, too many people calling themselves "financial planners" have conflicts of interest. And it's hard to find affordable help among the few planners who work on a conflict-free basis— because these planners usually manage money for the already rich and famous.

How to Use This Book

You can use this book in one of two ways:

- ✔ If you want to learn about a specific area, such as getting out of high-interest consumer debt or investing in mutual funds, you can flip to that section and get your answers quickly.

- ✔ If you want a crash course in personal finance, read it cover-to-cover. This will help to solidify major financial concepts and will get you thinking about your finances in a more comprehensive way.

Personal Finance For Dummies is basic enough for a novice to get his or her arms around the thorniest of financial issues. But advanced readers will be challenged as well to think about their finances in a new way and identify areas for improvement.

How This Book Is Organized

Personal Finance For Dummies is organized into five parts. The chapters within each part cover specific topic areas in detail. You can read each chapter and part without having to read what came before, which is useful if you have better things to do with your free time. It also makes for great reading anywhere you might be sitting for a length of time (perhaps the bathroom). You may be referred occasionally to somewhere else in the book for more detail on a particular subject.

Each part covers a major area of your personal finances. Here is a summary of what you'll find in each part:

Part I: Why You Can't Manage Your Finances

This part reveals common missing links in knowledge about personal finance and explains how to diagnose your current financial health. You may want to hire someone to help, so in this part you learn all you need to know to find the right person and avoid a lemon.

Part II: Saving More of What You Earn

Most people don't have gobs of extra cash. Therefore, this part shows you how to figure where all your dollars are going and how to reduce your spending. For example, I devote an entire chapter (Chapter 5) to solving the problem of getting out from under the burden of high-interest rate debt, such as on credit cards. I also provide specifics for reducing your tax burden, figuring out how much you should be saving if you want to retire someday, and getting the best deals on mortgages.

Part III: Investing What You Save

Earning and saving money is hard work. So you want to be careful when it comes to investing what you have worked so hard to save. Learning investment basics helps you to pick investments wisely. In this part, you learn how to hire a professional money manager through mutual funds (don't worry if you don't have much to invest). I recommend specific strategies and investments both inside and outside of tax-sheltered retirement accounts. I also discuss buying, selling, and investing in real estate (for all you Donald Trump wannabees).

Part IV: Protecting What You've Got

Even if you're *in* the insurance field, insurance can often be an amorphous topic (read: *boring*). Most people don't know which types of coverage they really need and which they should avoid. Odds are good that right now you're paying more than you should for insurance. This part tells you all you ever wanted to know (but were afraid to ask) about how to buy the right insurance at the best price.

Part V: The Part of Tens

I guess I'm still not sure whether IDG or David Letterman first came up with top ten lists. Although Dave's are just a *tad* funnier (partly because he has a team of professional joke writers), these lists of tens can help you out of a jam or keep you from getting in one. In this part, you can also find top products to dazzle and delight your friends.

Icons Used in This Book

This nerdy guy appears beside discussions that aren't critical if you just want to learn basic concepts and get answers to your financial questions. You can safely ignore these sections, but reading them will deepen and enhance your personal financial knowledge. This stuff can also come in handy if you're ever on *Jeopardy*.

This target flags strategy recommendations for making the most of your money (for example, *pay off your credit card with your lottery winnings*).

This highlights the best financial products in investment, insurance, and so on to implement strategy recommendations (for example, *call Ethical Bank & Trust for low-interest rate loans*).

This is a friendly reminder of information discussed elsewhere in the book or stuff you'll definitely want to remember.

This marks things to avoid and common mistakes people make in managing their finances.

This alerts you to scams and scoundrels that prey on the unsuspecting.

Where Do I Go from Here?

You may want to focus on certain sections of this book. I know you're just *champing at the bit* to read the whole thing, but you're busy and have better things to do with your free time. Maybe you have a specific question or issue that requires immediate assistance.

If so, check out the "Contents at a Glance" and the "Table of Contents" for a chapter-by-chapter rundown of what's in this book. You can also look up a specific topic in the Index and then flip to the page it lists. Or you can turn the page and start at the beginning: Chapter 1.

Part I

Why You Can't Manage Your Finances

"We were told to put our money into something that got more interest, so we started sticking it into this mason jar that's got some dang thing in it we bought from a traveling freak show."

In this part . . .

You learn the basic concepts that underlie sensible management of personal finances. You also find out why you didn't learn these concepts before now (and whom to blame). Here you'll undergo a (gentle) financial physical exam to diagnose your current economic health. You may discover that you need help, so I try to steer you toward those who can truly assist you and away from those who may have something else in mind.

Chapter 1

You're Not Dumb, but You May Be Financially Illiterate

*I*n the world of personal finance, we are not all created equal, of course. Some of us are born into poverty, a few into great wealth, and most of us somewhere in between. Because it's somewhat difficult (not to mention disrespectful) to put yourself up for adoption after you realize that your parents aren't wealthy, you need to figure out how to make do with what you've got. Money is one of those areas that reminds you that life isn't always fair.

Speaking of fairness, I would have preferred to go through life with a full head of hair. Yet, upon reflection, I see that good reasons exist for most things in life. For example, for me to have a full head of hair would require that I have different parents and grandparents, and I wouldn't like that. Plus I'd spend more on haircuts and shampoo.

As more and more industries open up to global competition, you need to be on your financial toes now more than ever. Job security is on the wane. Layoffs and retraining for new jobs are on the increase. Putting in 20 or 30 years for one company and retiring with the gold watch and lifetime pension are becoming as rare as never having computer problems.

Financial Illiteracy and Its Problems — You're Not Alone

What's most unfair is lack of education. Americans don't know how to manage our personal finances because in most cases we were never taught how to do so. Nearly 100 percent of our high schools and colleges offer not a single course to teach this vital skill.

Lucky people learn the financial keys to success at home or from knowledgeable friends. The rest of us never learn or learn the hard way: by making lots of costly mistakes. Lack of proficiency in personal financial management causes not only tremendous anxiety but also serious problems. Consider the following results of various studies:

- Last year, there were about one million personal bankruptcies in the United States. That's approximately one in every one hundred households.

- Studies show that less than 20 percent of baby boomers are saving adequately for retirement, and one-quarter of adults between the ages of 35 and 54 have not even *begun* to save for retirement.

- One in two marriages ends in divorce. Studies show that financial disagreement is one of the leading causes of marital discord.

- Less than 10 percent of American adults understand a 401(k) well enough to explain it to someone else. Fewer than one in four can explain what a municipal bond is.

- Nearly 80 percent of consumers do not know how the grace period on a credit card works. An even greater percentage don't understand that interest starts accumulating *immediately* for new purchases on credit cards with outstanding debts.

- People who have severe problems with credit and overspending can end up in poverty and, in some cases, get thrown in jail or become homeless.

The overall costs of personal finance illiteracy to our society are huge. The high rate of spending and low rate of saving in the United States lead to lower long-term economic growth and higher interest rates. Annually, billions of dollars are wasted through the purchase of inferior and inefficient financial products.

Uh-oh. Now I've *really* depressed you. You were feeling bad enough about your own financial situation, and here you are taking responsibility for the country's economic problems too!

TECHNICAL STUFF

Will this be on the test?

It's just common sense to urge that our schools teach the basics of personal finance. We should be teaching our children how to manage a household budget, about the importance of saving money for future goals, and about the consequences and dangers of overspending. Schools don't teach Personal Finance 101 for many reasons: They have a hard enough time teaching kids the basics — reading, writing, arithmetic, and not shooting your classmates.

Some people argue that it's the parents' job to teach their children the financial basics. However, this well-meant sentiment is what we rely on now, and it isn't working. In some families, financial illiteracy is passed on from generation to generation.

Some education professionals agree with me that schools should teach financial basics. But others say that they'd have to cut something vital out of the curriculum. To them, I echo what Paul Simon says in his song "Kodachrome": "When I think back to all the crap I learned in high school, it's a wonder I can think at all."

Giving due respect to schoolteachers who work hard and don't earn the pay or respect of other professions, I believe that personal finance should *at a minimum* replace the least important subject that schools are teaching now. (Of course, the hard part would be getting people to agree on the least important subject.)

We must recognize that education takes place in the home, on the streets, *and* in the schools. Therefore, schools must bear some responsibility for teaching this very important life skill.

If you think you're powerless to change the situation, you're mistaken. Many changes to our education system have started at the grass roots level. Lobby your schools!

Blame it on your parents

I was fortunate that my parents taught and instilled in me the importance of personal financial management. My folks never had the benefit of a college education. My dad took evening courses and learned the skills necessary on his own to become a mechanical engineer. Mom worked as a librarian and spent much of her career in what may be the hardest, lowest-paying job in the history of the world: raising children.

Mom and Dad taught me about earning, spending, and saving money. They had to know how to do these things because they were raising a family of three children on (usually) one income. They saw the importance of making the most of what you have and passing on those vital skills to the kids.

In many families, however, *money* is a taboo subject — parents don't level with their kids about the limitations, realities, and details of their budgets. In fact, it's not uncommon for kids to hear about money *only* when disagreements and financial crises bubble to the surface. Some studies have even shown that parents today are more likely to talk with their kids about sex than about financial matters!

On the other hand, some parents, with the best of intentions, do pass on their money-management habits. Some of those habits are, of course, *bad* habits. Now, I'm not saying that you shouldn't listen to your mother, but in personal finance, as in any other area, family advice can be problematic. Think about where these well-meaning parents learned about money management and consider whether they had the time, energy, or inclination to research choices before making their decisions.

In still other cases, Mom and Dad have the right approach, but the kids go to the other extreme out of rebellion. For example, if your parents spent money carefully and thoughtfully, you may tend to do the opposite, such as buying yourself a gift the moment any extra money comes your way.

You are what you read

Another cause of financial illiteracy is incorrect, biased, or just plain poor advice that you can get from reading. Surprisingly, written misinformation can come from popular and seemingly reliable information sources.

For example, one bestselling personal finance book (*Wealth Without Risk* by Charles Givens) advises you to "Buy disability insurance only if you are in poor health or accident prone." Putting aside the minor detail that *no* insurance company would issue you a disability policy *after* you fell into poor health, how do you know when you'll be accident prone? Because health-care problems and auto accidents cause many disabilities, unless you have a working crystal ball, you can't see them coming until it's too late!

I've also seen books describe how to send your kids to college "free." A few months before your child begins college, you're supposed to buy a four-bedroom property a few miles from campus. Then you're advised to rent out the house to students. The idea is that while your kid is completing a four-year degree, the value of your rental property will appreciate dramatically because of the shortage of off-campus housing in almost every college campus area.

You realize, I'm sure, that college students will give your property the same love and attention that people give to rental cars. And on the financial side, a modestly priced property would need to roughly *double in value over a four-year period* for this college-financing scheme to work. This is about as common as triplets (yes, it happens, but rarely).

Furthermore, this is a risky strategy that is more likely to cost you money than to pay for college. Many real estate markets *drop* in value over a four-year time period, and if that were to happen, it would only add to your college costs, not pay for them. Then factor in the hassles and expenses of locating, buying, and selling the property. Another minor detail: How many parents paying tuition bills also have piles of extra cash lying around available for the down payment on a property?

Scores of widely read financial publications offer predictive advice and commentary about investment markets. But such commentary is often wrong or misguided. For example, on October 16, 1987, just three days before the U.S. stock market crashed, here's what one of the most widely read daily business papers had to say about the prior day's stock market decline:

"But it is not yet time to pry the rubber seals out of the office windows . . . On September 22nd, it should be remembered, the market had a record 75-point one-day rise. The underlying economic news is mostly good, not bad."

Three days later, on Monday, October 19 (Black Monday), the market plunged 508 points — nearly 23 percent!

Also in 1987, one of the most widely read personal finance magazines ran a piece that purported to tell you where to get "safe, high yields." In addition to utility stocks and junk bonds, the article recommended real estate and oil and gas *limited partnerships* (LPs). LPs have *never* been safe investments. Over the past decade, most people who bought these problematic investment vehicles lost huge portions of their money.

Another popular business magazine ran an article in 1989 that touted life insurance as one of the best investments. The piece advocated the purchase of *cash-value insurance* — which contains an investment account as well as life insurance protection. The article went on to claim that life insurance should be the first consideration in most responsible investment programs. As you will learn in Parts III and IV of this book, this advice is *wrong, wrong, wrong* for the vast majority of working people who need life insurance. (They should buy *term insurance,* which is pure life insurance protection.) Any number of investment options would make a better first consideration than buying cash-value insurance, but you wouldn't have learned that from reading the article.

More reasons to tune out

More than a few writers and talk-show hosts claim to be personal finance experts but hardly address spending and debt issues. Instead, they focus almost exclusively on investments. For example, they may make you feel like an undisciplined failure for not saving through your employer's retirement savings program to reduce your taxes.

Saving through your employer's retirement program is all well and good, but the truth is, many people live paycheck-to-paycheck. So, unless you *first* learn how to reduce spending and get out from under high-cost consumer debt, the "experts" can talk until they're blue in the face about terrific investment strategies. If you don't have anything to invest in the first place, then they're not really helping you.

Information overload and its silver lining

Innovations in the finance field and advances in technology have resulted in a dramatic increase in the number of *financial products* and providers of those products. (A *financial product* is a catch-all term for any investment, insurance, or other vehicle that you put money into and that has some value.) Making informed financial decisions has become an overwhelming task, even for financially sophisticated people. For the financially illiterate, the task is over-whelming *and* confusing.

In the United States, thousands of mutual funds, banks, and insurers compete for your investment dollars with increasingly specialized and complex products — more than 80,000 banks and credit unions and 44,000 insurance companies, in fact. A few hundred different fund companies offer more than 4,000 individual mutual funds. Thousands of credit card options abound.

Under the circumstances, it's not surprising that flashy advertising campaigns can take you in. A catchy theme song or a cute comic strip can make all the difference when you're ready to buy. The good folks in the advertising industry know this and exploit it.

But now for the silver lining in this cloud of confusion: As more and more financial products and providers become directly available to you, you have a much larger world of opportunities in which to direct your own finances. Here are but three possibilities to whet your appetite (many more are forthcoming in this book):

- ✔ **Mutual funds** are widely available with no sales commissions.

- ✔ **Discount brokers** allow you to purchase securities at greatly reduced fees and without conflicts of interest. Avoiding salespeople enables you to save money on commissions. You also avoid a sales pitch that may lead to a decision not in your best interests.

- ✔ **Fee-based advisors** provide counsel for an explicit fee instead of from commissions hidden in products. Though still relatively small in number, fee-based advisors are increasing in strength as more commission-free financial products roll off the assembly line.

Beware media celebrities

One of the problems of the mass media is that the ethical and the less-than-ethical often get good coverage and publicity. Consider the example of Charles Givens. Givens got all sorts of free publicity by virtue of being quoted in the press and invited on a number of national programs such as the *Today* show, *Oprah*, *Donahue*, and *Larry King Live*.

Thousands of people went to seminars conducted by Givens, partly because of the credibility Givens built through media appearances. As has been well documented by now, many unsuspecting investors were sold commission-laden products, including risky iimited partnerships, through his organization.

For example, there is the widely-publicized case of Helen Giszczak, a 69-year-old retired secretary. She invested nearly two-thirds of her modest life savings in limited partnerships, which were described to her as "probably the most conservative investments we know of." Some of her limited partnerships ended up in bankruptcy and the others lost much of their value.

Helen Giszczak appeared on the *Donahue* show with John Allen, a former investment broker-turned-securities lawyer who helped her sue Givens's organization to get her money back. After a lengthy dialogue with Giszczak and Allen, Phil Donahue asked Helen how a smart person like her could get sucked in like that. She replied, "He was on your show and Oprah's. You gave him credibility. You gave him free advertising."

Helen has the right idea. Don't assume that because someone with something to sell is getting good press that he'll take care of you. He could just be good at press relations and self-promotion. Certainly, talk shows and the media at-large can and do provide useful information on a variety of topics, but be aware that sometimes bad eggs turn up on them.

Even you can get more from your dollars

Regardless of your income, you can make your dollars stretch farther if you learn good financial habits and avoid mistakes. In fact, the lower your income, the more important it is that you make the most of your income and savings (because you don't have the luxury of falling back on your next fat paycheck or dividends check to bail you out).

You probably want to work toward a number of big-ticket items or goals. The three most common major expenses are

- ✔ **Buying a home** and fulfilling the American Dream
- ✔ **Education** for you and/or your kids
- ✔ **Retirement** to allow you to cease full-time work

In addition, cars, vacations, entertainment, and hobbies are costly, too. How will you pay for all this? Don't you have to be rich?

No. You don't have to be rich, but you *do* have to be willing to take control of and plan your financial life.

What the heck is financial planning, and why do I need to do it?

Contrary to public perception, financial planning involves much more than just managing and investing money. Financial planning includes making all the pieces of your financial life fit together. It means lifting yourself out of financial illiteracy. Like planning a vacation, it means developing a plan to make the best use of your limited time and dollars.

Here are a few areas you may need to include in your plan:

- ✔ **Tracking and reducing spending.** If, like most people, you're not saving sufficiently to meet your future financial goals, then financial planning also involves tracking and reducing your spending.

- ✔ **Investing what you save.** Investing your savings is, of course, an important part of financial planning. So, too, are understanding and making the best use of tax incentives, tax breaks, and your employer's benefits.

- ✔ **Making informed real estate and insurance purchases.** You need to ensure that you invest in real estate intelligently, that you have the right types of insurance coverages, and that you're not paying more than necessary.

Financial planning has little to do with your gender, ethnicity, or marital status. We *all* need to do it. Some aspects of financial planning become more or less important at different points in your life, but for the most part, the principles remain the same for all of us.

Before you can take control, though, you first have to take stock. In medicine, doctors must examine before they can diagnose. The same holds true in personal finance. Where are you financially? To find out, turn to the next chapter to begin your financial physical exam. (Don't worry, I don't use rubber gloves or needles.)

Chapter 2

Measuring Your Financial Health

. . . .

In This Chapter

▶ The difference between bad debt and good debt

▶ Figuring if you have too much debt

▶ Assets, liabilities, and your (financial) net worth

▶ How much you really saved last year

▶ Investment and insurance check-ups

▶ Looking on the bright side

. . . .

A doctor takes your height, weight, pulse, and blood pressure and evaluates your cholesterol level and mental health.

How healthy are you? You may already know the bad news. The good news is that, like many medical problems, financial problems are best detected early (clean living doesn't hurt either). Most problems can be fixed over time and with changes in your behavior. That's what the rest of the book is all about.

This chapter puts you through a *financial physical* to help you detect problems with your current financial health.

Bad Debt versus Good Debt

Why do you borrow money? Usually, it's because you don't have enough to buy something you want or need — like a college education. If you want to buy a four-year college education, you could easily spend $50,000 – $100,000 or more. Not too many people have that kind of spare cash lying around. So, borrowing money to finance part of that cost enables you to buy the education.

How about a new car? A trip to your friendly local car dealer shows you that a new set of wheels will set you back $10,000 – $15,000 or more. Although more people have the money to pay for that than, say, the college education, what if you don't? Should you finance the car the way you'd finance the education?

NO! NO! NO!

There's a *big* difference between borrowing for something that represents a long-term investment and borrowing for consumption.

Take a vacation (no, I don't mean right now). If you spend, say, $1,500 on a vacation, the money is gone. Poof! You may have fond memories and even some Kodak moments, but you'll have no financial value to show for it. "But," you say, "vacations replenish my soul and they make me more productive when I return. In fact, the vacation more than pays for itself!"

Great. I'm not saying don't take a vacation. By all means, take one, two, three, or as many as you can afford yearly. But that's the point — *what can you afford.* If you have to borrow money to take the vacation in the form of an outstanding balance on your credit card for many months, then you *could not afford* the vacation you took. This is *bad debt.* Don't get me wrong — you're not a bad person for having the debt, but the debt is bad for your long-term financial health.

You'll be able to take many more vacations during your lifetime if you save the cash in advance to afford them. If you get into the habit of charging them and paying all that interest, you'll spend more of your future income paying back the debt and interest. So, you'll have *less* money available for vacations and all your other goals in life.

Borrowing to purchase a car or clothing is also detrimental to your long-term financial health. This is bad debt, too.

On the other hand, borrowing to pay for educational expenses can make sense. Education is generally a good long-term investment. It should increase your earning potential. This is *good debt.* Likewise, taking on a reasonable amount of debt to buy or start a business or to purchase real estate can be good debt. If properly and smartly managed, these should increase in value, too.

Lending rates and taxes

It's interesting to note that banks and other lenders charge more for bad debt — that is, credit cards, auto loans, and so on. Good debt, such as for real estate and business, is generally available at lower interest and is usually tax-deductible. So, bad debt is not only bad for your long-term financial health but is also *more expensive* than good debt.

Auto loans and leasing

Don't be fooled by the unusually low interest rates that car dealers offer. Sometimes they'll even offer 2 or 0 percent loans! They can only afford to do that by selling you the car at a higher price. In other words, you could have bought the car for less and taken a higher interest rate. Which is better? Neither! Don't buy a car on credit!

Leasing is also generally a bad financial move. Auto dealers know how people treat rental cars (that's basically what a lease is) and price a lease accordingly. Unless you're getting new cars for work every couple of years and taking tax deductions, leasing is even more expensive than buying a car on credit. Neither is a good option. Save and pay cash. Buy what you can afford.

How Much Bad Debt Is Too Much?

A useful but perhaps painful way to size up your debt load is to calculate how much debt you have relative to your annual income. Ignore, for now, good debt — the loans you may owe on real estate, a business, education, and so on. I'm focusing on bad debt, the higher-interest stuff used to buy items that depreciate in value.

For example, let's suppose that you earn $30,000 per year. Between your credit cards and an auto loan, you have $15,000 of debt. In this case, your debt represents 50 percent of your annual income.

$$\frac{\text{debt}}{\text{annual income}} = \text{debt danger ratio}$$

When your debt danger ratio starts to push beyond 25 percent to 33 percent of your income, that can spell trouble. High-interest debt on credit cards and auto loans is like cancer when it gets to those levels. As with cancer, the growth of the debt can snowball and get out of control unless something significant intervenes. If you have this much debt, turn to Chapter 5 to find out how to get out of debt.

Avoid borrowing money for consumption (bad debt) — for spending on things like cars, clothing, vacations, and so on that decrease in value and eventually become financially worthless. Borrow money only for investments (good debt) — for purchasing things that retain and hopefully increase in value over the long term, such as education, real estate, or your own business.

The financially healthy amount of bad debt is zero.

Your Financial Net Worth

Before we crunch any numbers here, before you experience the thrill of bigness or the agony of nothingness, let's get one thing perfectly clear. Sit down. Take a deep breath. And repeat after me:

"My financial net worth has absolutely, positively *no* relationship to my worth as a human being."

This is not a test. You don't have to compare your number with your neighbor's. It's not the scorecard of life. So, do we have an understanding? Good!

Your *net worth* is your financial assets minus your financial liabilities.

> Financial Assets – Financial Liabilities = Net Worth

Financial assets

What is a *financial asset,* you ask? A financial asset is worth real money or is something that you plan to convert to hard dollars that you can use to buy things now or in the future.

Financial assets generally include money in bank accounts, stocks, bonds, and mutual fund accounts (see Chapter 11 for more on mutual funds). Also included is money that you have in retirement accounts, including those with your employer. You should also include the value of a business you own and real estate, but usually not your personal residence.

You should include your home *only* if you expect to someday sell it (or take a *reverse mortgage*) in order to live off the money you now have tied up in it. If you plan on selling it, add that portion of the money from the sale that you expect to realize and use to your list of assets.

Assets also include your future expected social security benefits and pension payments if your employer has such a plan. These are usually quoted in dollars per month rather than in a lump sum value.

Personal property such as your car, clothing, stereo, wine glasses, and straight teeth do not count. I know adding these things to your assets makes your assets *look* larger, but you can't live off them unless you hock them at a pawn shop. (Technically, your smile might be able to charm others, so your teeth may actually have some value, but you shouldn't count on it.)

Financial liabilities

Your *financial liabilities* must be subtracted from your assets to arrive at your financial net worth.

Liabilities include loans and debts outstanding, like credit card and auto loan debts. Include money you've borrowed from family and friends (unless you're not gonna pay it back — I won't tell). Include mortgage debt on your home *only* if you include the value of your home in your assets, but include debt owed on other real estate no matter what.

Your net worth calculation

Ready? Table 2-1 provides a place for you to figure your financial assets. Go ahead and write in the spaces provided (unless you plan to lend this book to someone and you don't want to put your money situation on display — in that case, photocopying may be a good idea).

Important Note: We're ignoring your social security benefits here even though they are part of your assets. So if you don't have any assets, don't be totally depressed. Social security, as I discuss in Chapter 8, is something.

Table 2-1	Your Financial Assets: Savings and Investment Accounts (Including Retirement Accounts)
Account	**Value**
(Example: Bank savings account	$ 5,000)
_____	$ _____
_____	$ _____
_____	$ _____
_____	$ _____
_____	$ _____
_____	$ _____
Total =	$ _____
Benefits earned that pay a monthly retirement income:	
Employer's pensions	$ _____ / month
Total =	$ _____ / month
	x 240
Total =	$ _____
Grand Total Financial Assets =	$ _____

In Table 2-1, to convert benefits that will be paid to you monthly into a total dollar amount, let's assume that you will live 20 years in retirement. (Ah, think of two decades of lollygagging around — vacationing, harassing the kids, spoiling the grandkids, starting another career, maybe just living off the fat of the land.) As a shortcut, multiply the benefits that you'll collect monthly in retirement by 240 (12 months in a year times 20 years). Inflation may reduce the value of your employer's pension if it doesn't contain a cost-of-living increase each year in the same way that social security does. Don't sweat this now — we'll take care of this in the section on planning for retirement (Chapter 13). Add the result to the sum of the asset accounts total to arrive at your Grand Total Financial Assets.

Now comes the potentially depressing part — your debts and loans in Table 2-2:

Table 2-2	Your Financial Liabilities
Loan	*Balance*
(Example: Gouge 'Em Bank Credit Card	$ 4,000)
_____	$ _____
_____	$ _____
_____	$ _____
_____	$ _____
_____	$ _____
_____	$ _____
Total Financial Liabilities =	$ _____

Now, you can put it all together to figure your net worth in Table 2-3:

Table 2-3	Your Net Worth
Find	*Write It Here*
Grand Total Financial Assets (from Table 2-1)	$ _____
	—
Total Financial Liabilities (from Table 2-2)	$ _____
Net Worth =	$ _____

Your net worth is an important barometer of your financial health. It indicates your capacity to achieve major financial goals such as buying a home, retiring, and withstanding unexpected expenses or loss of income.

You'll need to crunch some more numbers in the chapters on financial independence and retirement planning to determine your status more precisely. In the meantime, find where you fit within the three following areas:

- ✔ **Your net worth is less than half your annual income or even negative.** You've got lots of company — in fact, you're in here with the majority of Americans. If you're in your twenties and just starting to work, this is less concerning. It's most important to get rid of your debts, the highest–interest ones first. Then you need to build a safety reserve equal to three to six months of living expenses. You should definitely learn more about getting out of debt, reducing your spending, and developing tax-wise ways to save and invest your future earnings.

- ✔ **Your net worth is more than half your annual income but less than a few years' annual income.** If you're less than 40, and especially if you own a home, consider yourself in good shape at this point. If you're older and still renting, you may be in okay shape, but you probably need to reduce your spending and accelerate your savings if you want to retire by your 60s and/or buy a home.

- ✔ **Your net worth is more than a few years' annual income.** You're probably on track to meet reasonable financial goals and may actually be ahead of the game, especially if you haven't reached your 40s yet.

Savings Analysis

In the past year, how much money have you actually saved? Most people don't know or have only a vague idea. The answer may sober, terrify, or pleasantly surprise you. In order to calculate your savings over the past year, you need to calculate your net worth as of today *and* as of one year ago.

The amount you actually saved over the past year is equal to the change in your net worth over the past year — in other words, your net worth today minus your net worth from one year ago. If you own your home, ignore this in the calculations. Do not include personal property such as car, computer, clothing, and so on with your assets.

It wouldn't be fair to count as savings the appreciation of investments you owned over the past year. Suppose that you bought 100 shares of a stock a year ago at $17/share and now it's at $34/share. Your investment increased in value during the past year by $1700. Although you would be the envy of your friends at the next party if you casually mentioned your investments, that $1700 is not really savings. Instead, it represents appreciation on your investments, so we must remove this appreciation from the calculations.

Note: Just so you know, I'm not unfairly penalizing you for your shrewd investments — you also get to add back the decline in value of your less–successful investments.

I know it's enough of a pain to find statements showing what your savings and investments were worth a year ago in order to do this exercise. But I'm willing to push my luck and ask you to do a *little* bit more in Table 2-4.

Table 2-4	Your Savings over the Past Year	
Today		*One Year Ago*
Step 1: Figuring your savings.		
Savings & investments $_____		Savings & investments $_____
– Loans & debts $_____		– Loans & debts $_____
= Net worth today $_____		= Net worth 1 year ago $_____
Step 2: Correcting for changes in value of investments you owned during the year.		
Net worth today	$_____	
– Net worth 1 year ago	$_____	
– Appreciation of investments	$_____	
+ Depreciation of investments	$_____	
= Savings rate	$_____	

If all this gives you a headache or if you get stuck or if you just hate crunching numbers, try the intuitive, seat-of-the-pants approach: Do you save a regular portion of your monthly income? You may save it in a separate savings account, retirement account, and so on.

How much do you save in a typical month? Get out your statements for accounts that you contribute to or save money in monthly. It doesn't matter if it's a retirement account that you can't access. Money is money. Savings is savings.

Note: If you're able to save, say, $200 per month for a few months but then spend it all on auto repairs, you're not saving. If you contributed $2000 to an *individual retirement account* (IRA), for example, but depleted money that you had from long ago (in other words, it wasn't saved during the year), you shouldn't count the $2,000 as savings.

As you'll see later, you very likely should be saving at least 8 – 10 percent of your annual income for longer-term financial goals such as retirement. If you're not, be sure to read Chapter 6 on how to reduce your spending so that you can increase your savings.

How Are You at Investing?

Regardless of how much or how little money you have invested in bank, mutual fund, or other types of accounts, you, of course, want your money invested in the wisest way possible. Recognizing that no one can predict the future, the following questions will help you size up how much time you need to spend with the sections on investing.

Note: The more *No* answers you reluctantly scribbled, the more you need to learn about investing, and the faster you should turn to Part III.

_____ Do you understand the investments you're currently in? (Y/N)

_____ Is the money that you would need to tap in the event of a short-term emergency in an investment where the principal does not fluctuate in value? (Y/N)

_____ Do you know what income-tax bracket you're in, and do you factor that into which investments you choose? (Y/N)

_____ For money outside of retirement accounts, do you understand how those investments produce income and gains and whether these types of investments make the most sense from the standpoint of taxes? (Y/N)

_____ Do you have your money in different, diversified investments that aren't dependent on one or a few securities or one type of investment (that is, bonds, stocks, U.S. investments, and so on)? (Y/N)

_____ Is the money that you will need for a major expenditure in the next few years invested conservatively rather than in riskier investments such as stocks, real estate, or pork bellies? (Y/N)

_____ Is the money that you have earmarked for longer-term purposes (more than five years) invested to keep you ahead of inflation (currently 3 percent)? (Y/N)

_____ Is the bulk of your long-term money invested inside retirement accounts, and have you exhausted possibilities for directing more money into these tax-sheltered accounts? (Y/N)

_____ Is your longer-term money, particularly what is inside of retirement accounts, invested more for growth rather than preservation of principal in the short-term? (Y/N)

_____   If you work with a financial advisor, is that person compensated in a way that eliminates potential conflicts of interest in the investments they recommend or when they recommend that you sell a current investment? (Y/N)

_____   Do you have a healthy portion of your money invested in commission-free, professionally managed mutual funds at the leading companies such as Fidelity or Vanguard, or through discount brokers like Charles Schwab or Jack White? (Y/N)

How's Your Insurance Savvy?

The last part of your financial physical covers *insurance*. If you're like most people, reviewing your insurance policies and coverages is about as fun as a root canal. Open wide!

_____   Did you recently (last year or two) shop around for the best price on your policies? (Y/N)

_____   Do you know if your insurance companies have good track records regarding paying claims and keeping their customers satisfied? (Y/N)

_____   On each policy that you have, do you understand the individual coverages and protection types and amounts? (Y/N)

_____   Does your current insurance protection make sense given your current financial situation (as opposed to when you bought the policies)? (Y/N)

_____   If you couldn't make it financially without your income, do you have adequate long-term disability insurance coverage? (Y/N)

_____   If you have family members who are dependent on your continued income, do you have adequate life insurance coverage to replace that income should you die? (Y/N)

_____   If you bought life insurance (and have a net worth of less than $2 million to $3 million), did you buy term insurance? (Y/N)

_____   Do you buy insurance through companies that sell direct to the public (bypassing agents) and through discount brokers and fee-for-service advisors? (Y/N)

_____ Do you carry enough liability insurance on your home, car (including umbrella/excess liability), and business to protect all your assets? (Y/N)

That wasn't so bad, was it? If you answered *No* more than once or twice, don't feel dumb — more than nine out of ten people make major mistakes when buying insurance (see Part IV for your salvation). If you answered *Yes* to all the preceding questions, you can spare yourself from reading Part IV, but bear in mind that most people need help in this area as much as they do in other areas of personal finance.

Look on the Bright Side

From the movie *Arthur* (1986)*:*

ARTHUR BACH (Dudley Moore):

(*Contemplating whether or not to accept his mom's $750 million.*) I don't know, Mom. Money has screwed me up my whole life. I've always been rich, and I've never been happy.

LINDA MAROLLA (Liza Minelli):

Well, I've always been poor, and I've usually been happy.

ARTHUR'S MOM:

(*Indignantly/insistently.*) I've always been rich, and I've always been happy!

Money can't buy happiness

It is tempting to think that if you could make only 10 or 20 percent more money, you'd be happier and less stressed out over your bills. You'd have more money to travel, eat out, and buy that new car you've been eyeing, right? Not so fast. A great deal of thoughtful research suggests that there is little relationship between money and happiness.

"Wealth is like health: Although its absence can breed misery, having it is no guarantee of happiness," summarizes Dr. David Myers, Professor of Psychology at Michigan's Hope College, in his book *The Pursuit of Happiness: Who Is Happy and Why*. (This guy has it good! Imagine studying happiness for a living.)

Despite cheap air travel, VCRs, compact discs, microwaves, computers, voice mail, and all the other stuff that's supposed to make our lives easier and more enjoyable, Americans aren't any happier than they were three decades ago.

According to research conducted by the National Opinion Research Center, 35 percent of Americans in 1957 said they were "very happy," whereas in 1991 *only 31 percent said the same.* These unexpected results occurred even though incomes more than doubled during that time (after adjusting for inflation).

As Dr. Myers observes in *The Pursuit of Happiness,* ". . . if anything, to judge by soaring rates of depression, the quintupling of the violent crime rate since 1960, the doubling of the divorce rate, and the tripling of the teen suicide rate, we're richer and less happy."

Being happy with what you have

Think of all that you have to be grateful for:

- Family and friends who love you and laugh at your jokes.
- People you can do things with.
- The freedom to catch a movie or play or read a good book.
- Some terrific talent or gift: a great singing voice, sense of humor, great smile, a full head of hair, or something else unique and wonderful.
- The fact that you live in a country not at war with any other country (at least at the time of this writing).
- The fact that you live in a country where a truck driver can balance a canoe vertically on his chin on the *Late Show with David Letterman.*

God bless America!

Statistically, you are spoiled rotten

Now let's talk about how financially spoiled you are. Yes, *you.*

Two-thirds of the people in the world have a standard of living that is a mere 20 percent of the U.S. average. Think about that. In other words, the average American is five times better off financially than two out of every three people in the world.

Be happy with what you have and content with the things that you can't change. Focus on what you have rather than on what you don't. Some financially wealthy people who have all the material goods they want are emotionally poor. Likewise, I know financially poor people who are very happy, contented, and emotionally wealthy.

Now, if you want, compare what you have in Table 2-5 to the average American (and remember how financially spoiled we Americans are).

Table 2-5 Average American Households and Their Stuff

Thing	% That Own It
Color TV	93
Motor vehicle	88
Motor vehicle 3 years old or less	21
Clothes washer	75
Clothes dryer	66
VCR	67
Video camera (Camcorder)	8
Dishwasher	44
Microwave	61
Home (not rented)	65
Investment real estate	21
Four or more years of college	22

Well, you survived your financial physical! Just like health exams, they can make you a little uncomfortable. The good news is that now you know more about your current financial health. The rest of this book can help you to improve on it.

Chapter 3
Hiring Financial "Help"

● ●

In This Chapter

▶ Learning from poor Alice's mishaps in Financial Planner Land

▶ Why it's hard to find good financial help

▶ Top ten conflicts of interest for financial planners

▶ Your financial management options

▶ Deciding whether you need help and how to find it if you need it

● ●

*N*ow that you've recovered from your financial physical, you may be considering hiring help to whip you back into shape. For some people, hiring help is a practical choice because they're busy or because they'd simply rather spend time on other things.

Hiring a financial planner or advisor to help you make and implement financial decisions *can* be money well spent. But if you pick a poor planner or someone who really isn't a financial planner but a salesperson in disguise, things could get worse instead of better. So, before we talk about the different types of help to hire, let's take a little journey with Alice to give you an idea of what you're up against.

Alice in Financial Planner Land

Alice is a client who landed on my doorstep a few years ago. She struck out the first four times she sought financial help. Her story illustrates many of the pitfalls in finding a good financial planner.

Alice's adventures

First, on the recommendation of her accountant, Alice called a *financial consultant,* who was a *certified financial planner* (CFP) at a well-known brokerage firm. Although Alice explained that she wanted a conservative investment, the broker sold her a mutual fund that primarily held aggressive growth (volatile) stocks.

After buying the fund and getting her first account statement a few days later, Alice noticed that there were several thousand dollars less in the fund than she had invested. The broker had told her he earned a 4 percent commission but assured her that she need not concern herself with it because the fund paid him and it wouldn't affect her investment.

After a little investigation, Alice discovered that the fund had, in fact, paid the broker out of her investment — a 6.5 percent commission. Thus, the broker had not only lied about where the commission dollars come from (all brokers' commissions come from the investors' money), but he had also understated the size of his commission.

Understandably steamed, Alice called the Securities and Exchange Commission (SEC), and after jumping through many hoops, the brokerage firm coughed up nearly $2,000 for the broker's lie about the commission amount.

Thinking that perhaps men and women simply don't communicate well, Alice next turned to a female planner on the recommendation of a friend, who said to Alice: "Women need to stick together." This financial planner promptly tried to sell Alice a limited partnership that, according to the planner, was *sure* to return upwards of 20 to 40 percent per year.

Alice took a gander at the *prospectus* — a delightfully long document written by attorneys — and saw in black-and-white on page 2 that the partnership paid the selling broker a 10 percent sales commission (which, she now knew, would be deducted from her investment).

Because Alice is a conscientious investor, she did more research in financial books and magazines and learned that limited partnerships are also handicapped by high, ongoing management fees. Alice did not return the dozen or so follow-up calls ("to see how you are doing") from her "sister" financial planner.

Wanting to learn more before her next attempt to get help, Alice enrolled in an "adult education class" at a local college. Alice, a student eager to learn, attended all the classes but soon felt only more confused. The world of finance and investments, her teacher said, is *very, very complicated.* Unless, of course, you're a financial expert.

The teacher, a "certified financial planner," was just such an expert. The teacher offered a free, one-hour consultation to all of his students at the end of his "course". During her free session, Alice was told that she should invest in an *annuity*. Investigation, however, revealed (you guessed it) high sales commissions and management fees.

Alice was also uncomfortable because planner number three hadn't inquired about other aspects of her situation and seemed intent on selling her an annuity. Annuities did not make sense for her, she later learned, because she was nearly retired and was in a very low tax bracket.

At this point, most people probably would have bought a good investment book or put their money in a mattress, but Alice really wanted to talk to someone about issues and ideas.

After listening to a financial planner on a radio call-in program, she had the planner mail his background materials to her. In addition to a certified financial-planning degree, *this* planner had a seemingly endless list of lofty-sounding credentials, such as RIA, BSCE, LLB, and MBA.

Quite wary of sales commissions by now, Alice also liked the sound of the planner's charging $350 for his time to help with her investment decisions and to discuss her other financial questions. Partway through their two-hour, $350 consultation, planner number four started to try to persuade Alice that what she really needed was to hire him as an ongoing manager of her money. For just $2,000 per year for the service (which didn't include commissions and management fees), he would trade her in and out of investments based on his economic analyses and expert prognostications.

That seemed like a lot of money to Alice, who had $150,000 to invest, and she did not like the thought of turning over her money to someone who could move it around among various investments without her approval. Besides, she was interested in learning more, and this "planner" kept telling her how complicated it is to make financial decisions. She therefore declined planner number four's sales pitch for managing her investments, whereupon he stormed out of her house complaining that she had wasted his time (for which he had his $350 check in hand!).

Lessons learned from Alice's trip to Financial Planner Land

Alice's case highlights two major problems that people often encounter when hiring financial help:

- ✔ **First, you absolutely, positively *must* do your homework before hiring any financial advisor.** Just look at Alice: Despite enthusiastic recommendations from her accountant and another from a friend, Alice ended up with bad advice.

- ✔ **Secondly, the financial planning and brokerage fields are mine fields for consumers.** The fundamental problem is the enormous conflict of interest that is created when "advisors" sell products that carry commissions for them to people they purport to advise.

For an analogy, imagine that you have flu symptoms. Would you be comfortable seeing a physician who didn't charge for office visits but made money only by selling you drugs? Maybe you don't *need* the drugs, or at least not so many expensive ones. Maybe what you really need is Mom's chicken soup and 16 hours of sleep.

What's truly amazing about Alice's situation is that none of the so-called financial "planners" ever bothered to ask about her insurance and debt situation. As it turns out, Alice not only lacked adequate homeowner's insurance, but she also had no health insurance!

Alice also had some relatively high-interest consumer debt that none of the "planners" ever asked about, probably because it would have diminished the funds that she would have available for investment. She could afford both the insurance and debt payoff. In short, no one had taken the time to explain to Alice the costs and risks of not getting her financial house in order.

Why It's Hard to Find Good Financial Help

Overwhelmed and undereducated consumers, especially those in low- and middle-income brackets, have few attractive options if they want to hire financial help. Over 90 percent of *financial planners* and *financial consultants* sell products and work on commission, which creates enormous conflicts of interest.

The few financial advisors who are *fee-only* make most of their fees from money-management services. (*Fee-only* or *fee-based* means that the advisors' fees are paid by their clients, not by companies whose products they recommend.) Thus, fee-based advisors tend to focus on those who have already accumulated significant wealth.

What business publications and others say about the financial planning industry and Certified Financial Planners (CFPs)

"When picking a financial planner, pay a lot of attention to how the planner is compensated. Pay no attention to CFPs earned at the College for Financial Planning."

— *Forbes,* "Meaningless Label"

"Financial planners often end up being wolves in sheep's clothing with hidden agendas to sell mutual funds, for example, or life insurance."

— *Consumer Reports,* "Financial Planners: What Are They Really Selling?"

"There is no effective regulation of planners, no accepted standard for admission into their ranks — a dog got into one trade group. All anyone need do is hang up a shingle and start planning."

— *The Wall Street Journal,* "Costly Counsel: The Best Financial Planner May Be No Planner At All"

"The financial planning business has two problems. One is credibility, and the other is conflict of interest. Both are spreading."

— *Fortune,* "The Financial Planning Jungle"

"Planners are supposed to pull apart your finances and suggest better ways of meeting your goals. They purport to be objective. But they can't be, if they work for brokerage firms or insurance companies or if their income depends on sales commissions from the products they sell."

— *Newsweek*

"Today's investors go up against a deadly combination of abusive securities industry practices and regulatory inattentiveness when investing their money."

— Consumer Federation of America

Regulatory problems

A pretty basic problem of oversight afflicts the financial planning field: There is minimal oversight *at best.* In many states, anyone can hang out a shingle and call him- or herself a financial planner. The U.S. Securities and Exchange Commission (SEC) polices only registered investment advisors (RIAs). Anyone who provides investment advice is required to register with the SEC as an RIA. To register, you must complete some forms and pay a fee. There are no courses, no midterms, and no exams.

Several studies have shown that because the SEC has so few investigators, and because there are so many RIAs, the typical RIA is investigated on the order of every 15 years or so. The SEC believes that the states should police the approximate 300,000 people who call themselves financial planners. But most states have done little to monitor planners and protect consumers.

What is a Certified Financial Planner (CFP)?

Nearly 100,000 planners have earned the certified financial planning (CFP) credential. This is basically a home-study course that isn't difficult to pass. It tests nothing of a planner's business ethics or how the planner earns income. The vast majority of people with CFPs work on commission and are employed by securities and insurance brokerage firms, so they're not really financial planners so much as salespeople with a "credential."

Financial planners *should* have to disclose in writing, prior to working with a client, how they are compensated. This would make it easier for consumers to know how the planner earns a living. And it would eliminate much of the need for more formal government regulation. Several bills introduced in state and federal government with this sort of common-sense provision have been squashed. Financial planners, insurance brokers, and others selling products with commissions that are hidden to the public have lobbied successfully (by spending and contributing money to politicians' campaigns) to kill such bills.

Letting the Big Bad Wolf guard the Three Little Pigs

The International Association of Financial Planners (IAFP) and the Institute of Certified Financial Planners (ICFP) are the two primary trade associations that represent most financial planners. Unfortunately, these organizations promote the status quo in the industry because they *are* the industry. Their membership and leadership are policing themselves. In fact, the associations lobby government to defeat legislation that opposes their membership's sales practices rather than advocate what's ethical or best for the public.

Financial planners' top 10 conflicts of interest

All professions have conflicts of interest. Some fields have more than others, and the financial planning field is one of those fields. Knowing where some of the land mines lie can certainly help. Here, then, are the most common reasons planners may not have 20/20 vision when they give you financial directions.

Selling products that pay commissions

If a financial planner isn't charging you a fee for his time, you can rest assured he is earning commissions on the products he'll try to sell you. To make it even harder for you to discern their agenda, you can't assume that planners who do charge fees for their time don't also earn commissions selling products. Compensation *double-dipping* seems to be more and more common.

Selling products that provide a commission tends to skew a planner's recommendations. Products that carry commissions mean you have less of your dollars working in the investments and insurance you buy. Because a commission is earned only when a product is sold, this inevitably makes such a product or service more attractive in the planner's eyes than any other option. For example, if the planner sells disability insurance that you could obtain through your employer at lower cost, he may overlook or criticize your employer's plan.

Pushing the highest-commission products

Another danger of trusting the recommendation of a commission-based planner is that she may steer you toward the products that have the biggest payback for her. These are among the *worst* for you because they siphon off even more of your money up front to pay the commission. They also tend to be among the costliest and riskiest financial products available.

Planners who are also commission-greedy may try to *churn* your investments. They'll encourage you to buy and sell, attributing the need to changes in the economy or the companies you've invested in. More trading means — big surprise — more commissions for the broker.

Taking a narrow view

Because of how they earn their money, many planners are biased in favor of certain strategies and products. As a result, they do not typically keep your overall financial needs in mind. For example, if you have a problem with accumulated credit card debts, some planners may never know (or care) because they're focused on selling you an investment product. Likewise, a planner who sells a lot of life insurance tends to develop recommendations that require its purchase.

Ignoring debts

Sometimes, your best investment is to pay off loans you have, be they credit card, auto, or even mortgage debts. But some financial planners don't recommend this strategy because paying down debts depletes your capital that you could invest. Paying off debts reduces your need to buy investments or turn your money over to the planner to manage.

Not recommending saving through your employer's retirement plan

One of your best financial options is to take advantage of saving through your employer's retirement savings plan. Although it's not as exciting as a stock portfolio, it's not as dull as watching paint dry — and it's tax-deductible. Planners are reluctant to recommend taking full advantage of this option because most people lack the monthly income to save and invest beyond their employer's plans.

Selling ongoing money-management services

Most financial planners who don't work on commission make their money by managing your money for an ongoing fee percentage (typically 1 - 3 percent). Although this removes the incentive to churn your account to run up more commissions, it's a service that you're unlikely to need or benefit from.

The latest rage, particularly among brokerage firms, is the *wrap account* (a.k.a. the *managed account*). Wrap accounts can cost you upwards of 3 percent of your assets. As you learn in Chapters 10 and 11, you can hire *professional money managers* for 1 percent per year or less.

Not recommending real estate

Like paying off debts, investing in real estate takes away from your interest and ability to invest elsewhere. Most planners won't help with these choices. They may even tell you tales of real estate investing disasters to give you cold feet. Sure, the value of real estate can go down just like any other investment. Yet owning a home makes good financial sense in the long haul for most people.

Selling legal services

More and more planners are getting into the business of drawing up *trusts* for their clients to increase their fee income. Trusts may be right for you. On the other hand, you may not need such devices. And even if you do, you can do it yourself at far lower cost if your situation is not complicated.

If you want advice on whether you need these legal documents, do a little investigating: Check out a book on the subject from the library or consult an advisor who won't actually perform the work. Legal matters are complex enough that the competence of someone who doesn't specialize in it full-time should be carefully scrutinized.

Scaring your pants off (with your wallet still in the pocket)

Some planners put together nifty computer-generated projections showing you that you will need $2 million by the time you retire to maintain your standard of living. Or that tuition will cost $200,000 by the time your two-year-old is ready for college. Look: Don't worry, be happy. Besides, your child may join the circus and never need a $200,000 college fund after all. (See Chapter 14 for more.)

Waking up a client to the realities of his or her financial situation is an important and difficult job of a good financial planner. Some unscrupulous planners take this task to an extreme and deliberately scare you into buying what they're selling. They paint a bleak picture and imply that you can fix your problems only if you do what they say. Don't let them scare you — you've got *Personal Finance For Dummies* on your side!

Creating dependency

As with any consultant, another conflict a planner has to work with is to make things seem so complicated that you can't possibly manage your finances or make major financial decisions without the planner. If an advisor is reluctant to recommend how you can learn more about a topic or implies that your time would be better spent learning yoga, then you've probably found a *self-perpetuating consultant.*

Financial Management Options

Everyone has three basic choices about how to approach managing money: You can do nothing, you can do it yourself, or you can hire someone to help you.

Doing nothing

The *do-nothing* approach has a large following (and you thought you were the only one!). People who fall into this category may be leading terribly exciting, interesting lives and are therefore too busy to attend to something so mundane. Or they may be leading terribly mundane lives but are too busy fantasizing about more appealing ways to spend their time. For both types, everything from a major UFO sighting to taking out the garbage captures the imagination more than thinking about personal finances.

But the dangers of doing nothing are many. Problem areas, left to themselves, get worse. Gaps in saving for retirement or ignoring your buildup of debt eventually come back to haunt you. Not carrying adequate insurance becomes harmful when an accident occurs. In the last few years, fires and earthquakes in California, flooding in the Midwest, and hurricanes in the South and East all show how precariously we live in paradise.

Even if the do-nothing approach has been yours for all your life, you are now officially promoted out of it! (You bought this book to learn more about personal finance and to make changes in your money matters, right?)

Doing it yourself

The do-it-yourselfers not only learn enough about financial topics to make informed decisions, but they actually implement some or all the changes on their own. Doing anything yourself, of course, requires investment of your precious free time to learn the basic concepts and keep up with changes. For some, this is a challenge and an absorbing interest. Others learn just enough to evaluate the judgment, knowledge, and ability of someone they hire.

Hiring help

Realizing that you need to hire someone to help you make and implement financial decisions can be a valuable insight. Even if you have a modest income or assets, spending a few hours of your time and a few hundred dollars to hire a professional can be a good investment.

Financial planners/advisors make money in one of three ways: They can earn commissions based on sales of financial products, they can charge a percentage of your assets that they are investing, or they can charge by the hour. As you learned from Alice's journey into this area, hiring assistance can be anything but a tea party.

Commission-based planners

Commission-based planners aren't really planners, advisors, or counselors — they are salespeople. Many of the *stock brokers* and *insurance brokers* of the 1970s and 1980s are now called *financial consultants* or *financial service representatives* in order to glamorize the profession and obscure how they are compensated. I've even seen insurance salespeople call themselves *estate planning specialists*.

That's like a Honda dealer calling himself a *transportation consultant*. A Honda dealer is a Honda salesperson who makes a living selling Hondas, period. He's definitely not going to tell you nice things about Ford, Chrysler, or Toyota cars — unless, of course, he happens to sell those, too. He also has no interest in educating you about public transit possibilities.

Salespeople and brokers masquerading as planners have an enormous bias to push certain products, particularly those that pay generous commissions. This arrangement tends to skew their recommendations towards certain strategies (such as selling investment or life insurance products) and causes them to ignore or downplay other aspects of your finances. For example, they'll gladly sell you a Gee-whiz-bang investment product rather than convince you to pay off your high-cost debts or to save and invest instead through your employer's retirement plan to reduce your taxes.

Table 3-1 gives you an idea of the commissions that a financial planner/salesperson can earn through selling financial products.

Table 3-1	Financial Product Commissions
Product	*Commission*
Life Insurance ($250,000, age 45):	
Term Life	$140 to $565
Universal/Whole Life	$1020 to $2580
Disability Insurance:	
($4,000/month benefit, age 35)	$345 to $1200
Investments ($20,000):	
Mutual Funds	$800 to $1700
Limited Partnerships	$1400 to $2000
Annuities	$1000 to $1800

Fee-based planners

A better choice than a commission-based planner is a financial planner who charges a percentage of the assets that are being managed or invested. This compensation system removes the incentives to sell you products with high commissions and churn your investments through lots of transactions to generate more of those commissions.

Although it is an improvement over product-pushers working on commission, the fee-based system has flaws, too. First off, suppose that you're trying to decide to invest in stocks, bonds, or real estate. A planner who earns her living managing your money won't recommend real estate because that would deplete your investment capital. The planner also won't recommend paying down your mortgage for the same reason — she'll claim that you can earn more investing your money (with her help, of course) than it will cost you to borrow.

Fee-based planners are also only interested in managing money for those who have already accumulated a fair amount of it — which rules out most people. According to the Boston Company, an economics research firm, the median household (*median* means half have more, half have less) headed by a person aged 35–49 has just $6000 in financial assets.

If what you really do need is someone to manage your money (you lucky dog), mutual funds or private money managers (discussed in Chapter 11) are what you should look for, not a financial planner who also tries to manage money. Increasing numbers of fee-based planners can help you with selecting money managers, particularly mutual funds.

Hourly-based planners

Your best bet for professional help with your personal finances is a planner who charges for his time. Because he doesn't sell any financial products, his objectivity is maintained. He doesn't perform money management, so he can help you make comprehensive financial decisions dealing with real estate, loans, retirement planning, and selecting good mutual funds.

The primary risk in selecting an hourly-based planner is incompetence. You can address this by checking references and learning enough yourself to discern between good and bad financial advice. Another risk comes from not clearly defining the work to be done and the approximate total cost before you begin. You should also review some of the other key questions outlined in Chapter 20 ("Ten Questions to Ask Financial Planners Before You Hire").

A drawback of an entirely different kind occurs when you don't follow through on the recommendations of your advisor. You paid for her work but didn't act on it, so you didn't capture its value. This situation is why your hourly-based planner should make provisions to ensure that she is there to help with implementation. After she presents her recommendations, you need time to digest them and will probably have more ideas and questions later.

You might also need some hand-holding to help get the job done. If part of the reason that you hired the planner in the first place was because you're too busy or not interested enough to make changes to your financial situation, then you should look for this support in the services you buy from the planner.

If you just need someone as a sounding board for ideas or to recommend a specific strategy or product, you can hire an hourly-based planner for one or two sessions of advice. You save money doing the legwork and implementation on your own. Just make sure the planner is willing to give you specific enough advice that you can implement on your own.

Who Should Hire a Financial Planner, and Who Shouldn't?

Not everyone reading this book should hire a financial planner. By the same token, even if you are financially savvy, don't be too quick to write off the value of hiring help.

Good reasons to hire a financial planner can be the same reasons for hiring someone to clean your home or do your taxes. If you're too busy or don't enjoy doing it, that's a good reason to hire help. If you're uncomfortable making decisions on your own, using a planner for a second opinion makes good sense. And if you shy away from numbers and bristle at the thought of long division, a good planner can help you.

Ten ways a good financial planner can help you

The following gives you a run-down of some of the *good* things a financial planner can do for you.

Identifying problems and goals

Many otherwise intelligent people have a hard time being objective about their financial problems. They may ignore their debts or have unrealistic goals and expectations given their financial situations and behavior. And many are so busy with other aspects of their lives that they never take the time to think about what their financial goals are.

Surprisingly, some people are in better financial position than they thought in relation to their goals. Good counselors really enjoy this aspect of their jobs — good news is easier and much more fun to deliver.

Identifying strategies to reach your financial goals

If your mind is like mine, it's a jumble of various plans, ideas, and concerns, along with a cobweb or two. A good counselor can help you sort out and straighten your thoughts and can propose alternative strategies for you to accomplish your financial goals.

Setting priorities

You could be doing dozens of things to improve your financial situation, but making a few key changes would probably have the greatest value. Equally important is to identify those changes that fit with your overall situation and that won't keep you awake at night fretting about them.

Saving research time and hassle

Even if you know what major financial decisions are most important to you, doing the research can be a major drag. A good planner researches to match your needs to the best available strategies and products. So much lousy information is out there on various financial topics that you can easily get lost, discouraged, sidetracked, or swindled. A good advisor can keep you from making a bad decision based on poor or insufficient information. Your free time is precious. (Does your car license plate holder say *I'D RATHER BE . . .*? If so, you're a great candidate to hire a financial planner — unless, of course, it says *I'D RATHER BE MANAGING MY OWN MONEY.*)

Purchasing commission-free financial products

If you hire a planner who charges for her time, you can easily save hundreds or thousands of dollars by avoiding the cost of commissions in the financial products you buy. This commission-free situation is especially valuable when it comes to purchasing investments and insurance.

Avoiding lousy financial products and strategies

A good counselor can keep you from doing something really dumb — particularly if a commission-based salesperson is giving you the *hard sell.* A conflict-free planner can recommend what is in your best interests.

Being an objective voice for major decisions

Deciding when to retire, how much to spend on a home purchase, and where to invest your money are big decisions. Getting swept up in the emotional up-heaval of these issues can cloud your perspective and objectivity. A competent and sensitive advisor can cut through this cloud to raise issues and provide sound counsel.

Helping you to just do it

It's not enough to decide what you need to do — you have to actually do it, of course. And although you can use a planner for advice and make all the changes on your own, a good counselor makes sure you follow through. After all, part of the reason you hired the counselor in the first place may be that you're too busy or disinterested to manage your finances. If the counselor merely produces a nice-looking report and disappears, all you're left with is something to lean against a book end.

Mediating

If you have a spouse or partner, financial decisions can produce real fireworks, and some financial decisions involve the extended family. Although a counselor can't be a therapist, a good one can be sensitive to the different needs and concerns of each party and can try to find middle ground on the financial issues you're grappling with.

Making you money and allowing you peace of mind

The whole point of financial planning is to make the most of your finances and help you plan for and attain your financial and personal goals. In the process, the planner should show you how to enhance your investment returns; reduce your spending, taxes, and insurance costs; increase your savings; improve your catastrophic insurance coverage; and achieve your financial independence goals. And last but not least: Putting your financial house in order should give you some peace of mind — like that clean, light-headed feeling after a haircut.

Not for everyone

Although many people can benefit from the advice of a knowledgeable and ethical financial planner, you should consider your personality type before you decide to hire help. My experience has been that some people (believe it or not) enjoy the research and number crunching. If this is you, or if you're not really comfortable taking advice, you'd be better off doing your own homework and calling your own shots.

Likewise, if you have a specific tax or legal matter, you're better off hiring a professional who specializes in that field.

How to Find a Good Financial Planner

As you may suspect by now, locating a good financial planner can be like finding a needle in a haystack. Two methods that can serve as good starting points are personal referral and associations.

Personal referral

One of the best ways to find a good financial planner is to get a personal referral from a satisfied customer who is someone you trust. A referral from an accountant or an attorney whose judgment you've tested can help as well.

Never *ever* take a recommendation from anyone as gospel. I don't care *who* is making the referral — even if it's your mother. You must do your homework. Ask the planner the ten questions in Chapter 20. I've seen people get into real trouble because of blindly accepting someone else's recommendation. Remember: The person making the recommendation is (probably) not a personal finance expert. He or she could be just as bewildered as you are.

It may happen that you get referred to a planner or broker who returns the favor by sending business to the tax, legal, or real estate person who referred you. On more than a few occasions, professionals in other fields have made it clear that they would refer business to me if I referred business to them. Good professionals don't do this. You should hire professionals who make referrals to others based on their competence and ethics.

Associations

Associations of financial planners are more than happy to refer you to planners in your area. But, as we discussed earlier in this chapter, the major trade associations are comprised of planners who sell products and work on commission.

Two better — but in no way ideal — places to start include the following:

✔ **The National Association of Personal Financial Advisors**
   1130 Lake Cook Road
   Buffalo Grove, IL 60089

   The NAPFA is comprised of fee-only planners. Its members are not supposed to earn commissions from products they sell, so at least you don't have to worry about the planners selling products. However, most of the planners in this association earn their living by providing money-management services and charging a fee that is a percentage of assets under management.

✔ **The American Institute of Certified Public Accountants**
   1211 Avenue of the Americas
   New York, NY 10036

   The AICPA is the professional association of CPAs that can provide names of members who have completed the Institute's Personal Financial Specialist program. Many, but certainly not all, of the CPAs provide financial advice on a fee basis. Competent CPAs have the advantage of understanding the tax consequences of different choices, which are important components of any financial plan. On the other hand, it is hard for a professional to keep current in two broad fields.

How financial planners get clients

You have no interest in becoming a financial planner (presumably), so why should you waste your time reading about how planners cultivate clients? Simple: The method by which you hear of a planner may not be the one that steers you in the direction of the best planners and may provide clues to a planner's integrity and way of doing business.

Cold calling

You've just come home after a hard day. No sooner has your posterior hit the chair to settle in for the night, then the phone rings. It's Joe the financial planner, and he wants to help you achieve all your financial dreams. Cold calling is the most inefficient way a planner can get new clients. It's also intrusive and is typically used by aggressive salespeople who work on commission.

Keep a log beside your telephone. Record the date, time, name of organization, and name of caller every time you receive a cold call. Tell cold callers to never call you again. Then, if they do call you again, you can sue them for $500 in small claims court! (This goes for "phantom faxes" as well.)

Here's an idea that's more fun: Tell Joe you just inherited a lot of money and ask him to hold on a moment while you get the account statement. Listen to him drool and then, keeping the receiver off the hook, go fix yourself dinner.

"Adult education classes"

These classes are often given at local universities. Here's what often happens: You probably pay a reasonable fee for the course. You go to class giddy at the prospect of learning about how to manage your finances. And then the instructor ends up being a broker or financial planner hungry for clients. He confuses more than he conveys. He's short on specifics. But he'll be more than happy to show you the way if you contact (and hire) him outside of class.

Instructors for these courses are paid to teach. It should be noted, however, that part of the problem is that some universities take advantage of the fact that they know the "teachers" want to solicit business. So, the universities set the pay at a very low level, thinking, erroneously, that they'll save money. Of course, they don't save money because fewer students are attracted to such courses. Ethical instructors who are there to teach do *not* solicit clients and may actively discourage students from hiring them. Smart universities pay their instructors well and weed out the instructors who are more interested in building up their client base than teaching.

Free seminars

This is a case of "you get what you pay for." Because you don't pay a fee to attend "free seminars," and the "teachers" don't get paid either, these events tend to be clear-cut sales pitches.

Note: Be *especially* wary of seminars targeted at selected groups, such as special seminars for people who have received retirement plan distributions or those touting "Financial Planning for Women." Financial planning is not specific to gender, ethnicity, or marital status.

Don't assume that the financial planner giving a presentation at your employer's office is the right planner for you, either. It's surprising how little investigation some corporate benefits departments conduct on the people they let in. In most cases, planners are accepted simply because they don't charge. One organization I'm familiar with gave preference to planners who, in addition to doing free presentations, also brought in a catered lunch!

Word-of-mouth

This is how the best financial planners continue to build their practices. Satisfied customers are any professional's best and least costly marketers.

Part II

Saving More of What You Earn

ORIGINAL
VAN-GOGH-OF-THE-MONTH
CLUB

"I just don't know where the money's going."

In this part . . .

1 show you how to identify where your hard-earned dollars are going. I pinpoint numerous ways to make those dollars go toward helping you build up your savings instead of going to wasteful spending. What? You're buried in debt with little to show for it? Well, it's never too late to start digging out. Here you'll find out how to reduce your taxes and credit-card burden, how to save for retirement, how to get the best deal on a mortgage, and lots more.

Chapter 4
Where Did It Go?

. . . .

In This Chapter
▶ Who me? Overspend?
▶ Ten leading causes of overspending
▶ Analyzing your spending
▶ Ten consequences of overspending
▶ The road to salvation

. . . .

> *Pay yourself first.*
>
> *It's not what you make, it's what you keep.*
>
> *A penny saved is a penny earned.*

These little sayings are good, common-sense advice.

Most people have a hard time living within their financial means. Living within your means requires more than spending less than you earn. Some folks have a hard time even doing that — they spend more than they make. The result of spending more than you make, of course, is accumulation of debt. The U.S. government is a good example.

Living within your means requires that you *spend, save,* and *invest* your money so that you can accomplish your financial goals. At a minimum, this implies that you must save some money — that is, spend less than you earn.

Whatever your financial dreams, you need to save. (That is, unless you expect to win the lottery or count on a large inheritance.)

Why You Overspend

As you know, it's very easy to spend your money. Thanks to innovations in technology like bank machines and credit cards, your money is always available for spending, 24 hours a day, 365 days a year. Major retailers are willing to extend their own loans and lines of credit. Sometimes, it may seem like somebody's trying to give away money by making credit so easily available. But this is a dangerous illusion. (Especially when it comes to financing a car, as you soon will learn.)

You're a consumer

Think about it. In the media and in the hallowed halls of our government, more often than not, you're referred to as a *consumer*. Not a person, citizen, or human being — a consumer.

In fact, some people I've worked with feel unpatriotic or inadequate if they don't spend enough. "Saving too much and not spending enough could hurt the economy," they say. "People could be thrown out of work, and it could be a friend or family member. My favorite politician might not get reelected if I don't single-handedly prop up the economy by spending. I wouldn't be doing my part if I didn't consume by spending as much as possible."

Balderdash! Ultimately, *you* are the one who suffers the consequences of spending more than you can afford.

Monthly payment mentality

Let's suppose that you're tired of driving around the old clunker. The car is battlescarred and boring, and you don't like to be seen in it. Plus, it's likely to only need more and more repairs in the months ahead. So, off you go to your friendly local car dealer.

Ooooh, look! It has A/C, stereo, and power everything. No problem there!

No money? No problem there, either! Only $249 a month.

That's not bad, you think. They run a credit report on you, have you sign a few things, and minutes later you're driving home, the proud owner of a spanking new car.

See, the dealer wants you to think in terms of monthly payments because it *sounds* so cheap: $249 for a car. But, of course, that's $249 per month, every month, for many, many months. You're gonna be payin' forever. You just bought a car that cost half a year's income!

But it gets worse. What does the total sticker price come to when interest charges are added in? And how about insurance and registration and maintenance over the seven or so years that you'll own it? Now you're probably up to more than a *year's* worth of your income. Yikes!

Access to credit

Easy and convenient access to credit allows you to spend more than you can actually afford. Credit cards, auto loans, and other lines of credit allow you to borrow against your future earnings. (It's hard enough to hop out of bed knowing that a third or more of your income goes to pay taxes.)

You never would have bought that grand sedan if you'd had to pay cash — you couldn't have afforded it. That's the point. Credit is most dangerous when you make consumption purchases that you couldn't afford in the first place.

Ten leading causes of overspending

Here are some of the opponents you're up against as you attempt to control your spending.

Credit cards

The modern-day bank credit card was invented by Bank of America near the tail end of the baby boom. Credit cards make it easy and tempting to spend money that you don't have. If you pay your bill in full every month, credit cards offer a convenient way to buy things with an interest-free, short-term loan. But they encourage you to live beyond your means, carrying debt over month-to-month at high interest rates.

There's only one solution: Get rid of them. Go cold turkey. You *can* function without them (see next chapter for details).

Minimum monthly payments

If you pay just the minimum monthly payment on your credit cards, interest continues to pile up on the bulk of your outstanding debt. **Note:** You'll *never* get your credit card paid off if you keep charging on your card and make only the minimum monthly payment. That's like using a Dixie cup to bail water from a sinking boat that has a basketball-sized hole in its bottom.

Cars

It's too easy to walk onto a car lot and go home with a new car that you could never afford if you had to pay cash. The dealer gets you thinking in terms of monthly payments that sound very small compared to what that four-wheeler is *really* gonna cost you. Auto loans are easy for just about anyone to get (except maybe a recently paroled felon).

Peer pressure

You go out with the guys or the gals (or both) to dinner, a movie, and then club-hopping. Try to remember the last time one of you said, "Let's go someplace cheaper. I can't afford to spend this much." On the one hand, you don't want to be a stick in the mud. But on the other, some of your friends have more money than you do — and the ones who don't may be running up debt even faster than you are.

Spending to feel good

Life is full of stress, obligations, and demands. "I work hard," you say. "And darn it, I deserve to indulge!" Especially after your boss took the credit for your last great idea or blamed you for the last major screwup. So, you buy something expensive or go to a fancy restaurant. Feel better? You won't when the bill arrives.

Becoming addicted to spending

Just as people can become addicted to alcohol, tobacco, TV, and even love, some become addicted to the high they get from spending. A number of psychological causes can be identified for spending addiction, some of them dating back to how your family handled money and spending. (And you thought you'd identified all the problems you can blame on Mom and Dad!)

If your spending and debt problems are chronic, Debtors' Anonymous, a 12-step support group program patterned after Alcoholics Anonymous, can help. See the next chapter for more information.

Trying to keep current

You just *have* to see the latest hit movie or have the latest designer clothes or get the new, superimproved, oversized tennis racquet with shock-absorbers, double-wishbone suspension, polyxylitol handgrips, and whatnot. All your friends are getting one, so you'd better get one, too. Right?

Wrong. Besides, some new technologies or products don't live up to their billing. Be smug and wait until a product is proven and until you can afford it.

Ignoring your financial goals when buying

When was the last time you heard someone say that they decided to forego a purchase because they were saving toward retirement or a home purchase? Doesn't happen, right? It's very tempting to just deal with the here and now and to forget your long-term needs and goals. That's why people toil away for too many years in jobs they dislike.

Living for today has its virtues: Tomorrow *may* not come. But odds are very high that it will. Will you still feel the same way tomorrow about today's spending decisions? Or will you feel guilty that you again failed to stick to your goals?

Wanting the best for your children

For children, many of the best things in life are free, just as they are for you. Junior *can* live without the latest $100 sneakers. Later on in life, your children will thank you: Better to pass on sound judgment and planning than the worship of material goods.

Thinking that money can buy happiness

Recall the handful of moments in your life that you wouldn't trade for anything. Odds are, they don't include the moment of buying a car or anything else. It is true: The most enjoyable and precious things of value in your life can't be bought.

Spending Analysis

If you aren't saving any money or not enough to meet your financial goals, you need to figure out where your hard-earned income goes each month by doing a little spending analysis.

Washing your face, brushing your teeth, and exercising are good habits. The financial equivalents of these habits are spending less than you earn and saving enough to meet your future financial objectives.

The immediate goal of a spending analysis is to figure out what you typically spend your money on. Its long-range goal is to establish a good habit: to maintain a regular, automatic savings routine.

Note: The good habit is *not* month after month of keeping track of exactly where you spend your money. Once you can establish the habit of saving first and spending only what's left over, continually tracking your spending is unnecessary.

Notice the first four letters in the word *analysis*. (You may never have noticed, but I felt the need to bring it to your attention.) It is very useful to know where your money is going each month. It's terrific to make changes in your spending behavior and to cut out the fat so you can save more money and meet your financial goals. But you'll make yourself and those around you into very unhappy campers if you try to be anal-retentive about documenting precisely where you're spending every single dollar and cent. It doesn't really matter — what *matters* is that you save what you want and need to achieve your goals. If you do that, who cares where the rest goes?

Tracking your spending on paper

Unless you keep meticulous records detailing every dollar you spend, you will not have perfect information. Don't sweat it! You have a number of available sources that should allow you to reconstruct where you have been spending the bulk of your money.

Doing your spending analysis is a little bit like being a detective. Your goal is to reconstruct the crime of *spending*. You probably have some major clues at your fingertips or piled somewhere on your desk or on the table where you plop yourself down to pay bills. Get out your

- Recent pay stubs
- Tax returns
- Checkbook register or canceled checks
- Credit and charge card bills

Ideally, you should assemble one year's worth of these documents so that you can track one year's spending.

If your spending patterns don't fluctuate greatly from month to month (or if your dog ate some of the old bills), you can reduce your data gathering to one six-month period or to every other or every third month for the past year. If you take a major vacation or spend a large amount on gifts during certain times of the year, make sure to include these months in your analysis.

The hardest transactions to track are cash transactions because they don't leave a paper trail. Over the course of a week or perhaps even a month, you *could* keep track of everything you buy with cash. Tracking cash can be an enlightening exercise — it can also be a hassle. If you're lazy like I am or lack the time and patience, try *estimating*. Think about a typical week or month — how often do you buy things with cash? For example, if you eat lunch out four days a week at work at around $5 a shot, that's $80 a month.

Next, try to separate your expenditures into as many useful and detailed categories as possible. Table 4-1 gives you a suggested format — you can tailor it to fit your needs. Remember, if you lump too much of your spending into broad, meaningless categories like *Other,* you'll be handicapped in gaining insights about where you spend your money and how you can improve your habits.

Table 4-1	Categorizing Your Spending	
Category	**Monthly Average**	**Percent of Total**
Taxes, taxes, taxes	_____	_____
Social Security	_____	
Federal	_____	
State and local	_____	
The roof over your head	_____	_____
Rent	_____	
Mortgage	_____	
Property taxes	_____	
Gas/electric/oil	_____	
Water/garbage	_____	
Phone	_____	
Cable TV	_____	
Furniture/appliances	_____	
Maintenance/repairs	_____	
Food, glorious food	_____	_____
Supermarket	_____	
Restaurants and takeout	_____	
Getting around	_____	_____
Gasoline	_____	
Maintenance/repairs	_____	
State registration fees	_____	
Tolls and parking	_____	
Bus or subway fares	_____	

(continued)

Table 4-1 *(continued)*

Category	Monthly Average	Percent of Total
Style	_____	_____
Clothing	_____	
Shoes	_____	
Jewelry (watches, earrings)	_____	
Dry cleaning	_____	
Debt repayments	_____	_____
Credit/charge cards	_____	
Auto loans	_____	
Student loans	_____	
Other	_____	
Fun stuff	_____	_____
Entertainment (movies, concerts)	_____	
Vacation and travel	_____	
Gifts	_____	
Hobbies	_____	
Pets	_____	
Other	_____	
Personal care	_____	_____
Haircuts	_____	
Health club or gym	_____	
Makeup	_____	
Other	_____	
Personal business	_____	_____
Accountant	_____	
Attorney	_____	
Financial advisor	_____	
Health care	_____	_____
Physicians and hospitals	_____	
Drugs	_____	

Category	Monthly Average	Percent of Total
Dental and vision	_____	
Therapy	_____	
Insurance	_____	_____
Homeowners/renters	_____	
Auto	_____	
Health	_____	
Life	_____	
Disability	_____	
Educational expenses	_____	_____
Courses	_____	
Books	_____	
Supplies	_____	
Children	_____	_____
Day care	_____	
Toys	_____	
Child support	_____	
Charitable donations	_____	_____
Other	_____	_____
_____	_____	
_____	_____	
_____	_____	
_____	_____	
_____	_____	
_____	_____	

Tracking your spending on the computer

More and more software packages are being developed and improved to help you track your spending and pay bills. The main advantage of these software packages is that they continually track your spending as long as you keep entering the information. But you don't need a computer and fancy software packages to figure where you're spending money. More than a few software purchasers give up entering the data after a few months. Like home exercise equipment and exotic kitchen appliances, some software ends up in the consumer graveyard.

Paper, pencil, and a calculator work just fine.

In addition to tracking expenses and making you feel hip and hi-tech, a major benefit of the software is that it can save you time paying your bills by automating the process. However, setting up and learning the software definitely requires an *investment* in time.

If you do want to try computerizing your bill payment and expense tracking, the the best software packages currently available are recommended in Chapter 22.

Ten consequences of overspending

Here are some things to consider that you won't find printed anywhere on your credit card statement.

Your future income is already claimed

As your spending and debt grow, so does your lack of control over where you'll be able to spend your future earnings. You have connected several Hoover Deluxe vacuum cleaners to your paycheck, and the giant sucking sound is the sound of your creditors getting their share of your money.

Our federal government is having problems with the vacuum cleaner effect, too. With more than $4 trillion in national debt outstanding, the annual interest *alone* on that debt guarantees that we'll keep adding to the debt at the rate of a couple hundred billion annually. The same can happen in your personal situation (though, hopefully, on a much smaller scale).

The greater the share of your income already claimed for future debt repayment and interest, the less you'll have available to put toward your financial and personal goals. Every dollar that goes toward interest is one less dollar to have fun with, resulting in fewer cappuccinos, fewer rap CDs, and fewer Howard Stern books. (Now that I think about it, maybe you should keep on spending after all!)

Living beyond your means becomes a habit

As you overspend, not only do you accumulate more debt — you become *spoiled* by a certain lifestyle that you can't really afford. You get used to spending that extra money: Eating out a few times a week, buying a new wardrobe every season, and employing a maid suddenly become necessities. Taking an annual vacation abroad becomes an expectation.

Pretty soon you'll have to buy an extra fanny pack just to carry all your credit cards.

Reduced future standard of living

Save today and you'll have more to spend tomorrow. Spend too much today and you'll have much less to spend tomorrow.

If you want to save enough to retire by, say, your mid-60s, you must save a reasonable portion (about 8 – 10 percent) of your income annually. If you don't, you'll be forced to work into your 70s or accept a lower standard of living than you've been accustomed to.

Americans are great at dreaming. We're also terrific at setting unrealistic expectations. Most say they want to retire but don't start to save until middle age — that's like training for a marathon by smoking a pack of cigarettes a day.

Harder time buying real estate

The less savings and more debt you have, the more difficult you will find it to convince a banker or others to lend you the money you'll need to buy a home. Would *you* want to own a bank that lent debt-heavy shopaholics more money to buy real estate?

Pay higher taxes

If you spend more, you have less left to save. That's common sense. But to add insult to injury, you also pay more taxes. By not taking full advantage of retirement savings plans, you miss easy ways to cut your income taxes. And because you pay sales tax on many purchases, you pay more taxes the more you spend.

More pressure and stress

Living from paycheck to paycheck is difficult enough. Counting on your next paycheck just to meet debt and spending obligations you're already committed to is the worst: More of your time and emotional energy is devoted to earning money and parceling it out. Then you fret about your current checking account balance and worry that you're about to bounce another check. And then the bank charges you more for falling below the minimum account balance, not to mention dinging you for the bouncing checks. And so on.

Ball and chain

Maybe you want to change careers, go back to school, or own your own business. Perhaps your boss is a grumpy tyrant, or maybe you'd like to work for a more successful company in your field. Or maybe you'd just like to take a year's leave, travelling, spending more time with your family, or reading . . . *For Dummies* books. You're less able financially and emotionally to do these things the closer you live to the edge.

Money can't buy you happiness or love, but it *can* give you the luxury and piece of mind you need in order to pursue a different path.

Increased odds of homelessness

If you don't have a financial cushion or a family member to turn to for a loan, unexpected expenses or loss of your job could put you into a financial emergency. **Note:** The only difference between someone without a financial safety net and some homeless people is a few months of unemployment.

To guard against financial emergencies, you should maintain the equivalent of six months of living expenses in an account that is safe and liquid. If you have a family member or someone who can reliably loan you money or a retirement account that you can borrow against, three months' worth may suffice.

More waste

The more you spend, the more you consume. Not only do you consume your earnings but also the resources that went into producing what you bought. You may think of yourself as environmentally friendly — you recycle and try not to pollute the air or water. But there's no getting around the fact that just by buying and using manufactured products, you ultimately add to the planet's waste.

More bill payment clutter

The more you spend and owe, the more bills you receive and have to pay each month. Everybody likes to get mail, but bills aren't the kind of mail you look forward to. So, save some trees, check-writing, and stamps. Eliminate the terrible taste of licking 20 stamps and envelope flaps. Spend less and you'll have fewer bills to pay each month *and* a happier tongue.

Spending less: the secret to growing rich on your income

As a financial counselor, I work with people who bring in tiny incomes, incomes of $200,000 and more, and everything in between. At every income level, people fall into one of the following three categories:

- People who spend more than they earn (accumulate debt)
- People who save nothing
- People who save 2, 5, 10, even 20 percent (or more!)

I've seen $30,000 earners save 20 percent of their income ($6,000) and $60,000 earners save just 5 percent ($3,000).

Let's say that you currently earn $30,000 per year and spend all of it. How can you save money? Good question!

Rather than knocking yourself out at a second job or hustling for that next promotion, you could try living below your income. In other words, spend less than you earn. (I know it's hard to imagine, but you can do it.) Consider that for every discontented person earning and spending $30,000 per year, someone else is out there making due on $27,000 (and someone else making $60,000 may be discontented as well).

A great many people live on less than you make. If you spent as they do, you could save and invest the difference.

Chapter 5

Getting Out of Debt

∙ ∙

In This Chapter

▶ Using your savings to reduce your debt

▶ Getting out of debt when you have no savings

▶ Swallowing your pride and doing the unthinkable: filing bankruptcy

▶ Ten ways to resist credit temptation

▶ Finding help for chronic debt problems

∙ ∙

*B*orrowing money can be good and productive. It can also lead to financial and emotional strains that can cause a lot of problems.

Borrowing money has a lot in common with eating. You need to eat to live, but some foods are better for you than others. It's tempting to eat too much of the bad foods.

Getting rid of your debts may be even more difficult than giving up the foods you love, but in the long run you'll be healthier financially. To decide which financial diet strategies make sense for you, you first must consider your overall financial situation and total debts relative to your income.

Using Savings to Reduce Your Debt

Psychologically, many people think of their savings as separate from their debts. Using savings to pay off debts makes it seem like somehow you're losing money.

You're *not* losing, you're gaining. Remember that the growth of your money is determined by your *net worth* — the difference between your assets and your liabilities (see Chapter 2). Hopefully, your savings and investments are growing, but if your debts are *also* growing, you're not making much headway.

If you have the savings to pay down high-interest credit card and auto loans, do it. You diminish your savings, true, but you also reduce your debts. Make sure to pay off the loans with the highest interest rates first.

You benefit financially because the interest on your savings is far less than the interest your debt accrues. Even if you're a financial wizard and think you can earn more on your savings, swallow your ego and pay down the debts anyway. In order to chase that higher potential return from investments, you need to take substantial risk. You *may* earn more investing in your uncle's company that makes contact lenses for cats, but then again you may lose your shirt.

If you have loans at, say, 12 percent, paying them off is like finding an investment with a guaranteed return of 12 percent — *tax-free*. You would actually need to find an investment that yielded even more — around 18 percent — to net 12 percent after paying taxes to justify *not* paying your 12 percent loans. Good luck!

If you use your liquid savings to pay down debts, be careful to leave yourself enough of an emergency cushion. You want to be in a position to withstand an unexpected large expense or temporary loss of income. On the other hand, if you use savings to pay down credit card debt, you can always run your credit card balances back up in a financial pinch (or turn to a family member or wealthy friend for a low-interest loan).

Savings you may be overlooking

Perhaps you have a life-insurance policy that has a cash-value balance. Your parents may have purchased it for you back when you were sucking your thumb. Borrow against the cash value to pay down your debts. (If you do this, paying back the life-insurance policy loan and continuing the policy may not be the best thing to do — see Chapter 17 for more details.)

Some employers' retirement accounts allow you to borrow a portion of your account value. You pay back the interest on the loan into the account as you repay the loan. What a deal — you get to be the bank as well as the borrower!

Did your Aunt Mary give you a few shares of stock when you graduated from high school? If so, even if they have sentimental value, consider selling them to raise more cash to pay down your loan balances. Aunt Mary will still love you, and if you explain to her why you did it, she may even wind up proud of you.

If you're a homeowner, you may be able to tap the equity in your home. You can generally borrow against real estate at a lower interest rate and get a tax deduction to boot.

Living on borrowed (family) money

Consider borrowing the savings of a family member (with permission, of course) to pay off your high-interest debts. Split the difference in interest rates: You benefit by getting a lower interest rate, and your relative benefits by getting a better savings rate. That way, it's a win/win situation. (You *will* return the money with interest, won't you?)

Yes, sometimes it's hard to ask for a loan. You may fear that your spending habits will be questioned, or you may feel irresponsible. I know that there are good reasons that your debt piled up. Just pretend you're asking me for the loan. (Sorry, I'm not making any new loans just now. I said *pretend*.)

Money borrowed from family members can have strings attached, of course. It's important to treat the obligation seriously. It's also best to write up a simple agreement listing the terms and conditions of your loan to avoid misunderstandings. Keep it to a page or less.

Getting Out of Debt If You Lack Savings

"I don't have any savings, you nincompoop," you may be shrieking. "That's why I have all this debt!"

Your quandary is quite common. (But it's surprising how many people with consumer debt *can* pay it down with savings. I know this because of all the people who come to me for help.)

If you don't have savings to get rid of your debts, you have some work to do. If you're currently spending all your income, you need to figure out how you can decrease your spending (see Chapter 6 for lots of great ideas) and/or increase your income. In the meantime, you need to slow the growth of your debt.

Indulge in low-fat interest rates

First, you should look at ways to reduce the interest rate you're paying on your debt. Think of it as putting your debt on a low-interest rate diet.

Different credit cards charge different interest rates. Why in the world should you pay 14, 16, 18 percent or more when you can pay less? Once approved, you can transfer your balance to a lower-interest card. If you're earning a decent income, are not *too* burdened with debt, and have a clean credit record, qualifying for lower-rate cards is relatively painless. Some persistence may be required if you have nicks in your credit report or have income and debt problems.

Something that you might want to try is simply calling the bank that issued your card and saying that you want to cancel your card because you found a competitor that offers no annual fee and a lower interest rate. Your bank may choose to match the terms of the "competitor" on the spot rather than lose you as a customer.

The credit card business has become quite competitive. Gone are the days when all banks charged 18 percent or more for VISA and MasterCards. Table 5-1 lists some of the consistently low-interest rate credit cards. Please note that these cards charge interest rates that are variable and are offered by banks that are somewhat picky about who they accept for a low-rate card. But you've got nothing to lose if you apply.

Table 5-1	Low-Interest Rate Credit Cards	
Bank	**Interest Rate**	**Annual Fee**
AFBA Industrial Bank 800-776-2265	8.9% first year, 12.5% thereafter	None
Arkansas Federal 800-477-3348	7.75%	$35
Consumer's Best Bankcard 800-952-3388	6.9% first year, 11.9% thereafter	$29
USAA Federal Savings 800-992-9092	12.5%	None
Wachovia Bankcard 800-842-3262	6% first year, 9.9% thereafter	$18

For a complete, quarterly-updated listing of low-interest rate credit cards, send a check for $4 to the following nonprofit organization:

Bankcard Holders of America,
560 Herndon Parkway, Suite 120
Herndon, VA 22070

Cut 'em up, cut 'em all up

You should also seriously consider drastically reducing or even eliminating your access to credit. Access to credit is probably how you got into your current predicament.

Stop making new charges on cards that have outstanding balances. Many people don't realize that interest starts to accumulate *immediately* when they carry a balance. *There is no grace period* — the 20-odd days you normally have to pay your balance in full without incurring interest charges doesn't apply if you carry a balance.

The world worked fine back in the years B.C. (Before Credit). Think about it: Just a couple of generations ago, credit cards didn't even exist. People paid with cash and checks — imagine that. *Pay with cash or check.* If you can trust yourself, keep a separate card *only* for new purchases that you absolutely can pay in full each month. Be careful, though — you may be tempted to run up a balance on that card you obtained only for new purchases. Better yet, consider getting a debit card (see later in this chapter) while you pay off your credit card debt.

If you have a pattern of living beyond your means by buying on credit, get rid of the culprit — the credit, that is. To kick the habit, a smoker needs to toss the cigarettes, an alcoholic needs to get the booze out of the house, and Larry King needs to lose Ross Perot's phone number.

Honestly, you *can* function in the 1990s without buying anything on a credit card. In certain cases, you may need a card as collateral — like when you rent a car. When you bring back the rental car, however, you can pay with cash or check, so leave the card at home in the back of your sock drawer and only pull it out for the occasional car rental.

Debit cards: the best of both worlds

Debit cards truly offer the best of both worlds. You say that you're hooked on the convenience that a credit card offers? Carrying your checkbook or cash can be a hassle or costly if you're mugged? Well, you can have your cake and eat it too with a debit card.

Debit cards (VISA's card is called the Check Card) look just like credit cards. They come with the widely accepted VISA or MasterCard logos on them. But they *act* like your ATM card. The debit card is directly connected to your checking account. When you buy something with your debit card, the amount is taken electronically from your checking account within a few days — just like when you write a check.

The beauty of the debit card is that it gives you the convenience of a credit card without tempting you to spend money you don't have. Nifty, huh?

Finding a debit card is the challenging part. Banks have been slow to offer them. Because moving your checking account can be a hassle, first check with the bank where you currently have a checking account to see whether they offer VISA or MasterCard debit cards.

The following banks are among the larger issuers of debit cards (according to *POS News*). By opening a checking account at one of them, you can also obtain a debit card.

- ✔ Bank of America
- ✔ Bank One
- ✔ BayBanks
- ✔ Chase Manhattan
- ✔ First Bank
- ✔ First Chicago
- ✔ First Interstate
- ✔ First National Bank of Maryland
- ✔ First Tennessee
- ✔ Fleet/Fleet/Norstar
- ✔ Norwest Banks
- ✔ Meridian Bankcorp
- ✔ U.S. Bank
- ✔ Wachovia
- ✔ Wilmington Trust

A number of investment firms offer debit cards with their asset-management accounts. For example, Charles Schwab & Co. (800-421-4488) offers a VISA debit card with its SchwabOne account, and Fidelity Investments (800-343-8721) offers a VISA debit card with its U.S.A. account. **Note:** Fidelity requires a higher minimum initial opening balance ($10,000) than does Schwab ($5,000).

These investment firm "checking accounts" also allow you to invest in securities. Having this type of account can not only help you break the credit card overspending habit but may also get you thinking about saving and investing your money. (Even if you don't go that far initially, you'll still impress friends and family by having a brokerage account.)

Last Resort: Filing Bankruptcy

Note: Most people with consumer debt should *not* consider bankruptcy because of the long-term (seven years) damage it inflicts on credit reports. On the other hand, if the ratio of your bad debt to annual income is high — 40 – 50 percent or more — filing bankruptcy may be your best option.

Every year, nearly one million Americans (that's about 1 in every 100 households) file personal bankruptcy.

The value or benefit of bankruptcy is that certain types of debts can be completely eliminated or discharged. Debts that may be discharged typically include

- ✔ Credit card balances
- ✔ Medical bills
- ✔ Auto loans
- ✔ Utilities
- ✔ Rent

Depending on the amount of debt outstanding relative to income, paying off large debts can take decades. Through bankruptcy you eliminate your debt, which enables you to start working toward your financial goals.

Debts that may *not* be canceled include

- ✔ Child support
- ✔ Alimony
- ✔ Student loans
- ✔ Taxes
- ✔ Court-ordered damages (drunk driving settlements, for example) and debt repayments

Pick a number: 7 or 13

There are two forms of bankruptcy:

- ✔ **Chapter 7** allows you to discharge or cancel certain debts. Chapter 7 bankruptcy makes the most sense when you have significant debts that you are legally allowed to cancel.

- ✔ **Chapter 13** comes up with a repayment schedule that requires you to pay off your debts over several years. Besides being an unlucky number, Chapter 13 stays on your credit record just like Chapter 7 *but doesn't eliminate debt,* so its value is limited (usually to dealing with debts like taxes that cannot be discharged through bankruptcy). Chapter 13 can keep creditors at bay, though, until a repayment schedule is worked out in the courts.

They can't take everything, can they?

In every state, you can retain certain property and assets even though you're filing for bankruptcy. Property that you are allowed to keep is called *exempt.*

You may be surprised to learn that in some states (such as Florida, Iowa, Kansas, Minnesota, and Oklahoma) you can keep your home regardless of its value! On the other hand, Maryland, Pennsyl-

vania, and Rhode Island provide no exemption for homeowners. Most states allow you to protect a certain amount of equity in your home.

Additionally, you're allowed to retain some other types and amounts of personal property and assets. For example, most states allow you to retain household furnishings, clothing, pensions, and money in retirement accounts.

Bankruptcy drawbacks

Filing bankruptcy, needless to say, has a number of potential drawbacks.

It trashes your credit record

Bankruptcy appears on your credit report for a minimum of seven years, so you will have difficulty obtaining credit during that time period. But, of course, if you already have problems on your credit report because of late payments or failure to pay previous debts, the damage has already been done.

If you do file bankruptcy, it is not impossible to get credit in the future. You'll probably be able to obtain a *secured credit card,* which requires you to deposit money in a bank account equal to the credit limit on your credit card.

But not having credit isn't so bad anyway because the temptation to run up debt is removed. And without savings, you're probably not going to be making major purchases (such as a house) in the next seven years anyway.

It costs money

I know it seems terribly unfair. You're already in financial trouble — that's why you're filing bankruptcy! Nevertheless, filing bankruptcy will probably set you back from several hundred dollars up to $1000 in court filing fees — in *addition* to legal fees to prepare your bankruptcy forms.

It causes major emotional stress

Admitting that your personal income can't keep pace with your debt obligations is a painful thing to do. Although filing bankruptcy clears the decks of debt and gives you a fresh financial start, it's only human to feel a profound sense of failure. Some people also feel that they're shirking responsibility.

Most banks make gobs and gobs of money from their credit card businesses. As a former consultant who worked in the industry, I can tell you that credit cards are one of the most profitable lines of business for banks. That's why your mailbox is always filled with solicitations for more cards even though you're already up to your eyeballs in them.

So, if you file for bankruptcy, don't feel *too* bad about not paying back the bank. The nice merchants where you bought the merchandise have already been paid. *Chargeoffs* — the banker's term for taking the loss on debt that you discharge through bankruptcy — are part of the business. This is another reason why the interest rate is so high on credit cards.

To file bankruptcy, you must open your personal financial affairs to court scrutiny and court control during the several months it takes to administer a bankruptcy. A court-appointed bankruptcy trustee oversees your case and tries to recover as much of your property as possible to satisfy the *creditors* — those to whom you owe money.

Bankruptcy advice

Be very careful where you get advice about whether to file for bankruptcy. Many people make the mistake of turning to bankruptcy attorneys or Consumer Credit Counseling Services (CCCS).

Attorneys who earn a legal fee from doing bankruptcy filings have a major conflict of interest. All things being equal, their bias is to — you guessed it — *recommend bankruptcy,* which generates their fees.

CCCS faces the opposite conflict. CCCS says that it is a nonprofit, educational service to help consumers who are in debt. Although it's true that CCCS has many loyal and well-intentioned employees, it's also true that CCCS is funded by credit-card issuers. Thus, CCCS counselors are loathe to recommend bankruptcy.

Bankruptcy resources

If you want to learn more about the pros, cons, and details of filing bankruptcy, pick up a copy of *How to File for Bankruptcy* (Elias, Renauer, and Leonard, Nolo Press, 800-992-6656). The authors are attorneys. (You could, I suppose, charge it with your credit card over the phone and then discharge *that* expense when you file bankruptcy.)

In filing bankruptcy, hiring an attorney makes sense when you have major assets (such as a home) to protect. Attorney fees can easily exceed several hundred dollars to over $1,000 for complicated cases.

If you're comfortable with your decision to file and think you can complete the paperwork, you may be able to do it yourself. The Nolo Press book mentioned a few paragraphs ago comes with all the forms necessary to file. An intermediate approach would be to hire a paralegal typing service to prepare the forms, which can be a cost-effective way to get help with the process if you don't need heavy-duty legal advice. Check your local yellow pages under *Paralegals* or call the National Association of Independent Paralegals (707-935-7951) for members in your area.

Regardless of the approach you use to deal with paying off your debt, you're in real danger of falling back into old habits. Backsliding happens not only to people who file bankruptcy but also to those who use savings or home equity to eliminate their costly debt.

If history has shown that you are likely to fall into this trap, the best and only solution is to go cold turkey. Eliminate your access to credit and pay for everything with cash, checks, or debit cards.

Ten Surefire Ways to Reduce Credit Temptation

The following are tactics you can use to limit the influence credit cards hold over your life.

Put that seaside mansion on my VISA

Think you have a lot of credit cards? Maybe you do, but I *know* you don't have as many as Walter Cavanagh of Santa Clara, California. According to the *Guinness Book of Records,* Walt lays claim to holding the most credit cards — 1,356, to be exact, each one different and valid, totaling $1,600,000 in credit! Guess where he keeps them? In the world's longest wallet, of course — 250 feet long.

Get rid of your extra credit cards

You don't need three, five, or ten credit cards to function — even in our plastic society. You only "need" one, given the wide acceptance of most cards. Count 'em up, including retail store and gas cards, and get rid of 'em. (See the nearest sidebar if you think you have a lot of cards.)

Reduce your credit limit

Just because your bank keeps raising your credit limit to reward you for being such a good (read: *lucrative*) customer doesn't mean that you have to accept the increase. Call your credit-card service's 800 number and have them lower your credit limit to a level you're comfortable with. Remember, they aren't giving you money — they're making a killing off you.

Replace your credit card (s) with a charge card

A *charge card* (such as the American Express Card) requires you to pay your balance in full each billing period. It gives you no credit line and charges no interest. Of course, it's possible to spend more than you can afford to pay when the bill comes. But you'll be much less likely to overspend if you know you have to pay each bill in full.

Get a VISA or MasterCard debit card

As I discussed earlier, debit cards are accepted by merchants who accept credit cards, so they give you the same convenience as credit cards. However, unlike a credit card, when you use a debit card, the money gets sucked out of your checking account within a few days, just as though you'd written a check. So, there's no credit line or interest charges.

Destroy retailer credit cards

Cancel the credit line, too. Retailers, like department stores and gas stations, just love to give you one of their cards. Not only do these cards charge outrageously high interest rates, they duplicate VISA and MasterCards. Virtually all retailers that accept credit cards (including Sears, which has finally given in) accept VISA and MasterCard. Remember, more credit lines mean more temptation to spend what you don't have and can't afford.

Leave home without it

Leave your credit card in your underwear drawer, your pet's bed, or the freezer (especially if you're going to be anywhere near a store). You can't use what you don't have.

Never buy on credit anything that depreciates

Meals out, even at world-renowned restaurants, new cars, clothing, shoes, and so on all depreciate in value. Never buy these things on credit. Borrow money only for investments — education, real estate, or your own business, for example.

Think in terms of total cost

Everything sounds cheaper when you think of it in terms of monthly payments. That's how salespeople hook you into buying things you don't have the money in hand to pay for and therefore can't afford. Bring a calculator along if necessary to tally up the sticker price, interest charges, and upkeep. The total cost will scare you. *It should.*

Stop the junk mail avalanche

Your friendly neighborhood postal carrier is one of the primary causes of your spending temptations. He or she brings all those solicitations and mail-order catalogs that beg for your credit card number. Toss the catalogs away as soon as you get them (or recycle them or put them out by the firewood pile). You can remove yourself from most mailing lists by writing to the following address:

Direct Marketing Association
Mail Preference Service
1101 17th St. NW, Suite 900
Washington, DC 10036-4704

Don't drive near shopping malls

I know that this is getting harder to do — there are malls on practically every corner these days. It's hard to bypass them on the highway because they strategically locate themselves in the most-visible locations. You *could* pretend that malls are actually Top Secret germ-warfare research facilities. Or you could try driving with horse blinders on (but the likely increase in your auto insurance bill would probably wipe out most of the savings of avoiding the mall).

Where to Turn When the Problem Becomes Chronic

As hard as they try to repent, some people become addicted to spending and debting. It becomes a chronic problem that starts to interfere with other aspects of their lives. Financial problems can lead to problems at work and with family and friends.

Officially started in 1976, Debtors Anonymous (DA) is a nonprofit organization that provides support, primarily through group meetings, to people trying to break their debting and spending habits. It is modeled after the 12-step Alcoholic Anonymous program. Like AA, Debtors Anonymous works with people from all walks of life and socioeconomic backgrounds. It's typical to find people who are financially on the edge, $100,000-plus income earners, and everybody in between at a DA meeting. Even former millionaires join the program.

DA has a simple questionnaire to help determine whether you are a problem debtor. If you answer *yes* to more than half of the following 15 questions, you may be developing or already have a compulsive debting habit:

1. Are your debts making your home life unhappy?

2. Does the pressure of your debts distract you from your daily work?

3. Are your debts affecting your reputation?

4. Do your debts cause you to think less of yourself?

5. Have you ever given false information in order to obtain credit?

6. Have you ever made unrealistic promises to your creditors?

7. Does the pressure of your debts make you careless of the welfare of your family?

8. Do you ever fear that your employer, family, or friends will learn the extent of your total indebtedness?

9. When faced with a difficult financial situation, does the prospect of borrowing give you an inordinate feeling of relief?

10. Does the pressure of your debts cause you to have difficulty in sleeping?

11. Has the pressure of your debts ever caused you to consider getting drunk?

12. Have you ever borrowed money without giving adequate consideration to the rate of interest you are required to pay?

13. Do you usually expect a negative response when you are subject to a credit investigation?

14. Have you ever developed a strict regimen for paying off your debts, only to break it under pressure?

15. Do you justify your debts by telling yourself that you are superior to the "other" people, and when you get your "break," you'll be out of debt?

To find a Debtors Anonymous support group in your area, check your local phone directory. Or write to DA's national headquarters for meeting locations in your area and a literature order form at the following address:

Debtors Anonymous
P.O. Box 400, Grand Central Station
New York, NY 10163-0400

Chapter 6

Putting Your Spending on a Diet

· ·

· ·

*P*eople go on food diets for all sorts of reasons. Someone makes a joke about your baby fat. Perhaps the old jeans just don't fit the way they used to. Whatever the specific precipitating event, most people need a little nudge or motivation to make changes in a major aspect of their lives.

If you've taken stock of your financial health, including your savings rate or lack thereof (see Chapter 2), and if you've analyzed where your money is being spent (see Chapter 4), then you should have a sense of whether and to what extent you need to go on a spending diet. The recommendations in this chapter don't require that you do any analysis in advance — they just require that you want to cut your expenses.

Some Assumptions

Telling people how and where to spend their money is a dangerous job because

▸ Most people like to spend money.
▸ Most people hate to be told what to do.

You'll be glad to hear that I'm not going to tell you exactly where you must cut spending. I'm simply going to give you strategies that have worked for other people. **Note:** *You* have to make the judgment call. What's important to you and what's dispensable? Should you cut out your weekly poker games or cut back on your shoe collection?

I assume throughout these recommendations that you value your time. Therefore, I'm not going to tell you to scrimp and save by doing things like cutting open a tube of toothpaste so that you can use every last bit of it. And I won't tell you to have your spouse do your ironing to reduce your dry-cleaning bills (no point in having money in the bank if you lose your Significant Other).

Probably, part of the reason you spend money the way you do is that you're busy. Therefore, the recommendations in this chapter focus on methods that don't involve a lot of time but that produce big savings. In other words, these strategies provide a lot of bang for the buck. I happen to believe in saving pennies, but small change is awfully heavy to cart around — better to save the big bucks.

Four Keys to Successful Spending

For most, spending money is a whole lot easier and more fun than earning it. Far be it from me to tell you to stop having fun and to turn into a penny-pinching, stay-at-home miser. Of course you can spend money. But there's a world of difference between spending money *carelessly* and spending money *wisely*.

Spending too much and not spending wisely or efficiently puts too much pressure on a limited income. Savings dwindle, debts accumulate, and you can't achieve your financial goals.

Sometimes, when you dive into details too quickly, you miss the big picture. So before I jump into how to spend less in specific areas of your budget, here are the four keys to successful spending:

- ✔ Live within your means
- ✔ Find the best value
- ✔ Eliminate fat
- ✔ Avoid buying on credit

These four principles run through most of the recommendations coming up in this chapter.

Living within your means

Spending too much is a *relative* problem. Two people could each spend $30,000 per year yet be in drastically different financial circumstances. How? Suppose that one of them earns $40,000 annually, and the other makes just $25,000. The $40,000 income earner saves $10,000 each year. The $25,000 earner, who spends more than he or she earned during the year, accumulates $5,000 of new debt (or spends that amount from prior savings). Spend within your means.

Finding the best value

You can find high quality and low cost in the same product. Conversely, paying a high price is no guarantee that you're getting high quality. Cars are a good example. Whether you're buying a subcompact, sportscar, or luxury four-door sedan, some cars are more fuel efficient and cost less to maintain than rivals that carry the same sticker price.

The good news is that you don't even have to do the tiresome research to know what's good and what's not. Independent evaluation services such as *Consumers Reports* do it for you.

Eliminating fat

If you want to reduce your overall spending by, say, 10 percent, you could just cut all current expenditures by 10 percent. Or you can reach your 10 percent goal by cutting some categories a lot and others not at all. You need to set priorities and make choices about what you can and can't live without.

What you spend your money on is sometimes a matter of habit rather than what you really want or value. For example, some people shop at whatever store is closest because they know where the store is and never bother to look elsewhere.

Eliminating fat doesn't necessarily mean cutting back on your purchases. Buying in bulk is a good example. Some stores specialize in selling larger packages or quantities of a product at a lower price because they save money on the packaging and handling. You save money by buying in bulk. And even though that 20-pound bag of rice means more cash up front than the little box of Uncle Ben's, every meal from now on that you make from the 20-pound bag will be a great deal cheaper than the meal out of the box would have been.

Avoid buying on credit

As discussed in Chapters 4 and 5, buying items that depreciate — such as cars, clothing, and vacations — on credit is hazardous to your long-term financial health. Buy today only what you can afford today. If you'll be forced to carry a debt for months or years on end, then you can't really afford it today.

Consumer credit is expensive and reinforces a bad habit: spending more than you can afford.

Strategies for Reducing Your Spending

Note: Some of these strategies will make sense for you, and some of them won't. Start your spending reduction plan with the ones that come easily first. Work your way through them. Keep a list of the options that are more challenging for you — ones that require more of a sacrifice but that you *could* make work if necessary to achieve your spending and savings goals.

Food

One way to reduce your food expenditures is to stop eating. However, this tends to make you weak and dizzy, so it's probably not a viable long-term strategy. The following culinary strategies will keep you on your feet for less money (and perhaps even improve your health).

Join a wholesale superstore

Superstores such as PriceCostco, Sam's Club, and Pace enable you to buy groceries in bulk at wholesale prices. And, contrary to popular perception, you *don't* have to buy 1000 rolls of toilet paper at once — just 24.

I've done price comparisons between these kinds of stores and retail grocery stores and found that wholesalers charge 30 to 40 percent less *for the same stuff*. Next time you see TV commercials comparing prices at several of your area's retail grocers, you'll know that they missed the real competition!

Besides saving lots of money, you'll find that you make fewer shopping trips. Buying in bulk means that you have more supplies around your humble abode — so there is less need to eat out (which is costly) or make trips to the local grocer, who may be really nice but who charges you out the wazoo.

Perishables run the risk of living up to their name, so don't buy what you can't use. Repackage bulk packs into smaller quantities for the freezer if possible.

Check your local phone directory for superstores. PriceCostco has a toll-free number to help you locate their store nearest you (800-544-1108). Most of these stores charge a small membership fee and are, frankly, somewhat of a hassle to join. PriceCostco, for example, charges $30 per year and asks for proof that you're a small-business owner or that you work for a nonprofit health-care organization, utility, bank, savings and loan, airline, or the media. You can also join if you hold a professional license or are a member of a credit union.

The reason you need to jump through these hoops is that if *anyone* could join the warehouse stores, retailers who sell similar merchandise would be upset. Anyone could get the better deals that the warehouse clubs pass on from manufacturers. That's why people with a potential business reason can join.

The reality, though, is that if you really want to join you can. Many community organizations that you may belong to, such as the YMCA/YWCA or Big Brothers/Big Sisters, can get you a membership. A small business owner whom you know well can sponsor you. Or shop with a friend who's a member. Don't give up — the savings you can reap make it well worth the hassle.

Be careful shopping at the warehouse clubs — you might be tempted to buy things you don't really need. These stores carry all manner of items, including wide-screen TVs, computers, furniture, clothing, complete sets of baseball cards, and giant canisters of M&M's and biscotti — beware! Try not to make impulse purchases, and be especially careful when you have kids in tow.

Clipping coupons can save you money. It also takes time and may steer you into lousy products you wouldn't buy otherwise. It's easier and usually cheaper to shop at wholesale warehouses that have lower prices overall.

Eat out more frugally

Eating meals out or getting takeout can be a time-saver but can rack up big bills if done too often and lavishly. Eating out is a luxury — think of it as hiring someone to cook for you. Of course, some people hate to cook or don't have the time or space or energy to do much in the kitchen. If this is you, choose restaurants carefully and order from the menu carefully. A couple of tips:

- ✔ **Avoid beverages, especially alcohol.** Most restaurants make big profits there. Drink water instead. (Water is healthful and reduces the likelihood of your wanting a nap after a big meal.)

- ✔ **Order vegetarian.** Vegetarian dishes, including pasta and rice dishes, generally cost less than meat-based entrees (and are better for you).

I don't want to be a killjoy. I'm not saying you should live on bread and water. You can have dessert — heck, try the wine too! But perhaps not *every* time. Try eating appetizers and dessert at home, where they're a lot less expensive (especially if you follow my advice on shopping for food).

Shelter

Housing and all the costs associated with it (utilities, furniture, appliances, and maintenance and repairs if you're a homeowner) can gobble a large chunk of your monthly income. I'm not suggesting that you live in an igloo or teepee (even though they're probably less costly and more energy-efficient), but people often overlook common opportunities to save money in this category.

Think about going veggie

Not only is meat expensive, but it is coming under increasing scrutiny as bad for your health.

In a landmark report entitled "The Surgeon General's Report on Nutrition and Health" (produced under former U.S. Surgeon General C. Everett Koop, M.D.), reliance on a meat- and dairy-based diet—with it's fat and cholesterol—was found to be the cause of the majority of premature deaths in the United States. In developing countries that are poorer economically, people eat mainly grains, beans, and vegetables and have significantly lower rates of heart disease and diet-related cancers, such as cancer of the prostate and colon.

Meat is expensive, so the less you eat, the more money you save. Even if you choose to merely reduce your meat consumption rather than eliminate it, you can still save some significant dough. If you decide to eliminate meat from your diet, don't try to shift from burgers, pork chops, and meatloaf to tofu and sprouts overnight. Make changes in your diet gradually. For example, I first gave up beef, pork, and lamb, but I still eat some chicken, fish, and low-fat dairy products.

(Besides saving you money and your health, a vegetarian diet is also friendlier to the environment. For example, cattle need a great deal more land and water to raise than do veggies. Livestock also produce a great deal of flatulence, which adds more methane to the atmosphere. Here's a statistical tidbit sure to liven up a dull cocktail party conversation: 100 million tons of the world's annual methane emissions — 20 percent of the total — are from cattle!)

A number of good books can teach you more about the benefits of a vegetarian-based diet and provide recipes, too. Among my favorites are

Diet for a New America by John Robbins (Stillpoint Publishing)

Eat for Life by The Food and Nutrition Board (National Academy Press)

Eat More, Weigh Less by Dr. Dean Ornish (Harper-Collins)

Shop wholesale for appliances and other household goods

As with groceries, try to do most of your shopping at wholesale warehouse clubs, such as PriceCostco, Sam's Club, Pace, and Home Depot.

You can also buy things wholesale via mail order. A terrific resource book worth checking out is the *Wholesale by Mail Catalog* (Print Project, 800-242-7737). It's packed with companies that sell everything from abrasives, accordions, and air compressors to woodworking tools, yarn, and zippers. Items cost less than retail and are just a phone call away. There's no headache in navigating traffic and finding parking at the mall, so you save time, gas, and wear and tear on the car, too.

Retailers running sales can sometimes save you money. But everybody knows that "sales" are often nothing more than markdowns on items that were overpriced to begin with. Warehouse wholesalers and mail-order companies maintain *everyday* low prices, eliminating the need to shop around to find a good deal.

Don't take rent for granted

Rent can take up a sizable chunk of your monthly take-home pay. Many people consider rent to be a fixed and an inflexible part of their expenses. It's not. Here are some things you can do:

Move to a lower-cost rental

Of course, a lower-cost rental may not be as nice — it may be smaller or lack a private parking spot. Make the tradeoff and shave $50 to $100 or more off your monthly rent. Don't forget: The less you spend renting, the more you can save toward buying your own place.

Share a rental

Living alone has some benefits, but financially speaking, it's a luxury. Rent a larger place with roommates. Your rental costs should go way down, and you'll get more home for your rental dollars. You have to be in a sharing mood, though. Roommates can be a hassle at times but can also be a plus — you meet all sorts of new people and have someone else to blame if the kitchen's a mess.

Negotiate your rental increases

Every year, like clockwork, your landlord bumps up your rent a certain percentage. If your local rental market is soft or your living quarters are deteriorating, stand up for yourself! You have more leverage and power than you probably realize.

If you pay your rent on time and are otherwise a good tenant, a smart landlord doesn't want to lose you. Filling vacancies takes time and money. State your case: You've been a responsible tenant, and your research shows comparable rentals going for less. Crying poor may help, too. At the very least, if you can't reduce your rent or the rent increase, maybe you can wrangle some improvements to the place.

Buy rather than rent

No, I haven't lost my mind. Purchasing your own place can be costly, yes, but in the long run, owning should be cheaper than renting, and you'll have something to show for it in the end. If you purchase real estate with a 30-year fixed-rate mortgage, your mortgage payment, which is your biggest ownership expense, remains constant. Only your property taxes, maintenance, and insurance costs are exposed to the vagaries of inflation.

As a renter, your entire monthly housing cost can rise with increases in the cost of living (unless you are a beneficiary of a rent-controlled building). If you lack money for the down payment required to buy, don't despair. In Chapter 15, you learn how to get around this obstacle. One way to build a down payment, of course, is to slash your current spending and bump up your savings rate.

Save on homeowner expenses

As every homeowner knows, houses suck money. You should be especially careful to watch your money in this area of your budget.

Don't overspend

If you're on the verge of buying your first home or trading up to a more costly property, crunch some realistic numbers before you jump. The most common mistake people make is overstretching when buying a home. If too little money is left over for other needs — such as taking trips, eating, enjoying hobbies, or saving for retirement — your new dream house may become a financial prison. Overspending on housing can cause unhappiness by blocking other personal and financial goals.

Calculate how much you can afford to spend monthly on a home by figuring your other needs first. (Doing the exercises in Chapter 4 about where you're spending your money and in Chapter 8 about saving for retirement will help.)

Rent out a room

If you already own your place, selling it and buying a less expensive place can be a big hassle and can cost you some taxes if you sell it for a profit. Have you considered taking in a tenant to reduce your housing expenses? Check out the renter thoroughly: Get references, run a credit report, and talk about ground rules and expectations before sharing your space.

Don't forget to check with your insurance company to see whether your homeowner's policy needs adjustments to cover potential liability from renting.

Refinance your mortgage to save on interest

This step may seem like common sense, but surprisingly, many people don't keep up-to-date on mortgage rates. At the time of this writing, you may be able to save enough to justify the costs of refinancing if you have a fixed-rate mortgage at 8 percent or higher or an adjustable mortgage with a lifetime cap over 10 percent (see Chapter 9 for more information about how to save on mortgages).

Appeal your property-tax assessment

In many areas of the country, housing prices have gone down in recent years. If you're still paying property taxes based on a higher valuation, you may be able to save money by appealing your assessment. Check with your local assessor's office for the procedure to follow. You may need to prove that your property is worth less today, and you can prove that by using sales of comparable homes in your area. An appraiser's recent valuation of your property would do — you can get one when you refinance the mortgage.

Reduce utility costs

Sometimes you have to spend money to save money. Old refrigerators, for example, can waste a lot of electricity. Insulate an attic to save on heating and air-conditioning bills. Install water flow regulators in shower heads and toilet bowls. Even if you don't live in an area susceptible to droughts, why waste water unnecessarily (which isn't free)? If you live in an area where garbage rates depend on the amount of stuff you toss, recycle. Recycling means less garbage, which means lower trash bills. (Even if you don't pay extra, recycle anyway — it benefits the environment by reducing landfill.)

Telephone expenses are a good example of not needing to reduce your usage to save money. Just adjust *when* you place your calls. In most areas, the most expensive time to place local or long-distance calls is weekdays between 8 a.m. and 5 p.m. From 5 p.m. to 11 p.m. is cheaper, and the cheapest time to call is late at night (usually 11 p.m. to 8 a.m.), which can save you 50-60 percent (and as a bonus, you get the thrill of waking up the other party). This bargain rate is also available all weekend, usually beginning after 11 p.m. Friday night and ending Sunday at 5 p.m.

You may be able to save money on your long-distance calls by switching companies. Despite (or perhaps because of) the millions of dollars that AT&T pours into advertising to convince you that its quality is better and prices are comparable, consider moving to MCI (800-444-3333) or Sprint (800-877-4000). Quality is virtually the same from company to company, and AT&T is more expensive in most cases.

Sometimes sending a thoughtful letter is cheaper, more appreciated, and longer-lasting than placing a phone call. Just block out an hour, grab pen and paper, and rediscover the lost art form of letter-writing. Formulating your thoughts on paper can be clarifying and therapeutic to boot.

Transportation

America is a car-driven society. In many other countries, cars are a luxury. If more people in the United States thought of cars as a luxury, there might be far fewer financial problems (and accidents). Cars not only pollute the air and clog the highways, but they also cost you a bundle. Purchasing the best car you can and using it wisely can save you big dollars. So can using other transportation alternatives.

Research before you buy a car

Just as cars differ in terms of sticker price, they also differ significantly in other aspects as well. When you buy a car, you not only pay the initial sticker price, but you're also on the hook for gas, insurance, registration fees, maintenance, and repairs. You also are trusting your life to the car. With more than 40,000 Americans killed in auto accidents annually, safety should be an important consideration as well. Air bags, for example, may save your life.

The magazine *Consumers Reports* annually reviews cars — new and used — and includes information such as repair records and safety ratings. Their annual *Buying Guide* summarizes all the latest information and includes a list of the most-reliable used cars in price ranges from $2,500 on up. Call 800-234-1645 to order a subscription to this terrific magazine for a mere $22 per year. Be sure to request the annual *Buying Guide* when you order — otherwise, the next one won't come to you until the next December. If you just want the *Buying Guide,* most bookstores carry it for $8.95.

For you data jocks, *The Complete Car Cost Guide* by Intellichoice (800-227-2665) is packed with information about all categories of ownership costs, warranties, and dealer costs. It rates new cars based on total ownership costs. But can you *really* afford a new car?

Buy your car with cash

The main reason people end up spending more than they can really afford on a car is that they finance it. As discussed in Chapter 2 and elsewhere, you should avoid borrowing money for consumption purchases, especially for items that depreciate in value like cars. A car is most definitely *not* an investment.

For most situations, leasing is even more expensive than borrowing money to buy a car. It's like a long-term car rental. We all know how well rental cars get treated — so do car dealers, which is one of the reasons leasing is so costly.

Replace high-cost cars

Maybe you've realized by now that your car is too expensive to operate because of insurance, gas, and maintenance costs. Or maybe you bought too much car — people who borrow money to buy a car frequently buy a far more expensive car than they can realistically afford.

Nothing says that you're stuck with it until the bitter end. *Dump* your expensive car and get something more financially manageable. The sooner you switch, the more money you'll save.

Sell unnecessary cars

I've seen households that have one car per person. Four people, four cars! In most cases, this is unnecessary and *very* costly. As I mentioned earlier, in developing countries like China, cars are a luxury. Everybody rides bikes and carries groceries, the kids, and even large pieces of furniture on them, thereby reducing transportation costs and the need for exercise!

Maintaining two or more cars for most middle-income households is an expensive extravagance — *especially* if you live in an area well served by public transportation. Try to find ways to make do with fewer cars. One advantage of living close to work, or at least close to public transit systems, is that you may be able to do without a car altogether.

Buy regular unleaded gas

A number of studies have shown that superduperultrapremium gasoline is not worth the extra expense. Fill up your tank when you're on a shopping trip to the warehouse wholesalers (see earlier in this chapter). These superstores are usually located in lower-cost areas, so the gas is usually cheaper there, too.

Service your car before problems develop

Sure, servicing your car (for example, changing the oil every 5,000 miles) costs money, but it saves you dough in the long run by extending the operating life of the car. It also reduces the chances that your car will crap out in the middle of nowhere, which requires a humongous towing charge to a service station. Even worse is stalling on the freeway during peak rush hour and having thousands of angry commuters stuck behind you.

Take public transportation and carpool

One of the ways to move beyond the confines of a car is to ride buses or trains or carpool to work. Some employers give incentives for taking public transit to work, and some cities and counties offer assistance in setting up vanpools or carpools along popular routes. By leaving the driving to someone else, you can catch up on reading or just relax on the way to and from work. And it's ecologically sensible.

Buy commuter passes

In many areas, you can purchase train, bus, or subway passes to reduce the cost of commuting. Many toll bridges also have booklets of tickets that you can buy at a discount. Some booths don't advertise that they offer these plans — maybe as a strategy to keep revenues up. It took me several years to figure out that the Golden Gate Bridge — the world's most beautiful bridge — had these booklets.

Clothing and accessories

When you buy clothing, try to stick with cottons and machine-washable synthetics rather than wools or silks that require dry cleaning. Check labels before you buy stuff.

Jack Bogle, CEO and founder of the Vanguard Group of mutual funds, still wears wool ties to work. He proudly declares that his ties are more *efficient,* and he's right. They last longer and require less cleaning than silk ties.

In most cases, there is simply no need to buy racks of new clothes or an entire new wardrobe yearly. If you haven't worn some of your clothes for over a decade, you're probably tossing them before their time or buying clothing that's not durable enough. Buy basic, buy classic — don't let fashion be your guide or you'll be the best dresser in the poorhouse.

Shoes, jewelry, handbags, and the like can gobble large amounts of money. Again, how many of these accessory items do you *really* need? The answer is probably very few, and each one should last many years.

Go to your closet or jewelry box and tally up the loot. What else could you have done with all that cash? See the things you regret buying or forgot you even had? Don't make the same mistake again.

Have a garage sale if there's a lot of stuff you don't want.

Debt repayment

In Chapter 5, I discussed strategies to reduce the cost of carrying consumer debt (and Chapter 9 covers mortgages). The *best* way to reduce the costs of debt is to avoid it in the first place. You can avoid it by eliminating your access to credit and only buying what you can pay off each month.

Learn when to borrow

As I've said, you should only borrow to buy something when it's a long-term investment. Examples include financing an education, starting or expanding a business, or purchasing real estate. A car, vacation, or new wardrobe is not an investment but a consumption. (See Chapter 2 for more information.)

Manage credit cards

If you pay your balance in full each month, there's no need to keep a credit card that charges you an annual fee. There are many no-fee credit cards.

The following cards do not charge annual fees:

- Discover Card (800-347-2683) rebates 0.25–1 percent of purchases in cash. No annual fee.

- GM Card (800-947-1000) puts credits worth 5 percent of charges toward the purchase of a GM-manufactured vehicle (Saturns excluded).

- AFBA Industrial Bank (800-776-2265).

- Bank of New York (800-235-3343).

- USAA Federal Savings (800-922-9092).

If you have a credit card that charges an annual fee, try calling the company and saying that you want to cancel the card because you can get a competitor's card without an annual fee. Many banks will agree to waive the fee on the spot. Some require you to call back yearly to cancel the fee — a hassle that can be avoided by getting a no-fee card.

If you pay in full each month and charge $10,000 or more annually, consider a card that gives you credits toward a purchase, such as a car or airline ticket. **Note:** Be careful, however, because some people are tempted to charge more on a card that rewards them for more purchases. If you spend more than you would otherwise, it defeats the purpose of getting the credits.

The following cards *may* rebate enough to justify a fee:

- ✔ American Advantage (800-359-4444) credits one American Airlines frequent-flier mile per dollar charged. Annual fee: $50.

- ✔ United Mileage Plus (800-537-7783) credits one United Airlines frequent-flier mile per dollar charged. Annual fee: $60.

- ✔ Continental (800-446-5336) credits one Continental frequent-flier mile per dollar charged plus gives 5,000-mile credit as a bonus for signing up. Annual fee: $45.

- ✔ Ford Card (800-374-7777) credits 5 percent of charges toward the purchase of a Ford-manufactured vehicle. Annual fee: $20.

Fun stuff

Having fun, taking time out for R & R, and lavishing gifts on those you love is good. But in these areas, financial overindulgence can wreck an otherwise good budget.

Gifts

Think about how you approach buying gifts throughout the year — and especially during the holidays. I know people who spend so much money on credit cards at this time of year that it takes them until late spring or summer to pay it off!

Although I don't want to deny your loved ones gifts from the heart — or you the pleasure of giving them — spend wisely. Homemade gifts are less costly to the giver and may be more dear to recipients. Many children actually love durable, classic, basic toys that aren't necessarily advertised on Saturday morning TV. Or you can organize white elephant gift exchanges to rotate unwanted gifts of the past among your loving family members — just don't give Uncle Chester the tie-organizer/paperweight that he gave you!

Entertainment

Entertainment doesn't have to cost a great deal of money if you adjust your expectations. Especially in metropolitan areas, many movies, theaters, and museums offer discount prices on certain days and times. Same goes for restaurants.

Cultivate some interests and hobbies that are free or low cost. Seeing friends, reading, hiking, and playing sports can be good for your finances as well as your health.

Vacations

For many people, vacations are a luxury. For others, regular vacations are essential parts of their routine. Regardless of how you recharge your batteries, remember that vacations are not investments, so you shouldn't be living on credit cards while you're away. After all, how relaxed will you feel when you have to pay all those bills?

Try vacations that are shorter and closer to home. Have you been to a state or national park recently? Take a vacation at home and see the sights in your local area. There are probably great places within fifty miles that you've always wanted to see but haven't got around to for one reason or another.

If you do travel far, head to a popular destination during the off-season for the best deals on airfares and hotels. Keep an eye out for discounts and "bought-but-unable-to-use" tickets advertised in your local paper. Be sure to shop around even when working with a travel agent. Travel agents work on commission, so they may not work very hard to find you the absolute best deals. Tour packages, when they meet your interests and needs, can also save you money. If you have flexible travel plans, courier services can cut your travel costs significantly (but make sure that the company is reputable).

Personal care

You have to take care of yourself, but as with anything else, there are ways to do it that are expensive, and there are ways that can save you money.

Hair care

One way to save money in this category is to go bald. I'm working on this one myself.

A number of no-frills, low-cost, hair-cutting joints can do the job — Supercuts is one of the larger chains. I know that some of you will insist that your stylist is the *only* one who can manage your hair the way you like it. At the prices charged by some of the trendy hair places, you have to *really*, *really* adore what they do to justify the cost. Consider going periodically to a no-frills stylist for maintenance after getting a fabulous cut at a more expensive place. If you're daring, you could try getting your hair cut at a local training school.

As long as we're on the subject of outward beauty, I have to say that in my personal opinion, the billions spent on cosmetics annually are a complete waste of time and money. Now, deodorant and perfume I can understand, but beyond that, you should pay close attention to your spending in this area.

As for other personal-care services: Having regular massages, facials, pedicures, and manicures can add up quickly. Same goes for other service providers, including housekeepers and personal trainers. Why not take an aerobics class instead of paying a personal trainer? Why not get a massage from your Significant Other?

Health club expenses

Expenditure on exercise is almost always money well spent. But you don't have to belong to a trendy club to get benefits. If you belong to a gym or club for the social scene, whether it's for dating or business purposes, you have to judge whether it's worth the cost.

Low-cost exercise facilities are everywhere — look for them anywhere you see children. Local schools, colleges, and universities almost always have tennis courts, running tracks, swimming pools, basketball courts, and exercise rooms, and often provide instruction. Community centers offer fitness programs and classes, too. Metropolitan areas that have lots of health clubs undoubtedly have the widest range of options and prices. **Note:** When figuring the cost of membership, be sure to factor in the cost of travel to and from these clubs (and the realistic likelihood of going there regularly to work out).

Don't forget that lots of healthy exercise can be done indoors or out, free of charge. Isn't biking in the park at sunset more fun than peddling away on a stationary bike, anyway? If you're dedicated, you may want to buy some basic gym equipment for use at home. Be careful, though, that your home gym (like many a kitchen) doesn't become a graveyard for appliances that are a better match for your dreams and aspirations than for actual use. Lots of rowing machines and free weights — like bread makers and pasta machines — languish in a closet after their first week at home.

Personal business

Accountants, lawyers, and financial advisors can be worth their weight in gold if they're good. But be wary of professionals who create or perpetuate work. This is one of the dangers of hiring someone who works by the hour.

The best way to use professionals for tax, legal, or financial advice is to get organized before you meet with them. Do some background research to evaluate their strengths and biases. Make sure you set goals and estimate fees in advance so you know what you're getting yourself into.

Self-help guides and software (see Chapter 22) can be terrific low-cost alternatives to hiring professionals.

Medical care

Health care is a big topic nowadays, and the cost of it is going up fast. Your health insurance — if you have health insurance, that is — probably covers most of your health care needs. But many plans require you to pay for certain expenses out of your own pocket. Medical care and supplies are like any other services and products — price and quality vary.

Medicine in the United States, like any other profession, is a business, and there is a conflict of interest whenever the person recommending treatment benefits financially from providing that treatment. Many studies have documented unnecessary surgeries and other medical procedures. Always get a second opinion for any major surgery. Most health insurance plans, out of economic self-interest, require one anyway.

Therapy can be useful and even lifesaving. Have a frank talk with your therapist about how much total time and money you can expect to spend and what kind of results you expect. As with any professional service, a competent therapist should be able to give you a straight answer if he or she is looking out for your psychological *and* financial well-being.

Alternative medicine (holistic and chiropractic, for example) is gaining attention because of its focus on preventative care and treatment of the whole body or person. Although it can be dangerous to undertake if you are in critical condition, alternative treatment for many forms of chronic pain or disease may be worth your investigation. It may lead to better *and* lower-cost health.

If you must take certain drugs on an ongoing basis and pay for them out-of-pocket, ordering through a mail-order company can bring down your costs and be more convenient for refilling prescriptions. Your doctor may be able to provide more information about this. The following companies also offer generic drugs, which are medically equivalent to brand-name drugs:

- Family Pharmaceuticals of America (800-922-3444)
- Pharmail Corp. (800-237-8927)
- Retired Persons Services, Inc. (AARP) (800-456-2277)

If you don't have health-insurance coverage, you may end up paying a larger amount out of your own pocket. (You should really investigate buying minimal coverage.) Just remember — as with any other service or product that you buy — shop around. Don't take any one physician's advice as gospel.

Insurance

Insurance is a vast mine field. Part IV explains the different coverages, suggests what to buy and avoid, and reveals how to save on policies. The following are the most common ways people waste money unnecessarily on insurance.

Keeping low deductibles

The *deductible* is how much of a loss comes out of your pocket. On an auto insurance policy, for example, if your collision deductible is $100, you pay for the first $100 toward coverage of an accident and your insurance company picks up the rest. Low deductibles, however, translate into much higher premiums for you. In the long run, you should save money with a higher deductible, even factoring in the potential for greater losses. If you have a lot of claims, you still don't come out ahead with lower deductibles. Plus, low deductibles mean more claim forms to file for small losses (more hassle).

Covering small potential losses or unnecessary needs

You shouldn't buy insurance for anything that wouldn't be a financial catastrophe if you had to pay for it out of your own pocket. Insuring small gifts sent in the mail or buying dental or home warranty plans generally don't make sense for this reason. If no one is dependent on your income, then you don't need to buy life insurance either (who will be around to collect when you're gone?).

Failing to shop around

Rates vary *tremendously* from insurer to insurer. In Part IV, I recommend the best companies to call first for quotes.

Taxes

Taxes probably represent one of the largest — if not the largest — of your expenditures. (So why is it last here? You will soon see.)

Retirement savings plans are one of the best and simplest ways to reduce your tax burden. You learn a lot more about them in Chapter 8. Unfortunately, most people can't take full advantage of these plans because they spend everything they make. So, not only do they have less savings, they also pay higher income taxes — a double whammy.

I've attended many presentations where a fast-talking investment guy in an expensive suit lectures about the importance of saving for retirement and explains how to invest your savings. Yet details and tips about *finding* the money to save (the hard part for most people) are left to the imagination.

In order to take advantage of the tax savings that come with saving through retirement savings plans, *you must first spend less than you earn*. Only then can you afford to contribute to these plans. That's why the first part of this chapter is all about strategies to reduce your spending.

Another benefit of spending less and saving more is reduced sales tax. When you buy most consumer products, you pay sales tax. Therefore, the less money you spend and the more you save in retirement accounts, the more you reduce income *and* sales taxes. (See Chapter 7 for other tax-reduction strategies.)

Ten Costly Habits and How to Break Them

Humans are habitual creatures. All of us have habits we wish we didn't have, and breaking those habits can be very difficult. Costly habits are the worst. Here are some tidbits that may nudge you in the right direction toward breaking your own financially draining habits.

Abusing credit cards

Credit cards are like tobacco and alcohol. Using credit excessively and carrying balances from month to month can be bad for your financial health. Credit cards and credit lines encourage you to spend more than you can really afford and to live beyond your means. You're literally borrowing against (stealing from) your future.

Charging and running up balances on multiple credit cards can too easily fool you into thinking in terms of monthly payments rather than total debt owed. Having retailer cards from department stores and specialty shops is usually a danger sign for anyone trying to reduce spending, because retailers usually accept VISA and MasterCard anyway. Carrying balances on these retailer cards is a sure sign of danger!

Too much high-interest debt is like financial cancer. Once the debt tumor starts to grow, the interest begins to compound rapidly. At some point, debt minimum payments and interest charges can begin to hamper your ability to meet your basic living expenses.

Treatment for this financial cancer must be decisive and swift. If the debt gets too large, bankruptcy may be the best and only solution. In the United States, nearly one million people (roughly one in every 100 households) declare personal bankruptcy annually. (See Chapter 5 for a full discussion of options for getting out of debt.)

If you're a smoker

Despite the decline over the past few decades in smoking, 30 percent of all Americans still smoke. Using smokeless tobacco, which also causes long-term health problems, is on the increase. Americans spend more than $45 billion annually on tobacco products — that's a staggering $900 per year per tobacco user. The increased medical costs and lost work time costs are even greater, estimated at more than $50 billion every year.

Check with local hospitals for smoking cessation programs. The American Lung Association (check your local phone directory) also offers Freedom from Smoking clinics around the country. The National Cancer Institute (800-4CAN-CER) and the Office on Smoking and Health at the Centers for Disease Control (1600 Clifton Rd., Atlanta, GA 30333, phone 404-488-5705) offer free information guides containing effective methods to stop smoking.

Practicing poor eating habits

Five out of the ten leading causes of death — heart disease, certain types of cancer, stroke, diabetes, and arteriosclerosis — are caused largely by a diet high in fat and cholesterol. Cut out junk food and move away from a meat-based diet. You'll save money and feel better and look better (what more could you want?).

Abusing alcohol and other drugs

Nearly three-quarters of a million Americans seek treatment annually for alcoholism or drug abuse. These addictive behaviors, like bankruptcy, transcend all educational and socioeconomic lines in our society. Even so, studies have demonstrated that only one in seven alcoholics or drug abusers seeks help. Three of the ten leading causes of death — cirrhosis of the liver, accidents, and suicides — are associated with excessive alcohol consumption.

The National Clearinghouse for Alcohol and Drug Information (800-729-6686) can refer you to local treatment programs such as Alcoholics Anonymous. They also have pamphlets and other literature available on various types of substance abuse. The National Drug Abuse Information and Treatment Hotline (800-662-HELP) can refer you to local drug treatment programs and has literature available as well.

Shopping with spendthrift friends

Certain people bring out the big spender in you. Do something else with them besides shopping. If you can't find any other activity to share with them, try shopping with limited cash and no credit cards. That way you can't overspend on impulse.

Taking extravagant vacations you can't afford

You may be able to save $50 a week only to blow it all on one vacation. Vacations don't happen very often — not as often as most people would like. You can take time away from work and have a good time in ways that need not cost a small fortune. Go hiking, camping, or do the tourist thing where you live sometime. Or just block out some time and do what my cats do: take a lot of naps.

Cars and new cars

Contrary to advertising slogans, cars are not built to last — car manufacturers don't want you to stick with the same car year after year. They want you to have to buy a new one. New models are constantly introduced with new features and styling changes. Getting a new set of wheels every few years is an expensive luxury.

Some professionals like to use their cars to project a successful image. Picking up a prospective client in your spiffy new car is sure to make an impression, all right. I ask my counseling clients what they think when a salesperson arrives in a gleaming new sedan. My clients say that a new car is a sign that the person behind the wheel makes a lot of money — probably at their clients' expense! Many also wonder whether the person is a good financial manager. I don't think either image is one you want to project.

Don't try to keep up with the Joneses as they show off their new cars every year — for all you know, they're running themselves into financial ruin just to try to impress you. Let your neighbors admire you for your thriftiness and priorities instead.

The "money pit" house

Although real estate can be a good long-term investment, a great deal of your discretionary dollars can end up being poured into your home. Besides decorating and remodeling, some people feel the need to trade up to a bigger (therefore "better") home every few years. Of course, after they're in the better home, the remodeling and renovation cycle simply begins again, which costs even more money.

Be happy with what you have. The world will always have people with bigger, nicer houses and toys than you have.

Gambling

The house *always* comes out ahead in the long run. Why do you think so many governments run lotteries? Because they make money on people who gamble, that's why.

Casinos, horse and dog racetracks, and other gambling establishments are sure long-term losers for you. It's easy and tempting to get hooked on the dream of winning. And sure, occasionally you win a little bit (just enough to keep you coming back). Every now and then a few folks win a lot. But it's built into the odds that your hard-earned capital *mostly* winds up in the pockets of the gambling place's owners.

If you go just for the entertainment, bring only what you can afford to lose.

Clothing and style

If you want the effect of a new wardrobe every year, store last year's purchases away next year and then bring them out the year after! Or rotate your clothing inventory every third year. Either way, you can and should dramatically reduce shopping binges throughout the year. Your budget is tight, yet look at all the loot that sits in your closet!

Fashion designers and retailers are constantly working to tempt you to buy more. Don't do it. Toss the magazines that pronounce this season's look (or donate them to a local clinic's waiting room). Fashion, as defined by what people wear, changes quite slowly. In fact, the classics don't ever go out of style. Set your own standards.

An Inspiring Story

The story of one fellow I met, Ruben, can teach you something about how to save more of what you earn. At age 27, Ruben has managed to save more than $100,000. He accomplished this feat without the benefit of an inheritance or even a high-income job. In fact, he's never held a job with an annual salary above $30,000. And he's not a penny-pinching hermit who has no fun. He's taken two vacations outside the continental U.S., he enjoys tennis, karate, music, and going to movies, and indulges in meals out every now and then.

How can he do these things while living in the high-cost Bay Area, let alone San Francisco, which is one of the most expensive cities in the country? Simple: He's done it the old-fashioned way. At an early age, he learned to spend much less than he earns and to let the savings accumulate over the years.

I've run across other people that have Ruben's spending and saving discipline, although there seem to be fewer Rubens among younger people today. In his case (as with others like him), family members were powerful financial influences.

As early as age nine, Ruben remembers saving money in a bank account. He got a weekly allowance of $5. He would spend part of it, but part of it he always added to his savings. He also stashed away birthday and holiday gifts.

During junior high and high school, Ruben held a variety of part-time jobs, including a paper route and stints in a bowling alley and a restaurant. Ruben enjoyed working and saving money, but money was by no means an end in itself. "I wanted to buy a Mustang and wanted to go to Europe," Ruben recalls. By the end of high school, Ruben had saved $20,000 and had his car.

Ruben temporarily postponed his trip to Europe because he feared it would cost too much. He went to Hawaii instead, where he stayed free with a friend.

His patience toward traveling to Europe was rewarded. Several years later, Ruben finally got to go. An aunt in the travel business helped him buy a companion ticket, and he lived cheaply by staying with family and friends.

Setting financial goals and working toward them has carried over into Ruben's adult life. He looks ahead: "To people my age, it seems strange to be thinking about retirement 40 years ahead of time, but I see my mom entering her golden years without adequate money," he says. Thanks to his concern and prodding about saving for retirement, Ruben's aunt, too, recently started contributing to her 401(k) plan at the age of 42.

Thriftiness is not always valued in our culture. Like other thrifty folks, Ruben often faces pressure to loosen his wallet and "live it up." The teasing and criticism has changed over the years, but the song remains the same. In high school, he was "brutally teased" for wearing shoes with holes in them. Even today, "my friends think I'm much too frugal and don't enjoy life enough," he says.

Ruben has resisted the pressure to spend in several ways. First, having his own savings makes him feel independent and proud. When he was 12 years old, he got a paper route. His earnings were about $30 a month. "I would be a 50-percent saver — half got added to my savings and I spent the rest," he remembers. "Having money allowed me to buy things like presents for my family."

Secondly, he has been able to have his cake and eat it, too. By doing his homework, Ruben has been able to make his dollars go further. Rather than foregoing purchases, he makes sure he spends in smart ways. "The first question I ask myself is, 'Is this something I really need?,'" he says. Anything deemed to be a luxury gets paid for with cash. Meals out, considered by some to be a weekly necessity, fall into Ruben's luxury category. He treats himself to a restaurant meal once a month.

Once he decides to buy something, he takes his time buying it. For example, when he recently bought tennis shoes, he asked a clerk when the store would be closing out the model he was interested in. He waited until the end of the season to get what he wanted at a 50-percent discount.

He goes to see many of the best movies, but he gets 50–75 percent off the ticket price by going to matinees or by waiting for first-run movies to hit local discount theaters. Ruben indulges his music habit by buying used CDs at discount stores where he can get them for less than half the price of new ones.

He makes the most of what he has. For example, he still drives a '78 Toyota that has more than 200,000 miles on it. Thanks to regular preventive maintenance, his other operating costs beyond gas and insurance are negligible.

He's always had roommates to keep his living costs down. Despite living in San Francisco, his share of monthly rent has remained below $300.

Ruben's frugality has helped him build a solid financial foundation for his future. Of course, what works for Ruben may not be the answer for everyone. But if you want to save money towards future financial goals, you must save *first*, and *then* you can spend whatever's left over. "Automatic payroll deduction works great — that way your savings goes into a separate account without any thinking or work on your part," he says.

Making the most of one's income is a highly useful and underrated skill. With finances, as with dieting, too many people consume too much (and then regret it). Yet they rarely make the effort to unlearn old habits and acquire the knowledge to keep fit financially.

Do your homework before you spend and be resourceful. Recognize bad habits and overcome them. If you are living beyond your means because of overdependence on credit, then do yourself a favor and eliminate access to it. Your future is worth it.

Chapter 7

Taxes, Taxes, and More Taxes

• •

In This Chapter

▶ Dealing with the baffling tax system

▶ Figuring your marginal income tax rate

▶ Reducing the taxes on your employment income

▶ Lowering the taxes on your investment income

▶ Increasing your deductions

▶ Preparing your return with and without help

▶ What to do if you get an audit notice

▶ Ten costly financial planning and tax preparation mistakes

• •

> "The nation should have a tax system that looks
> like someone designed it on purpose."
>
> — Former Treasury Secretary William E. Simon, 1977

*T*he Winchester Mystery House is a bizarre tourist attraction near San Jose, California. It is named for its former owner, Sarah Winchester, widow of the rifle-manufacturing magnate. As the story goes, Sarah believed that she would not die so long as she continued to build on her property.

Proving that the prospect of death can be a very powerful motivator, Sarah Winchester kept builders working on her house around the clock for 38 years. Without a plan in mind, contractors added one room at a time. One hundred and sixty rooms later, you can imagine the result. Some staircases appropriately lead upstairs, but others dead end at ceilings. Some doors and windows open only to reveal walls.

The Winchester Mystery House provides tour guides to lead you through the property. If you were on your own, of course, you'd need a detailed map and a lot of patience and persistence to get from one end of the house to the other.

It's Not You, It's the System

And so it is with our tax system, which has quite a bit in common with the Winchester Mystery House. There is no master plan. The U.S. tax code has been changed incrementally over the years but has never been examined globally or given an overhaul.

Our tax system is so complicated because we don't like it yet can't seem to leave it alone. Nearly every year, elected officials make revisions to the tax code, changing, amending, deleting, and adding to the written rules and regulations that determine what is taxable, which deductions are legal, which aren't, and so forth. The revisions are the results of political bargaining that often doesn't factor in you, the taxpayer, at all (or common sense, for that matter).

Of course, not everyone suffers at the hands of the confusing, cumbersome tax code. Accountants and tax preparers are guaranteed employment as long as bewildered taxpayers need help. And the category of bewildered taxpayers includes most of us.

You might be interested to know that almost all of the congressional members who sit on the tax-writing committees — the Senate Finance Committee and the House Ways and Means Committee — *hire tax help, too.* A 1992 article in *Forbes* magazine found that 11 of the 12 members of the tax-writing committees don't prepare their own tax returns!

So, don't feel like an idiot when it comes time to fill out tax forms, because it's not you, it's the system. Nevertheless, even if you hire a tax advisor to help you navigate the tax morass, it's worth some of your time to understand how the system treats certain financial moves you make.

The value of understanding the system

You pay a lot of money in taxes, probably more than you realize. Most people remember only whether they got a refund or owed money on their return. But you *should* care about the *total* taxes you pay.

When you file your tax return, all you're doing is balancing your checkbook, so to speak, against the federal and state governments' version of your checkbook. You're settling up with tax authorities over the amount of taxes you paid during the year versus the total tax that you still owe based on your income and deductions. Some people feel lucky when they get a refund, but really, all a refund indicates is that you overpaid in taxes during the year. You should have had this money in your own account all along.

The only way to know the *total* taxes you pay is to get out your federal and state tax returns. On each of those returns is a line that shows the *total tax:* This is line 53 on federal 1040 returns. Add up the totals from your federal and state tax returns, and you'll probably see one of the single largest expenses of your financial life (unless you have an expensive home or a huge gambling habit).

If you don't understand the tax system, you probably pay more in taxes than necessary. Your tax ignorance can lead to mistakes, which can be costly if the IRS and your state government catch errors in your favor. With the proliferation of computerized information and data tracking, discovering mistakes has never been easier.

The tax system, like other public policy, is built around incentives to encourage "desirable" behavior and activity. Home ownership, for example, is considered desirable because it encourages people to take more responsibility for maintaining buildings and neighborhoods. Clean, orderly neighborhoods are supposed to be the result of home ownership. Therefore, the government offers all sorts of tax benefits (allowable deductions) to homeowners to encourage people to buy and own homes.

To understand the tax system is to understand what your government thinks you should be doing. Naturally, not all people follow the path the government encourages — after all, it's a free country. You've spent years rebelling against your parents. Why should the government get better treatment?

The difference between rebelling against your parents and being a rebellious taxpayer, of course, is that as a taxpayer, the cost comes out of your pocketbook (I haven't heard of many parents who penalize kids' defiance in *cash*). The *fewer* desirable activities that you engage in, the *more* you pay in taxes. If you understand the options, you can choose those that meet your needs as you approach different stages of your financial life.

Many people resent the taxes they pay — they feel that they pay too much and get too little in return. Therefore, another benefit to understanding the tax system is that you can become a more informed voter and citizen in the democratic process.

Your marginal income tax rate: the single most important tax number

"What's marginal about my taxes?" I hear you asking. "They're huge! They're not marginal in my life at all!" *Marginal* is a term often applied to those things that are small or minimally acceptable. Sort of like getting a C- on a school report card (or an A- if you're from an overachieving family).

Marginal tax rates are a powerful concept. Once you understand them, you can understand the value of many financial strategies that affect the amount of taxes you pay. And because you pay taxes on your employment income as well as on the earnings from your investments held outside of retirement accounts, a lot of personal financial decisions are at stake.

First, you must understand that when it comes to taxes, *not all income is treated equally.* This fact is not self-evident. If you work for an employer and have a constant salary during the course of a year, a steady and equal amount in federal and state taxes is deducted from your paycheck. It sure looks as though all that earned income is being taxed equally.

In reality, however, you pay less tax on your *first* dollars of earnings and more tax on your *last* dollars of earnings. For example, if you're single and your taxable income totaled $30,000 during 1993, you paid federal tax at the rate of 15 percent on the first $22,100 of taxable income and 28 percent on income from $22,100 up to $30,000.

Table 7-1 gives federal tax rates for singles and married households filing jointly.

Table 7-1   1993 Federal Income Tax Brackets and Rates

Singles Taxable Income	Married-Filing-Jointly Taxable Income	Federal Tax Rate
Less than $22,100	Less than $36,900	15%
$22,100 to $53,500	$36,900 to $89,150	28%
$53,500 to $115,000	$89,150 to $140,000	31%
$115,000 to $250,000	$140,000 to $250,000	36%
Over $250,000	Over $250,000	39.6%

Taxable income is defined as the amount of income on which you actually pay taxes. You don't pay taxes on your total income for the following two reasons:

- ✔ **Not all income is taxable.** For example, you pay federal tax on the interest you earn on a bank savings account but not on the interest from municipal bonds.

- ✔ **You get to subtract deductions from your income.** Some deductions are available just for being a living, breathing human being. In 1994, single people get an automatic $3800 standard deduction and married couples filing jointly get $6350. (People over age 65 and those who are blind get a slightly higher deduction.) Other expenses, such as mortgage interest and property taxes, are deductible to the extent that your total deductions exceed the standard deductions.

Your *marginal tax rate* is the rate of tax that you pay on your *last* or so-called *highest* dollars of income. In the example of a single person with taxable income of $30,000, that person's federal marginal tax rate is 28 percent. In other words, she effectively pays 28 percent federal tax on her last dollars of income — those dollars in excess of $22,100.

Your marginal tax rate allows you to quickly calculate additional taxes that you would pay on additional income. Conversely, you can delight in quantifying the amount of taxes that you save by reducing your taxable income, either by decreasing your income or by increasing your deductions.

If you don't particularly feel like figuring your marginal tax rate, or if you just want to test your accountant's competence, ask him or her what it is. These folks should be able to tell you in a flash. If they can't, you'd better find someone else to prepare your taxes.

As you are painfully aware, you don't pay only federal income taxes, you also pay state income taxes — that is, unless you live in Alaska, Florida, Nevada, South Dakota, Texas, Washington, or Wyoming. Those states have no state income taxes at all. Your *total marginal rate* includes your federal *and* state tax rates.

You can look up your state tax rate by getting out your most recent year's state income tax-preparation booklet.

Alternative minimum tax (say what?)

You may find this hard to believe, but (as if the tax system weren't already complicated enough) there is actually a *second* tax system. This second system may raise your taxes higher than they would have been. Let me explain.

Over the years, as the government has grown hungrier for revenue, taxpayers who slash their taxes by claiming lots of deductions have come under greater scrutiny. So, the government created a second tax system — the *alternative minimum tax* (AMT) — to ensure that those with high deductions pay at least a certain amount of taxes on their income.

If you have a lot of deductions from state income taxes, real estate taxes, certain types of mortgage interest, and passive investments (for example, limited partnerships and rental real estate), you may fall prey to AMT.

At the federal level lurk two AMT tax brackets: 26 percent for AMT income up to $175,000 and 28 percent for everything over that amount. AMT restricts you from claiming certain deductions and requires *adding items of income back*. So, you have to figure your tax under the AMT system *and* under the other system and pay whichever amount is higher. Sorry to depress you.

Strategies to Reduce Taxes on Employment Income

You are supposed to pay taxes on any income you earn from work. Countless illegal ways are available to reduce your employment income — for example, not reporting it — but you could very well end up with a heap of penalties and extra interest charges on top of the taxes you owe. And, of course, you could get tossed in jail.

I don't want you to lose even more money by paying unnecessary penalties and serving jail time to boot, so I'll focus on the many *legal* ways to reduce your taxes.

Retirement plan contributions

A retirement plan is one of the few painless and completely legal ways to reduce your taxable employment income. Besides reducing your taxes, you build up a nest egg so that you don't have to work for the rest of your life.

Money that you tuck away through employer-based retirement plans, such as 401(k) plans or 403(b) plans, and through SEP-IRAs or Keoghs for the self-employed, is deducted from your taxable income. Therefore, if you contribute $1,000 to one of these plans, and your combined federal and state marginal tax rate is 32 percent, you reduce your federal and state taxes by $320. Like the sound of that? How about this: Contribute another $1,000, and your taxes drop *another* $320.

If this process sounds easy, that's because it is. In fact, everyone should invest in a retirement plan. You benefit both in the short-term and the long-term. So, why don't more people take advantage of this tax break?

Many people cannot reduce taxes this way because they *spend* all of their current employment income and, therefore, have nothing left to put into a retirement account. If this scenario sounds familiar, you need to reduce your spending first in order to be able to contribute money to a retirement plan. Take a tour through Chapter 6, which is all about how to reduce your spending.

If your employer does not offer the option of saving money through a retirement plan, see whether you can drum up support for it. Lobby the benefits and human resource departments. If they resist, you might add this to your list of reasons to consider other employment (but don't leave for this reason alone). Many employers offer this valuable benefit, but others don't. Some company decision-makers themselves don't understand the value of these accounts. Other employers think that they cost an arm and a leg to set up and administer.

Individual retirement account (IRA) contributions may or may not be tax-deductible, based on your circumstances. You should first exhaust contributions to the previously mentioned accounts that are tax-deductible. Chapter 8 contains all the details you need to determine whether your IRA contribution is tax-deductible.

Income shifting

This tax-reduction technique is more esoteric and is available only to those who can control *when* they receive their income.

For example, suppose that your employer tells you in late December that you're eligible for a bonus. You are offered the option to receive your bonus in either December or January. Looking ahead, if you're pretty certain that you will be in a higher tax bracket next year, you should choose to receive your bonus in December.

Or suppose that you run your own business and think that you'll be in a lower tax bracket next year. Perhaps you plan to take time off to be with a newborn or take an extended trip. You can send out some invoices later in the year so that your customers won't pay you until January, which falls in the next tax year.

Strategies to Reduce Taxes on Investment Income

For investments that you hold in *tax-sheltered* retirement accounts [IRAs and 401(k) plans, for example], you don't need to worry about taxes. These moneys are not taxed until you actually withdraw funds from the retirement account.

Distributions and profits from investments that you hold outside of tax-sheltered retirement accounts are exposed to taxation. Interest, dividends, and other profits from the sale of an investment at higher than purchase price (called *capital gains*) can be taxed.

Taxes on investment income should definitely concern you if you are in a relatively high tax bracket. If you're in the 31 percent or higher federal bracket (which kicks in for singles with taxable income over $53,500 and couples filing jointly over $89,150), you should pay attention to the rest of this section.

If you're in the 28 percent federal tax bracket, these strategies may or may not help. Pay close attention to the issues that increase or decrease the benefits of following each of the strategies.

If you're in the 15 percent federal bracket, you can probably skip this section. Or you may sit quietly at your desk and amuse yourself until the rest of the class is finished.

In this section are some of the best methods to reduce the taxes on investments exposed to taxation. (Chapter 12 discusses in detail how and where to invest money held outside of tax-sheltered retirement accounts.)

Directing more money into retirement accounts

Make sure that you take advantage of opportunities to direct your employment earnings into retirement accounts. You get two possible tax bonuses by investing more of your money in retirement accounts. First, your contributions to the retirement account may be immediately tax-deductible (see Chapter 8 for complete details). Second, the distributions and growth of the investments in the retirement accounts aren't taxed until withdrawal.

This strategy makes particular sense if you're currently in a high tax bracket and can allow the money to compound over many years (at least 10 years, preferably 15 – 20 years or more).

Having a comfortable chunk of money outside of retirement accounts increases your ability to contribute more to retirement accounts. Even if you need all of your monthly work earnings to meet living expenses, you should still fund a retirement account by taking money from other investments.

Investing in tax-free money market funds and bonds

If you're in a high enough tax bracket, you may find that you come out ahead with tax-free investments. Tax-free investments yield less than comparable investments that produce taxable earnings. But because of the difference in taxes, the earnings from tax-free investments *can* end up being greater than what you're left with from taxable investments.

Tax-free money market funds can be a better alternative to bank savings accounts that pay interest subject to taxation. Likewise, tax-free bonds are longer-term investments that pay tax-free interest. (Read Chapter 12 for more specifics on which tax-free investments may be right for your situation.)

Selecting other tax-friendly investments

What you get to keep is what matters in the long run. Too often, when selecting investments, people mistakenly focus on past rates of return. We all know that the past is no guarantee of the future. But an even worse mistake is choosing an investment with a reportedly high rate of return without considering tax consequences.

Mutual funds

Mutual funds are a good example. When comparing two similar funds, most people prefer a fund that averages returns equaling 14 percent per year to one earning 12 percent. But what if the 14-percent-per-year fund causes you to pay a lot more in taxes? What if, after factoring in taxes, the 14-percent-per-year fund nets just 9 percent, while the 12-percent-per-year fund nets an effective 10-percent return? In such a case, you'd be unwise to choose a fund solely on the basis of the higher reported rate of return.

Investments that appreciate in value and don't distribute much in the way of taxable income are considered *tax friendly*. Examples include stocks and mutual funds that invest in growth-oriented securities. (See Chapter 12 for specific investment ideas for non-retirement account investments.)

Real estate

Real estate is one of the few areas with privileged status in the tax code. In addition to deductions allowed for mortgage interest and property taxes, you can depreciate rental property to reduce your taxable income.

If your rental property shows a loss for the year (when you figure your properties' income and expenses), you may not be able to take this loss on your tax return. If your *adjusted gross income* (AGI) is less than $100,000, and you actively participate in managing the property, you are allowed to deduct your losses on operating rental real estate of up to $25,000 per year. (Your AGI is your total wage, interest, dividend, and all other income minus retirement account contributions and losses from investments.)

If you make more than $100,000 per year, you start to lose these write-offs. At an income of $150,000 or above, you cannot deduct rental real estate losses from your other income. People in the real estate business (for example, agents and developers) who work more than 750 hours per year in the industry may not be subject to these rules (check with a tax advisor).

You should be aware of tax consequences related to your investments, but don't go overboard. In their glee to reduce taxes, some investors in the lower tax brackets focus too much on tax-free funds when they might do better with taxable funds.

Strategies to Increase Your Deductions

Deductions are just that: You subtract them from your income before you calculate the tax you owe. To make things more complicated, the IRS gives you two methods for determining your total deductions. The good news is that you get to pick the method that leads to the best solution for you — whichever way offers greater deductions.

Standard deductions

The first method for deductions requires no thinking or calculations. If you have a relatively uncomplicated financial life, taking the so-called standard deduction is generally the better option. Symptoms of a simple tax life are not earning a high income, renting your house or apartment, and lacking unusually large expenses, such as medical bills, moving expenses, or loss due to theft or catastrophe. As mentioned earlier, single folks qualify for a $3800 standard deduction, and married couples filing jointly get a $6350 standard deduction in 1994. If you're 65 or older or blind, you get a slightly higher standard deduction.

Itemized deductions

The other method of determining your allowable deductions is itemizing them on your tax return. This method is definitely more of a hassle, but if you can tally up more than the standard amounts above, itemizing saves you money. Use Schedule A of IRS Form 1040 for summing up your itemized deductions (see Figure 7-1).

Many of the categories on Schedule A, such as line 9a, "Home mortgage interest and points reported to you on Form 1098," are reasonably self-evident. If you own your home and have a mortgage, early in the new year your bank should send you Form 1098, which tells you to the penny how much deductible interest you paid.

Organizing to deduct

The hard part for most people is locating Form 1098 and all the other scraps of paper you need when you're completing your tax return. Setting up a filing system can be a *very* big time-saver.

If you have limited patience for setting up neat file folders and you lead an uncomplicated financial life (that is, you haven't saved receipts throughout the year that you need for tax purposes), you can confine your filing to January and February. During those months, you get tax summary statements on wages paid by your employer (Form W-2), investment income (Forms 1099), and home mortgage interest (Form 1098) in the mail. Set up a folder that's labeled with something easy to remember ("1994 Taxes" is a brilliant choice) and dump these papers as well as your tax booklet into it. When you're ready to crunch numbers, you should have everything you need to complete the form.

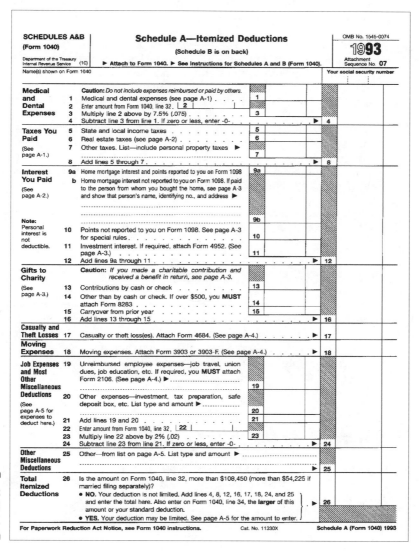

Figure 7-1:
IRS
Schedule A.

A more thorough approach is to organize the bills you pay into individual folders during the entire year. This method is essential if you own your own business and need to tabulate your expenditures for office supplies each year. No one is going to send you a form totaling your office expenditures for the year — you're on your own. You might also have a folder marked "1994 Mortgage" to collect monthly mortgage bills. This method isn't as critical because you do get a summary. Yes, banks sometimes make mistakes, so the more detail you have, the better off you are in the event of an audit.

Software programs can be a godsend for organizing your tax information during the year and can save you time and accounting fees come tax-preparation time. My favorite is Quicken by Intuit. Intuit also has a terrific software program for small-business accounting and business management called QuickBooks. (See Chapter 22 for more information about financial software.)

A number of available resources explain in excruciating detail what you can and cannot deduct on Schedule A. These include IRS instructions, preparation guide books, and software, which are reviewed later in the chapter. They are a delightful read — when you're tired of twiddling your thumbs and just can't think of anything else to do, that is.

The following are the most *overlooked* deductions and strategies (some are listed on Schedule A, and others are on Form 1040 itself).

Purchasing real estate

When you buy a home, two big ongoing expenses of home ownership — the interest on your mortgage and your property taxes — are deductions you can claim on Schedule A. You are allowed to claim mortgage interest deductions for a primary residence (where you actually live) and on a second home for mortgage debt totaling $1,000,000 (and a home equity loan of up to $100,000). You can also write off the full amount of your property taxes, even if you live in a multimillion-dollar mansion.

Shifting or bunching deductions

If, when you total up your itemized deductions on Schedule A, the total is lower than the standard deduction, then you should take the standard deduction. This total is worth checking each year, because you may have more deductions in some years than others, and you may occasionally be able to itemize.

Because you can control when you pay particular expenses that are eligible for itemizing, you can *shift* or *bunch* more of them into the select years when you have enough deductions to take advantage of itemizing. Suppose, for example, that you are using the standard deduction this year because you don't have many itemized deductions. Late in the year, though, you become certain that you'll be buying a home next year. With mortgage interest and property taxes to write off, you also know that you can itemize next year. It makes sense, then, to shift and collect as many deductible expenses as possible into next year. For example, if you typically make more charitable contributions in December because of the barrage of solicitations you receive when you're in the giving mood, you may want to write the checks in January rather than in December.

If you're sure that you won't have enough deductions in the current year to itemize, try to shift as many expenses as you can into the next tax year.

Trading consumer debt for mortgage debt

If you own real estate and haven't borrowed the maximum that you can and if you've run up high-interest consumer debt, you may be able to trade one debt for another. If you can refinance your mortgage and pull out extra cash to pay off your credit card, auto loan, or other costly credit lines, you may be able to save yourself money.

You can usually borrow at a lower interest rate for a mortgage and get a tax deduction as a bonus, which lowers the effective borrowing cost further. Consumer debt, such as on auto loans and credit cards, is not tax deductible.

This strategy involves big danger. Borrowing against the equity in your home can be an addictive habit. I've seen cases in which people run up significant consumer debt three or four times and then refinance their home the same number of times over the years to bail themselves out.

An appreciating home creates the illusion that excess spending isn't really costing you. But debt is debt, and all borrowed money has to be repaid. In the long run, you wind up with greater mortgage debt, and paying it off takes a bigger bite out of your monthly income. Refinancing and establishing home equity lines cost you more in terms of loan application fees and other charges (points, appraisals, credit reports, and so on).

At a minimum, continued expansion of your mortgage debt handicaps your ability to work toward other financial goals. In the worst case, easy access to borrowing encourages bad spending habits that can lead to bankruptcy or foreclosure against your debt-ridden home.

Deducting charitable contributions and expenses

If you itemize, you can deduct contributions made to charities. For example, most people know that when they write a check for $50 to their favorite church or college, they can deduct it. **Note:** Make sure to get a receipt, because a cancelled check is no longer sufficient documentation.

Many taxpayers overlook the fact that you can also deduct expenses for work you do with charitable organizations. For example, when you go to a soup kitchen to help prepare and serve meals, you can deduct your transportation costs to get there. You just need to keep track of your bus fares or driving mileage. The IRS currently allows a deduction of 12 cents per mile.

You also can deduct the fair market value of donations of clothing, household appliances, furniture, and other goods to charities, many of which will even drive to your home to pick up the stuff. Rather than throwing things in the garbage, which just adds to the pile up in a landfill, see whether the Salvation Army, Goodwill, or other similar organization is interested in your donation. Just make sure to keep some documentation — write up an itemized list and get it signed by the charity. Consider taking pictures of more valuable donations.

Deducting auto registration fees and state insurance

If you must pay a fee to the state to register and license your car, you can itemize the expenditure as a deduction (line 7, "Other Taxes"). The IRS only allows you to deduct that part of the fee that relates to the value of your car. The state organization that collects the fee should be able to tell you what portion of the fee is deductible. If it's a user-friendly organization, they'll even show this figure for a fee on your invoice.

Several states — California, New York, New Jersey, and Rhode Island — have state disability insurance funds. If you pay into these funds (check your W-2), you can deduct this fee as state and local income taxes on line 5 of Schedule A.

Deducting miscellaneous expenses

A number of so-called *miscellaneous expenses* are deductible on Schedule A. Most of these relate to your job or career and managing your finances.

Educational expenses

You may be able to deduct your tuition, books, and travel costs to and from classes if your education is related to your career. Specifically, you can deduct these expenses if your course work improves your work skills. Continuing education classes for professionals may be deductible. If the law or your employer requires you to take courses to maintain your position, they are deductible. **Note:** Educational expenses that allow you to change or move into a new field or career are not deductible.

Job search and career counseling

After you obtain your first job, you may deduct legitimate costs relating to finding another job within your field. For example, suppose that you're a chef in a steak house in Chicago and decide that you want to do stir fry in Los Angeles. You take a crash course in vegetarian cooking and then fly to L.A. a couple of times for interviews. You can deduct the cost of the course and your trips — *even if you don't change jobs.* If you hire a career counselor to help you figure everything out, you can deduct that cost, too. On the other hand, if you're burned out on cooking and decide that you want to become a professional volleyball player in L.A., that's a new career. You might get a better tan, but you won't generate deductions from changing jobs.

Unreimbursed expenses related to your job

If you pay for your own subscriptions to trade journals to keep updated in your field or buy a new desk and chair to ease back pain, you can deduct these costs. If your job requires you to wear special clothes or a uniform, you can write off the cost of purchasing and cleaning them, as long as the clothes aren't suitable for wearing outside of work. (I wonder what the IRS would do in the case of Cliff Clavin?)

If you buy a computer for use outside the office at your own expense, you may be able to deduct the cost if it's for the convenience of your employer, is a condition of your employment, and is used more than half the time for business.

Union dues and membership fees for professional organizations are also deductible.

Investment and tax-related expenses

Investment and tax-advisor fees are deductible, as are subscription costs for investment-related publications. Accounting fees for preparing your tax return or conducting tax planning during the year are deductible, as are legal fees related to your taxes. If you purchase a home computer to track your investments or prepare your taxes, you can deduct that expense, too.

When you deduct miscellaneous expenses, you only get to deduct the total of these costs that exceed 2 percent of your *AGI.* To refresh your memory, AGI (adjusted gross income) is your total wage, interest, dividend, and all other income minus retirement account contributions and losses from investments. That's what the calculations on lines 21-24 of Schedule A make you figure out.

Deducting self-employment expenses

If you are self-employed, you deduct a variety of expenses from your income before calculating the tax that you owe. If you buy a computer or office furniture, you can deduct those expenses (sometimes they need to be gradually deducted or *depreciated* over time). Salaries for your employees, office supplies, rent or mortgage interest for your office space, and phone expenses are also generally deductible.

Although some business owners cheat on their taxes, some self-employed folks don't take all the deductions they should. In some cases, people simply aren't aware of the wonderful world of deductions. For others, large deductions raise the risk of an audit. Taking advantage of your eligible deductions makes sense and saves you money.

The following are common mistakes made by people who are their own bosses.

Being an island unto yourself

If you're self-employed, it's usually a mistake to go it alone around tax time. Many issues can trip up even the sharpest solo shop. It's worth the money to hire tax help — either in the form of a tax professional or by using the better self-help or computer software packages on the market (see the section on software later in this chapter).

Tax administrative screwups

When you are self-employed, you are responsible for correct and timely filing of all taxes owed on your income or on that of your employees. Without an employer and a payroll department to handle the paperwork for withholding taxes on a regular basis, you need to make estimated tax payments on a quarterly basis.

If you have employees, you also need to withhold taxes on their income from each paycheck they receive and make timely payments to the IRS and appropriate state authorities. In addition to federal and state income tax, you also need to withhold and send in social security and any other state or locally mandated payroll taxes.

For paying taxes on your income, you can obtain Form 1040-ES with instructions from the IRS (call 800-TAX-FORM). This form comes complete with an estimated tax worksheet and the four payment coupons to send in with your quarterly tax payments.

To learn about all the amazing rules and regulations of withholding and submitting taxes from employees' paychecks, ask the IRS for Form 941. Once a year, you also need to complete Form 940 for unemployment insurance payments to the feds.

Unless you're lucky enough to live in a state with no income taxes, don't forget to call for your state's estimated income tax package. Check your local telephone directory for the number of your state tax authorities. If, like me, you have trouble remembering their silly name (in California the responsible body is the Franchise Tax Board — just what you would have guessed, right?), you can also find their number by getting out the instruction booklet that you used to prepare last year's state income taxes.

Start-up expenses

Many small-business owners use some of their personal assets when starting a business. For example, perhaps you owned a home computer that you put to service for your new business. When you convert the computer to business use, you can deduct some of the original costs of purchase.

Receipts, receipts, and more receipts

When you pay with cash, it's hard to follow the paper trail for all the money you spend. At the end of the year, how are you going to remember how much you spent for parking or client meals if you keep no record? For purchases under $25, you don't need a receipt as proof, but you do need a system or written record of your daily petty cash purchases. Most pocket calendars or daily organizers include ledgers that allow you to jot down these small purchases. If you can't be that organized, at least get a receipt for cash transactions and stash them in a file folder in your desk. Or keep receipts in envelopes labeled with the month and year.

Depreciating what is deductible

One of the goodies in the 1993 tax bill was a provision that allows you to deduct up to 75 percent more of your equipment purchases annually. Now you can take up to $17,500 as a current year deduction (the previous limit was $10,000).

Choosing the wrong entity or form of organization

When you set up your own business, you can structure its legal and tax organization in a variety of ways. To incorporate or not to incorporate is the first question you want to answer. Those motivated to incorporate do so not out of a love of paperwork (which can be considerable) but out of the desire to shield themselves from liabilities and lawsuits that might be brought against the business.

A *corporation* is a separate legal entity from you, the individual. For example, if a customer slips on a stray banana peel at your office and decides to sue, if you're incorporated, the customer can sue your company but can't go after your personal assets.

Incorporating makes more sense if you have employees, customers who visit the office, or if you do business with many vendors.

Incorporating is not always the right answer. For professional servicers, such as self-employed attorneys, physicians, or financial planners, incorporating may not necessarily be useful as protection against professional negligence suits related to their work. In such cases, the law treats the business and the professional as one and the same. The answer for these folks is *professional liability insurance*. Check with the professional association(s) in your field.

Not funding a retirement plan

I am always shocked and amazed by the number of accountants who do not encourage their clients to contribute to retirement plans to reduce taxes. You should be saving money toward retirement anyway, and you can't beat the tax break. People who are self-employed are allowed to save up to about 20 percent of their net income on an annual basis. To learn more about SEP-IRAs, Keoghs, and other retirement plans, see Chapter 8.

Not using numbers to help manage business

If you go to all the time, trouble, and expense of keeping records and filing tax returns, make sure you reap the rewards of all your work. Some small-business owners track their income, expenses, and data on their customers and staff performance quarterly or even monthly. But many don't. If you don't, your tax return may be the one and only time during the year when you take a financial snapshot of your business.

Some bookkeepers and tax preparers can provide you with management information reports on your business from the tax data they compile for you. Just ask! Likewise, software like Quicken, QuickBooks, and tax-preparation packages can help, too (see Chapter 22).

Not paying family help

If your children, spouse, or other relatives help with some aspect of your business, consider paying them for the work. Besides showing them that you value their work, this practice may reduce your family's tax liability. For example, a child is likely not in as high an income tax bracket as you are. So by shifting income to the child, you cut your tax bill.

Sideline businesses, deductions, and audits

Some "financial experts" claim that you can slash or even completely eliminate your tax bill by setting up a sideline business. You can sell your services while doing something you enjoy (something legal, of course!). The problem, they argue, is that as a regular wage earner who receives a paycheck from an employer, you can't write off many of your other (that is, personal) expenses. The experts usually promise to show you the secrets of tax reduction if you shell out a few bucks for their audiotapes and notebooks of inside information.

My wife, for example, is a terrific photographer. She could take pictures at a friend's wedding or on our next vacation and then sell the pictures, which "experts" claim allows her to deduct many expenses that she previously couldn't, including airfare for travel. According to these "experts," you can write off part of your utility bills and rent for your home office. Turn your restaurant meals with potential clients (that is, your friends) into tax deductions. Entertain them at your health club and deduct those dues, too! Before you know it, you have wiped out most of your taxes. You're entitled, they say, because lots of big corporations and wealthy people also pay next to nothing in taxes.

The pitch is enticing, but the reality is that sideline or hobby businesses are audited at a very high rate by the IRS, so you're more than likely to get caught deducting personal expenses. Furthermore, the IRS has significantly tightened the rules for writing off meals, entertainment, club dues, and the like. The bottom line is that you need to be operating a legitimate business for the purpose of generating income and profits, not tax deductions. For example, your sideline business, in most cases, must realize a profit three out of the last five years of operation to allow for deductions. Even if your sideline business meets this as well as other IRS requirements, it's illegal to deduct any expenses not directly applicable to your sideline business.

Tax Preparation and Planning Options

You should be planning throughout the year to make sound strategic decisions about taxes. By the time you actually file your return, it's usually too late to take advantage of many tax-reduction strategies. You do, however, have an array of choices about how you prepare your returns. Which approach makes sense for you depends on the complexity of your situation and your level of interest and knowledge about taxes.

Doing it yourself

Odds are, you do many things for yourself, such as cooking, shopping, and home repairs. You may do these chores because you enjoy them, because you save money by doing them, or because you want to develop particular skills.

By preparing your own tax return, you develop a better understanding of the ins and outs of the tax code and of your own situation. Reading the list of deductions that don't apply to you might motivate you to take some action before you go at it again next year. If your financial situation doesn't change much from year to year, neither does your return. You may need to do a little reading to keep up with the small number of changes in the tax system and laws that might affect your situation.

IRS publications and phone assistance

If you have a simple, straightforward tax return, filing it on your own using only the IRS instructions is fine. This approach is as cheap as you can get. The only costs are time, patience, photocopying expenses (you should always keep a copy for your files), and postage to mail the completed tax return.

This approach has a lot in common with an Easter egg hunt. If you've ever hunted Easter eggs, you know the prizes are well hidden (from a child's perspective, anyway) and require some real searching to ferret out. In my own egg-hunting experience, I don't recall any large, flashing neon signs reading "DON'T MISS THIS ONE!" pointing to hidden eggs. Likewise, IRS publications don't, in general, have Tip or Warning icons like this book. For example, here's something you don't usually see in an IRS publication:

STOP! ONE OF THE MOST COMMONLY OVERLOOKED DEDUCTIONS IS A TAX-DEDUCTIBLE RETIREMENT ACCOUNT CONTRIBUTION. YOU STILL HAVE TIME TO START ONE AND WHACK OFF HUNDREDS, MAYBE *THOUSANDS* OF DOLLARS FROM YOUR TAX BILL! HURRY!

Another danger of relying on the IRS is that it has been known to give wrong information on a more-than-infrequent basis. If you call the IRS with a question, be sure to take notes about your conversation to protect yourself in the event of an audit. Date your notes and include the name of the tax employee you talked to, what you asked, and the employee's responses. File your notes in a folder with a copy of your completed return.

In addition to the standard instructions that come with your tax return, the IRS offers some free and helpful books that you can call to request. Publication 17, *Your Federal Income Tax,* is designed for individual tax-return preparation. Publication 334, *Tax Guide for Small Businesses,* is for (you guessed it) small-business tax-return preparation. These guides serve as useful references and provide more detail and insight than the basic IRS publications. Call 800-TAX-FORM to have the guides sent to you free of charge. (Actually, nothing is free. You've already paid for IRS guides through your taxes.)

Other preparation and advice guides

Books about tax preparation that are written in clear, simple English and that highlight common problem areas are invaluable. They supplement the official instructions not only by helping you to complete your return correctly but also by saving you as much money as possible.

Quite a number of preparation guides are on the market. My favorites are

- *JK Lassers Tax Guide*
- *Consumer Reports Books Guide to Income Tax*
- *Price Waterhouse Personal Tax Advisor*

Software

If you have access to a computer, tax-preparation software can be a great tool. Think of it as having a squadron of excellent accountants living on your desktop. Plus, you don't have to go to the library to get all the forms for your particular return only to discover that the library is out of them and then call the IRS and wait for weeks for your forms to arrive in the mail — they're all in the software!

Software also has the virtue of automatically recalculating all the appropriate numbers on your return when one of them changes — no more whiting out math errors because your dog was sleeping on some of the receipts.

Among the better tax preparation software packages on the market are

- TurboTax (for Windows and DOS)
- MacinTax (for the Macintosh)

Hiring help

Some people hire a contractor to help with a home-remodeling project because they lack the time, interest, energy, or skill to do it themselves. For the same reasons, some choose to hire a tax advisor.

A competent tax specialist can save you money — sometimes more than enough to pay their fees — by identifying tax-reduction strategies you may overlook. They can also reduce the likelihood of an audit, which can be triggered by blunders you might make.

Tax practitioners come with varying backgrounds, training, and credentials. One type of professional is not necessarily better than another. Think of them as different types of specialists who are appropriate for different circumstances. The four main types are preparers, enrolled agents (EAs), Certified Public Accountants (CPAs), and tax attorneys.

Preparers

Among all the tax practitioners, preparers generally have the least amount of training, and a greater proportion of them work part-time. As with financial planners, no national regulations apply to preparers, and no licensing is required.

H&R Block is the largest and most well-known tax-preparation firm in the country with nearly 9,000 offices nationwide. In addition to Block and other national firms such as Jackson Hewitt and Triple Check, there are also lots of mom-and-pop shops. The appeal of preparers is that they are relatively inexpensive — they can do most basic returns for $100 or less. The drawback, of course, is that you may be hiring a preparer who doesn't know any more than you do.

Preparers make the most sense for folks who don't have a lot of complications in their financial lives, who are budget minded, and who hate doing their own taxes. If you're not good about hanging onto receipts or don't want to keep your own files with background details about your taxes, you should definitely shop around for a tax preparer who's going to be around for a few years. You may need all that stuff someday for an audit, and many tax preparers keep and organize their clients' documentation rather than return everything each year. (Can you blame them for keeping it after they went to the trouble of sorting it all out of the shopping bags?) Also, it may be safer to go with a firm that is open year-round (some small shops are only open during tax season) in case tax questions or problems arise.

Enrolled agents (EAs)

A person must pass IRS scrutiny in order to be called an *enrolled agent*. This license allows the agent to represent you before the IRS in the event of an audit. Continuing education is also required. Training to become an EA is generally longer and more sophisticated than that for a typical preparer.

Enrolled agents' prices tend to fall between those of a preparer and a CPA. Returns with a few of the more common schedules (such as Schedule A for deductions and Schedule B for interest and dividends) shouldn't cost more than a couple hundred dollars to prepare.

EAs are best for people with moderately complex returns who don't necessarily need tax-planning advice throughout the year (although some EAs provide this service as well as prepare returns). You can get names and telephone numbers of EAs in your area by contacting the National Association of Enrolled Agents (800-424-4339).

Certified public accountants (CPAs)

Certified public accountants go through significant training and examination to receive the CPA credential. In order to maintain this designation, a CPA must also complete a fair number of continuing education classes every year.

CPA fees vary tremendously. Most charge around $100 per hour, but CPAs at large companies and in high cost-of-living areas tend to charge somewhat more.

CPAs are of greatest value to people completing some of the more unusual and less user-friendly schedules, such as K-1 for partnerships, Schedule C for self-employed folks, or Form 8829 for home office deductions. CPAs are also helpful for people who had a major or first-time tax event during the year, such as the sale of a home, retirement, or childcare tax-credit determination.

If your return is uncomplicated and your financial situation is stable, hiring a high-priced CPA year after year to fill in the blanks is a waste of money. A CPA once bragged to me that he was making about $500 per hour from some of his clients' returns that only required 20 minutes of an assistant's time to complete.

Paying for the additional cost of a CPA on an ongoing basis makes sense if you can afford it and if your situation is reasonably complex or dynamic. If you are self-employed and/or file lots of other schedules, it may be worth hiring a CPA. But you needn't do so year after year. If your situation grows complex one year and then stabilizes, consider getting help for the perplexing year and then using preparation guides, software, or a lower-cost preparer or enrolled agent in the future.

Tax attorneys

Tax attorneys are hired guns that can tackle major tax problems and issues. Unless you're a superhigh-income earner with a complex financial life, it's prohibitively expensive to hire a tax attorney to prepare your annual return. In fact, many tax attorneys don't prepare returns as a normal practice.

Because of their level of specialization and training, tax attorneys tend to have the highest hourly billing rates — $200 – $300 per hour is not unusual.

The more training and specialization a tax practitioner has (and the more affluent his clients), the higher his hourly fee is. Select the one that best meets your needs. Fees and competence at all levels of the profession vary significantly. If you're not sure of the quality of work performed and the soundness of the advice, try getting a second opinion.

Help, I Got an Audit Notice!

On a list of real-life nightmares, most people would rank tax audits right up there with rectal exams.

The primary trauma of an audit is that it makes many people feel like they're on trial and are being accused of a crime. Don't panic.

First of all, you may be one of the tens of thousands of taxpayers whose returns are audited at random. No, the IRS isn't headed by sadists. Random audits help the IRS identify common areas on tax forms where taxpayers make mistakes or try to cheat.

Secondly, you might be getting audited simply because a business that reports tax information on you, or someone at the IRS, made an error regarding the data on your return.

About 20 percent of audited returns are left unchanged by the audit — that is, you don't end up owing more money. In fact, if you're the lucky sort, you may be one of the 5 percent of folks who actually gets a refund because the audit finds a mistake in your favor!

Unfortunately, it's more likely that you'll be one of the roughly 80 percent of audit survivors who end up owing more tax money. The amount of additional tax that you owe in interest and penalties hinges on how your audit goes.

Audit preparation

Preparing for an audit is sort of like preparing for a test in school. The IRS informs you of which sections of your tax return the agency wants to examine.

The first decision you face when you get an audit notice is whether to handle it yourself or turn to a tax advisor to represent you. Hiring representation costs money out-of-pocket but saves you time, stress, and possibly money.

If you normally prepare your own return and are comfortable with your understanding of the areas being audited, then do it yourself. If the amount of tax money in question is small in comparison to the fee you'd pay the tax advisor to represent you, self-representation is probably the answer. However, if you're likely to turn into a babbling, intimidated fool and are unsure how to present your situation, hire a tax advisor to represent you (see the "Hiring help" section earlier in this chapter for information about who to hire).

If you decide to handle the audit yourself, get your act together sooner rather than later. Don't wait until the night before to start gathering receipts and other documentation. You may find, for example, that you can't find certain documents and need to contact others to get copies.

You need to document and be ready to speak with the auditor only about the areas the audit notice said were being investigated. Organize the various documents and receipts into folders. You want to make it as easy as possible for the auditor to review your materials. *Don't* show up, dump shopping bags full of receipts and paperwork on the auditor's desk, and say, "Here it is — *you* figure it out."

Don't bring documentation for parts of your return not being audited, either. Besides creating more work for yourself, you're required to discuss only those areas mentioned in the audit letter.

Whatever you do, *don't ignore your audit request letter.* The IRS is the ultimate bill-collection agency. And if you end up owing more money (the unhappy result of most audits), the sooner you pay, the less interest and penalties you'll owe.

The day of reckoning

Two people with identical situations can walk into an audit and come out with very different results. The loser can end up owing much more in taxes and have the audit expanded to include other parts of the return. The winner can end up owing less tax money than he or she really should pay under the tax laws.

Here's how to be a winner:

Treat the auditor as a human being

Obvious advice, but very often not practiced by taxpayers. You may be resentful or angry about being audited. You're a busy person with better things to do with what little free time you have, so you might be tempted to gnash your teeth and tell the auditor how unfair it is that an honest taxpayer like you had to spend scores of hours getting ready. You might feel like ranting and raving about how the government wastes too much of your tax money or that the party in power is out to get you.

Bite your tongue.

Believe it or not, most auditors are decent people just trying to do their job. They are well aware that taxpayers don't like seeing them. Don't suck up, either — just relax and be yourself. Behave as you would around a boss whom you like — with respect and congeniality.

Stick to the knitting

You're there to discuss *only* the sections of your tax return in question. The more you talk about other areas or things that you're doing, the more likely the auditor will probe into other items.

Don't argue when you disagree

State your case. If the auditor wants to disallow a deduction or otherwise increase the taxes you owe and you don't agree, state once why you don't. If the auditor won't budge, don't get into a knock-down, drag-out confrontation. He or she may not want to lose face and is inclined to find additional tax money — that's the auditor's job. Remember: You can plead your case with several layers of people above your auditor. If that fails and you still feel wronged, you can take your case to tax court.

Don't be intimidated

Most auditors are not tax whizzes. The work is stressful — it's not easy being in a job in which people dislike seeing you. Turnover is quite high. Thus, many auditors are fairly young, just-out-of-school types who majored in something like English, history, or sociology. They may know less about tax and financial matters than you do. The basic IRS tax boot camp that auditors go through doesn't come close to covering all the technical details and nuances in the tax code. So, you may not be at such a disadvantage regarding knowledge after all, especially if you work with a tax advisor (most of whom know more about the tax system than the average IRS auditor).

Chapter 8
Financial Independence (Retirement)

- -

In This Chapter

▶ Misers, spendthrifts, and everyone in between

▶ What you'll need to get through retirement

▶ Ten ways to make up for lost time

▶ Types of retirement accounts

▶ The advantages of saving in retirement accounts

▶ Keys to a happy retirement

- -

Do not wait until you are thirsty to dig a well.
— Chinese proverb

*M*any people toil away at work, dreaming idealized dreams about the day they can give it all up and do what they want when they want. People often assume that this magical day will arrive when they retire or win the lottery, whichever comes first.

The odds for hitting the jackpot in the lottery aren't very good. And I've never cared much for the term *retired.* It seems to imply idleness or the end of usefulness to society. But if retirement means not having to work at a job (especially one you don't enjoy) and having financial flexibility and independence, then I'm all for it.

Part of the American dream is to be able to retire sooner rather than later. But this idea has some obvious problems.

First, you set yourself up for disappointment. If you want to retire by your mid-sixties (when social security kicks in), you'll need enough money to live for an additional 20 years, maybe longer. Two decades is a long time to be living off your savings. You're going to need a good-sized chunk — more than most people realize. The earlier you hope to retire, the more money you need to set aside and the earlier you have to start saving. Either that, or plan to work part-time in retirement to earn more income!

More than half of Americans between the ages of 18 and 34 and a quarter of those aged 35 to 54 have not begun to save for retirement. This kind of planning is like preparing to be an Olympic swimmer by hauling your lawn chair to the beach to watch the waves come crashing in.

Retirement-planning illiteracy is another classic area in which lack of education causes people much financial harm. The government instituted programs like social security to ensure a minimal retirement income for subsistence purposes. Social security literature talks about the importance of supplementing social security with additional personal savings, but people rarely read this stuff until they are just about to retire. This oversight is yet another reason why schools should be teaching Personal Finance 101.

A Tale of Two Extremes

When it comes to money, you're a hardworking miser, a free spirit or spend-thrift, or something in between.

Misers

Some people want to make and save a lot of money in order to retire early. I see people pursuing higher-paying jobs and increasingly demanding careers to accomplish this goal. They make many personal sacrifices in exchange for income today.

The problem is that tomorrow might not come. Even if all goes according to plan, will you know how to be happy when you're not working if you spend your entire life making money? More importantly, who will be around to share your leisure time? One of the costs of engaging in an intense career is time spent away from friends and family. You may indeed realize your goal of retiring early, but you may be putting off too much living today in expectation of living tomorrow.

As Charles D'Orleans said in 1465, "It's very well to be thrifty, but don't amass a hoard of regrets."

Spendthrifts

At the other extreme are those who live only for today. A friend of mine once said, "I'm not into delayed gratification." *Shop till you drop* seems to be the motto of this personality type. "Why bother saving when I might not be here tomorrow?" reason these people.

The danger of this approach is that tomorrow may come after all, and most people don't want to spend all their tomorrows working for a living. The earlier neglect of saving, however, handicaps the possibility of *not* working when you are older.

A happy medium

Neither extreme is good, obviously.

You may be surprised to hear me say that if you must pick an extreme, I think it's better to pick the spendthrift approach. (Do I hear a collective sigh of relief?) As long as you have a financial safety net, a nest egg of some kind or relatives or friends you can really count on, and you don't mind continuing to work (assuming your health allows), you should be okay. At least you're making use of your money and, hopefully, deriving value and pleasure from it.

The only difference between a person without savings or access to credit and some homeless people is a few months of unemployment.

Postponing doing what you love and being with people you love until retirement can be a mistake. It may never come. Retirement can be a great time for some people; for others, it is a time of boredom, loneliness, and worry. You won't know what it will be like for you until you get there. In the meantime, you need to figure out where you stand financially regarding retirement planning. If you're like most working people, you need to increase your savings rate for retirement.

What You Need for Retirement

If you hope to stop working someday or reduce the time you spend working for an income, you will need sufficient savings to support yourself. Most people — particularly young people and those who don't work well with numbers — underestimate the amount of money needed to retire.

And what about today? Are you prepared to meet unexpected expenses?

Many people don't think about saving for retirement until middle age rolls around. As you'll soon see, this mistake can be costly. To figure out how much you should be saving per month given your retirement goals, there's no way to avoid crunching a few numbers (but don't worry, it's easier than doing your taxes).

Luckily for you, you don't have to start cold. Studies have shown how people typically spend money before and during retirement. On average, most people need about 70 to 80 percent of their preretirement income throughout retirement to maintain their standard of living.

For example, if your household earns $40,000 per year before retirement, you're likely to need $28,000–$32,000 (70–80 percent of $40,000) per year during retirement to live the way that you're accustomed to living. The 70–80 percent is an average. Some people may need more money simply because they have more time on their hands to spend their money. Others adjust their standard of living and need less.

You, of course, are a shining example of the diversity that makes our country great. You're unique! You're not average in any way! So, how do you estimate what *you* will need?

I'll start with the simplest and easiest way and simply tell you what percentage you'll need. (I know we've only known each other a short time, but let me have a chance to offer some friendly counseling.)

The following three profiles can give you a rough estimate of the percentage of your preretirement income that you'll need during retirement. Pick the one that most accurately describes your situation. If you fall between two of the descriptions, pick a percentage in the middle.

- **65 percent.** You save a large amount (15 percent or more) of your annual earnings, are a high-income earner, will own your home free of debt by retirement, and do not anticipate leading a lifestyle in retirement that reflects your current high income.

- **75 percent.** You save a reasonable amount (5 to 10 percent) of your annual earnings, will still have some mortgage debt or a small rent to pay by the time you retire, and anticipate having a standard of living in retirement that is comparable to what you have today.

- **85 percent.** You save little or none of your annual earnings, will have a significant mortgage payment or growing rent to pay in retirement, and anticipate wanting or needing to maintain your current lifestyle throughout retirement.

Of course, there is a more precise approach to figuring out how much you'll need per year in retirement. Those who are more data oriented may feel comfortable tackling this method. You need to figure out where you're spending your money today (worksheets are located in Chapter 4) and then work up some projections for your financial situation in retirement.

This more precise method is far more time-consuming, and because you're making projections into an uncertain future, it may not yield information any more accurately than the first method. But the figure it yields is personalized to your current lifestyle and your vision of yourself in retirement.

A final approach (for free spirits and the truly faithful) is simply to pick an annual dollar amount or percentage of your current income that you believe would allow the kind of retirement lifestyle you need. (A ouija board can come in handy for this approach!)

What You Have: Retirement Building Blocks

Did you play with Legos or Tinker Toys when you were a child? You start by building a foundation on the ground and then build up and out. Before you know it, you're creating bridges, castles, and panda bears. Planning for retirement isn't exactly like playing with blocks, but the concept is the same. You need a basic foundation for your necessary retirement reserves to grow.

If you have been working steadily, you may already have a foundation, even when you haven't been actively saving towards retirement.

Social security

Social security is the Rodney Dangerfield of government programs. Contrary to widespread cynicism, it's really not bad and will be there for you. If you think you can never retire because you have no cash saved, I'm happy to inform you that you're wrong. You've got some social security.

Social security is intended to provide you with a subsistence level of income in retirement to provide for basic necessities such as food, shelter, and clothing. It is *not* intended to be your sole source of income. Few people could maintain their current lifestyle without supplementing social security with personal savings and company retirement plans.

How does social security work?

Prior to changes made in social security regulations in 1983, if eligible, you could collect full social security payments at age 65. This rule no longer holds true. If you were born before 1943, you're still eligible to collect full social security benefits at age 65. If you were born in 1960 or after, you have to wait until age 67 for full benefits. If you were born between 1943 and 1959, full benefits are payable to you at age 66 plus or minus some number of months, depending on the year you were born.

The problem with social security is that when the system was created early in this century, its designers underestimated how long people would live in retirement (the Roosevelt administration must have included a lot of young people). Thanks to scientific advances and improved medical care, life expectancies have risen substantially during this century. As a result, many of today's retirees get back far more in benefits than they paid into the system.

For this reason, the age at which you can start collecting full benefits has been increased from 65 to 67 and may be increased again. It may seem unfair, but it's necessary to update the system for the realities of our increased longevity, large federal budget deficits, and aging baby boomers. Without changes, the social security system could collapse, because it is fed by a relatively small number of workers while supporting large numbers of retirees.

In addition to paying for retirement-income checks for retirees, your social security taxes also provide for disability insurance for you, survivor income insurance for your financial dependents, and Medicare, the health-insurance program for retirees.

The amount of social security benefits that you receive in retirement depends on your average earnings during your working years. Don't worry about the fact that you probably earned a lot less many years ago. The social security benefits calculations increase your older earnings to account for the lower cost of living and wages in the good old days.

How much will I get from social security?

Table 8-1 shows the approximate size of your expected monthly allowance from social security. The first column gives your average *yearly employment earnings* (in today's dollars) on which you paid social security taxes. The second column contains your approximate *monthly benefit amount* (in today's dollars) that you'll receive when eligible for full benefits.

Note: The benefit amounts in Table 8-1 are for an individual income earner. If you're married, and one of you doesn't work, the nonworking spouse collects 50 percent of what the working spouse collects. Working spouses are eligible for either individual benefits or half of their spouses' benefits, whichever amount is greater.

Table 8-1	Your Expected Social Security Benefits
Annual Earnings	*Approximate Monthly Benefit*
$10,000	$500
$20,000	$750
$30,000	$1,000
$40,000	$1,050
$58,000 or more	$1,120

When should I start collecting social security?

You *can* start collecting reduced retirement income benefits as early as age 62. But because the benefits are permanently reduced by 20 percent when you start drawing at age 62 rather than age 65, you should consider a few factors to determine the age at which you should start drawing benefits.

First is your health. If you knew exactly how long you were going to live, you could calculate what age would be best to start drawing benefits. To save you the drudgery of crunching numbers, you'll probably come out ahead by waiting until age 65 to start collecting benefits if you live into your late seventies or longer. Most people make it into their early sixties, some into their seventies, eighties, and nineties, and, of course, some make it to the century mark and end up on Willard Scott's weather report on the *Today* show.

Another consideration is the amount of employment income you're still earning. As of 1993, if you earn more than $7,680 during the year, your social security benefits get whacked down by one dollar for every two dollars you earn over this amount. This reduction is like an additional 50-percent income tax surcharge! Ouch! So, if you're still earning a good income, it's better to wait until you're 65.

How much work makes me eligible?

To be eligible to collect social security benefits, you need to have worked a minimum number of years. Just to keep you on your toes, the government counts quarters (¼ of a year) instead of years. If you will reach age 62 after 1990, you need 40 quarters of work credits to qualify for social security retirement benefits.

If for some reason you work only the first half of a year or only summer months, don't despair. You don't need to work part of every quarter to get a quarter's credit. You get credits based on the income you earn during the year. As of this writing, you get the full four quarters credited to your account if you earn approximately $2,500 or more in a year. In earlier years, folks got one quarter's credit for each actual calendar quarter in which they earned $50. To get 40 quarters of coverage, you basically need to work ten years.

To get credits, you must report the income and pay taxes on it, including social security. In other words, you encounter problems when you pay people under the table or neglect to declare income — you may be cheating others or yourself out of valuable benefits.

In order to get a more precise handle on your social security benefits, call the Social Security Administration at 800-772-1213 and ask for Form 7004, which allows you to receive a record of your reported earnings and an estimate of your social security benefits. Checking your earnings record is a good thing to do every few years, because occasional errors do arise.

Personal savings

Money that you are saving towards retirement can include money under the mattress as well as money in a retirement account such as an Individual Retirement Account (IRA), 401(k), or similar plan.

Equity in rental real estate can be counted as well. Deciding whether to include the equity in your primary residence (your home) is trickier. If you don't want to count on using this money in retirement (for example, you don't want to sell the house and move away), then don't include it when you tally your stash.

In reality, many people do sell their homes when they retire to move to a cheaper region of the country, to move closer to family, or to downsize to a more manageable household. So, you may want to count a portion of your home equity in your total assets for retirement.

Pensions

Pension plans are a benefit offered by some employers — mostly larger organizations and government agencies. Even if your current employer does not offer a pension, you may have earned pension benefits through a previous job (if you have become fully eligible for retirement benefits, the accumulated amount will still be yours when you leave the company).

The plans I'm referring to are known as *defined-benefit plans*. You qualify for a monthly benefit amount to be paid to you in retirement based on your years of service.

Although each company's plan differs, all plans calculate and pay benefits based on a formula. A typical one might credit you with 1.5 percent of your salary for each year of service (full-time employment). For example, if you work ten years, you earn a monthly benefit worth 15 percent of your monthly salary.

This type of benefit is quite valuable. In the better plans, an employer puts away 5–10 percent of your salary to pay your future pension. What the employer is effectively doing is putting money away in an account for your retirement. This money is not quoted as part of your salary — it's *in addition* to your salary. You never see it in your paycheck and it is not taxed.

To qualify for pension benefits, you don't have to stay with an employer long enough to receive the 20-year gold watch. Under current government regulations, an employee must be fully *vested* (entitled to receive full benefits based on years of service upon attaining retirement age) after five years of service.

Retirement planning

The following worksheet (Table 8-2 and minitable) assume that you will retire at age 66 and that your investments will grow 4 percent per year faster than inflation.

Table 8-2	Retirement Planning Worksheet
1. Annual retirement income needed in today's dollar (see earlier in this chapter)	$ _____ / year
2. Annual social security (see Table 8-1)	– $ _____ / year
3. Annual pension benefits (ask your benefits department). Multiply by 60% if your pension won't increase with inflation during retirement.	– $ _____ / year
4. Annual retirement income needed from personal savings (subtract lines 2 and 3 from line 1)	= $ _____ / year
5. Savings needed to retire at age 66 (multiply line no. 4 by 15)	$ _____
6. Value of current retirement savings	$ _____
7. Value of current retirement savings at retirement (multiply line 6 by Growth Multiplier in following minitable)	$ _____
8. Amount you still need to save (line 5 minus line 7)	$ _____
9. Amount you need to save per month (multiply line 8 by Savings Factor in following minitable)	$ _____

To get a more precise handle on where you stand in terms of retirement planning, call Fidelity Investments (800-544-8888) or T. Rowe Price (800-638-5660) and ask for their retirment planning booklets. I recommend retirement planning software in Chapter 22 that can save you a great deal of number-crunching.

Your Current Age	*Growth Multiplier*	*Savings Factor*
26	4.8	.001
28	4.4	.001
30	4.1	.001
32	3.8	.001
34	3.5	.001
36	3.2	.001
38	3.0	.002
40	2.8	.002
42	2.6	.002
44	2.4	.002
46	2.2	.003
48	2.0	.003
50	1.9	.004
52	1.7	.005
54	1.6	.006
56	1.5	.007
58	1.4	.009
60	1.3	.013
62	1.2	.020
64	1.1	.041

Defined-benefit pension plans are becoming rarer for two reasons. First, they are very costly for employers to maintain. Many employees don't understand how these plans work and why they're so valuable, so companies don't get mileage out of their expenditures here — employees don't see the money, so they don't appreciate how generous the company is being. Secondly, most of the new jobs being generated in the U.S. economy are with small companies that typically don't offer these types of plans.

More and more employers are offering plans like 401(k)s, in which employees elect to save money out of their own paychecks. Known as *defined-contribution plans,* these plans allow you to save toward your retirement at your own expense rather than at your employer's expense. Thus, more of the burden and responsibility for saving for retirement falls on your shoulders in 401(k) and similar plans. You need to be educated about how these plans work.

Employers offering defined-contribution plans should educate employees about how to save by using these plans. Defined-contribution plans transfer the burden of planning for retirement from the employer to the employee. Most people are ill equipped to know how much to save and how to invest the money.

Ten Ways to Make Up for Lost Time

Now that you're motivated to save for retirement, you know that you should have started sooner. It's okay, all is not lost. In fact, there are some tried-and-true ways to make up for lost time. Saving money doesn't have as much sex appeal as spending it does, so don't expect much help or praise from your friends and neighbors. But your mother will think she brought you up well, and you'll have the satisfaction of knowing that you're doing the right thing.

Turbocharge your savings rate by slashing your spending

There are only two ways to boost your savings: Earn more money or cut your spending (or do both). Become a lean, mean, spending machine to boost the rate at which you're saving money. Chapter 6 offers suggestions for a spending diet that won't leave you hungry.

Be more realistic about your retirement age

If you extend the age at which you plan to retire, you get a double financial benefit. You're earning and saving money for more years and spending your nest egg over fewer years. Of course, if your job is making you crazy, this option may not be too appealing.

Statistics show that people change careers three to five times during their adult working lives. Try to find work that makes you happy and that provides income now, and consider working, at least part-time, during the years typically considered the retirement years.

Use home equity

Psychologically, the prospect of tapping the cash in your home can be troubling. After getting together the down payment, you probably worked for many years to pay off that sucker. You're delighted not to have to mail a mortgage payment to the bank anymore. You've been released from that particular prison. But what's the use of owning a house free and clear when you have no cash? All that money tied up in the house can help to increase your standard of living in retirement.

There are a number of ways to tap your home's equity. You can sell your home and either move to a lower-cost property or rent. If you're over 55, you may be eligible to take a once-in-a-lifetime $125,000 capital-gains tax exclusion. Another option is a *reverse mortgage* — where you get a monthly income check as you build a loan balance against the value of your home. The loan is paid when your home is finally sold (see Chapter 9 for more information about reverse mortgages).

Get aggressive with your investments

The faster the rate at which your money grows and compounds, the less you need to save each year to reach your goals. Earning just a few extra percentage points per year on your investments can dramatically slash the amount you need to save. The younger you are, the more powerful the effect.

For example, if you're in your mid-30s, were your investments to appreciate 6 percent per year faster than the rate of inflation rather than 4 percent, the amount you need to save each month to reach your retirement goals drops by about 40 percent!

Turn a hobby into supplemental retirement income

My father just retired at age 64. Over the years, he has built many things for recreation, including a two-story, four-bedroom house. He's a perfectionist — some of his stuff is real art! He'll soon realize that he can make a small fortune by selling handmade furniture or consulting on repair and remodeling projects for homeowners who are all thumbs (like me).

Even if you've earned a living in the same career over many decades, you have skills that are portable and can be put to profitable use. Pick something you enjoy and are good at. Go to the library and do some research on how to market your services and wares. Remember, as people get busier, more specialized services are being created to support their hectic lives. There's also demand for quality, homemade goods of all varieties. Be creative! You never know — you may wind up on the covers of *Business Week* and *Inc.*

Invest in a tax-wise way

A free way to boost the effective rate of return on your investments without taking on additional risk is to insulate more of your money from taxation. Many people who are able to save money do not do so in a way that minimizes their taxes.

By directing your savings into a tax-favored retirement account like a 401(k) plan, you get an immediate tax deduction for your contribution. For a typical person, a third or more of your contribution represents money you would have had to pay in federal and state taxes. This money gets to work for you, rather than the government, in the years ahead. Plus, the money compounds over the years without taxation.

As for money outside of tax-sheltered retirement accounts, if you're in a relatively high tax bracket, you may earn more by investing in tax-free investments and other vehicles that do not make a great deal of taxable distributions. (Chapter 12 discusses these investments in detail.)

Take a look at jobs that offer retirement plans

When evaluating employers, cash is usually king. As long as the position includes health insurance, most people are concerned only about the salary. But having access to a retirement savings plan is a valuable benefit. Even more beneficial is a pension plan, which pays you a monthly retirement benefit based on your years of service (a completely pain-free way to plan for retirement). If you're lucky enough to have choices, check out these plans when considering a job offer.

What's a retirement savings plan such as a 401(k) worth in the long run? A lot. Suppose that a person who is 40 years old earns $35,000 per year and pays 35 percent in federal and state taxes on her last dollars of income. If she can contribute 10 percent of her salary, or $3,500 per year, into a retirement savings plan, she reduces her current year's taxes by $1,225. Assume further that the money she contributes this year grows at the rate of 8 percent per year until she withdraws the money at age 65. If she pays taxes at the same rate she is paying today when she withdraws the money at age 65, she'll have about $15,580 left.

If she hadn't saved this money through a retirement plan, she would have only $8,080 at 65. In other words, on *just one year's contribution* of $3,500, she nets $7,500 more in retirement because of the tax-deferred compounding allowed in the retirement account. On top of that, if she's like most people, she probably would have been tempted to spend the money if she had had access to it, so she might not have saved even the $8,080 if she hadn't used the retirement account.

Put saving for junior's college expenses on the back burner

It may sound selfish, but you need to take care of *your* future first. If you're not taking advantage of saving through tax-sheltered retirement accounts, you should be doing so before setting aside money in custodial savings accounts for your kids. You're missing out on terrific tax savings! You and your kids can always borrow more money when it comes time for college, and if you want to pay more then, withdraw money from your retirement account to pay down student loans. (See Chapter 14 for more details).

Stop funding cash-value life insurance plans

Most people who invest in these insurance plans should get out of them (see Chapter 17 for tax-wise ways to do this). They are inferior ways to save in comparison to retirement savings plans that are tax deductible. Premiums paid into a cash-value life insurance plan are *not* tax deductible. If you need life insurance, buy term life insurance (see discussion of life insurance in Chapter 17).

Think about inheritances

First, let's be clear: I don't endorse knocking off rich relatives whom you don't care for. But people do die every day, and their estates (large or small) typically go to their children or grandchildren. Although you should never count on an inheritance to support your retirement, in reality, you may inherit money someday. If you want to see what impact an inheritance has on your retirement calculations, simply add the amount (use a conservative estimate) that you expect to inherit to your current total assets.

Retirement Accounts

If you're like most people, you may not fully appreciate all the benefits of contributing to *retirement accounts.* And you may have a number of objections or reasons not to. I'll get to the objections in a moment. In the meantime, check out the following goodies you get by saving and investing in the many types of retirement accounts that are available.

The advantages of retirement accounts

Contributing to retirement accounts confers numerous advantages: Contributions are generally tax-deductible, earnings compound without taxation over time, you can save less money and spend more, and you incur penalties for early withdrawal (I'll explain why this is an advantage).

Contributions to retirement accounts are (generally) tax deductible

Retirement accounts are misnamed. They should really be called *tax-reduction accounts.* If they were, people might be more excited about contributing to them. For many, avoiding higher taxes is the motivating force that opens the account and starts the contributions.

When I got my first job out of college, retirement was the last thing on my mind. But when I got around to preparing my first tax return, I found that I owed Uncle Sam an additional couple hundred dollars, which hurt after paying taxes all year. I did some research and learned about Individual Retirement Accounts (IRAs).

I took $2,000 out of my savings and deposited it into a newly opened IRA at a mutual fund company. I immediately got to subtract $2,000 from the income on which I had to pay taxes. After plugging in my brand-new $2,000 deduction, my tax return showed that I merited a *refund* of a few hundred dollars. So, by putting money in a retirement account, not only are you planning wisely for your future, but you get an immediate financial reward: lower taxes.

Earnings and growth on your investment compound without taxation over time

Once money is in a retirement account, any interest, dividends, and appreciation add to your account without being taxed.

Of course, there's no such thing as a free lunch — these accounts don't allow for *permanent* avoidance of taxes. Yet you can get a really great lunch at a discount — you get to defer taxes on all of the accumulating gains and profits until you withdraw the money down the road. Thus, more money is working for you over a longer period of time.

You can save less money and spend more

That's right! Because of all of the terrific tax benefits you get by saving and investing in retirement accounts, you end up with more money now than if you had saved the money elsewhere.

You incur penalties for early withdrawal

If you withdraw funds from retirement accounts before age 59 ½, you not only have to pay income taxes on the withdrawals, but you also must pay early withdrawal penalties — 10 percent in federal and varied state charges.

Yes, this *is* an advantage! The system is built to save you from your bad habits!

Retirement accounts are there for just that reason — saving toward retirement. If you could easily raid them without penalties, then the money wouldn't be there when you really need it. And if you have an emergency or want to retire early, there are ways to avoid this early withdrawal penalty (detailed in the "Ten objections to saving in retirement accounts" section, next).

Ten objections to saving in retirement accounts

Despite all the great tax benefits of saving in a retirement account, many people aren't psyched to take advantage of them. Everyone has unique priorities. Maybe you're saving for a home purchase or paying off student loans. Some reasons, however, stem from a lack of knowledge and understanding. The following are the objections to contributing to tax-favored accounts that I hear most frequently. Some of these objections can be overcome, whereas others are legitimate excuses.

Why your taxes probably won't go up when you retire

You may get an added bonus from deferring taxes on your retirement account assets if you are in a lower tax bracket when you withdraw the money. You may very well be in a lower tax bracket in retirement, because most people have less income when they're not working.

Some people fret that their taxes will increase when they retire. Although it could happen, the following simple example shows you why your time is better spent worrying about more important issues.

Earlier in this chapter, I created the scenario of a woman earning $35,000 per year who pays 35 percent in federal and state taxes on her last dollars of income. She contributes 10 percent, or $3,500, per year into a retirement savings plan, thereby decreasing her current year's taxes by $1,225. Assume that the money she contributes grows at the rate of 8 percent per year until she withdraws the money at age 65. After paying taxes at the same rate on her withdrawal at age 65 as she pays today, she'll have about $15,580 left. If she hadn't saved this money through a retirement plan, she would have had only $8,080 at age 65.

Now, suppose that her career takes off and she earns more money (and pays more taxes) as she gets closer to retirement. How high would her retirement tax rate have to be before she should regret having saved in the retirement account? Answer: She would have to pay about 67 percent in taxes on the retirement account withdrawals to be worse off, a very unlikely occurrence.

The only people who may not want to start saving money in retirement accounts are those who are close to retirement. For these people, the small number of years available for funds to compound tax deferred before withdrawal may not be worthwhile, especially if they can expect their tax rate to increase in retirement.

Note: If you are near retirement and already have money in a tax-sheltered type of retirement account — for example, at your employer — by all means continue to keep it in a tax-sheltered account if you leave. You can do this, for example, by rolling the money over into an IRA account. *Never* pass up an opportunity to continue the tax-deferred compounding of your money.

Retirement's a long way away

When you're in your twenties or thirties, age 65 seems like the distant future. For many people, it's not until middle age that some warning bells start to stimulate thoughts about one's golden years.

Delaying the age at which you start to sock money away is usually a financial mistake. The sooner you start to save, the less painful it is each year, because your contributions have more years to compound. Ideally, you should start saving a small portion of your employment earnings with your very first paycheck. Start your kids' saving habits while they're young!

Only losers who don't know how to have a good time save for retirement

Some people really believe this statement. But I also know losers who don't save for retirement and still don't know how to have a good time (none of my counseling clients, of course). This attitude is just a rationalization. The reality is that if you manage your finances efficiently and start working towards your goals sooner, you can spend more in the long run. Besides, who says spending all your money is the only way to have fun?

Withdrawing money before age 59 ½ incurs penalties

I like nice, round numbers. But the IRS never has — personally, I think it's a conspiracy to make our lives more difficult and keep accountants employed. Age 59 ½ is the magic age. After that, you can withdraw money from your retirement accounts without penalty.

If you save enough to retire before 59 ½, there's a way to take money out of your retirement account without triggering penalties. The IRS allows you to withdraw money before 59 ½ as long as you do so *in equal, annual installments based on your life expectancy*. The IRS (this is slightly chilling) even has a little table that allows you to look up your life expectancy.

I need to reserve emergency money

What if you have catastrophic medical expenses or a disability? You can legally make early withdrawals from retirement accounts for these reasons.

What if you just run out of money because you lose your job? Although you can't bypass the penalties, if you're earning so little income that you need to raid your retirement account, you'll surely be in a low tax bracket. So, even though you pay some penalties to withdraw retirement account money, the lower income taxes you pay as compared to the taxes you would have paid when you earned the money originally should make up for most or all of the penalty.

If you get in a financial pinch while you're still employed, some company retirement plans allow you to borrow against your cash balance (it's like loaning money to yourself).

Another strategy to meet a short-term financial emergency is to withdraw money from your IRA and return it within 60 days to avoid paying penalties. I don't generally recommend this because of the penalties invoked if you don't make the 60-day deadline.

If your only borrowing option right now is a high-interest credit card, you should save three to six months' worth of living expenses in an accessible account before funding a retirement account (see Chapter 12).

I'm saving for my children's education

It's perfectly natural to want to provide for your child's future. But doing so can be a financial mistake.

You need to provide for your retirement first and then worry about the kids. This practice isn't selfish — do you really want to have to leach off your kids when you're old and frail because you didn't save any money for yourself? Retirement savings accounts are a smart investment for the future of the entire family, and they give you immediate tax breaks. As you'll learn in Chapter 14, the financial-aid system effectively penalizes you for saving money outside of retirement accounts. And loans are available to make up for insufficient college savings. (See Chapter 14 for more information.)

There are greener investment pastures elsewhere

Real estate is a good example. Some people find retirement accounts boring and believe that they can get a better return in the real estate market. Rental real estate can appreciate in value and produce increasing rental income over the years. This is a legitimate reason for not maximizing retirement plan contributions.

However, although real estate provides some tax breaks, it also has drawbacks. First, while you accumulate the down payment, you may pay higher income taxes if you're sacrificing contributions to retirement accounts that are tax deductible.

Secondly, rental real estate produces income that is taxable and is added to all your other income during the year. In a retirement account, the earnings continue to compound without taxation and you decide when you want to start drawing on the money.

There may be a way for you to have your cake and eat it, too. Many types of investments — stocks, bonds, mutual funds, precious metals, and even real estate — can be held in retirement accounts. (See Chapter 13 for more details.)

I'm funding a life insurance policy with a cash value instead

Money contributed into cash-value life insurance gives you no immediate tax deduction. By contrast, a retirement savings plan like a 401(k), 403(b), SEP-IRA, or Keogh allows you to deduct your contributions from your taxable income. Even if you don't have access to these plans, you're better off saving in an IRA or annuity plan.

The only reason to buy cash-value life insurance is because you're wealthy and are using the life insurance as a way to shelter your assets from inheritance taxes. Don't buy cash-value life insurance for tax-deferred compounding of the excess contributions in it (see Chapter 17 for a more complete discussion of your life insurance options).

I'm saving for a home down payment

When you're starting out financially, deciding whether to save money to buy a home or to put it in a retirement account presents a real dilemma. In the long run, owning your own home is a wise financial move. On the other hand, starting to save earlier for retirement makes saving easier.

The bottom line is that you should be doing both. If you're really eager to own a home, then you can throw all of your savings toward achieving that goal and put retirement savings on the back burner. If you're not in such a rush, you can save for both purposes simultaneously.

You may be able to have the best of both worlds if you work for an employer that allows borrowing against retirement account balances. You can save money in the retirement account and then borrow against it for the down payment. Be careful, though. Retirement account loans typically must be paid back within a set number of years (check with your employer), or immediately when you quit or lose your job.

I have no cash left over to save

This reason is the most common one faced by people who don't save enough and who don't take advantage of the great tax savings that come with retirement accounts. In a very real sense, the extra taxes that you pay are an additional cost of overspending today. So, if you can reduce your expenditures, you can more easily meet your retirement goals. You'll have more money to contribute to retirement accounts and you'll save on your taxes to boot!

In some cases, people have a pile of money not earmarked for specific future needs that's invested outside of tax-sheltered retirement accounts. They may use all of their monthly employment income to meet their ongoing living expenses. As a result, they think that they can't afford to save in a retirement account. But they *can* afford to make retirement account contributions even if they can't save any new money!

If you think this way, you're compartmentalizing your finances. Look at the big picture. For example, what if you save $300 per month through your tax-deductible retirement plan? Suppose that doing so reduces your taxes by $100 and thus really costs you only $200 a month. You then can take $200 from your savings outside the retirement account and put it toward living expenses.

What you're effectively doing is transferring your savings from outside retirement accounts to inside a retirement account. You're not really saving *new* money, but you're getting terrific tax savings by playing this perfectly legal investing shell game. Just be careful not to drain your emergency savings reserve down too far. (See Chapter 12 for a discussion of how big a reserve you should keep.)

I love my job and will work forever

Are you one of those people who loves his or her work? You don't plan to retire and therefore don't need to amass a pile of money to live on for 20-plus years? If so, that means you can get away with saving a lot less than your eager-to-retire friends.

You may not, however, be *able* to work at your current job forever. What if you lose your job? What if something happens to your health? You can't assume that you will always be able to work — plan ahead for these what-ifs.

I've saved enough already

Congratulations! This is the single best excuse for not saving more for retirement. If you have a lot of money outside of tax-sheltered retirement accounts, you may want to contribute to retirement accounts anyway for the tax deductions.

Types of retirement accounts

You have the option to put money away in a retirement-type account that compounds without taxation until you withdraw the money. And in most cases, your contributions are tax deductible. The following list includes the major types of accounts and explains how to determine whether you are eligible for them.

Employer-sponsored plans

Your employer sets up these plans. No muss, no fuss — the employer does all the work, including selecting investment options. All you have to do is collect the cash!

401(k) plans

For-profit companies offer 401(k) plans. The silly name comes from the section of the tax code that establishes and regulates these plans. The 401(k) generally allows you to save up to approximately $9,000 per year or 20 percent of your salary, whichever is less. Your contributions to a 401(k) are excluded from your reported income and thus are free from federal and state income taxes. Your employer's plan may have lower limits, though, because not enough employees save enough.

Some employers don't allow you to start contributing to a 401(k) plan until you've worked for them for a full year. Others allow you to start contributing right away. Some employers also match a portion of your contributions. They may, for example, match half of your first 6 percent of contributions, so in addition to saving a lot of taxes, you get a bonus from the company. Check with your company's benefits department for your plan's specifics.

Thanks to technological innovations and the growth of the mutual fund industry, smaller companies (those with fewer than 100 employees) can consider offering 401(k) plans, too. In the past, it was prohibitively expensive for smaller companies to administer 401(k)s. If your company is interested in this option, contact a mutual fund organization, such as T. Rowe Price, Vanguard, or Fidelity, or a discount brokerage house, such as Charles Schwab or Jack White.

403(b) plans

Nonprofit organizations offer 403(b) plans to their employees. As with a 401(k), your contributions to these plans are federal and state tax deductible. The 403(b) plans are more often known as *tax-sheltered annuities*, the name for insurance company investments that satisfy the requirements for 403(b) plans. For the benefit of 403(b) retirement-plan participants, *no-load* (commission-free) mutual funds can now be used in 403(b) plans.

Nonprofit employees are allowed to contribute up to 20 percent or $9500 of their salary, whichever is less. Employees who have 15 or more years of service may be allowed to contribute a few thousand dollars beyond the $9500 limit. Ask your employee benefits department or the investment provider for the 403(b) plan about eligibility requirements and details about your personal contribution limit.

Nonprofit organizations have no excuse not to offer a 403(b) plan to their employees. Unlike a 401(k), this type of plan includes virtually no out-of-pocket expenses to the employer for accounting and administrative fees. The only requirement is that the organization must deduct the appropriate contribution from employees' paychecks and send the money to the investment company handling the 403(b) plan. If you work for a nonprofit or public-sector organization that doesn't offer this benefit, make a fuss and insist on it.

Self-employed plans

If you work for yourself, then you obviously don't have an employer to do the legwork to set up a retirement plan. You need to take the initiative. Although there's more work for you, the good news is that you can select and design a plan that meets your needs. Self-employed retirement savings plans allow you to put *more* money away on a tax-deductible basis than most employers' plans do.

If you have employees, you are required to provide coverage for them under these plans with contributions comparable to the company owners' (as a percentage of salary). Some part-time (fewer than 1,000 hours per year) and newer employees (less than a few years of service) may be excluded. Not all small-business owners know about this requirement — or choose to ignore it, setting up plans for themselves but failing to cover their employees. The danger is that the IRS and state tax authorities may discover it if you neglect to make contributions for eligible employees and may sock you with big penalties and disqualify your prior contributions. Because self-employed people and small businesses get their taxes audited at a relatively high rate, it's dangerous to muck up this area.

Don't avoid setting up a retirement savings plan for your business just because you have employees and you don't want to make contributions on their behalf. If you look at contributions for your employees as an additional cost of doing business, you need to take a fresh look at the world.

In the long run, you build the contributions you make for your employees into their total compensation package — which includes salary and other benefits like health insurance. Making retirement contributions need not increase your personnel costs.

To get the most from contributions as an employer, consider the following:

- Educate your employees about the value of retirement savings plans. You want them to understand, but more importantly, you want them to appreciate your investment.

- Select a Keogh plan that requires employees to stay a certain number of years to vest in their contributions.

- Offer a 401(k) plan if you have more than 20 employees.

SEP-IRAs

Simplified employee pension individual retirement account (SEP-IRA) plans require little paperwork to set up. They allow you to sock away the lesser of about 13 percent (13.04 percent, to be exact) of your self-employment income (business revenue minus deductions), up to a maximum of $22,500 per year. Each year, you decide the amount you want to contribute — there are no minimums. Your contributions to a SEP-IRA are deducted from your taxable income, saving you big-time on federal and state taxes. As with other retirement plans, your money compounds without taxation until withdrawal.

Keoghs

Keogh plans require a bit more paperwork to set up and administer than SEP-IRAs. The appeal of certain types of Keoghs is that they allow you to put away a greater percentage (20 percent) of your self-employment income (revenue less your deductions), up to a maximum of $30,000 per year.

All types of Keogh plans allow *vesting schedules,* which require employees to remain with the company a number of years before they earn the right to their retirement account balances.

Keogh plans also allow for *social security integration.* Without going into all the gory tax details, *integration* effectively allows those in the company who are high-income earners (usually the owners) to receive larger percentage contributions for their accounts than the less highly-compensated employees. The logic behind this idea is that social security benefits top out once you earn more than $60,600 (for 1994). Social security allows you to make up for this ceiling.

Just to make life complicated, Keoghs come in four main flavors:

- ✔ **Profit-sharing plans.** These plans have the same contribution limits as SEP-IRAs. So why would you want the headaches of a more complicated plan when you can't contribute more to it? These plans appeal to owners of small companies who want to minimize the contributions they make on behalf of employees, which is done through use of vesting schedules and social security integration.

- ✔ **Money purchase pension plans.** You can contribute more to these plans than you can to a profit-sharing plan or SEP-IRA. The maximum tax-deductible contribution here is the lesser of 20 percent of your self-employment income or $30,000 per year. While allowing for a larger contribution, there is no flexibility allowed on the percentage contribution you make each year — it's fixed. Thus, these plans make the most sense for high-income earners who are comfortable enough financially to know that they can continue making large contributions.

If the simplicity of the money-purchase pension plan appeals to you, don't be overly concerned about the consequences of some unforeseen circumstance that might make you unable to make the required contribution. You can amend your plan and change the contribution percentage starting the next year.

As long as you have a reason, the IRS generally allows you to discontinue the plan altogether. Prior contributions can remain in the Keogh account — you can even transfer them to other investment providers if you like. Discontinuing the plan simply means that you won't be making further contributions. You don't lose the money.

Usually, the reason people reduce contributions is that their business income drops off. The silver lining to your shrinking income is that Keogh plan contributions are set as a percentage of your earnings. So, less income means proportionately smaller contributions.

- ✔ **Paired plans.** These plans combine the preceding profit-sharing and money-purchase plans. Although it requires a little more paperwork to set up and administer, a paired plan takes the best of both individual plans.

> # What's with the oddball percentages you can contribute to these plans?
>
> I prefer round numbers, too, but there's a reasonable explanation. SEPs, for example, actually allow you to contribute 15 percent of your *net* self-employment income. However, you need to subtract your SEP contribution and half of your self-employment (social security) taxes to arrive at your net self-employment income. In the real world, people normally think of their self-employment income, which doesn't adjust for this subtraction. Your maximum permissible SEP contribution is 13.04 percent of this unadjusted figure.

You can attain the maximum contribution possible (20 percent) that you get with the money-purchase pension plan but have some of the flexibility that comes with a profit-sharing plan. You can fix your money-purchase pension plan contribution at 8 percent and contribute anywhere from 0 to 13.04 percent to your profit-sharing plan.

✔ **Defined-benefit plans.** These plans are for people who are able and willing to put away more than $30,000 per year. As you can imagine, only a very small percentage of people can afford them. Consistently high-income earners older than 45 or 50 who want to save more than $30,000 per year in a retirement account should consider these plans. If you are interested in defined-benefit plans, hire an actuary to crunch the numbers to calculate how much you can contribute to such a plan.

Individual Retirement Accounts (IRAs)

Anyone with employment income can contribute to IRA accounts. You may contribute up to $2,000 each year. If you don't earn $2,000 a year, you can contribute as much as you'd like (and can afford) up to that amount. If you are a nonworking spouse, you're eligible to put $250 per year into a so-called *spousal IRA.*

One exception to earning employment income makes you eligible to contribute to an IRA: Receiving alimony also qualifies you for an IRA contribution.

Your contributions to an IRA may or may not be tax deductible. If you're single and your adjusted gross income is $25,000 or less for the year, you can deduct your IRA contribution. If you're married and file your taxes jointly, you're entitled to a full IRA deduction if your AGI (adjusted gross income) is $40,000 per year or less.

TIP

If you make more than these amounts, you can take a full IRA deduction if and only if you (or your spouse) are *not* an active participant in any retirement plan. The only way to know for certain whether you're an active participant is to look at your W-2 Form: that smallish (4 by 8 ½-inch) document your employer sends you early in the year to file with your tax returns. Little boxes in box number 15 on that form indicate whether or not you are an active participant in a pension or deferred-compensation plan. If either of these boxes is checked, you're an active participant.

If you are a single income earner with an adjusted gross income above $25,000 but below $35,000 or part of a couple with an AGI above $40,000 but below $50,000, you're eligible for a partial IRA deduction, even if you're an active participant. The size of the IRA deduction that you may claim depends on where you fall in the income range. For example, a single income earner at $30,000 is entitled to half ($1,000) of the full IRA deduction because his or her income falls halfway between $25,000 and $35,000.

A couple earning $42,500 loses just a quarter of the full IRA amount because their incomes are a quarter of the way from $40,000 to $50,000. Thus, they can take a $1,500 IRA deduction. The IRS 1040 instruction booklet comes with a worksheet that allows you to do the calculations for your situation.

Even if you can't deduct a portion or all of a $2,000 IRA contribution, you can still contribute to an IRA. This misunderstanding is common among people who used to contribute to IRAs before tax laws changed in 1986 (before, anyone could deduct their IRA contributions, but lots of restrictions on deductions were added in 1986).

An IRA contribution that is not tax deductible is called, not surprisingly, a *nondeductible* IRA contribution. The benefit of this type of contribution is that the money can still compound and grow without taxation. For a person who plans to leave contributions in the IRA for a long time (a decade or more), this tax-deferred compounding makes even nondeductible contributions worthwhile. However, you should consider such an IRA *only* after you have exhausted the possibilities of contributing to retirement accounts that do provide an immediate tax deduction (for example, 401(k)s, SEPs, Keoghs, and so on).

To put everyone on more-equal footing, those who don't work for employers with retirement savings plans should be allowed to contribute more to their IRAs. It's not fair that people who work for companies that have no retirement savings plans can deduct only $2,000 per year from their taxable income for an IRA.

Take an example of two households that each have annual employment income of $50,000. One household has access to a 401(k) plan, while the other household has no access to retirement plans other than an IRA. The household with the 401(k) can put away and deduct from their taxable income thousands of dollars more per year than the household with just the IRA.

This inequity has persisted because of the federal government's budget deficit. Allowing more people to make larger tax-deductible contributions to retirement accounts would reduce government revenue in the short-term. Tax deductions for retirement savings are included in the tax system to encourage people to provide for their own retirement. But it's hypocritical to tell people the importance of saving for retirement and not give them more equal access to do so.

Annuities

Annuities, like IRAs, allow your capital to grow and compound without taxation. You defer taxes until withdrawal. Annuities carry the same penalties for withdrawal prior to age 59 ½ as do IRAs.

Unlike an IRA that has a $2,000 annual contribution limit, you can deposit as much as you want in any year into an annuity — even a million dollars if you've got it! As with a so-called nondeductible IRA, you get no up-front tax deduction for your contributions.

Annuities are peculiar investment products. They are contracts that are backed by an insurance company. If you, the annuity holder (investor), die during the so-called *accumulation phase* (that is, prior to receiving payments from the annuity), your designated beneficiary is guaranteed to receive the amount of your original investment. In this sense, annuities look a bit like life insurance.

Because the initial contribution to an annuity is not tax deductible, it makes sense to contribute to an annuity only *after* you have exhausted contributing to employer-sponsored and self-employed plans. And because annuities carry higher fees (which reduce your investment returns) because of the insurance that comes with them, you should also make the maximum contribution that you can to an IRA first, even if it's not tax deductible.

For more details about other investment options and the best places to purchase annuities, see Chapter 12 about investing money you currently have outside of retirement accounts.

If you have access to more than one type of retirement account, prioritize which accounts to use first by what they give you in return. Your first contributions should be to employer-based plans that match your contributions. After that, contribute to any other employer or self-employed plans that allow tax-deductible contributions. If you've contributed the maximum possible to tax-deductible plans or do not have access to such plans, contribute to an IRA. If you've maxed out on contributions to an IRA, or don't have this choice because you lack employment income, consider an annuity.

Where to set up a retirement account

No-load, or commission-free, mutual funds and discount brokerage firms are your best bet. (You'll find specific recommendations of companies to contact about investing in retirement accounts in Chapter 11 and details about investments to use inside of your retirement account in Chapter 13.)

Investments and account types are different issues. People sometimes get confused when discussing the investments they make in retirement accounts, especially people who have a retirement account, such as an IRA, at a bank. They don't realize that you can have your IRA at a variety of financial institutions (for example, a mutual fund company or brokerage firm). At each financial institution, you can choose among the firm's investment options for putting your IRA money to work.

Ingredients for Happy Financial Independence

Having sufficient financial resources gives you flexibility to change careers, quit working altogether, or do volunteer work. But money isn't the only thing — it's just one ingredient for a happy future.

I've noticed the following common themes among the successful, happy, financially independent or retired people with whom I work.

Health

Few things are more important than your health. Without your health, it's hard to enjoy the good things in life. Unfortunately, many people are not motivated to care about their health until after they discover problems. By then, it may be too late.

Although regular exercise, a balanced and healthy diet, and avoidance of substance abuse cannot guarantee that you won't have future health problems, they go a long way toward prevention of many of the most common causes of death and debilitating disease. Regular medical exams also are important in detecting problems early.

Friends and family

No, I'm not talking about the MCI program to lower your phone bill. It is well documented that people live longer and are happier and healthier when they have a circle of people around them for support. Unfortunately, as we grow older, many people, especially retirees, become ever more isolated because they lose regular contact with business associates, friends, and family members.

Retirees who are happy seem to be busy and involved in volunteer organizations and in new social circles. They may travel to see old friends or to visit younger relatives who may be too busy to visit them.

Thoughtful transitions

Abruptly leaving your job without some sort of plan for spending all that free time is an invitation to boredom and depression. Everyone needs a sense of purpose, even of routine. Establishing hobbies, volunteer work, or a sideline business while gradually cutting back your regular work schedule can be a terrific way to make the transition into retirement.

Financial order

You can't enjoy retirement when you don't know what you have to work with or when you're constantly worried about the bank. If you are already retired or plan to retire soon, all the accumulated years of good or bad financial habits have already had a significant impact on your current financial health. Although you can't undo the past, you still have time ahead of you to benefit from getting things in order.

Your savings, for example, need to be invested to ensure security of principal as well as growth to keep you ahead of the double bite of inflation and taxes. Wills and (when appropriate) trusts should be established, too. (See Chapter 18 for more on wills and trusts.)

Chapter 9

The Mortgage:
Debt with a Lot of Zeros Behind It

● ●

In This Chapter

▶ The various flavors of mortgages

▶ Selecting a mortgage

▶ Finding a lender

▶ Determining how much to borrow

▶ Knowing when to refinance

▶ What to do when you can can't qualify for a mortgage

▶ The reverse mortgage

● ●

*I*t's somewhat ironic that a major part of the American dream is to own a home, because a big part of owning a home is acquiring a large amount of debt. The *mortgage* is the loan from a bank or other source that makes up the difference between the cash you have already and the agreed-upon selling price of a piece of real estate.

Mortgages — the monthly payment of which consists of interest and principal to repay your loan balance — are huge expenses. Taking the time to educate yourself about how to get the best possible deal on a mortgage and ancillary fees is a very wise financial move.

If you have already purchased a home, you may have recovered from the initial shock of agreeing to pay more money than you ever imagined to buy property. But did you know that you may end up paying more for the *interest* on your mortgage than you will for your humble abode itself?

Assume that your new pad costs $150,000. To buy it, you borrow $120,000 and contribute $30,000 from your savings for the down payment. If you borrow that $120,000 with a 30-year fixed-rate mortgage at 7 percent, you end up paying more than $167,000 *in interest* over the life of your loan. Of course, you'll pay back some of these interest dollars many years from now when the dollar will likely (thanks to inflation) be worth less than it is today. Even so, you're going to spend a truckload of dollars in interest. And as anyone who has ever acquired a mortgage knows, just about everybody has a hand in your wallet when you buy a home, figuring "Hey! They're spending a *big* chunk of change — they probably won't even notice a few extra thousand gone!"

Important Note: This chapter assumes that you are already in the real estate game and are considering a refinance *or* that you're ready to move and have done some homework about a particular property. If you haven't yet decided how much you should spend on a house or if you want help deciding whether real estate is a good investment for your financial situation, *stop!* — turn to Chapter 15 to learn more about real estate purchases and investments.

An Overview of Mortgage Flavors

For many households, mortgage payments are the single largest monthly expenditure (besides taxes). Like many other financial products, zillions of different mortgages are available to choose from. The differences can be important or trivial, expensive or cost-free. Selecting among these mortgage bells and whistles is what this chapter is all about.

First, the big differences. So that you don't miss the forest for the trees (to risk a metaphor), we're going to take one swoop over it in a helicopter. If you start comparing different individual trees (mortgages) before considering the forest as a whole (your financial situation), you're going to get lost in the woods.

There are two major types of mortgages — those with a *fixed interest rate* and those with a *floating* or *variable rate*. Your choice depends on your financial situation and how much risk you're willing to accept.

Fixed-rate mortgages

Fixed-rate mortgages are the standard mortgages that ruled the whole marketplace before variable-rate mortgages came into being. Usually issued over a 15- or 30-year period, these mortgages have interest rates that never, ever change. The interest rate you pay the first month is the same one that you pay the last month and every month in between. Not all fixed-rate mortgages offered by different banks have the same interest rate, but with a fixed-rate mortgage, you lock in an interest rate that won't change over the life of your loan.

Because the interest rate stays the same, your monthly mortgage payment amount does not change. There's nothing complicated to track, and there is no uncertainty. If you like getting your daily newspaper delivered at the same time everyday, you're gonna like fixed-rate mortgages.

Fixed-rate loans are not without risks, however. If interest rates fall significantly after you obtain your mortgage, you face the danger of being stuck with your higher-cost mortgage. The answer for some people in this situation is to *refinance* their mortgage.

But what if, because of a deterioration in your financial situation or a decline in the value of your property, you don't qualify for a refinance? Even if you are eligible to refinance, you'll probably have to spend a good amount of time and money to complete it.

Comparing different fixed-rate mortgages is easier than comparing adjustables. But picking a fixed-rate mortgage is no walk in the park either. *Points, application fees, appraisal fees,* and *prepayment penalties* can quickly multiply your confusion (stay tuned).

Balloon loans

Balloon loans start out the way traditional fixed-rate mortgages start out. You make level payments based on a long-term payment schedule, over 15 or 30 years, for example. But at a predetermined time — and well before the traditional end of such a loan — the remaining loan balance becomes fully due. Balloons typically need to be paid off within the first three to ten years.

Why, then, would anyone want a balloon loan? One motivation is to save money. All things being equal, a balloon loan has a lower interest rate than a fixed-rate mortgage. Sometimes, balloon loans may be the only option for the buyer (or so the buyer thinks). Buyers are more commonly backed into these loans during periods of high interest rates. When a buyer can't afford the payments on a conventional mortgage and really wants a particular property, a seller may offer a balloon loan.

Balloon loans are dangerous. Like the balloons that you inflate with your breath, balloon loans can blow up in your face. The explosion happens when you're unable to refinance into a new loan to pay off the balloon loan when it comes due. The *what-ifs* can hurt: What if you lose your job or your income drops? What if the value of your property drops, and the appraisal comes in too low to qualify you for a new loan? What if interest rates rise and you can't qualify for the higher rate on a new loan? Taking a balloon loan is a high-risk maneuver that can backfire.

Avoid balloon loans. You should take such a loan *only* if the following three conditions are true:

✔ You *really, really* want a certain property.

✔ The balloon loan is your *only* financing option, and you've really done your homework to exhaust other financing options.

✔ You're *positive* that you'll be able to refinance when the balloon comes due.

If you take a balloon loan, get one with as much time as possible — preferably seven to ten years — before it becomes due. Don't get suckered into a balloon loan because you fall in love with a place and you just have to buy it. Remember: There are other fish in the sea and other times to buy. You have to live not just with the house but also with the mortgage, and for a long time.

Adjustable-rate mortgages (ARMs)

In contrast to a fixed-rate mortgage, an *adjustable-rate mortgage* (ARM) carries an interest rate that varies. Like a fidgeting child, it moves, jumps, rises, falls, and otherwise can't sit still.

Some adjustables are more hyperactive and prone to get you into trouble than others — again, like kids. You can start with one interest rate this year and have different ones for every year, possibly every month, during a 30-year mortgage. Thus, the size of your monthly payment fluctuates. Because a mortgage payment makes an unusually large dent in most homeowners' checkbooks anyway, signing up for an adjustable without understanding its risks is dangerous.

The advantage of an adjustable-rate mortgage is that if you purchase your property during a period of relatively high interest rates, you can start paying your mortgage with the artificially depressed initial interest rate. And if interest rates start to decline, you can capture the benefits over the next few years.

A decline in interest rates can prompt a refinance for a homeowner with a fixed- or adjustable-rate loan. In both cases, however, it costs money to do a refinance. The good news for homeowners with an adjustable, however, is that if you're financially unable to refinance, you probably already capture a lot of the benefit of the lower rates. With a fixed-rate loan, you must refinance to realize the benefit of a decline in interest rates.

Mumbo-jumbo about adjustable-rate mortgages

To understand why adjustables came into being, you need to understand just a wee bit of banking history. Adjustable-rate mortgages are a relatively recent lending invention.

When inflation and interest rates skyrocketed in the 1970s and early 80s, mortgage lenders (primarily banks) that had previously issued only fixed-rate mortgages got — how shall we say it? — screwed. They had lots of mortgage balances at fixed rates — 4, 5, and 6 percent — while they were having to pay depositors interest rates that were almost double those levels. You can fool some bankers some of the time, but you can't fool them all for long. It didn't take the banks too long to figure out that they were losing a lot of money and risked bank failure.

Bankers created adjustable-rate mortgages to reduce *their* risk in lending money over a long period of time. They were smart enough to realize that they couldn't predict the future course of interest rates. They wanted flexibility in their rates, because interest rates were no longer puttering around the 3 – 5 percent range as they did during most of the 1940s, 50s, and 60s.

Given the uncertainty that comes with adjustable-rate mortgages, why would a borrower take on such an unstable and precarious payment system? Well, inveterate gamblers love this kind of life adventure. Others who seek excitement in an otherwise quiet and boring existence may also relish the thrill.

Other thrill-seekers in the form of home buyers, particularly first-time buyers or those stretching themselves to trade up to a pricier property, are financially forced into adjustable-rate mortgages. ARMs are all they can qualify for given the home and accompanying mortgage amount they want.

Some home buyers, however, have a choice and opt for the adjustable. The reason they do so is simple — *adjustables can save you money; sometimes quite a lot.* On most adjustables, paying less in interest in the first few years than you would on a comparable fixed-rate loan is virtually guaranteed. After that, it depends on the overall trends in interest rates. When interest rates drop, stay level, or rise just a little, you continue to pay less for your adjustable. On the other hand, when rates rise more than a percent or two and stay elevated, the adjustable is going to cost you more than a fixed-rate loan.

How to Choose a Mortgage

Choosing between a fixed rate or adjustable-rate loan is the single most important nail-biter of a decision you'll ever make (not to put any pressure on you) when choosing a mortgage.

Should I get a fixed-rate or adjustable-rate mortgage?

Ideally, you should weigh the pros and cons of each mortgage type and decide what's best for your situation *before* you go out to purchase a piece of real estate or refinance.

In the real world, most people ignore this advice. The excitement of purchasing a home tends to cloud one's judgment. My experience has been that few people look at their entire financial picture before making major real estate decisions.

Consider the following issues before you decide which kind of mortgage — fixed or adjustable — is right for you.

How willing and able are you to take on financial risk?

Forget for the moment which size or style of property is really you or which town you have your heart set on. Take stock of how much of a gamble you can take with the size of your monthly mortgage payment. If you start making offers on properties before you resolve this issue, you're putting the cart before the horse. You may end up with a mortgage that could someday seriously over-shadow your delight in your little English herb garden out back.

For example, if your job and income are unstable and you need to borrow a lot, you can't afford much risk. I define *a lot* as close to the maximum that a bank is willing to lend you. *A lot* can also mean that you have no slack in your monthly budget — that is, you're not saving any money on a regular basis. If you're in this situation, stick with fixed-rate mortgages.

When interest rates rise, a mushrooming adjustable mortgage payment may test the lower limits of your checking account balance. If you don't have emergency savings that you can tap to make the higher payments, how can you afford the monthly payments — much less all the other expenses of home ownership?

If you can't afford the highest allowed payment on an adjustable-rate mortgage, you have no business taking one. You shouldn't take the chance that it might not rise that high — it could, and you could lose your home! Ask your lender to calculate the highest possible *maximum monthly payment* on your loan. That's the payment you would face if the interest rate on your loan went to highest level allowed, or the *lifetime cap.*

And what about your stress level? If you have to start reading the daily business pages to check interest rates, it's probably not worth gambling on rates. Life is too short! Take a fixed-rate mortgage and keep up with *Calvin and Hobbes* or *Seinfeld* instead! (That is, unless interest-rate watching has become a real hobby for you, in which case, go for it! This could be the start of a new career!)

Another potential risk and stress factor is your personal life. Are you planning to start a family soon? Your income may fall when you take a leave or reduce your workload (the kind that pays, that is — your total workload's gonna go up in a big way with kids). Your expenses will surely rise, especially if you expect to keep going full tilt with your job. An adjustable may not work for you in this case.

On the other hand, maybe you're in a position to take the financial risks that come with an adjustable-rate mortgage. A floating interest rate places more (but not all) of the risk of fluctuating rates on you. Almost all adjustables limit, or *cap,* the rise in the interest rate allowed on your loan. Typical caps are 2 percent per year and 6 percent over the life of the loan.

You have better chances of saving money with an adjustable than with a fixed-rate loan. Your interest rate starts lower and stays lower if the overall level of interest rates stays unchanged. Even if rates go up, they will probably come back down over the life of your loan. So if you can stick with your adjustable for better and for worse, you may still come out ahead in the long term.

If you do choose an adjustable loan, you may feel more financially secure if you have a hefty financial cushion that is accessible in the event that rates go up. Maybe you took out a smaller loan than you're qualified for. Or perhaps you're able to save a sizable chunk — more than 10 percent — of your monthly income. If you've got some wiggling room in your spending, you'll feel less anxiety about fluctuating interest rates. On the other hand, maybe you're certain that your income is destined to soar to the moon. Will your mood fluctuate with Federal Reserve changes in interest-rate policy? Will you drive family members crazy by trying to clamp down on their spending with each increase in rates? Will you become a nervous wreck?

Consider an adjustable-rate mortgage only if you're financially secure enough to handle the maximum possible payments over an extended period of time. You must also be emotionally secure enough to handle volatile rates. Don't take an adjustable because the initially lower interest rates allow you to afford the property you want to buy (unless you're absolutely certain that your income will rise to meet future payment increases). Try setting your sights on a property that you can afford — with a fixed-rate mortgage.

How long do you plan to keep the mortgage?

A mortgage lender takes extra risk in committing to a constant interest rate for 15 to 30 years. Lenders don't know any better than you or I what may happen in the intervening years, so they charge you a premium for their risk. If you aren't going to keep your mortgage more than five to seven years, you're probably paying unnecessary interest costs to carry a fixed-rate mortgage.

Savings on most adjustables is usually guaranteed in the first two or three years. An adjustable-rate mortgage starts at a lower interest rate than a fixed one. When the adjustable does what it does best — adjusts — it's almost always limited or capped in the amount of each interest-rate change. If rates rise, you can end up giving back or losing the savings you achieve in the early years of the mortgage.

If you're pretty sure that you'll hang onto a property for less than five years, you should come out ahead with an adjustable.

Which way are interest rates going?

Some people ask, "Shouldn't the likelihood of interest rates going up or down determine whether I take a fixed-rate or adjustable-rate mortgage?" (The logic goes that if rates are on their way up, then you're better off locking in a fixed-rate mortgage before it goes any higher.) A recent book written by an MBA about mortgages asserts, "Interest rate forecasts should be the major factor in deciding whether or not to get an ARM."

Forget it. You can't predict the future course of interest rates. If you could, you could make a fortune investing in bonds and interest-rate futures and options. Even the pros on Wall Street can't make these predictions with any consistent accuracy, as you'll learn in Part III.

Too many people take adjustables when they can't really afford them. Those who can afford adjustables can save money. But sooner or later, interest rates will go up, and sometimes they go up a lot. When they do, people who can't really afford much higher payments may face a financial crisis.

Should I go for a 15-year or 30-year mortgage?

Many people don't have a choice. To afford the monthly payments, they need to spread the loan payments over a longer period of time, and a 30-year mortgage is the only answer. A 15-year mortgage has higher monthly payments because you pay off more quickly. With fixed-rate mortgages hovering around 7 percent, a 15-year mortgage comes with payments that are about 30 percent higher than those for a 30-year mortgage.

If you can afford these higher payments, it's not necessarily better to take the 15-year option. The money for making extra payments doesn't come out of thin air. You might have better uses for your excess funds.

If you opt for a 30-year mortgage, you maintain the flexibility to pay it off faster (except in those rare cases where there is a prepayment penalty). By making additional payments, you can create your own 15-year mortgage. But you can fall back to making only the payments required on your 30-year schedule when the need arises.

There's a risk in locking yourself into higher monthly payments with a 15-year mortgage. If money gets too tight in the future, you can fall behind in your mortgage payments. You *may* be able to refinance your way out of the predicament, but you can't count on it. If your finances worsen or your property declines in value, odds are that you'll have trouble qualifying for a refinance.

Suppose you can qualify for a 15-year mortgage and you're financially comfortable with the higher payments. The appeal of paying off your mortgage 15 years sooner is enticing. Besides, the interest rate is lower on a 15-year mortgage. So if you can afford the higher payments on the 15-year mortgage, you'd be a dummy not to take it, right? Not so fast. You're really asking whether you should pay off your mortgage slowly or more quickly. And the answer isn't as simple as you think. Read on!

Mortgages don't always come in 15-year and 30-year versions. There can be 20-year and 40-year options, for example. These are quite rare and don't change the above logic.

Should I pay off my mortgage faster?

It depends. You need to think through this decision.

If you have the extra cash to make larger-than-required mortgage payments, consider yourself fortunate. The desire to pay off your mortgage sooner rather than later is understandable.

For many people, the temptation to add to the mortgage payment comes the day after they realize that they aren't excited about working for another decade or two — or the day after they return from an invigorating vacation. "The sooner I get that mortgage paid off," you think, "the less work I have to do and the more free time I can have." The sooner the debt is paid back, the less total interest you pay.

Entire books have been written extolling the virtues of owning your home free and clear as soon as possible. They come complete with endless rows and columns of numbers so that you can look up how much you'll save through a quicker payback.

It's not that simple.

If you have the time and inclination (and a good financial calculator), you can calculate how much interest you can save or avoid through a quicker payback. I have a friendly word of advice about spending hours crunching numbers: *don't.* You can make this decision by considering the qualitative issues.

First, think about *alternative uses* for the extra money you're throwing into the mortgage payments. What's best for you depends on your overall financial situation and what else you can do with the money. If you would end up blowing the extra money at the racetrack, on an expensive car, or on gummy bears, pay down the mortgage. That's a no-brainer.

Suppose that you take the extra $100 or $200 per month that you were planning to add to your mortgage payment and contribute it to a retirement account instead. That step may make financial sense. Why? Because additions to 401(k)s, SEP-IRAs, Keoghs, and other types of retirement accounts (discussed in Chapter 8) are tax deductible.

When you add $200 to your mortgage payment to pay off your mortgage faster, you get no tax benefits. Zero, *nada,* zippo! When you dump that $200 into a retirement account, you get to subtract that $200 from the income on which you pay taxes. If you're paying 35 percent in federal and state income taxes, you shave $70 (that's $200 multiplied by 35 percent) off your tax bill. (You're going to pay taxes when you withdraw the money from the retirement account someday. In the meantime, you've got the money that would have gone to taxes growing on your behalf.)

If the investments in your retirement account plummet in value, then the impact of the tax-deferred compounding of your capital may be negated. Paying down the mortgage, on other hand, is just like investing your money in a sure thing — but with a modest rate of return.

In most cases, you get to deduct your mortgage interest on your tax return. So, if you're paying 7 percent interest, it really may only cost you around 5 percent after you factor in the tax benefits. If you think you can do better by investing elsewhere, go for it. Investments such as stocks and real estate have generated better returns over the long haul. These investments carry risk, though, and are not guaranteed to produce any return.

If you're uncomfortable investing and would otherwise leave the extra money sitting in a money market fund or savings account, you're better off paying down the mortgage. On the other hand, if you can save money in retirement accounts and reduce your taxes, you should come out ahead in the long haul by not paying your mortgage off faster. Master Part III on investing your money for better long-term growth.

If you have children

With kids, you have an even greater reason to fund your retirement accounts before you consider paying down your mortgage quickly. Under current rules for determining financial aid for college expenses, money in your retirement accounts is not counted as an asset.

Equity in your home (the difference between its market value and your loan balance) is still counted by many schools as an asset. Thus, your reward for paying down your mortgage balance may be less financial aid!

When you pay down your mortgage balance faster, you're building more equity in your home. On paper, you appear wealthier to financial aid officers than when you save the money in a retirement account.

Particularly sad are the cases I've seen of middle-income families who can't afford to do it all financially. They want the best for their kids, so they save money outside retirement accounts (and pay down their mortgage) to prepare to pay for their educational costs. Saving for their own retirement seems selfish and so it gets neglected. When the kids apply for financial aid, they don't get much. The parents get saddled with more debt and deplete their assets, and then the parents have nothing to show for their efforts in their retirement accounts.

 Therefore, given a choice between funding your retirement account and paying down your mortgage, you're better off funding the retirement account. Money contributed to retirement accounts provides you with substantial tax benefits. Paying down your mortgage doesn't.

 Paying down your mortgage faster, especially when you have children, is rarely a good financial decision when you haven't exhausted contributions to retirement accounts. Save first in retirement accounts and get the tax benefits.

When retirement accounts aren't available

If you *don't* have a burning investment option, it's usually wise to pay down your mortgage as your cash flow allows. If you have extra cash and have contributed the maximum allowed for retirement accounts, you may want to invest in real estate or perhaps a business. You have to decide whether it is worth the extra risk to make that particular investment instead of paying less interest on your mortgage.

Paying off your mortgage early makes sense especially when you are retired or nearing retirement. Just make sure that you retain enough of a cash reserve to meet emergency and other important expenses.

How Do I Select the Best Fixed-Rate Mortgage?

You've decided that you want a fixed-rate mortgage. The good news is that shopping for a fixed-rate loan is easier than shopping for an adjustable. Fixed-rate loans don't come with all the bells and whistles that adjustables do.

Still, the many different lenders in a given market try to differentiate themselves. And lenders have just enough bells and whistles on fixed-rate loans to give you a minor migraine.

The following are the primary ways in which fixed-rate mortgages may differ.

Interest rate

This one is easy. The *interest rate* is the rate of interest that a lender charges you for borrowing their money. Unlike credit-card interest rates, which are usually double-digit rates, fixed-rate loans are much lower. As of this writing, fixed-rate loans can be found for around 7 percent.

Just as a seesaw doesn't work with one rider missing, an interest rate quote on its own is completely meaningless. The interest rate on a fixed-rate loan must always be quoted with the points on the loan. If one lender offers 30-year mortgages at 6.75 percent and another lender offers them at 7 percent, the 7-percent loan is not necessarily worse. You need to know how many points each lender charges, too.

Points

Points are fees paid up front to your lender when you close on your loan. Points are actually percentages: One point is equal to 1 percent of the loan amount. So when a lender tells you that there are 1.5 points on a quoted loan, you pay 1.5 percent of the amount you borrow as points. On a $100,000 loan, for example, 1.5 points cost you $1,500.

The seesaw analogy explains how the interest rate and points on a fixed-rate loan go together and move in opposite directions. If you are willing or want to pay more points on a given loan (one end of the seesaw goes up), the lender should reduce the interest rate (the other end of the seesaw goes down).

If you want to pay fewer points, your interest rate increases. You may want to take a higher interest rate on your mortgage if you don't have enough cash to pay a lot of points, which are paid up front when you close the loan. On the other hand, if you're willing to pay more points, you can lower your interest rate. You might want to do so because the interest rate on your loan determines your payments over a long, long time — 15 – 30 years.

Suppose lender X quotes you 6.75 percent on a 30-year fixed-rate loan and charges one point (1 percent). Lender Y, who quotes 7 percent, doesn't charge any points. Which is better? The answer depends mostly on how long you plan to keep the loan.

The 6.75-percent loan is .25 percent less than the 7-percent loan. Year in and year out, the 6.75-percent loan saves you .25 percent. But because you have to pay 1 percent (one point) up front on the 6.75-percent loan, it will take you about four years to earn back the savings to cover the cost of that point. So if you expect to keep the loan less than 4 years, go with the 7 percent option.

To make it easier to perform an apples-to-apples comparison of mortgages from different lenders, get interest rate quotes at the same point level. For example, ask each lender for the interest rate on a loan for which you pay one point.

Some lenders advertise no-point loans as though they're offering something for nothing. There are no free lunches. If a loan has no points, it's *guaranteed* to have a higher interest rate. That's not to say that it's better or worse than comparable loans from other lenders. But don't get sucked in by a no-points sales pitch. Many lenders who spend big bucks on advertising these types of loans don't have the best deals, anyway.

All things being equal, no-point loans make more sense for refinances since the points aren't immediately tax-deductible. On a mortgage for a property that you're purchasing, a no-point loan may help if you are cash poor at closing.

Consider a no-point loan if you can't afford more out-of-pocket expenditures now or if you think that you'll only keep the loan a few years. Make sure to shop around and compare different lenders' no-point loans when you decide that you want one.

Other lender fees

In addition to points and the ongoing interest rate, lenders tack on all sorts of other up-front charges in processing your loan.

When two lenders are in a dead heat with regards to interest rate and points, these other fees can help break the tie. Besides, you need to know the total of all lender fees so that you can determine how much closing on your loan should cost you. Get an itemization of charges in writing from all lenders you are seriously considering.

Lenders can nickel and dime you with a number of fees other than points. Actually, you pay more than nickels and dimes — $300 here and $50 there adds up in a hurry! Here are the main culprits:

- **Application and processing fees.** Most lenders charge a couple hundred dollars to complete your paperwork and process it through their under-writing (loan evaluation) department. The justification for this fee is that if your loan is rejected or you decide not to take it, the lender needs to cover the costs. Some lenders return this fee to you upon closing when you go with their loan (after you're approved).

- **Credit report.** Many lenders charge a fee to pay for the cost of obtaining a copy of your credit report. This report tells the lender whether you've been naughty or nice to other lenders in the past. If you have problems on your credit report, get them cleaned up before you apply for a mortgage.

- **Appraisal.** The property for which you are borrowing money needs to be valued. If you default on your mortgage, a lender doesn't want to get stuck with a property worth less than you owe. The cost is typically several hundred dollars for most residential properties.

- **No-point, no-fee loans.** Some lenders offer loans without points or other lender charges. Remember: Lenders aren't charities. If they don't charge points or other fees, they have to make up the difference by charging a higher interest rate on your loan. Only consider such loans when you lack the cash to close a loan or when you're planning to hold onto the loan for just a few years.

You pay many of these other fees when you apply for your mortgage. To minimize your chances of throwing money away on a loan for which you might not qualify, ask the lender whether you might not be approved for some reason. Be sure to disclose any problems on your credit report or problems with the property that you are aware of. Don't expect them to run through a list of qualities on which they don't like taking risks. Lenders don't take the time to ask about these sorts of things in their haste to get you to complete their loan applications.

For example, I once obtained a loan for a property with a partial brick foundation. Brick foundations make California lenders wary because of the danger of earthquake damage. Fortunately, I talked about the brick foundation in my preliminary search for lenders and quickly eliminated some lenders who would have rejected the loan on that basis. If I had just filled out the nearest lender's loan application and waited for the appraisal report to come in and tell the bank what I already knew about the foundation, I would have wasted several hundred dollars and weeks of time.

How Do I Select the Best Adjustable-Rate Mortgage?

So, you're committed to the roller coaster ride of an adjustable-rate mortgage, and you're comfortable with that fact. Now comes the real fun. Adjustables come with all sorts of options — *caps, indexes, margins,* and *adjustment periods* — that aren't issues with fixed-rate loans. You can spend weeks comparing them.

If you're clueless about personal finances — or just think that you are — shopping for and understanding adjustables scores a 9.9 degree of difficulty on the financial frustration scale.

Unfortunately, you have to wade through a number of details to understand and compare one adjustable to another. Bear with me. If you have a map of the forest, navigating among the trees gets a lot easier. It is vital to understand these details, because they determine how the interest rate adjusts over the life of your loan.

It is virtually impossible to calculate exactly which adjustable mortgage should cost you the least under different circumstances. If you're the type who insists on cold, hard facts and numbers, you'll just get frustrated. Loosen up or the excitement may kill you!

Selecting an adjustable-rate mortgage has a lot in common with selecting a home to buy. You have to make trade-offs and compromises. And you can't make them until you prioritize what's important to you.

Start (initial) rate

Just as the name implies, this interest rate is the one that your mortgage begins with. Don't judge a loan by this rate alone. You won't be paying this attractively low rate for long — the start rate is always low on an adjustable-rate loan. You can be absolutely certain that the interest rate will rise as soon as the terms of the mortgage allow.

Start rates are probably one of the least important items to focus on when comparing adjustables. You'd never know this from the way lenders advertise adjustables — you'll see ads with the start rate in 3-inch bold type and everything else in microscopic footnotes! The formula (which includes index and margin) and rate caps are far more important in determining what a mortgage is going to cost you in the long run.

Some people have labeled the start rate a *teaser rate*. This term implies that the initial rate on your loan is set artificially low to entice you. In other words, even if the market level of interest rates doesn't change, your adjustable is destined to increase. An increase of 1 – 2 percent is not uncommon.

The formula

The formula should be the first thing that a mortgage lender or broker tells you about. More likely, though, they'll tease you with how low the initial interest rate is.

You'd never (I hope) agree to a loan if your lender's whim and fancy determined your future interest rate. You want to know exactly how a lender figures how much your interest rate will increase. All adjustables are based on the following formula, which specifies how the interest rate will be set on your loan in the future:

Index + Margin = Interest Rate

The *index* measures the overall level of interest rates that the lender chooses to calculate the specific interest rate on your loan. Indexes are generally (but not always) widely quoted in the financial press.

For example, the six-month treasury bill rate is an index used on some mortgages. As of this writing, the going rate on six-month treasuries is approximately 3 percent.

The *margin* is the amount added to the index to determine the interest rate you pay on your mortgage. Most loans have margins of around 2.5 percent.

The rate of a mortgage, driven by the following formula,

Six-month treasury bill rate + 2.5 percent

is set at the going rate for six-month treasuries plus 2.5 percent. So when six-month treasuries are yielding 3 percent, the interest rate on your loan should be 5.5 percent. This figure is known as the *fully indexed rate.* If this loan starts out at 4 percent, you know that if the rate on six-month treasuries stays the same, your loan should eventually increase to 5.5 percent.

Note: The margin is very important. When you are comparing two loans that are tied to the same index and are otherwise the same, the loan with the lower margin is better. The margin determines the interest rate for every year you hold the mortgage.

Representatives at one large mortgage lender in California told me that their market research shows that most borrowers care more about the start rate than the margin on their mortgage. So, they happily jacked up their loans' margins and lowered the start rates. Rather than educating their borrowers about the longer-term importance of the margin, they choose to pursue short-term profits.

Another way to think about the index and margin is to look at loans from the perspective of a banker making them. Bankers are in the business of lending money that they take in from depositors. The index is like the bankers' cost of funds — the rate they pay depositors on their deposits. The margin is like a markup on the bankers' cost of funds. This markup goes toward covering the bank's other expenses — executive and staff salaries, advertising, rent for office space, and so on. What's left over is profit — which bankers like.

The number of different indexes differ mainly in how rapidly they respond to changes in interest rates. The following are the more common ones:

- **Treasury bills (T-bills).** These indexes are issued by the U.S. government. Because they are government IOUs, there are a whole lot of them out there. Most adjustables are tied to the interest rate on six-month or twelve-month T-bills.

- **Certificates of deposit (CDs).** Certificates of deposit are interest-bearing bank investments that lock you in for a specific period of time. Adjustable-rate mortgages are usually tied to the average interest rate banks are paying on six-month CDs. Like t-bills, CDs tend to respond quickly to changes in the market level of interest rates. Unlike t-bills, CD rates tend to move up a bit more slowly when rates rise and come down faster when rates decline.

- **11th district cost of funds (cost of funds).** This index tends to be among the slower moving indexes. Adjustable-rate mortgages tied to 11th district cost of funds tend to start out at a higher interest rate. A slower moving index has the advantage of moving up less quickly when rates are on the rise. On the other hand, you have to be patient to benefit from falling interest rates when rates are on the decline.

Adjustment period or frequency

Every so many months, the mortgage-rate formula is applied to recalculate the interest rate on an adjustable-rate loan. Some loans adjust monthly. More typical is an adjustment every six or twelve months.

In advance of each adjustment, the lender should send you a notice telling you what your new rate will be. All things being equal, the less frequently your loan adjusts, the less financial uncertainty you have in your life. Less-frequent adjustments usually indicate that your loan starts at a higher interest rate, though.

Increasingly common are *hybrid loans* — which combine features of fixed- and adjustable-rate mortgages. For example, the initial rate may hold constant for a number of years — three to five years is common — and then adjust once a year or every six months thereafter.

These hybrid loans may make sense for you if you foresee a high probability of keeping your loan seven years or less but want some stability in your monthly payments. The longer the initial rate stays locked in, the higher the rate will be.

Rate caps

Once the initial interest rate expires, the interest rate fluctuates based on the formula of the loan. Almost all adjustables come with a rate cap, which limits, or *caps,* the maximum rate change (up or down) allowed at each adjustment. This limit is usually referred to as the *adjustment cap.* On most loans that adjust every six months, the adjustment cap is 1 percent. In other words, the interest rate can move up or down no more than 1 percent in a given adjustment period.

Loans that adjust more than once per year usually limit the maximum rate change allowed over the entire year as well. On the vast majority of such loans, 2 percent is the annual rate cap.

Finally, almost all adjustables come with lifetime caps. These caps limit the highest rate allowed over the entire life of the loan. It's common for adjustable loans to have lifetime caps of 5 – 6 percent higher than the initial start rate.

When you want to take an adjustable-rate mortgage, you must identify the maximum payment you can handle. If you can't handle the payment that comes with a 10- or 11-percent interest rate, for example, then you shouldn't look at adjustables that may go that high.

Negative amortization

As you make mortgage payments over time, the loan balance you still owe is gradually reduced — this process is known as *amortizing* the loan. The reverse of this process — increasing your loan balance — is called *negative amortization.*

Negative amortization is allowed by some adjustable-rate mortgages. How can your outstanding loan balance grow when you're continuing to make mortgage payments? When your mortgage payment is less than it really should be.

Some loans cap the increase of your monthly payment but not that of the interest rate. The size of your mortgage payment may not reflect all the interest that you owe on your loan. So, rather than paying the interest that is owed and paying off some of your loan balance (or *principal*) every month, you're paying off some but not all of the interest you owe. Thus, the extra unpaid interest you still owe is added to your outstanding debt.

Taking on negative amortization is like paying only the minimum payment required on a credit card bill. You keep racking up finance charges (in this case, greater interest) on the balance as long as you make only the artificially low payment. Doing so defeats the whole purpose of borrowing an amount that fits your overall financial goals. And you may never get the mortgage paid off!

Avoid adjustables with negative amortization. The only way to know whether a loan includes it is to ask. Some lenders aren't forthcoming about telling you. You'll find it more frequently on loans that lenders consider risky. If you're having trouble finding lenders willing to deal with your financial situation, be especially careful.

Prepayment penalties

Avoid loans with prepayment penalties. You pay this charge, usually 2 – 3 percent of the loan amount, when you pay off your loan before you're supposed to. Typically, prepayment penalties don't apply when you pay off a loan because you sell the property. But when you refinance a loan with prepayment penalties, you have to pay the penalty. If interest rates drop, your hands will be tied financially to take advantage of the lower rates.

The only way to know whether a loan has a prepayment penalty is to ask.

Finding the Best Lender

As with other financial purchases, you can save a lot of money by shopping around. It doesn't matter whether you do so on your own or hire someone to help you. Just do it!

On a 30-year, $120,000 mortgage, for example, getting a mortgage that costs 0.5 percent less per year saves you about $13,000 in interest over the life of the loan (given current interest rate levels). That's enough to buy a nice car!

Doing it yourself

There are many mortgage lenders in most areas. Although having a large number to choose from is good for competition, it also makes shopping around a chore. The major lenders are banks, savings and loans, and mortgage bankers. Unlike banks, which are in many different businesses, mortgage bankers only do mortgages. The better ones offer some of the most competitive rates.

Large banks whose names you recognize from their advertising usually don't offer the best rates. Make sure that you check out some of the smaller savings and loans and credit unions in your area as well.

Real estate agents can also refer you to lenders with whom they've done business. Those lenders don't necessarily offer the most competitive rates — the agent simply may have done business with them in the past.

Hiring a mortgage broker

Insurance agents sell insurance, real estate agents sell real estate, and mortgage brokers sell mortgages. They buy mortgages at wholesale from lenders (usually banks and savings and loans) and then mark them up to retail to you. The difference, or *spread,* is their income.

Mortgage brokers can sell you a loan from a number of different lenders. The rate the broker charges you is generally the same rate you would pay a lender directly.

A mortgage broker gets paid a percentage of the loan amount — typically 0.5 to 1 percent. This commission is completely negotiable, especially on larger loans that are more lucrative. There's no reason not to ask a mortgage broker what her cut is. Many people don't, so some brokers may act taken aback when you inquire. Remember, it's your money!

The best mortgage brokers

- **Shop among lots of lenders to get you the best deal available.** There are many lenders with many different loan programs out there.

- **Educate you about various loan options and the pros and cons of available features**. They take the time to understand your overall financial situation and steer you toward loans that better meet your needs.

- **Hold your hand through the process by filling out all those yucky documents required by lenders and by hounding you to get your documents in so that your loan package is complete.**

- **Polish your loan package so that the information is presented in its most favorable, yet still truthful, light.**

The worst mortgage brokers are

- **Lazy and don't continually shop the market looking for the best mortgage lenders.** They place their business with the same lenders, who don't necessarily offer the best rates.

- **Salespeople who push certain loan programs that are not in your best interests to earn a large commission.** They aren't interested in taking the time to understand your needs and discuss your options.

- **Morons who don't understand the advantages and disadvantages of different types of loans themselves.**

Be especially careful to avoid getting pushed into a balloon mortgage, which I described earlier in the chapter. Loans that become fully due and payable several years after you get them are dangerous because you may not be able to get new financing and could be forced to sell the property.

Most mortgage brokers fall between the two extremes of resourceful helper and greedy moron. In particular situations, using a broker makes sense. If you're too busy or disinterested to shop around for a good deal on a mortgage, a competent mortgage broker can probably save you money.

Brokers can also help if you anticipate that lenders may be skittish about offering you a loan. Problems on your credit report make lenders uncomfortable. If you're borrowing a large amount (90 percent or more) of the value of a property, many lenders aren't interested. Certain types of properties, such as co-ops and tenancies-in-common, give many lenders cold feet, because these buildings tend to give them more problems.

If you don't anticipate having difficulties qualifying for your loan, you can find good mortgages by shopping either on your own or through a mortgage information service. A competent mortgage broker can be of greatest value to those who don't bother shopping around for a good deal or who may be shunned by most lenders.

Even if you plan to shop on your own, it may be worthwhile to talk to a mortgage broker. At the very least, you can compare what you find with what brokers say they can get for you. Just be careful. Some brokers tell you what you want to hear — that is, that they can beat your best find — and then aren't able to deliver when the time comes.

If your loan broker quotes you a really good deal, make sure to ask who the lender is. (Most brokers refuse to reveal this information until you pay the few hundred dollars to cover the appraisal and credit report.) You can check with the actual lender to verify the interest rate and points the broker quotes you and make sure that you're eligible for the loan.

Using mortgage information services

If you're a real do-it-yourself type, look in the real estate section of one of the larger Sunday newspapers in your area for charts of selected lender interest rates. These tables are by no means comprehensive or reflective of the best rates available. In fact, many of them are sent to newspapers for free by firms that distribute mortgage information to mortgage brokers. Use them as a starting point by calling the lenders who list the best rates.

HSH Associates (800-873-2837) publishes mortgage information for most metropolitan areas. For $20, they'll send you a list of dozens of lenders' rate quotes. You need to be a real data junkie to wade through all the numbers on the multipage report of abbreviations in small type. The loan programs quoted are for purchases, not refinances.

If you're looking for a *jumbo* loan (currently, a loan larger than $203,150), you may be out of luck — loans this size are only covered in New York or New Jersey.

Applying for back-up loans

It can take several weeks for a lender to complete your property appraisal and evaluation of your loan package. When you're under contract to buy a property, having your loan denied after waiting several weeks could mean that you lose the property as well as the money you spent applying for the loan and having the property inspected. Some property sellers may be willing to give you an extension, but others won't. It's also extremely disappointing to spend all that time and emotional energy getting so close to owning a special property.

When job hunting or applying to college, people rarely set their sights on just one position or college. It's foolish to put all your eggs in one basket. So why put your life savings and emotional energy on a house purchase at stake by applying for a single loan? I once submitted two separate loan applications for the same property because I really didn't want to lose the deal. And I'm glad that I did, because a mortgage broker I used didn't deliver what he promised.

Applying for a second loan means additional application fees. Completing two lenders' applications also involves more time and work. It's not a huge hassle, however, because lenders require many of the same types of documentation and forms.

Whether for a purchase or refinance, you want the best deal you can get. If a lender knows that you have no other options, he or she may be less willing to work hard to get you the best deal. You should consider getting a back-up loan for this reason as well.

It's best to alert each lender you apply with that you're applying elsewhere. The second lender to pull your credit report will see the other lender's recent inquiry on your report. You should tell both lenders that you are sincerely interested — just as you would all prospective employers. (You aren't lying — if one turns you down, the other automatically becomes your first choice, and you wouldn't have applied if you weren't interested, right?)

An alternative would be to hold off on applying for your second choice loan until it's clear your first choice won't pan out. This is a potentially less useful strategy because the delay could cause you to lose the property on a purchase. You also lose your ability to tell the first lender that you'll take the other loan if what they deliver isn't what they promised.

How Much Can I Borrow?

All mortgage lenders want to know your ability and the likelihood of your repaying the money you borrow. So you have to pass a few tests. The lender calculates the maximum amount you can borrow when taking out a real estate loan. For a home in which you will reside, lenders total up your monthly housing expense. They define your housing costs as

> Mortgage Payment + Property Taxes + Insurance

A lender couldn't care less about the money you spend for dog food, vacations, or supporting local restaurant owners. Good thing, or you might not get the loan!

Lenders will loan you up to about 33 percent of your monthly gross income (before taxes, that is) for the housing expense. If you're self-employed, this figure is the net income from the bottom line of your federal tax form Schedule C.

Although lenders don't care where you spend money outside your home, they *do* care about your other debt. A lot of other debt diminishes the funds available to pay your housing expenses. Lenders know that debt increases the possibility that you may not make your monthly mortgage payments. When you have auto, credit card, or other types of debt requiring monthly payments, lenders calculate another ratio to determine the maximum you can borrow. To your monthly housing expense they add the amount you need to pay down your other consumer debt. These total costs typically cannot exceed 38 percent — anything higher and most lenders will reject your loan application.

Lending ratios vary slightly from lender to lender. Some lenders, for example, may allow your housing expense to reach up to 36 percent of your monthly income. Others may allow the ratio of housing expenses plus other consumer debt payments to reach up to 40 percent of your gross income.

An old rule of thumb says that you can afford to borrow three times (or two and one-half times) your annual income when buying a home. But this is a really rough estimate.

The maximum that a mortgage lender will loan you depends on interest rates. If rates fall (as they have during much of the past decade), the monthly payment on a mortgage of a given size also drops. Table 9-1 gives you a ballpark idea of the maximum that you're probably eligible to borrow. Multiply your gross annual income by the number in the second column to determine the maximum size mortgage you can get.

Table 9-1	What's the Maximum I Can Borrow?
When Mortgage Rates Are	**Multiply Your Gross Annual Income by This Figure to Determine the Maximum You May Be Able to Borrow**
4%	4.6
5%	4.2
6%	3.8
7%	3.5
8%	3.2
9%	2.9
10%	2.7
11%	2.5

For example, if you're getting a mortgage with a rate around 7 percent and your annual income is $50,000, multiply 3.5 x $50,000 to get $175,000, the approximate maximum mortgage allowed. As you can see, lower interest rates make buying real estate much more affordable.

The maximum amount that you can borrow depends on the property taxes you pay. These taxes vary from area to area, so the preceding table is based on average property tax rates of about 1.25 percent of the property value per year. Table 9-1 also assumes that you plan to take a 30-year mortgage.

The only way to know what size mortgage you're eligible for is to talk to some lenders. Most are more than willing to prequalify you, which means that they take down some background data on you (income, debts, and so on) and run some numbers to tell you how much you can borrow. This preliminary meeting isn't a promise or guarantee, though — lenders won't commit to a loan until they have your documentation and property appraisal in hand.

When you're prequalified, the lender isn't committed to approving a loan for you. You're also under no obligation to work with a lender or mortgage broker who prequalifies you. Prequalification is part of marketing. It benefits lenders by allowing them to learn, after a small investment of their time, whether they should spend their time trying to get you a loan.

How Much Should I Borrow?

Lenders inform you of the maximum amount that you qualify to borrow, but you shouldn't necessarily borrow the maximum. The most common mistake people make when buying a home is failing to consider their overall financial situation and needs.

If you fall in love with a home and buy it without looking at your monthly expenditures and long-term goals, you may end up with a home that dictates much of your future spending. For example, how much should you be saving monthly to reach your retirement goals? How much do you spend (and want to continue spending) on fun stuff like travel and entertainment? If you would like to maintain your current lifestyle (and the expenditures inherent in it), you have to be honest with yourself about how much you can really afford to spend to support a new house.

First-time home buyers commonly run into financial trouble because they don't know their spending needs and priorities and don't know how to budget for them. Buying a home can be a wise decision, but it can also be a huge burden. Some people have trouble curtailing their spending despite the large amount of debt they incur and, in fact, spend even more because there are all sorts of nifty things to buy for a home. Many prop up their spending habits with credit, which is why a surprisingly large percentage of people — some studies say about half — borrow additional money against their home equity and use the funds to pay other debts.

Don't let your home control your financial future. Take stock first of your overall financial health (see Chapter 2), especially where you stand in terms of retirement planning if you hope to retire before age 70 or so (refer to Chapter 8), *before* you buy property or agree to a particular-size mortgage.

Private mortgage insurance (PMI)

Another factor to consider in deciding how much you should borrow is that most lenders require you to purchase *private mortgage insurance* (PMI) if your down payment is less than 20 percent. On a moderate-size loan, PMI can add hundreds of dollars per year to your payments.

If you have to take PMI to buy a home with less than 20 percent down, keep an eye on your home's value and your loan balance. With luck, your property will appreciate over time and your loan balance will decrease. Once the loan amounts to 80 percent or less of the market value of the home, you can get rid of the PMI. Removing PMI can be a costly hassle, because you must prove (with an appraisal) that you have at least 20 percent equity in the property.

What if I have plenty of cash around?

What if you have so much money that you can afford to put down less than a 20 percent down payment? (For most people, this problem doesn't usually arise — buyers generally struggle to get a down payment together. But if you just sold a house and are moving to a less-expensive area or if you won the lottery, you may face this problem.)

How much should you put down, then? The answer depends on what else you can or want to do with the money. If you're considering other investment opportunities, determine whether you can expect to earn a higher rate of return than the interest rate you'll pay on the mortgage.

During this century, stock market and real estate investors have enjoyed average annual returns of around 10 percent per year (just remember the past doesn't guarantee the future). So if you borrow mortgage money at around 7 percent today, you should come out ahead by investing in these areas. Besides possibly generating a higher rate of return, other real estate and stock investing can help you to diversify your investments, which is always a good thing.

There is, of course, no guarantee that you can earn 10 percent yearly. And don't forget that all investments come with risk. The advantage of putting more money down for a home and borrowing less is that a home is essentially a risk-free investment.

If you prefer to put down just 20 percent and invest more elsewhere, that's fine. Just don't keep the extra money under the mattress, in a savings account, or in bonds that pay less interest than your mortgage costs you in interest.

Should I Refinance Now?

Three reasons motivate people to refinance. One is obvious — to save money because interest rates have dropped. Refinancing also can be a way of raising capital for some other purpose. A final reason is to get out of one type of loan and into another. The following discussion should help you to decide upon the best option in each case.

Spending money to save money

Most people refinance for the same reason that they want a promotion — for the money. When you refinance a mortgage, you have to spend money and time to save money. So you need to crunch a few numbers to determine whether refinancing makes sense for you.

As of this writing, fixed-rate loans are in the neighborhood of 7 percent, and adjustables are around 4 percent with lifetime caps of around 9 to 10 percent. So, if your loan has a higher rate of interest, you may save money by refinancing. Because refinancing almost always costs money, it's a bit of a gamble whether you can save enough to justify the cost.

Your odds of saving money by refinancing go up a lot when

- ✔ Your current interest is quite high — above 8.5 percent on a fixed-rate loan or 6 percent plus on an adjustable with a lifetime cap above 10 percent.
- ✔ You're planning to keep the property for at least five years or more.

Not all refinances cost tons of money. So-called *no-cost* refinances or *no-point* loans are becoming more widely available. These may not be your best long-term options, however. As I explained earlier in the chapter, there are no free lunches. No-cost or no-point loans come with higher interest rates.

Ask your mortgage lender or broker how many months it will take you to recoup the costs of refinancing, such as appraisal, loan fees and points, title insurance, and so on. For example, if the refinance costs you $2,000 to complete and reduces your monthly payment by $100, the lender or broker typically says that it'll take 20 months for you to save back the refinance costs. This isn't accurate, however, because you lose some tax writeoffs if your mortgage interest rate and payment are reduced. You can't simply look at the reduced amount of your monthly payment (mortgage lenders like to look at it, however, because it makes refinancing more attractive).

If you want a better estimate but don't want to spend hours crunching numbers, take your tax rate as specified in Chapter 7 (for example, 28 percent) and reduce your monthly payment savings on the refinance by this amount. That means, continuing with the example in the preceding paragraph, that if your monthly payment drops by $100, you're *really* only saving around $72 a month after factoring in the lost tax benefits. So, it will take 28 months ($2,000 divided by $72) — not 20 — to recoup the refinance costs.

If you can recover the costs of the refinance within a few years or less, go for it. If it takes longer, it may still make sense if you anticipate keeping the property and mortgage that long. More than 5 – 7 years is probably too risky to justify the refinance costs and hassles.

Using money for another purpose

Refinancing to pull out cash from the house for some other purpose can make good financial sense because under most circumstances, mortgage interest is tax deductible.

A common reason for borrowing against a home is to pay off other higher-interest consumer debt — such as on credit cards or on an auto loan. The interest on consumer debt is not tax deductible. Plus, you can usually borrow at a much lower interest rate than that which consumer loans charge you.

If you're starting a business, consider borrowing against your home to finance the launch of your business. You can usually do so at a lower cost than on a business loan.

The most critical question is whether a lender is willing to lend you more money against the equity in your home (which is the difference between the market value of your house and the loan balance). You can "guesstimate" whether you can afford larger payments by using Table 9-1 to find the maximum loan for which you may qualify. But you also need to know the value of your property (comparable recent sales in your neighborhood can help you determine what it's worth) to understand how much more you can borrow.

Changing loans

Sometimes, saving money or raising more money isn't the objective. You might be forced to get a new loan. Balloon loans, which come due and payable in full at a predetermined time, may require you to get new financing. Or you may have bought property in partnership with others and now need to cash out one of your partners.

In these cases, you can determine which type of loan is best for you in the same way you do in getting a new loan. Go back and read the sections that deal with choosing a fixed- versus an adjustable-rate mortgage.

There are other cases in which you might want to refinance even though you're not forced to and won't save money. Perhaps you're not comfortable with your current loan — holders of adjustable-rate mortgages often face this problem. You may find out that a fluctuating mortgage payment makes you a nervous wreck in addition to wreaking havoc on your budget. The certainty of a fixed-rate mortgage can be your salvation.

Paying money to go from an adjustable into a fixed is a lot like buying insurance. The cost of the insurance in this case — the refinance — guarantees a level mortgage payment. Consider this option only if you want peace of mind and you plan to stay with the property for a number of years.

Sometimes it makes sense to consider jumping from one adjustable to another. Suppose you can lower the maximum lifetime interest rate cap and the refinance won't cost too much. Your new loan should have a lower initial interest rate than the one you're paying on your current loan. Even if you won't save megabucks, the peace of mind of a lower ceiling can make it worth your while.

Help, I Can't Get a Loan!

Being turned down for a mortgage is a bummer, especially when you lose a property you have your heart set on. I believe in trying to avoid as many situations of disappointment as possible. Not good for the ego, you know.

The best defense against loan rejection is to avoid it in the first place. You can sometimes head off potential rejection by disclosing to your lender anything that may cause a problem before you apply for the loan. That way, you have more time to correct problems and find alternate solutions.

If you are a lending risk because you don't have the income to qualify for the loan you want, you may need to get a cosigner. You can try parents, other relatives, or even rich friends as potential cosigners. As long as they aren't borrowed up to their eyeballs, they can help you qualify for a larger loan than you can get on your own. Be sure that all parties understand the terms of the agreement, including who is responsible for monthly payments! Here are some other ideas to try in different circumstances:

Get rid of other debt

The more credit card, auto loan, and other consumer debt you rack up, the less mortgage you qualify for. If you're turned down for the mortgage, consider it a wake-up call and a blessing. In addition to the high interest rate on consumer debt and the fact that it encourages you to live beyond your means, you now have a third reason to get rid of it. Hang onto the dream of a home and plug away at paying off your debts before you make another foray into real estate.

Clear up credit report problems

Late payments, missed payments, or debts that you never bothered to pay can come back to haunt you. Get a copy of your credit report from the lender who turned down your loan. Your consolation prize for not winning the mortgage game is a free copy of your credit report (much better than a case of Turtle Wax!).

If there are bona fide problems documented on your credit report, start by trying to explain them to your lender. If the lender is unsympathetic, try calling other lenders. Tell them your credit problems up front and see whether you can find one willing to give you a loan. Mortgage brokers (discussed earlier) can also help you shop for lenders in these cases.

It's not unusual for mistakes to crop up on credit reports. The only way to fix them, unfortunately, is to get on the phone to the credit bureaus and start squawking. If specific creditors have reported erroneous information, call them, too. If the customer service representatives you talk with are no help, dash off a nice letter to the president of each company. Let the head honcho know that his or her organization caused you problems in obtaining credit, and threaten to tell the Better Business Bureau, *Consumer Reports,* and me what dirty rotten scoundrels they are if they don't remove the derogatory information from your credit report.

Try renegotiating a lower price based on a low appraisal

Perhaps the value of the property comes in lower than necessary to qualify you for the loan. If this happens when you're purchasing, you may be lucky. Your lender may have saved you from paying too much for a property. Go back to the seller and renegotiate a lower price based on the appraisal.

If the appraisal on a refinance is too low, your best bet is usually to pay cash into the loan closing to get the loan balance down to a level for which you qualify. If you don't have the cash, you have to forego the refinance until you save more money or until the property value rises (either through home improvements or because the market improves).

Some critics have charged that lenders sometimes "low-ball" an appraisal to sabotage a loan. If you suspect that this may be the case, make sure to ask for a copy of your appraisal — which you are entitled to. If you have comparable sale prices from your area that support your case, go back to the lender and see what they have to say. If you're still not satisfied, you can take your beef to a state regulator of mortgage lenders. It may be a lot less hassle, though, to find another lender.

Work around low income

If you're self-employed or have been changing jobs, your recent economic history may be as unstable as a communist country trying out capitalism. One way around this problem is to make a larger down payment. If you put down 30 percent or more, you may be able to get a no-income verification loan. If you can put that much money down, lenders probably won't care what your income is. They'll just repossess your property if you can't make the payments! (For more ideas about buying real estate when cash is tight or when you have credit problems, be sure to read Chapter 15 about buying and investing in real estate.)

Questions You May Ask Yourself

In this section, I deal with some of the more common mortgage quandaries and dilemmas.

Should I take out a home equity loan?

This special type of mortgage loan allows you to borrow more against your home in addition to the mortgage you already have (a first mortgage). Home equity loans used to be known as *second mortgages,* a term that much better describes what they are.

Those who lived through the Great Depression of the 1930s can tell you why second mortgages have a bad rap. During the Depression, many homeowners were forced to take out second mortgages to pay monthly bills. At the peak of the Depression, one in four Americans was out of work. Many homeowners ended up losing their properties to foreclosure.

More recently, marketing folks figured correctly that they could entice people to borrow more against their homes if they avoided the term *second mortgages.*

Today, about 25 percent of homeowners have home equity loans. Unlike their predecessors during the Depression, most of these borrowers aren't desperate for additional funds. The majority of these second mortgages are for new cars or home improvements. A smaller number are for paying off credit card and other debts.

The allure of home equity loans is simple. Borrowing against real estate is relatively low cost and (generally) tax-deductible to boot. The problem I see with home equity loans is that they allow, and even encourage, people to overspend. It's no wonder that many people have them (and, in some cases, for frivolous reasons), because they can be as easy to use as credit cards — some home equity loans can be accessed simply by writing a check.

Borrowing more against your home makes financial sense in some cases: for example, when you decide to build an addition to your home instead of selling it to buy a larger one. But taking out a second mortgage is usually an inferior option. Second mortgages or home equity loans have higher interest rates than comparable first mortgages. They are riskier from a lender's perspective because the first mortgage lender gets first dibs if you file bankruptcy or the property ends up in foreclosure.

A home equity loan might be beneficial if you need more money for just a few years, or if your first mortgage is at such a low interest rate that refinancing to get more cash would otherwise be costly — otherwise, avoid home equity loans. If you've racked up high-interest credit card or other consumer debt, refinancing your mortgage to pay it off can be a good financial move. Mortgage interest costs less and is tax-deductible.

Should I lie to get a mortgage?

Some people lie to qualify for a mortgage. I know more than a few folks who have lied to get a mortgage. It's not that I associate with unethical people. I just hear the juicy tails in the course of work that I do in the financial services industry. Mortgage brokers, who end up working with more of the borrowers with less-than-perfect situations, can tell you lots of war stories of trickery and deception to close a deal. Some brokers even coach people into lying so they can qualify for a loan.

In most cases, it's for your own good that you can't qualify for the loan that you want. Lenders have lending criteria to ensure that you will be able to repay and don't get in over your head. On the other hand, I am sympathetic to some of the complaints I hear about bankers and other mortgage lenders who can some-times be as compassionate and flexible as a totalitarian government agency. They have their rules and regulations and qualifying ratios. You either meet them or you don't. It's black or white. They have their reasons, but sometimes their rules don't fit your situation.

Don't lie. Besides the obvious legal objections, you could end up with more mortgage debt than you can really afford and possibly worse. There are alternatives if you're cash constrained. For example, loans that don't require documentation of income are available when you make a large down payment, generally 30 percent or more. These loans cost a little more than conventional loans, but they also allow you to avoid lying. You could also get a cosigner. Go back and read the section earlier in the chapter, "Help I Can't Get a Loan!" to learn more about what you can legally do when you can't qualify for a mortgage.

Do I need mortgage life insurance?

Shortly after you buy a home or close on a mortgage, you start getting mail from all kinds of organizations who keep track of publicly available information about mortgages. Most of these organizations want to sell you something, and they don't tend to beat around the bush.

"What will your dependents do if you meet with an untimely demise and they are left with a gargantuan mortgage?" they ask.

Fair enough. In fact, it's a good financial-planning question. If your family is dependent upon your income, can they survive financially if you and your income disappear from life as we know it?

Don't waste your money on mortgage life insurance. You may need life insurance to provide for your family and help meet large obligations such as mortgage payments or educational expenses for children. But mortgage life insurance is grossly overpriced. (Read the life insurance section in Chapter 17 for recommendations about term life insurance protection.)

If you're not in good health and the insurer does not require a physical examination, then consider it. But make sure to compare it with term life insurance providers (Chapter 17).

Is getting a reverse mortgage a good idea?

Increasing numbers of homeowners are finding, particularly in their later years of retirement, that they are lack cash. Their largest asset is usually the home in which they live. Unlike other investments, such as bank accounts, bonds, or stocks, a home does not provide any income to the owner unless he or she decides to rent out a room or two.

A reverse mortgage allows a homeowner who's low on cash to tap into home equity. For an elderly homeowner, this can be a difficult thing to do psychologically. Most people work hard to feed a mortgage month after month, year after year, until finally it is all paid off. What a feat and what a relief after all those years!

Taking out a reverse mortgage reverses this process. Each month, a bank or other financial institution sends you a check that you can spend on food, clothing, travel, or whatever suits your fancy.

The money you receive each month is really a loan from the bank against the value of your home, which makes the monthly check free from taxation. Other advantages of a reverse mortgage are that it allows you to stay in your home and use its equity to supplement your monthly income.

The main drawback is that a reverse mortgage can deplete the estate that you may want to pass onto your heirs or use for some other purpose. Also, some loans require repayment within a certain number of years. The fees and the effective interest rate you are charged to borrow the money can also be quite high.

Because some loans require the lender to make monthly payments to you as long as you live in the home, lenders assume that you will live a very long time so that they don't lose money in making these loans. If you end up only keeping the loan for a few years because you move, for example, the cost of the loan is extremely high.

An excellent book that explores all the mechanics of reverse mortgages and how to shop for them is *Retirement Income on the House* by Ken Scholen. Call 800-247-6533 or write to him at 7373 147th St., Apple Valley, MN 55124. The American Association of Retired Persons (AARP) also publishes a free information booklet entitled *Home Made Money,* which can be requested by writing AARP at 1909 K St. NW, Washington, D.C. 20049 or by calling 202-434-2277.

You may be able to create a reverse mortgage within your own family network. This technique can work if you have family members who are financially able to provide you with monthly income in exchange for ownership of the home when you pass away.

There are also other alternatives to tapping home equity. One is to simply sell your home and buy a less expensive property or rent a place. Current tax laws allow homeowners 55 and older to take a once-in-a-lifetime $125,000 capital gains exclusion when they sell a home and buy a less expensive one.

Part III
Investing What You Save

"All right, ready everyone! We've got some clown out here who looks interested."

In this part . . .

You find out what you already know deep down, that earning and saving are hard work and that you should be careful where you invest the fruit of your labor. I lay out the basics of investing and show you how to pick your investments wisely. This part is where you find out the real story on such things as stocks, bonds, mutual funds, the differences between investing in retirement and non-retirement accounts, how to invest for college, and how to buy a home.

Investment Basics

· ·

· ·

*W*hether you're just starting to save money to invest or have millions to play with, mistakes can cost you dearly. Everyone makes at least one (and I have to admit, I've made a few more than that).

I don't define a mistake as an investment that doesn't turn a profit. No one has a crystal ball to predict which investments will produce great profits. Aside from doing your homework before making an informed investment decision, there's an occasional element of luck to yielding great results from some investment choices. No, an investment mistake is a bad decision that you could or should have avoided — either because there were better options or because the odds were heavily stacked against your making money. A mistake results from not doing your homework, surrendering to a sales pitch (or salesperson) against your better judgment, or being greedy and believing that you can get something for nothing.

Ten Common Investment Mistakes

This section is one of the most important of the book. As a financial counselor, I always ask new clients to tell me about their mistakes. Beginners make many of the same mistakes. The following are the most common blunders, costly errors, and regrets. If you can avoid major investment errors, you're more than halfway down the road to investment success. So, sit back, relax, swallow your pride, and learn from the mistakes of others.

Neglecting to pay off high-interest consumer debt

Psychologically, you want to feel like you're saving money and making it grow. Your best investment, however, may be as simple as looking at your credit card bill or auto loan. If you're paying 10, 14, or 18 percent interest on your outstanding balance, pay it off first. To get a comparable return on your own investments (after the government takes its share of your profits), you would have to start a new career as a loan shark.

Even people who have money languishing in savings or money market accounts at 2 or 3 percent interest resist this strategy, although they pay far more in interest charges on their loans than they earn on their savings. Invest your money by paying off high-interest debts as soon as possible.

Investing based on sales solicitations

Companies that advertise aggressively or sell investments by cold calling offer some of the worst financial products with the highest commissions. Companies with great products don't reach their audiences this way.

Another rule of thumb is never to seek out companies because they have a catchy theme song or because they promise you a piece of some rock. (That firm, by the way, sold billions of dollars of limited partnerships, which led to the loss of billions of investor dollars. If you don't know what a limited partnership is, consider yourself lucky.)

Purchasing investments you don't understand

This mistake usually follows from the preceding no-no. If you don't understand an investment, odds are good that it may not be right for you. Fast-talking brokers who earn commissions based on what they sell often talk you into these investments. You don't need to understand your investments well enough to become a financial counselor, but you should know the track record of the investment, its true costs, and how liquid it is.

Not understanding risks

No investment is without risk — some risks are just more apparent than others. When the stock market rises and falls like a yo-yo, it feels risky. You need to understand the likely volatility and fluctuations an investment may experience so that you don't have a nervous breakdown watching it. If you are investing for growth, then you must be willing to deal with good and bad periods.

Calculation of risk should include not only the volatility in the value of your investment but also the factors that influence the fluctuations. A mistake many investors make is keeping money they don't plan to use for many years in investments that are too conservative. Bank savings accounts seem safe, but they provide no growth potential and may not keep you ahead of inflation and taxes. Stocks and real estate have good track records of growth but can plunge in value periodically. If you can ride out down periods or add to your holdings in the meantime, these investments — if you choose wisely — should be fine in the long run.

Paying unnecessary commissions and high management fees

Avoid investments that carry high commissions and expenses (usually disclosed in a *prospectus*). Virtually all investments today can be purchased without a salesperson. Besides paying unnecessary commissions, the danger in investing through salespeople is that you're far less likely to make choices that are in your best interests (see Chapter 3 for information about hiring financial help).

Higher-fee investments, on average, perform worse than alternatives with lower fees because of the drag the expenses place on returns. High ongoing management fees often go toward supporting lavish offices, glossy brochures, and excessive salaries or toward supporting small, inefficient operations. Do you want your hard earned dollars to support either of these types of businesses?

Putting all your eggs in one basket

Diversification means putting your money in different investments that perform well under differing market conditions. A common mistake is investing too much retirement money in an employer's stock. If the employer falls on hard times, you may lose your job *and* the value of your investments. Remember when folks talked about IBM as a super safe investment? IBM may have been a blue chip stock for a while, but employees who were laid off now have more than bruised egos — they also have black-and-blue investment portfolios if they invested heavily in IBM stock.

Buying after major price increases

By the time an investment gets front-page coverage and everyone is talking about its stunning rise, it's time to take a reality check. The higher the value of an investment rises, the greater the danger that it's overpriced. Its next move may be downward. Don't follow the herd.

Selling after major price declines

When the New York Mets lost the majority of their games in 1968, their future prospects seemed bleak. But the very next year, the Mets won the World Series. When things look bleak, it's easy to give up hope — who wants to be associated with a loser? If you could have invested in the Mets, though, 1968 would have been a great time to do so. Things couldn't have gotten much worse for the team, and the price of stock would have been cheap. But you gotta have faith.

Likewise, investors who panicked and sold *after* the October 1987 stock market crash missed out on a tremendous buying opportunity.

You buy everything from clothing to cars to ketchup on sale — why should investments be any different? It takes a little more courage to buy when people are stampeding for the exits. Again, don't follow the herd. After all, lemmings die that way. (By the way, how is it that lemmings haven't gone out of existence?)

Ignoring tax consequences

Even if you never become an investment whiz, you're smart enough to know that the less money you pay in taxes, the more you have to invest and play with. Channeling investment money into retirement accounts allows your money to grow without taxation, and therefore faster, over time (see Chapter 8). For investments outside retirement accounts, you need to match the types of investments to your tax situation (see Chapter 12).

Believing self-proclaimed gurus and soothsayers

Ignore the predictions and speculations of self-proclaimed gurus (the Jeane Dixons of the investment world). No one has a crystal ball — and even if they did, they wouldn't waste time publishing a mass-market newsletter to tell you what they saw.

Of course, you want to believe that people can divine the future of the investment world. It makes it easier to accept the risk you know you're taking to make your money grow. But if you have to believe in something to offset your fears, believe in good information and proven investment managers. And don't forget the value of hope — regardless of What or Whom you believe in!

Setting Your Goals

It's more fun and exciting to jump right into picking a particular investment. (People like lots of action — if we can't look like Schwartzenegger, at least we can mobilize to action as though we do.) You may have an idea from some reading you've done. Or maybe Uncle Louie is whispering in your ear that he's gonna get you in on the ground floor of a great new idea — a real sure thing.

Stop! Wait! Hit the brakes!

Before you immerse yourself in a specific investment, you must first determine your investment needs and goals. Why are you saving this pile of money? What are you going to use it for? You can't earmark *every* dollar, but you should set some major objectives. Doing so is important because the future use of the money determines how much time you can stick with an investment. And that, in turn, may help determine which investment you choose to go with.

Suppose the money you plan on using for Uncle Louie's sure-win deal is all the liquid cash you have available. What if Louie's deal is a bust? What are you going to tap in the event of an emergency? In recent years, too many people have found out the hard way that the recession and natural disasters aren't just bad things that happen to other people. You need a safety net in case you lose your job or are hit with unexpected expenses.

If you've been accumulating money toward a down payment on a home you'd like to buy in a few years, for example, you can't afford much risk. You're going to need that money sooner rather than later. Putting that money in the stock market, then, is probably not a wise move. As you'll see later, the stock market can drop a lot in a year or over several consecutive years. So stocks are probably too risky a place to invest down payment money you plan on using soon.

Perhaps you're saving towards a longer-term goal, such as retirement, that is 20 or 30 years away. In this case, you're in a position to take more risk because you have more time to bounce back from temporary losses or setbacks. A retirement account that you leave alone for 20 years may be where you should consider investing in stocks. You can tolerate year-to-year volatility in the market — you've got time on your side.

For some people, the thought of putting retirement money in the stock market is horrifying. You want to make sure that your retirement nest egg is intact, and you know what a roller coaster the stock market can be. These concerns are valid, and you have to weigh these fears against the potential benefits. The risk level of your investments has to meet your comfort level as well as your time frame. The rate of return from your investments that you need to reach your goals can help you direct how much risk to take.

Tasting Different Investment Flavors

Remember your childhood friends who always aced their math tests or arranged alphabet soup into ten-letter words before eating it? Well, these little geniuses grew up, went to work on Wall Street, and cooked up hundreds of confusing names and acronyms for different investment products.

Forget all those buzzwords — in many cases, they're only meant to confuse and obscure what an investment really is.

Imagine a world with only chocolate and vanilla ice cream (or low-fat, non-dairy frozen dessert for you health-minded folks). Just two choices. Might make the ice cream shop a lot less interesting, but it would sure simplify your decision.

The investment world is really just as simple. If you have money to invest, you can either be a lender or an owner.

Lending investments

You're a *lender* when you invest your money in a bank certificate of deposit, a treasury bill, or a bond issued by General Motors, for example. In each case, you are lending your money to an organization — a bank, the federal government, or GM. You are paid an agreed-upon rate of interest for lending your money. You are also promised to have your original investment (the principal) returned to you on a specific date.

The best that can happen with a lending investment is that you are paid all of the interest in addition to your original investment as promised. This result isn't so bad given that the investment landscape is littered with carcasses of failed investments.

The worst that can happen is that you don't get everything you were promised. Promises can be broken under extenuating circumstances. When a company goes bankrupt, for example, you can lose all or part of your original investment.

Another risk is that you get what you were promised, but because of the ravages of inflation, your money is worth less — it has less purchasing power than you thought it would. Back in the 1960s, for example, high-quality companies were issuing long-term bonds that paid approximately 4 percent interest. At the time it seemed like a good deal, because the cost of living was increasing at the rate of only 2 percent a year. When inflation rocketed to 6, 8,10 percent and higher, those 4 percent bonds didn't seem so attractive. High-quality bonds paid annual interest of 4 percent and you got your principal back, but the interest and principal didn't buy nearly the amount it did years earlier when inflation was lower.

A final drawback is that you do not share in the success of the organization to which you are lending your money. If it doubles or triples in size and profits, it's good for the company and its owners and ensures that you'll get your interest and principal back. But you don't get any of it unless you get real friendly real fast.

Ownership investments

You're an *owner* when you invest your money in an asset, such as a company or real estate, that has the ability to generate earnings or profits. Suppose that you own 100 shares of Sears stock. With hundreds of millions of shares of stock outstanding, Sears is a mighty big company — your 100 shares represent a tiny piece of it.

What do you get for your small piece of Sears? As a stockholder, you share in the profits of a company in the form of annual dividends as well as an increase (you hope) in the stock price if the company grows and becomes more profitable. That's when things are going well.

The downside is that if Sears's business declines, your stock can become worth less (or even worthless!). Sears might be taken over by evil aliens who decide to sell all sorts of "socially irresponsible" products. Everyone boycotts the store and your stock plummets in value.

Real estate is another type of ownership investment. Most folks invest in real estate in order to earn a profit. (The two exceptions are homes you live in yourself, in which case you probably hope that it increases in value, and properties people buy for sentimental or conservation reasons.) Real estate can yield profits by being rented out for income (profits come when rental income exceeds the expense of owning the property) or by being sold at a higher price than that which you paid to buy it.

As with other ownership investments, the value of real estate depends on the health and performance of the economy as well as the specifics of the property you own. If the local economy grows and more jobs are being produced at higher wages, then real estate should do well. If companies in the community are laying people off left and right and excess housing is sitting vacant because of previous overbuilding, then rents and property values are likely to fall.

Other factors also affect property values. If the local planning board rezones your property and allows construction of a ten-story apartment building where you have a little duplex, the value of your property should skyrocket. On the other hand, if a toxic waste dump is discovered on your property's doorstep, booming economy or not, your real estate fortunes are sure to dwindle.

Rolling the dice

There's a difference between investing and gambling. The two may seem similar because people hope to make a lot of money in both arenas, if not by skill then by chance.

Gambling is putting your money into schemes that are sure long-term losers. That's not to say that everyone loses or that you lose every time you play. However, the deck is stacked against you. The house wins most of the time.

In some cases, as with horse racing, gambling casinos, and lotteries, the system is set up to pay out 50 – 60 cents on the dollar. The rest goes to administration of the system and — don't forget that these are businesses — profits. Sure, your horse may win a race or two, but in the long run, you're almost guaranteed to lose. The track is in business to make money from people with loose cash and high hopes. Of course, some horses are more likely to win than others. That's why the track sets odds to give you lower payoffs on the front-runners.

Gambling in the investment world is *speculation* — these opportunities are found in sales and trading of futures, options, and commodities.

You may have heard the radio ad by the firm of Fleecem, Cheatem, and Leavem, advocating that you buy heating oil futures because the cold weather months lead to the use of more heating oil. You call and are impressed by the smooth-talking vice president who spends so much time with little ol' you. His logic makes sense, and he's spent a lot of time with you, so you send him a check for $10,000.

Doing so isn't much different from blowing $10,000 at the craps tables in Las Vegas. Futures prices depend on short-term price movements. Commodities and futures are quite volatile in price. As with gambling, you occasionally win when the market moves the right way at the right time. But in the long run, you're gonna lose. In fact, you can lose it all.

Options are the same — you're betting on short-term movements of a specific security. If you have inside information, as Ivan Boesky did, such that you know in advance when a major corporate development is going to occur, you can get rich. But don't forget one minor detail — insider trading is illegal. You may end up in the slammer like Boesky.

Honest brokers who help their clients invest in stocks, bonds, and mutual funds tell you the truth about commodities, futures, and options. A former broker I know who used to work for Merrill Lynch and Shearson Lehman told me, "I had one client who made money in options, futures, or commodities for 12 years, but the only reason he came out ahead was because he had to pull money out to close on a home purchase just when he happened to be ahead. The commissions were great for me, but there's no way a customer will make money in them."

No way to fund government

More and more states are getting into the gambling business as a way to bring in more revenue. This business is sad and wrong for many reasons. First, it's been well documented that lotteries and casinos obtain the most business from those least able to afford them — primarily middle- and low-income earners. They end up creating an additional tax on the poor and operate on the basis of false hopes.

Secondly, government endorsement of gambling promotes the get-rich-quick mentality. Why get an education and toil away over the years when you may solve all your financial concerns with the next ticket you buy or slot you pull? Gambling is also a contributor to our nationally low personal savings rate.

Finally, gambling, like alcohol and tobacco, can be addictive and destructive. In the worst cases, gambling and gambling debts can split up families and lead to divorce or even suicide.

It's bad enough that legalized gambling exists. It's even worse that in the pursuit of short-term profits and a quick fix, more local governments are piling into this business. Government is fostering an irresponsible attitude toward money.

Investment Returns

Now you know the difference between ownership and lending investments. Hopefully, you can distinguish gambling and speculation from true investments.

"That's all well and good," you say, "but how do I choose which type of investments to put my money into? How much can I make and what are the risks?"

Good questions. I'll start with the returns you *might* make. I say "might" because I'm looking at history, and history is a record of the past. Using history to predict the future, especially the near future, is dangerous. History may repeat itself, but not always in exactly the same fashion and not necessarily when you expect it to.

Over time, ownership investments like stocks and real estate have returned around 10 percent per year, handily beating lending investments such as bonds (around 5 percent) and savings accounts (roughly 4 percent) in the investment performance race.

Wouldn't it be interesting to see where those who have some discretionary funds to toss around invest their money? They must know some secret. Many millionaires are financially savvy — that's how some of them make their millions. But others are financial dummies — the difference is that they are (or feel) wealthy enough to hire advisors.

Millionaires invest most of their wealth — nearly three-quarters of it — in ownership investments such as corporate stock, real estate, and businesses. The remaining quarter they invest mainly in lending-type investments.

Risks

We should put all of our money in stocks and real estate, right? The returns sure look great. So what's the catch?

Investments with a potential for higher returns carry greater risks.

The drawback to ownership investments is volatility. For example, during this century, stocks have declined by more than 10 percent in a year every five years. Drops in stock prices of more than 20 percent have occurred once every ten years. Thus, in order to earn those generous long-term returns, you must be willing to tolerate volatility. That's why you absolutely should not put all your money in the stock or real estate market.

Low-risk, high-return investments

Despite what they teach in the nation's leading business and finance graduate school programs, there *are* low-risk investments that are almost certain to lead to high returns.

They are:

Your health. Eat healthy, exercise, relax. Low risk, high return!

Friends and family. Improve your relationships with loved ones. Invest the time and effort in making them better. Low risk, high return!

Personal and career development. Learn a new hobby, improve your communication skills, read widely. Take an adult education course or go back to school for a degree. Your investment will surely pay off in higher paychecks and greater happiness. Low risk, high return!

Some types of bonds have higher yields than others. Nothing is free here, either. A bond generally pays you a higher rate of interest as compared to other bonds when it includes

- Lower credit quality — to compensate for the higher risk of default and higher likelihood of losing your investment

- Longer-term maturity — to compensate for the risk that you'll be unhappy with the bond's interest rate if interest rates move up

Investment Vehicles

In the investment world, there are many different types of investment vehicles in which you can place your money.

Decent ones work their way methodically around the race track, rarely deterred but also never at a fast rate. The best ones make their way through the course at a faster clip, only occasionally slowed by a bump or detour. The worst ones sputter in fits and starts and sometimes crash and burn in a flaming heap.

Which vehicle you choose for your trip depends on where you're going, how fast you want to get there, and what risks you're willing to take along the way. The following lists vehicles to choose from and offers thoughts on when each might be appropriate. There are also caution signs labeling the ones you should avoid.

Transaction/checking accounts

These accounts are best used for depositing your monthly income and paying for your expenditures. If you have to have unlimited privileges to write checks of all size denominations and access your money with your ATM card, checking accounts at local banks are your best bet. Make sure to shop around for accounts that don't ding you $1 here for use of an ATM machine and $10 there for a low balance.

With interest rates as low as they are now, focus on avoiding monthly service charges rather than chasing after an account with a slightly higher interest rate. Some banks, for example, do not require you to maintain a minimum balance to avoid a monthly service charge when you direct deposit your paychecks. In any event, you should keep only enough money in the account to service your monthly needs. If you consistently keep more than a few thousand dollars in a checking account, get it out. You can earn more in a savings or money market account.

If you don't need access to ATM machines on every other street corner, an option usually available through larger banks, you can generally get a better checking account deal at a credit union or a smaller bank.

Savings and money market accounts

Savings accounts can be found at banks; money market funds are available through mutual fund companies. They are nearly identical in that they generally pay a better rate of interest than checking accounts. The interest rate paid, also know as the *yield,* fluctuates over time, as the overall level of interest rates changes.

Bank savings accounts are backed by the federal government through Federal Deposit Insurance Corporation (FDIC) insurance. Money market funds are not. Should you prefer a bank account because your investment (principal) is insured? No.

Money market securities are extremely safe; many are guaranteed or backed by a federal government agency. The risk difference versus a bank account is negligible. General-purpose money market funds invest in very safe short-term bank certificates of deposits and corporate commercial paper (short-term debt), which is issued by the largest and most credit-worthy companies and U.S. government securities.

Money market funds are closely regulated by the U.S. Securities & Exchange Commission. There are hundreds of money market funds that invest over $500 billion of individuals' and institutions' money. Money market funds' investments can exist only in the most credit-worthy securities and must have an average maturity of less than 120 days. Money market funds maintain a constant $1-per-share price. In the unlikely event that an investment in a money market's fund portfolio goes sour, a large money market fund will certainly cover the loss.

Although these funds are not insured through FDIC insurance programs, no major money market mutual fund to date has lost investors' principal investments. In contrast, investors have lost billions of dollars due to bank failures, of which there were many during the 1980s. The 1980s highlighted how poorly much of the savings and loan industry was run and showed that banks are not perfectly safe, either. The FDIC insurance system is just an insurance system. If there were ever such an economic disaster in the U.S. that money market fund investments declined in value, the whole U.S. banking system could be in jeopardy and the FDIC insurance system could collapse.

If the lack of insurance on money market funds still spooks you, here's a way to get the best of both worlds: Select a money market fund that invests exclusively in U.S. government securities, which are virtually risk-free because they are backed by the full strength and credit of the federal government (as is the FDIC insurance system). These types of accounts typically pay less interest, usually 1/4 percent less (although the interest is state tax free).

Bonds

Bonds are the most common lending investment traded on securities markets. When a bond is issued, it includes a specified maturity date on which you will be repaid your principal. Bonds are also issued at a particular coupon or interest rate. That rate is fixed on most bonds.

Bonds fluctuate in value based mainly on changes in interest rates. If, for example, you're holding a bond issued at 8 percent, and rates increase to 10 percent, your bond decreases in value. (Why would anyone want to buy your bond at the price you paid if it yields just 8 percent and they can get 10 percent elsewhere?)

More bonds issued today are tied to variable interest rates. For example, you can buy bonds that are adjustable-rate mortgages, on which the interest rate can fluctuate. You, as a property owner, can get these as mortgages on a piece of real estate. As an investor, you're actually lending your money to a mortgage borrower — indirectly, you are the banker making a loan to someone buying a home.

Bonds differ from each other in the following dimensions:

- ✔ The type of institution to which you are lending your money — for example, state government (municipal bonds), federal government (treasuries), mortgage holder (GNMA), and corporations (corporate bonds).

- ✔ The credit quality of the borrower to whom you lend your money (in other words, the probability that they will pay you the interest and return your principal as agreed).

- ✔ The length of maturity of the bond. Bonds generally mature within 30 years. Short-term bonds are mature within a few years, intermediate bonds within 7 to 10 years, and long-term bonds within 30 years.

Bonds are rated by major credit-rating agencies for their safety, usually on a scale on which AAA is the highest possible rating. For example, high-grade corporate bonds (AAA or AA) are considered the safest (that is, most likely to pay you back). Next in safety are general bonds (A or BBB), which are still safe but just a little less so. Junk bonds (rated BB or lower), made popular by Michael Milken and Drexel Burnham, are actually not all that junky; they're just lower in quality and have a slight (1 or 2 percent) probability of default.

Some bonds are *callable,* which means that the lender can decide to pay you back earlier than the previously agreed-upon date. This event usually occurs when interest rates fall and the lender wants to issue new, lower-interest rate bonds to replace the higher-rate bonds outstanding. To compensate you for early repayment, the lender typically gives you a small premium or bonus over what the bond is really worth.

Stocks

Stocks are the most common ownership investment traded on securities markets. They represent shares of ownership in a company.

Companies that issue stock (called *publicly-held* companies) include automobile manufacturers, computer software producers, fast food restaurants, hotels, magazine and newspaper publishers, supermarkets, wineries, zipper manufacturers, and everything in between!

Companies differ in what industry or line of business they're in and also vary in size. In the financial press, you often hear companies referred to by their *market capitalization,* which is the value of their outstanding stock.

There are two very different ways to invest in bonds and stocks. You can purchase individual securities or you can invest in a portfolio of securities through a mutual fund.

The danger of individual securities

Investing in individual stocks and bonds generally should be avoided. There are many drawbacks to selecting and trading individual securities successfully, including the following:

- ✔ **Significant research time and cost required.** You should know a lot about the situation of the company you're investing in when you are considering purchase of an individual security. Relevant questions to understand are: What products do they sell? What are their prospects for future growth and profitability? How much debt does the company have? You need to do your homework not only before you make your initial investment but also on an ongoing basis as long as you hold the investment.

- ✔ **High transaction costs.** Even when you use a discount broker (described in the next section), the commissions you pay to buy or sell securities are quite high. It may cost you about $40 to buy 100 shares of a $20 security through a discounter, which amounts to 40 cents per share, or 2 percent of the amount invested. A large institution, such as a mutual fund, that buys securities in blocks of 10,000 shares or more pays a penny or two per share when trading. So you're effectively paying 20–40 times more than mutual fund companies do per share in commissions.

- ✔ **Less likely to diversify.** Unless you have several hundred thousand dollars or more to invest in dozens of different securities, you probably can't afford to develop a diversified portfolio. For example, when you're investing in stocks, you should hold companies in different industries, different companies within an industry, and so on. And not diversifying adds exponentially to the risk of losing your shirt.

- ✔ **Accounting and bookkeeping.** When you invest in individual securities outside retirement accounts, every time you sell a specific security, you must report that transaction on your tax return. Even if you pay someone else to complete your return, you still have the hassle of keeping track of statements and receipts.

The relative advantages of mutual funds

Mutual funds make better sense than individual securities for investors with small or large amounts of money to invest. To illustrate, imagine the following scenario. You just bought your first home. It's an older, lived-in property with barf-brown carpets that have accumulated 20-plus years of food spills and pet accidents. You want to tear out the yucky old carpet and install hardwood floors.

Imagine that you can either redo your flooring work yourself or pay a contractor just $200 to do it for you. You would hire the contractor if you could hire him this cheaply. The only type of person who would choose to go it alone is someone who really enjoys this type of work. You're not going to be able to do a faster, better job than a full-time contractor if you do a decent job searching for a good one.

The same thinking process should go into investing in stocks and bonds. Investing in individual securities should be done only by those who really enjoy doing it. Mutual funds are a low-cost way to hire professional money managers.

In the long haul, you're not going to beat full-time professional managers who are investing in the securities of the same type and risk level that you are. As with hiring a contractor, you need to do your homework to find a good money manager. Even if you think that you can do as well as the best, remember that superstar money managers like Peter Lynch have only beaten the market averages by a few percent per year.

My experience is that more than a few otherwise smart, fun-loving people choose to invest in individual securities because they think that they're smarter or luckier than the rest. I don't know you personally, but it's safe to say that in the long run, your investment choices are not going to outperform those of a full-time investment professional.

I've noticed a distinct difference between the sexes on this issue. Perhaps because of differences in how people are raised, testosterone levels, or whatever, men tend to have more of a problem swallowing their egos and admitting that they're better off not going with individual securities. Maybe it's genetically linked to not wanting to ask for directions.

If you derive sheer ecstasy from picking and following your own stocks or want an independent opinion of some stocks you happen to own now, probably the single best research reports available are from the *Value Line Investment Survey*. This superb publication provides concise, user-friendly, single-page summaries of about 1,700 stocks. Libraries with good business sections usually carry this publication. You can subscribe for $525 per year or on a 10-week trial basis for $55 by calling Value Line at 800-634-3583.

Dividend reinvestment plans for individual stock purchases

Increasing numbers of corporations allow existing holders of shares of stock to reinvest their dividends in more shares of stock without paying brokerage commission. In some cases, companies allow you to make additional cash purchases of more shares of stock, also commission-free.

In order to qualify, you must first buy some shares of stock in a company that seems strong and attractive. Ideally, you should purchase these initial shares through a discount broker to keep your commission burden as low as possible. The National Association Investor Corporation (NAIC) also has a plan that allows you to buy one or a few shares to get started.

Frankly, I couldn't be bothered with these plans for several reasons. First, investing this way is only available and cost-effective for investments held outside retirement accounts. You should know by now that I feel strongly about doing as much investing as possible through the retirement accounts that are available to you. Secondly, you need to complete a lot of paperwork to invest in a number of different companies' stock. Life is too short to bother with these plans for this reason alone. Thirdly, some that offer these plans are hungry — for whatever reason, they need to drum up support for their stock. These investments may not be the best ones for the future. Finally, you're probably better off in the long run using professional money managers such as those available through no-load mutual funds.

International securities

Not only can you invest in stocks and bonds in companies that trade on the U.S. stock exchanges, but you can also invest in securities overseas. Aside from folks with business connections abroad, why would the average citizen want to do so?

Several reasons. First, the majority of investment opportunities are overseas. If you look at the total value of all stocks and bonds outstanding worldwide, the value of U.S. securities is now in the minority. Note that because Americans are so good at spending and borrowing, we hold a larger share of the debt (bonds) outstanding!

Another reason for investing in international securities is that when you confine your investing to U.S. securities, you're missing a world of opportunities, not only because of business growth available in other countries but also because you get the opportunity to diversify your portfolio further (don't worry — it's not like you're betting against the home team — we're all on this planet together!). International securities markets don't move in tandem with U.S. markets. During the 1987 U.S. stock market crash, for example, most international stock markets dropped far less. Some actually rose in value.

Some people hesitate to invest in overseas securities because they feel that it hurts the U.S. economy and contributes to a loss of American jobs. I have two counterarguments. One is that if you don't profit from the growth of economies overseas, someone else will. If there is money to be made, Americans may as well be there to participate.

Also, you must recognize that we already have a global economy — making a distinction between U.S. companies and foreign companies is no longer appropriate. Many companies that are headquartered in the U.S. also have overseas operations. Some U.S. firms derive a large portion of their revenue from their international divisions. Conversely, many firms that are based overseas also have operations here. Increasing numbers of companies are worldwide operations.

It is not unpatriotic to buy from a company that is based overseas or that has a foreign name. In fact, that foreign product you buy may be made right here at home. I learned how little brand names tell us in buying cars. I was surprised to learn that a greater percentage of the Ford car I owned was assembled overseas, while my Honda was made more in America.

Finally, profits from a foreign company are distributed to all stockholders, no matter where they live. Dividends and stock price appreciation know no national boundaries.

Real estate

Real estate has made a lot of people wealthy. Besides producing consistently good rates of return (averaging around 10 percent per year) over long investment periods, you can buy real estate with lots of borrowed money. This leverage can help you to generate an even higher rate of return on your investment.

For investors with time, patience, and capital, real estate can make sense as part of an investment portfolio. Chapter 15 covers this investment opportunity in complete detail.

Precious metals

Gold and silver have been used by many civilizations as currency or as a medium of exchange. One advantage of precious metals as a currency is that they can't be debased by the government. With a paper-based currency, such as U.S. dollars, the government can print more to pay off debts. This process can lead to the devaluation of a currency and inflation. It takes a whole lot more work to make more gold. Just ask Rumpelstiltskin.

Holdings of gold and silver can provide a so-called *hedge* against inflation. In the U.S. in the late 1970s and early 1980s, inflation rose dramatically. This rise depressed stocks and bonds. Gold and silver, however, rose tremendously in value — in fact, more than 500 percent (even after adjusting for inflation) from 1972 to 1981.

Don't purchase precious metals futures contracts. They are not investments; they are short-term gambles on which way gold or silver prices might head over a short period of time. You should also stay away from firms and shops that sell coins and *bullion* (not the soup but bars of gold or silver). Even if you can find a legitimate firm (not an easy task), the cost of storing and insuring gold and silver is quite costly. You don't get good value for your money. I hate to tell you, but the Gold Rush is over.

Gold and silver can profit long-term investors. If you want to invest in precious metals, your best option is to do so through mutual funds. For more information about determining how mutual funds fit with the rest of your investments and how to buy them, be sure to read Chapters 11–13.

Annuities

Annuities are a peculiar type of insurance and investment product. They are a sort of savings-type accounts with slightly higher yields that are backed by insurance companies.

As in other types of retirement accounts, money that is placed in an annuity compounds without taxation until withdrawal. However, unlike most other types of retirement accounts [401(k)s, SEP-IRAs, and Keoghs], your contributions into an annuity give no tax benefits (deductions). Thus, it only makes sense to consider contributing to an annuity after you fully fund tax-deductible retirement accounts.

The best annuities available today are distributed by no-load (commission-free) mutual fund companies. For more information on deciding whether to invest in an annuity and determining which one you should buy, be sure to read Chapter 8.

Limited partnerships

Limited partnerships sold through brokers and financial planners should be avoided at all costs. They are inferior investment vehicles. That's not to say that no one has ever made money on one, but they are so burdened with high sales commissions and ongoing management fees that deplete your investment that you can do better elsewhere.

Limited partnerships invest in real estate and a variety of businesses, such as cable television, cellular phone companies, and research and development. They pitch that you can get in on the ground floor of a new investment opportunity and make big money. And they also usually tell you that while your investment is growing at 20 percent or more per year, you get handsome dividends of 8 percent or so per year. Sound too good to be true? It is.

Many of the yields on LPs have turned out to be bogus. In some cases, partnerships propped up their yields by paying back investors' principal (without telling them, of course). The other hook with LPs is tax benefits. What few loopholes did exist in the tax code for LPs have largely been closed. (Amazingly, some investment salespeople hoodwink investors to put their retirement account money — which is already tax-sheltered — into LPs!) The other problems with LPs overwhelm any small tax advantage, anyway. It you want tax-friendly investments, check out Chapters 8 and 12.

The investment salesperson who sells you such an investment stands to earn a commission of up to 10 percent or more — so only 90 cents per dollar you invest has a chance to be invested. Each year, LPs siphon off another several percent for management and other expenses. Most partnerships have little or no incentive to control costs. In fact, they have a conflict to charge more to enrich the managing partners. Efficient, no-load mutual funds, in contrast, put 100 percent of your capital to work and charge 1 percent per year or less in management fees.

Unlike a mutual fund, you can't vote with your dollars. If the partnership is poorly run and expensive, you're stuck. LPs are *illiquid.* You can't get your money that is left until the partnership is liquidated, typically seven to ten years after you buy in.

Some firms will buy your illiquid limited partnership from you, paying you pennies on the dollar. Don't bother unless you're totally desperate for cash. Otherwise, you're better off sticking it out.

The only thing limited about a limited partnership is its ability to make you money. If you want to buy investments that earn profits, stick with stocks (using mutual funds), real estate, or running your own business.

Life insurance with a cash value

Life insurance should not be used as an investment, especially if you haven't exhausted contributing money to retirement accounts. Life insurance that combines life insurance protection with an account that has a cash value is usually known as *universal, whole,* or *variable life.*

The advantage it has over pure life insurance (known as *term*), is that the proceeds paid to your beneficiaries can be free of inheritance taxes. You need to have a fairly substantial estate at your death to benefit from this feature. (See Chapter 17 for more on life insurance and why term is best for the vast majority of people.)

Diversification

Diversification is one of the most powerful investment concepts. All diversification really means is that you carry and save your eggs (or investments) in different baskets.

Diversification requires you to place your money in different investments with returns that are not completely correlated. This is a fancy way of saying that with your money in different places, when one of your investments is down in value, odds are that others are up.

To decrease the odds of all of your investments getting clobbered at the same time, you must put your money in different types or classes of investments. The different kinds of investments include money market funds, bonds, stocks, real estate, and precious metals. You can further diversify your investments by investing in domestic as well as international markets.

Within a given class of investments such as stocks, it's important to diversify by investing in different types of stocks that perform well under various economic conditions. For this reason, mutual funds, which are diversified portfolios of securities, are a highly useful investment vehicle. You buy into the mutual fund, which in turn pools your money with that of many others to invest in a vast array of stocks and bonds.

There are two ways to look at the benefits of diversification. First, it reduces or dampens the volatility in the value of your whole portfolio. In other words, you can achieve the same rate of return that a single investment can provide with dramatically fewer fluctuations in value. Also, diversification allows you to obtain a higher rate of return for a given level of risk.

Keep in mind that no one, no matter who they work for or what credentials they have, can guarantee returns on an investment. You can do good research and you can be lucky, but no one is free from the risk of losing. Diversification allows you to hedge the risk of your investments. See Tables 10-1, 10-2, and 10-3 to get an idea of how diversifying can reduce your risk (figures in these tables are adjusted for inflation). Notice that different investments did better during various time periods. Because the future can't be predicted, you are safer diversifying your money into different investments.

Table 10-1	1928–1937 — a Better Decade for Bonds (Starting with $10,000 Investment)	
Year	*Bonds*	*Stocks*
1928	$10,000	$10,000
1929	$10,309	$9,142
1930	$11,845	$7,304
1931	$12,840	$4,576
1932	$15,860	$4,683
1933	$17,422	$7,176
1934	$19,438	$6,937
1935	$20,683	$9,947
1936	$21,808	$13,161
1937	$21,744	$8,298

Table 10-2   1947–1956 — a Better Decade for Stocks (Starting with $10,000 Investment)

Year	Stocks	Bonds
1947	$10,000	$10,000
1948	$10,273	$10,136
1949	$12,427	$10,663
1950	$15,470	$10,290
1951	$18,114	$9,455
1952	$21,256	$9,698
1953	$20,917	$9,968
1954	$32,081	$10,559
1955	$42,050	$10,570
1956	$43,562	$9,573

Table 10-3   1972–1980 — a Better Time for Precious Metals (Starting with $10,000 Investment)

Year	Stocks	Bonds	Gold	Silver
1972	$10,000	$10,000	$10,000	$10,000
1973	$7,838	$9,292	$14,553	$13,923
1974	$5,134	$8,025	$20,479	$22,830
1975	$6,585	$8,595	$20,543	$20,023
1976	$7,779	$9,735	$15,219	$18,803
1977	$6,760	$9,270	$16,872	$18,699
1978	$6,611	$8,496	$20,185	$20,051
1979	$6,910	$7,184	$28,431	$36,345
1980	$8,138	$6,225	$50,342	$60,151

Places to Invest

Thousands of firms sell investments and manage money. Banks, mutual fund companies, securities brokerage firms, and even insurance companies vie for your money.

Just to make matters more complicated, each industry plays in the others' backyards. You can find mutual fund companies that offer securities brokerage; insurance firms that are in the mutual fund business; and mutual fund companies that offer banking-like accounts and services. You benefit somewhat from all this competition and one-stop shopping convenience. On the other hand, some firms are novices at particular businesses and count on the fact that you shop by brand-name recognition and will support them in entering new businesses.

The firms that you should do business with are those that do the following:

✔ Offer the best value investments in comparison to their competitors. Value combines performance and price. Given the level of risk you're comfortable with, you want investments that offer the highest possible rates of return, but you don't want to have to pay a small fortune for them. Commissions of all types (front-end, back-end, or ongoing), management fees, maintenance fees, and other fees and charges can turn a high-performance investment into a mediocre or poor one.

✔ Employ representatives that do not have an inherent self-interest in steering you into a single type of investment. This criterion has nothing to do with whether an investment firm hires nice, well-educated, or honest-looking people. The most important factor is the way the company compensates their employees. If salespeople are paid completely or in part based on commissions on the investments they sell to you, forget it. You want to work with firms that don't tempt their employees to push one investment over another because it's more profitable.

No-load (commission-free) mutual fund companies

As discussed in the preceding section, mutual funds are an ideal investment vehicle for most investors. No-load mutual fund companies are firms in which you can invest in mutual funds without paying sales commissions. In other words, every dollar you invest goes to work in the mutual funds you choose. Not one cent is siphoned off to pay sales commissions.

The entire next chapter is devoted to understanding and investing in mutual funds.

Discount brokers: brokers without conflicts of interest

Prior to May 1, 1974, when investors bought or sold stocks, bonds, and other securities, the commissions they were charged were fixed. In other words, no matter which brokerage firm an investor did business with, the cost of the firm's services was set.

In one of the most beneficial changes for investors in this century, the Securities and Exchange Commission (SEC) deregulated the retail brokerage industry. For the first time, brokerage firms could charge people whatever their little hearts desired. You may think that this change opened the door to exorbitantly high rates. In fact, it did the opposite. A fair and open free market is good for consumers. Competition inevitably results in more and better choices.

Most firms that were in business prior to that time, such as Merrill Lynch, Prudential, and E. F. Hutton, continued business as usual. Some firms raised their already high commissions. More importantly, they continued to pay their brokers based on the amount of trading their customers did and which investments they sold.

Fortunately, many new brokerage firms have been springing up since the mid-1970s. They were dubbed *discount brokers* because the fees they charged customers were substantially lower than what other brokers charged under the old fixed-fee system.

Even more important than saving you money, discount brokers established a vastly improved compensation system that effectively eliminated conflicts of interest. Discount brokers pay their brokers a straight salary. Therefore, they don't have an incentive to encourage you to trade, and they also won't steer you into one investment over another unless it is truly wiser.

The term *discount broker* is actually not an enlightening one. It is certainly true that this new breed of brokerage firm saves you lots of money when you invest. You can easily save 50–80 percent through the major discount brokers, such as Charles Schwab, Quick & Reilly, and Waterhouse Securities. Fidelity, which is better known for mutual funds, is also a major player in the discount brokerage market. But these firms' investments are not "on sale" or second rate. Discount brokers are simply brokers who lack a conflict of interest. Of course, like any other for-profit enterprise, they want your business, but they're much less likely to steer you wrong for their benefit.

Things to Avoid and Places Not to Invest

The worst places to invest are those that charge you a lot, have mediocre or poorly performing investments, and have major conflicts of interest.

The prime conflict of interest comes with investment firms that pay their brokers or other employees on the basis of how much and what they sell. The result: They sell lots of stuff that pays fat commissions and they churn your account (because there's a fee for each transaction, the more you buy and sell, the more money they make).

The major firms that historically have compensated their brokers almost exclusively on commissions from what they sell include Prudential, Merrill Lynch, Smith Barney Shearson, Paine Webber, Dean Witter, and Kidder Peabody.

You probably recognize the names of many of these firms. Think about that. Do you know many people who have made lots of money and beaten the securities market averages by investing with them? Or do you know of them because of all the advertising they do and the negative publicity so many of these firms have received in the press in recent years? Going by a catchy slogan or by brand-name recognition is _not_ smart shopping.

There are also folks who call themselves _financial planners_ or _financial consultants_ who work on commission (discussed in Chapter 3) outside the big brokerage firms. Many of them belong to so-called _broker-dealer networks,_ which can provide back-office support and products to sell. Representatives of the following larger broker-dealers (that sell more than $500 million per year) work almost exclusively on commission:

- Royal Alliance Associates
- Investment Management & Research
- New England Securities
- Financial Service Corporation
- NY Life Securities
- Financial Network Investment Corporation
- SunAmerica Securities
- MML Investor Services
- Cigna Securities
- Lincoln Investment Planning
- John Hancock Distributors

- ✓ Mutual Service Corporation
- ✓ Walnut Street Securities
- ✓ Cadaret, Grant & Co.
- ✓ Investacorp
- ✓ Mariner Financial Services

Commissions

Investment products bring in widely varying commissions. The products that bring in the highest commissions tend to be the ones that money-hungry brokers push the hardest.

Table 10-4 lists the commissions that you pay and that come out of your investment dollars when you work with brokers, financial consultants, and financial planners working on commission.

Table 10-4	Investment Sales Commissions	
Investment Type	*Avg. Commission on $20,000 Investment*	*Avg. Commission on $100,000 Investment*
Annuities	$1,400	$7,000
Initial public offerings (new stock issue)	$1,000	$5,000
Limited partnerships	$1,800	$9,000
Mutual funds	$1,200	$6,000
Options and futures	$2,000+	$10,000+

Besides the fact that you can never be sure that you're getting an unbiased recommendation from a salesperson working on commission, you're wasting unnecessary money. Most investments can be bought on a no-load (commission-free) basis. (Those that can't shouldn't be bought by an individual investor in the first place.) If you need advice about buying investments, hire a financial advisor for a fee. Or peruse the remaining investing chapters to learn where and how to do it yourself for the mere cost of this book.

If you're unsure about an investment product that's being pitched to you (and even when you *are* sure), ask for a copy of the prospectus. In the first few pages, check out whether the investment includes a commission. If it does, pitch it and the salesperson who recommended it.

Ten conflicts of interest for investment salespeople

Financial consultants (also known as stock brokers), financial planners, and others who sell investment products can have enormous conflicts of interest in the strategies and specific investment products they recommend. Commissions and other financial incentives can't help but skew the advice of even the most earnest and otherwise well-intentioned salespeople.

Numerous conflicts of interest can damage your investment portfolio. The following are the most common conflicts to watch out for (for more information about hiring financial advisors who don't have conflicts of interest, be sure to read Chapter 3).

Pushing high-commission products

As discussed earlier, commissions vary tremendously on investment products. At the worst end of the spectrum for you (and the best for a salesperson) are products like limited partnerships, commodities, options, and futures. At the best end of the spectrum for you (therefore, the worst for a salesperson) are investments such as no-load mutual funds and treasury bills.

Surprisingly, commission-based brokers and financial planners need not give you the prospectus (where commissions are detailed) before you buy a financial product that carries commissions (as with a load mutual fund). In contrast, commission-free investment companies such as no-load mutual fund companies have to send a prospectus in advance of taking a mutual fund order. Commission-based investment salespeople should have to disclose any commissions in writing up front and provide prospectuses in advance of sale.

Recommending active trading

Investment salespeople who advocate investing in individual securities may be tempted to get you to trade frequently into and out of different securities. Trades are usually advised based on current news events or an analyst's comments on the security. Sometimes, these moves are valid, but often they are not. In extreme cases, brokers trade on a monthly basis. They churn half (or all) of your portfolio and then some annually.

Diversified mutual funds (discussed earlier in the chapter and in detail in the next chapter) make more sense for most people. You can invest in mutuals free of sales commissions. Beside saving money on commissions, you earn better long-term returns by having an expert money manager work for you.

Failing to recommend investing through employer's retirement plans

If you're not taking full advantage of retirement savings plans (see Chapter 8), you may be missing out on valuable tax benefits. Your initial contributions to most retirement plans are tax-deductible, and your money compounds without taxation over the years. An investment salesperson is not likely to recommend that you contribute to your employer's retirement plan [for example, a 401(k)] that cuts into the total stash of money you have available to invest with him or her. If you're self-employed, salespeople are somewhat more likely to recommend that you fund a retirement plan because they can set up such plans for you. You're better off doing so through a no-load mutual fund company. If you need advice, consult with a conflict-free financial planner. (See Chapter 3.)

Pushing high-fee products

Many of the brokerage firms that used to sell investment products only on commission (for example, Prudential, Merrill Lynch, Smith Barney Shearson, Paine Webber, and Dean Witter) are moving into fee-based investment management. This change is an improvement for investors because it reduces some of the conflicts of interest caused by commissions.

On the other hand, these brokers charge extraordinarily high fees (which are usually quoted as a percentage of assets under management) on their managed investment (wrap) accounts.

Wrap or managed accounts

Wrap, or *managed,* accounts are all the rage among commission-based brokerage firms such as those I just mentioned.

These accounts go under a variety of names — Smith Barney Shearson calls them "Trak" and Merrill Lynch calls them "Consults." They are all the same, however, in that they charge a fixed percentage of the assets under management to invest your money through money managers.

There are two major problems with wrap accounts. First, their management expenses are extraordinarily high — often up to 3 percent (some even more) per year of assets under management. Remember that in the long haul, stocks can return about 10 percent per year before taxes. So, if you're paying 3 percent per year to have the money managed in stocks, 30 percent of your return (before taxes) is siphoned off. But don't forget — because the government sure won't — that you pay a good chunk of money in taxes on your 10 percent return as well. So the 3 percent wrap actually ends up depleting 40–50 percent of the profits you get to keep after payment of taxes!

Forbes magazine said it best in a recent article on wrap accounts: "Brokerage firms love wrap accounts because they're so lucrative — for them."

No-load (commission-free) mutual funds offer investors access to the nation's best investment managers for a fraction of the cost of wrap accounts. You can invest in dozens of top-performing funds for an annual expense of 1 percent per year or less. Companies like Vanguard offer many excellent funds for a cost as low as 0.2 – 0.5 percent.

So how do brokerage firms hoodwink investors into paying 3–15 times as much for access to investment managers? Marketing. Slick, seductive, deceptive, misleading pitches that include some outright lies. Here are the key components of the broker's pitch for wrap accounts — and then the real truth:

"You're getting access to investment managers who don't take money from small-fry investors (that is, who have less than a million) like you."

First off, not a single study shows that the performance of money managers has anything to do with the minimum account they handle. Secondly, no-load mutual funds hire many of the same managers who work at other money management firms. In fact, Vanguard — the nation's largest exclusively commission-free investment firm — contracts out to hire money managers to run many of their funds who typically handle only million-dollar-plus accounts. A number of other leading mutual funds do this as well.

"You'll earn a higher rate of return, so the extra cost is worth it."

Part of the bait money managers use to hook you into a wrap account is the wonderful rates of returns they generate. You could have earned 18–25 percent per year, they say, had you invested with the "Star of Yesterday" investment management company. The key word here is "had." History is history. Many of yesterday's winners become tomorrow's losers or mediocre performers.

Secondly, you must remember that, unlike mutual funds, whose performance records are audited by the SEC, wrap account performance records may include marketing hype. The most common ploy is showing only the performance of selected accounts — those that performed the best!

The expenses you pay to have your investments managed have an enormous impact on the long-term growth of your money. If you can have your money managed for 0.5–1 percent per year versus 2.5–3 percent, you've got a 2 percent per year performance advantage already. In the long run (ten or more years down the road), the majority of investment managers (around 70 percent) underperform broad-market indexes. I discuss index funds in Chapter 11.

"There's little difference in cost between wrap accounts and no-load mutual funds."

Baloney! True, the worst and most inefficient mutual funds can have total costs approaching that of a typical wrap account. But you're no dummy — you're not going to invest in the highest-cost funds. Chapters 11, 12, and 13 detail which mutual funds offer both top performance and low cost.

The value of brokerage research

One of the arguments frequently advanced by brokerage firms and financial planners who work on a commission basis is that their research is better. With their insights and recommendations, they say, you'll do better and "beat the market averages."

Don't believe them. A number of studies clearly demonstrate that their research is barely worth the cost of your morning paper (sometimes not even that)!

If the brokerage firms' research were superior, then their mutual fund returns should be exceptional, right? They're not.

Wall Street analysts are chronically overly optimistic. (Hey, it's better than being a sad sack all the time!) Every year since 1980 (with the exception of 1988), they have overestimated the increase in corporate earnings, as you can see in Figure 10-1.

If analysts were simply inaccurate or bad estimators, you would expect that they would sometimes underestimate and other times overestimate companies' earnings. The discrepancy identifies yet another conflict of interest among many of the brokerage firms that pay their brokers on commission.

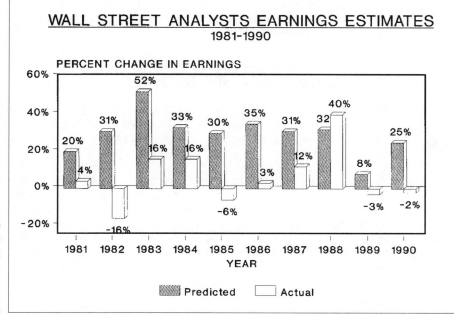

Figure 10-1: Wall Street analysts are a tad optimistic.

Source: Lynch, Jones & Ryan

Brokerage firm analysts are loathe to write a negative report about a company because the firms these analysts work for also solicit companies to issue new stock to the public. What better way to show your potential for selling shares at a high price to the public than by showing how much you believe in certain companies and writing up glowing reports about a their future prospects?

Brokerage analysts can't be objective. *Investment banking* (the business of helping companies sell new securities) cannot be done by companies evaluating the same securities for the investing public.

If you want research on individual securities, check out the *Value Line Investment Survey,* which I mentioned earlier in this chapter.

Experts who divine the future

A common mistake that many investors make is believing that they can greatly increase their chances of success if they follow the prognostications of certain gurus. The sage predictions in an investment newsletter or by an "expert" who is repeatedly quoted in financial publications make you feel protected. It's sort of like Linus and his security blanket.

I have some bad news for you newsletter subscribers and guru followers. Go buy yourself a warm blanket. It has a lot more value and costs a whole lot less. No one can predict the future. If they could, they would be so busy investing their own money and getting rich that they wouldn't have the time and desire to share their secrets with you.

Investment newsletters

Newsletters that purport to time the markets, telling you exactly the right time to get into and out of certain securities (or the market in general), are doomed to failure in the long run. By failure, I mean that they aren't going to beat a buy-and-hold approach.

I see many people paying hundreds of dollars annually to subscribe to all sorts of market-timing and stock-picking newsletters. One client, an attorney, had subscribed to several newsletters. When I asked him why, he said that their marketing materials claimed that if you followed their prior advice, you would make 20 percent per year return on your money. In the four years that Ken had followed their advice, he had actually *lost* money, despite appreciating financial markets overall.

An enlightening read is *Hulbert's Financial Digest*, written by Mark Hulbert, whose firm tracks the performance of the recommendations made by newsletter writers. Hulbert's organization looks at the cold, hard facts of actual returns and shows how your portfolio would have done if you had followed the recommendations of given newsletters.

If you had been so omniscient as to know in advance which five newsletters would give the best advice during the past decade, you would have barely beaten the overall rate of return of the Wilshire 5000, the broadest index value that tracks the performance of small, medium, and large companies' U.S. stocks. During the 10-year period from the end of 1983 to the end of 1993, the Wilshire 5000 gained 14.2 percent per year on average. See Table 10-5.

Table 10-5	The "Best" Newsletters
Newsletter	**Average annual performance vs. Wilshire 5000**
Systems & Forecasts	+1.1%
Zweig Forecast	+0.7%
Zweig Performance Ratings Report	+0.6%
The Chartist	+0.1%
Peter Dag Investment Newsletter	0.0%
BI Research	-0.1%

Source: *Hulbert Financial Digest*

Hulbert uses *risk-adjusted returns,* which are corrected for the differences in the amount of risk different newsletters took in their recommendations.

If by bad luck you had been suckered into following the worst newsletters' advice, your investment results would have been disastrous, especially in comparison to what you could have earned in treasury bills or the Wilshire 5000 stock index. Check out Table 10-6:

Table 10-6 The Worst Newsletters Compared to the Market	
Newsletter	**Total Return**
Granville Market Letter	-96%
Ruff Times	+61%
Professional Tape Reader	+67%
Dines Letter	+80%

(continued)

Table 10-6 *(continued)*	
Newsletter	**Total Return**
United & Babson Investment Report	+92%
Treasury bills	+172%
Wilshire 5000 index	+555%

Source: Hulbert's *Financial Digest*

Never use a newsletter for predictive advice. If people were that smart about the future of financial markets, they would be money managers making lots more money.

The only types of investment newsletters and periodicals that you should consider subscribing to are those that offer research and information rather than predictions. I discuss those that fit the bill in the subsequent chapters about investment.

Investment gurus

Investment gurus come and go. Some of them get their 15 minutes of fame on the basis of one or two successful predictions that someone in the press remembers (and makes famous). A classic example is a market analyst at Shearson named Elaine Garzarelli.

Now, I don't mean to pick on Ms. Garzarelli. I assume that she's a decent person who has done some good with the money she's been paid since becoming famous for predicting the stock market's plummet in the fall of 1987. Perhaps she happened to be in the right place at the right time (that is, she was out of the market just before the market crashed).

Garzarelli's fund, Smith Barney Shearson Sector Analysis, was established just before the crash. Supposedly, Garzarelli's indicators warned her to stay out of stocks, which she did, and in doing so saved her fund from the plunge.

Shearson, being a money-minded brokerage, quickly motivated its brokers to sell shares in Garzarelli's fund. In addition to her having avoided the crash, it didn't hurt that Shearson brokers were being paid a hefty 5 percent sales commission for selling her fund. By the end of 1987, investors had poured nearly $700 million into this fund.

In 1988, Garzarelli's fund was the worst-performing fund among funds investing in growth stocks. From 1988 to 1990, Garzarelli's fund underperformed the S&P 500 average by about 43 percent! In 1987 — the year of the crash — Garzarelli outperformed the S&P 500 by about 26 percent. So what she saved her investors by avoiding the crash she lost back and more in the years that followed.

Commentators and experts interviewed in the media can't predict the future. Don't make investing decisions based on any expert's advice. The very few people who have a slight leg up on everyone else aren't going to share their investment secrets — they're too busy investing their own money!

How Do I Invest This Lump of Money?

Whether through accumulation of funds over the years, inheritance, or a recent windfall from work that you've done, you've got a problem when you have a large chunk of cash to invest. Many people, of course, would like to have your problem. (You're not complaining, right?) You want to invest your money, but you're a bit skittish, if not outright terrified, about the prospect of investing the lump of money all at once.

If the money is residing in a savings or money market account, you may feel like it's wasting away. You want to put it to work!

My first words of advice are: Don't rush. There's nothing wrong with earning only a few percentage points on your money in a money market account (see Chapter 12 for recommendations). It beats the heck out of rushing into an investment in which you might lose 20 percent or more. I often get calls from people in a state of near panic. Typically, these folks have CDs coming due and feel that they must decide exactly where they want to invest the money in the 48 hours before the CD matures.

Take a *deeeep* breath. There's absolutely no reason to rush into an important decision. Instruct your friendly banker that when the CD matures, you'd like the proceeds to be put in their highest-yielding savings or money market account. That way it still earns some interest while you buy yourself some breathing room.

One approach to investing is called *dollar-cost averaging*. This term indicates that you're investing your money in equal chunks on a regular basis, such as once a month.

For example, if you have $60,000 to invest, you can invest $2,000 per month until it's all invested, which takes a few years. The money that's awaiting future investment isn't lying fallow. You keep it in a money market-type account earning a bit of interest while it's waiting its turn.

The attraction of dollar-cost averaging is that it allows you to ease into riskier investments instead of jumping in all at once. The benefit may be that if the price of the investment drops after some of your initial purchases, you can buy some later at a lower price. If you had dumped all your money into the "sure win" investment at once and then it dropped like a stone, you'd kick yourself for not waiting.

The flip side of dollar-cost averaging is that if your investments of choice appreciate in value, you may wish that you had invested your money faster. Another possible drawback of dollar-cost averaging is that you may get cold feet continuing to invest money in an investment that's dropping in value. Many people who are attracted to dollar-cost averaging out of fear of buying before a price drop are scared to continue boarding a sinking ship.

Dollar-cost averaging can also cause headaches with your taxes when it comes time to sell investments held outside retirement accounts. If you buy an investment at many different times and prices, accounting is muddied as you sell blocks of the investment.

Dollar-cost averaging has its advantages, but it also has its drawbacks. It's most valuable when the money you want to invest represents a large portion of your total assets and you can stick to a schedule. It's best to make it automatic so that you're less likely to chicken out. Most investment firms recommended in the next few chapters can provide automatic exchange services.

Help! I've Been Fleeced!

Losing money on lousy investments is hard on the ego and even harder on your financial situation. But there's no use crying over spilled milk.

There is a potential way for you to get a good chunk of your money back if a broker or financial planner has committed certain cardinal financial sins. Here are the major violations for which you may be able to collect damages:

- **Misrepresentation and omission.** If you were told, for example, that a particular investment guaranteed returns of 15 percent per year and the investment ends up plunging in value by 50 percent, you were misled. You should know that any investment that can produce double-digit returns can also drop significantly in value. Misrepresentation can also be charged if you're sold an investment with a hefty commission attached but were told that it was commission-free and that you could get all of your money out whenever you wanted it.

- **Unsuitable investments.** Retirees who need access to their capital are pitched to invest in limited partnerships (discussed earlier in this chapter) for safe, high yields. The yields on most LPs end up being anything but safe. LP investors have also discovered how illiquid their investments are — some can't be liquidated for up to ten years or more.

- **Churning.** If your broker or financial planner is constantly trading your investments, odds are that his or her his weekly commission check benefits at your expense.

- **Rogue elephant salespeople.** If your planner or broker buys or sells without your approval or ignores your request to make a change, you may be able to collect for losses caused by these actions.

You can't sue someone just because some or even all of their investment recommendations drop in value. That's life in the big city.

Two major types of practitioners — securities lawyers and arbitration consultants — stand ready to help you recover your lost money. You generally don't end up in a courtroom *L.A. Law* style. You'll probably go to arbitration to which you agreed (probably not realizing it) when you set up an account to work with the broker or planner.

The good news is that arbitration is usually much quicker, cheaper, and easier for you. You can even choose to represent yourself. Both sides present their case to a panel of three arbitrators who make a decision that both sides can't squabble over or appeal.

Most lawyers and consultants work on a contingency-fee basis — they get a percentage (about 20–40 percent of the amount collected) in damages. They also usually ask for an up-front amount ranging from several hundred to several thousand dollars to help them cover their expenses and time. If they take on your case and lose, they generally get to keep the up-front money.

If the amount of money you want to recover is small — less than $20,000 or so — you'll have a harder time finding someone to take your case on contingency. If you pay them an hourly fee, you may end up throwing even more money down the rat-hole.

Securities lawyers are usually a more expensive option, but they argue that they're worth the extra cost. Securities arbitration consultants say that they can do just as well at a lower cost. From my experience with people who try one or both routes, the truth falls somewhere in between. Capability depends on the specific person's background and experience.

Interview several securities lawyers and arbitration consultants. You can find securities lawyers by looking under "Attorneys — Securities" in the yellow pages or by calling your local bar association for referrals. Arbitration consultants can be found under "Arbitrators" in the yellow pages. If you come up dry, try contacting business writers at a major newspaper in your area or at your favorite personal finance magazine. These sources may be able to give you names and numbers of folks they know.

If you decide to prepare for arbitration yourself, the nonprofit American Arbitration Association can send you a background package of materials to help you with your case. Check your local phone directory or contact their headquarters at

American Arbitration Association
140 West 51st Street
New York, NY 10020
212-484-4000

Chapter 11

Mutual Funds

• •

In This Chapter
▶ Why mutual funds are kicking butt
▶ Selecting the best mutual fund
▶ Knowing where to invest in mutual funds
▶ Finding a good information source
▶ Making sense of fund performance numbers
▶ Tracking your funds

• •

Important note: I recommend specific mutual funds in Chapters 12 and 13. This chapter's focus is to help you understand mutual funds and to look at the best companies that sell them. If you want more background information on the basics of investing, read Chapter 10 first.

Understanding the Benefits of Mutual Funds

Mutual funds are investment companies that pool your money with that of thousands of other like-minded individuals and invest it in stocks, bonds, and other securities. It's kind of like a big investment club without the meetings or dues. When you invest through a typical mutual fund, several hundred million to a billion dollars or more is invested along with your money.

Mutual funds date back to the 1800s, when English and Scottish investment trusts sold shares to investors. They hit the U.S. in 1924. Today, thousands of mutual funds manage more than $2 trillion. That's a mighty big number (but still less than *half* the amount of the U.S. government deficit).

Mutual funds have been successful for many reasons. To understand why is to understand how and why funds can work for you. Read on to discover their main benefits.

Professional management

Mutual funds are managed by a portfolio manager and research team whose full-time jobs are to screen the universe of investments for those that best meet the stated objectives of the fund. The portfolio management team calls and visits companies, analyzes companies' financial statements, and speaks with companies' suppliers and customers. In short, the team does more due diligence and research than you can ever hope to do in all of your free time.

Fund managers are typically graduates of the top business and finance schools in the country, where they learn the principles of portfolio management and securities valuation and selection. (Despite this fact, most of them do a good job of investing money.) The best fund managers typically have five or more years of experience in analyzing and selecting investments.

Low cost

The most efficiently managed mutual funds cost less than 1 percent per year in fees (bonds and money market funds cost much less). *No-load funds* do not charge a fee for purchasing or redeeming shares. By comparison, the transaction fee and commission for buying and selling individual stocks and bonds is double to triple the cost of the annual management fee on a mutual fund.

Because mutual funds typically buy or sell tens of thousands of shares of a security at a time, their transaction fees are generally 80 – 90 percent less per share than what you pay to buy or sell a few hundred shares on your own.

Mutual funds are also able to manage money more efficiently through effective use of technology. Innovations in information management tools enable funds to monitor and manage billions of dollars from millions of investors at a very low cost.

If you decide that you want to withdraw money from a fund, most funds — particularly no-loads — do not charge you a redemption fee. (Think about that — some investments require that you pay to get your own money back!)

Diversification

Mutual fund investing enables you to diversify to an extent that you can't achieve on your own without several hundred thousand dollars and a lot of time to invest. To go it alone, you need to invest money in at least 8 – 12 different securities in different industries to ensure that your portfolio can

Why mutual funds are hurting banks and brokers

Mutual funds take a lot of dollars away from other financial intermediaries, including commission-based brokerage firms and banks. Years ago, most investors handed their money to brokers from firms like Prudential, Shearson, and E. F. Hutton, who recommended and traded individual securities. Because a broker could only work with so many people in a workday and had to share a big chunk of commissions with the firm, each trade cost an investor about 3 percent of his or her investment dollars.

Today, with mutual funds, investors can pool their money with tens of thousands of other investors and have their funds managed by the best money managers in the business for 1 percent or less per year.

Banks are losing out because more and more companies can go directly to financial markets to borrow money or issue bonds, thus bypassing the banks. Investors benefit because they can usually get a higher effective yield through a fund than a bank can offer.

The growth of mutual funds has received some bad press. If a fund's investors head for the exits at the same time, it has been implied, they may get stuck or trampled at the door. Some people lament the demise of banks as more and more money flows out of them.

Most of these concerns and fears are unwarranted. Mutual funds, for example, hold just 10 percent of outstanding U.S. stocks.

Just as computers have replaced typewriters because they allow for more efficient, enhanced word processing, mutual funds are replacing less-efficient institutions that manage money. That's not to say that all banks and commission-based brokerage firms are going to disappear — but you'll probably see fewer of them in the coming years.

withstand a downturn in one or more of the investments. A mutual fund is typically invested in 25 – 100 or more securities. Proper diversification ensures that the fund receives the highest possible return at the lowest possible risk given the objectives of the fund.

I'm not suggesting that mutual funds escape without share price declines during major market downturns. For example, mutual funds that invested in stocks certainly declined during the October 1987 market crash. However, the most unlucky investors that month were individuals who had all of their money riding on only one or a few stocks. Some shares plunged in price by as much as 80 – 90 percent that month.

Democracy in action

If you have $500 to invest, you should consider mutual funds. Most funds have low minimum-investment requirements, especially for retirement account investors. When you invest in a mutual fund, you get the same attention given to the rich and famous.

If you have a lot of money to invest, you should also consider mutual funds. Join the increasing numbers of companies and institutions with big bucks to invest who are turning to the low-cost, high-quality money-management services that you can get in a mutual fund.

Audited performance records and expenses

All mutual funds are required to disclose through their prospectus historical data on the returns earned by the fund, operating expenses and other fees, and rate of trading (turnover) in the fund's investments. The Securities and Exchange Commission (SEC) audits these disclosures for accuracy. Rest assured that someone is watching over the folks who are watching your money.

Flexibility in risk level

You can choose among a variety of different mutual funds to select those that accept a level of risk that you're comfortable with and that meet your personal and financial goals.

- **Stock funds.** If you want your money to grow over a long period of time, you may want to select funds that invest more heavily in stocks.

- **Bond funds.** If you need current income and don't want investments that fluctuate as widely as stocks in value, you may choose more conservative bond funds.

- **Money market funds.** If you want to be sure that your invested principal does not drop in value because you may need your money in the short-term, you can select a money market fund.

Virtually zero risk of bankruptcy

Mutual funds have a heck of a track record. Unlike banks and insurance companies, which have and will continue to fail, mutual funds have never failed and probably won't in the future. The situation in which the demand for money back (*liabilities*) exceeds the value of a fund's investments (*assets*) cannot occur with a mutual fund. Of course, the value of a fund fluctuates as the securities it is invested in fluctuate in value. But this variation doesn't lead to the failure or bankruptcy of a mutual fund company. In fact, since the Investment Company Act of 1940 was passed to regulate the mutual fund industry, no fund has ever gone under.

In contrast, hundreds of banks and dozens of insurance companies have failed in the past decade alone. Banks and insurers can fail because their liabilities can exceed their assets. When a bank makes too many loans that go sour at the same time that depositors want their money back, the bank fails. Likewise, if an insurance company makes several poor investments or underestimates the number of claims that will be made by insurance policy holders, it too can fail.

Where's my money?

The specific securities in which a mutual fund is invested are held at a *custodian* — a separate organization independent of the mutual fund company. The employment of a custodian ensures that the fund management company can't embezzle your funds and use assets from a better-performing fund to subsidize a poor performer.

Freedom from salespeople

Stock brokers (a.k.a. financial consultants) and commission-based financial planners make more money by encouraging trading activity and by selling you investments that provide them with high commissions — limited partnerships and mutual funds with high load fees, for example.

No-load (commission-free) mutual fund companies do not push products. Their toll-free telephone lines are staffed with knowledgeable people who earn a salary. Their recommendations don't carry inherent conflicts of interest.

The Major Types of Mutual Funds

One of the major misconceptions about mutual funds is that they are all invested in stocks. They're not. Here is roughly how the $2 trillion currently invested in mutual funds breaks down:

Type of fund	Percent of Funds
Stocks	33%
Bonds	38%
Money market	29%

So, as you can see, the majority of mutual fund money is *not* invested in stocks.

When you hear folks talk about the "riskiness" of mutual funds, even in the media, you'll know that they're overlooking this fact: All mutual funds are not created equal. Some funds, such as money market funds, carry virtually *no* risk that your investment will decline in value.

Throughout this discussion, it's important to remember that when mutual fund companies package and market their funds, the name they give their fund isn't always completely accurate or comprehensive. For example, a stock fund may not be *totally* invested in stocks. Twenty percent of it may be invested in bonds. Don't assume that a fund invests exclusively in U.S. companies, either — it may invest in international firms as well.

Money market funds

Money market funds are the safest type of mutual funds if you are worried about the risk of losing your principal. Money market funds are like bank savings accounts in that the value of your investment does not fluctuate.

Money market funds have several advantages over bank savings accounts.

- ✔ The best ones have higher yields.
- ✔ If you're in a higher tax bracket, you have the option of using tax-free money market funds. No savings account pays tax-free interest.
- ✔ Most money market funds come with free check-writing privileges. (The only stipulation is that each check must be written for a minimum amount — $250 is common.)

Note: Money market mutual funds are not insured by the federal government, but none of them has ever lost shareholders' money. For all intents and purposes, they are as safe as bank accounts.

Money market funds are suitable for money that you can't afford to let fluctuate in value. See Chapter 10 for more background on money market funds and Chapter 12 for specific money market fund recommendations.

Bond funds

Bonds are IOUs. When you buy a bond, you are lending your money, typically to a corporation or government agency. A bond mutual fund is nothing more than a large group (pack, herd, gaggle, whatever) of bonds.

Most bond funds invest in bonds of similar *maturity* (the number of years to elapse before the borrower must pay back the money you lend). The names of most bond funds include a word or two to provide clues about the average length of maturity of their bonds. For example, a short-term bond fund concentrates its investments in bonds maturing in the next few years. An intermediate-term fund generally holds bonds that come due within 7 – 10 years. The bonds in a long-term fund usually mature in 20 years or so.

In contrast to an individual bond that you buy and hold until it matures, a bond fund is always replacing bonds in its portfolio to maintain its average maturity objective.

Like money market funds, bond funds can invest in tax-free bonds, which may be appropriate for investing money you hold outside retirement accounts if you're in a reasonably high tax bracket.

Bond funds are useful when you want to live off dividend income or when you don't want to put all your money in riskier investments such as stocks and real estate (perhaps because you plan to use the money soon). For more complete background on bonds, refer to Chapter 10. Specific bond funds for meeting different investment objectives are recommended in Chapters 12 and 13.

Hybrid funds

Hybrid funds invest in a mixture of different types of securities. Most commonly, they invest in bonds and stocks. These funds are usually less risky and volatile than funds investing exclusively in stocks. In an economic downturn, bonds usually hold up better in value than stocks do.

Hybrid mutual funds are typically known as *balanced* or *asset allocation* funds. Balanced funds generally try to maintain a fairly constant percentage of investment in stocks and bonds. (Some funds are exceptions to this rule — the Fidelity Balanced Fund, for example, fund makes major shifts in strategy despite its name.)

"Asset allocation" funds tend to adjust the mix of different investments according to the portfolio manager's expectations. You should note that most have done a dismal job in beating the market averages by shifting money around rather than staying put in good investments.

Hybrid funds are a terrific way to make investing simple. They also make it easier for investors who are skittish about the stock market to invest in stocks yet avoid the high volatility that normally comes with pure stock funds. Specific hybrid funds are recommended in Chapters 12 and 13.

Stock funds

Stock mutual funds, as their name implies, invest in stocks. These funds are often referred to as *equity* funds. Equity (not to be confused with equity in real estate) is another word for stocks. Stock mutual funds are usually categorized by the type of stocks they invest in. (For more background on stocks, refer to Chapter 10. I recommend specific stock funds in Chapters 12 and 13.)

U.S., international, and global funds

Most funds focus their investments in the U.S. unless they have words like *international, global, worldwide,* or *world* in their names. But you cannot assume that a fund that has *U.S.* in its name invests solely in the U.S.

The only way to know for sure where a fund is currently invested (or where the fund may invest in the future) is to ask. You can start by calling the 800 number of the mutual fund company that you're interested in.

The term *international* typically means that a fund can invest anywhere in the world except the U.S. The term *worldwide* or *global* generally implies that a fund can invest anywhere in the world, including the U.S. I generally recommend avoiding worldwide or global funds for two reasons. First, it's quite difficult for

Fund-investing styles

In the fashion world, a certain style is "in" during a given season, while everything else is too tacky to talk about. The same can hold true for investments.

With stocks, styles are usually defined by size of company (small, medium, and large). The categories are defined by the total market value (capitalization) of a company's outstanding stock. Small-company stocks, for example, are usually defined as companies with total market capitalization of less than $1 billion.

Money managers are further categorized by those who invest in growth or value stocks. *Growth stocks* are companies that are experiencing rap-

idly expanding revenues and profits. These companies tend to reinvest most of their earnings in the company to fuel future expansion and thus pay low dividends.

At the other end of the spectrum are *value investors.* These folks look for good buys. They want to invest in stocks that are cheaply priced in relation to the assets and profits of the company.

Styles can be combined so that a fund can focus on large-company growth stocks or small-company value stocks. These categories can be further subdivided into even more categories and fund types by adding in U.S., international, and worldwide funds.

a fund manager to follow the financial markets and companies in so many parts of the world thoroughly. It's hard enough to do so solely in U.S. or international markets. Secondly, most of these funds charge high operating expenses — often well in excess of 1 percent per year — which puts a drag on returns.

The only exceptions I've seen to this rule are the outstanding Fidelity Balanced and Fidelity Asset Manager funds offered by Fidelity Investments. Although these fund names don't contain the words _global_ or _worldwide,_ both funds diversify their investments worldwide. And they deliver top-notch performance with an expense fee of about 1 percent per year. Fidelity is one of the few companies that has the research capabilities to allow a fund manager to invest intelligently in so many different markets.

Index funds

Index funds are funds that can be (and are, for the most part) managed by a computer. An index fund's assets are invested so as to replicate an underlying index, such as Standard & Poor's 500 Index — the 500 companies with the greatest market value of stock outstanding in the U.S.

Unlike other mutual funds, in which the portfolio manager and a team of analysts scour the market for the best securities, an index fund manager simply invests to match the performance of an index.

Over long periods (ten years or more), index funds outperform about three-quarters of their peers! How is that possible? Because most other so-called active fund managers cannot overcome the handicap of high operating expenses that pulls down their funds' rates of return.

For example, the average U.S. stock fund has an operating expense ratio of 1.2 percent per year. So, a U.S. stock index fund with an expense ratio of just 0.2 percent per year has an advantage of 1 percent per year.

For money invested outside retirement accounts, index funds have an added advantage: Fewer taxable distributions (discussed later in this chapter) are made to shareholders because less trading of securities is conducted and a more stable portfolio is maintained. Index funds seem downright boring. When you invest in them, you give up the opportunity to brag to others about your shrewd investments. On the other hand, there's no chance of doing much worse than the market, which more than a few mutual fund managers do.

Index funds make sense for a portion of your investments, especially bond funds, where it's very difficult for portfolio managers to beat the market.

Bowser stock funds

Woof. If you were unfortunate enough to have been involved in the following loser mutual funds in the past ten years, you probably fared more than 15 percent worse per year in your rate of return than if you had invested in a boring old index fund (Vanguard S&P 500 Index over the same time period provided an average annual rate of return of +14.6 percent). See Table 11-1.

Table 11-1	Mutual Funds That Will Fetch a Stick
Fund	*Average annual rate of return (10 yrs.)*
Steadman Ocean Tech. & Growth	– 9.3%
Steadman American Industry	– 7.7%
Lexington Strategic Investments	– 7.6%
United Services Gold	– 4.9%
Centurion Growth	– 1.6%

Specialty funds

Specialty funds don't fit neatly into the previously discussed categories. These funds are often known as *sector* funds because they tend to invest in stocks in specific industries.

Specialty or sector funds should be avoided in most cases. Investing in stocks of a single industry defeats a major purpose of investing in mutual funds — you're giving up the benefits of diversification.

Another good reason to avoid sector funds is that they tend to carry much higher expenses than other mutual funds.

The only types of specialty funds that may make sense for a small portion (10 percent or less) of your investment portfolio are funds that invest in real estate (discussed in Chapter 15) or precious metals (try Vanguard or Benham). These types of funds can help diversify your portfolio because they can do better during times of higher inflation.

Selecting the Best Mutual Funds

Although investing in the stock and bond markets through mutual funds has significant potential rewards, it also involves risks.

When you go camping in the wilderness, you can do a number of things to maximize your odds of happiness and success. You take maps to keep you on course, food and entertainment to keep you from hunger and boredom, proper clothing to stay dry and warm, and perhaps some first-aid gear. But regardless of how much advance preparation you do, you may have a less-than-perfect experience. You may get sick, trip on a rock and break your ankle, or not get any sleep because your neighbors in the park play heavy metal music until the wee hours of the morning.

And so it is with mutual funds. There are no guarantees. You can, however, use a number of simple, common sense criteria to increase your chances of investment success and happiness. The following issues are the main ones you should consider.

Cost

For a particular type of mutual fund, for example, short-term bonds, dozens — in some cases, hundreds — of choices are available. The charges you pay to buy or sell a fund, as well as the ongoing fund operating expenses, can have a big impact on the rate of return you earn on your investments.

The biggest mistake that novice investors make when buying mutual funds is looking first (and sometimes only) at the prior performance of the fund or with too much attention paid to the current bond fund yield. Doing so is dangerous because there are many (risky) ways that a fund can inflate its return or yield. And what worked yesterday may flop tomorrow.

Fund costs are an important factor in the return that you earn from a mutual fund. Fees are deducted from your investment. All other things being equal, high fees and other charges depress your returns.

Sales loads

Sales loads are commissions paid to financial planners and brokers who sell mutual funds. They typically range from 4 percent to as high as 8.5 percent of the amount you invest.

Sales loads have two problems. First, they are an additional and unnecessary cost that is deducted from your investment money. Those with a vested interest in sales loads, not surprisingly, have made a number of misleading arguments in favor of funds that carry sales loads. Some of their statements are downright silly.

A common argument is that load funds perform better than no-load (commission-free) funds because you buy access to better managers through these funds. No objective studies support this claim. Because commissions are paid to the salesperson and not to the fund manager, there is no reason to think that these managers work any harder or are in any way better. Common sense suggests and studies confirm that load funds perform worse, on average, than no-loads when the load is taken into account.

The second problem with sales loads is, again, the power of self-interest. This issue is rarely talked about but is even more important than the extra costs you pay. When you buy a load fund through a salesperson, you miss out on the opportunity to assess objectively whether you should be buying a mutual fund at all. Maybe, for example, you're better off paying off debt or investing somewhere else. But salespeople almost never advise you to pay off your credit cards or invest through your company's retirement plan instead of buying an investment through them.

I've seen too many people purchase investment products without understanding what they're buying and the risks the investments entail. Salespeople who sell mutual funds usually push other stuff as well. Limited partnerships, life insurance, annuities, futures, and options hold the allure of big commissions. Salespeople tend to exaggerate the potential benefits and obscure the risks and drawbacks of what they sell; they don't seem to take the time to educate investors.

Just as some jewelers flog fake diamonds on late-night TV commercials, increasing numbers of brokers and financial planners are selling bogus funds that they *call* no-loads, but these funds are *not* no-loads — they just hide the sales commission.

You're told something along the lines that as long as you stay in a fund for five to seven years, you needn't pay the back-end sales charge that would apply upon sale of the investment. This claim may be true, but it's also true that these funds pay investment salespeople a hefty commission. They are able to receive this commission because the fund company charges you a very high ongoing operating expenses (usually 1 percent more per year than the best funds). So one way or another, they get their pounds of flesh (that is, commissions) from your investment dollars.

Invest in no-loads and avoid load funds and investment salespeople. The only way to be sure that a fund is truly no-load is to look at the prospectus for the fund. Only there, in black and white and without marketing hype, must the truth be told about sales charges and other fund fees. If you need advice about investing, hire a financial advisor on a fee-for-service basis. Doing so ends up costing you less and eliminates potential conflicts of interest in product sales and recommendations.

Operating expenses

All mutual funds charge ongoing fees. The fees pay for the operational costs of running a fund — employees' salaries, marketing, servicing the toll-free phone line, printing and mailing published materials, computers for tracking investments and account balances, accounting fees, and so on. Running a business costs money!

A fund's operating expenses are quoted as a percentage of your investment. The percentage represents an annual fee or charge. You can find this number in a fund's prospectus in the fund expenses section, where there should be a line that says something like "Total Fund Operating Expenses." Alternatively, you can call the mutual fund's 800 number and ask a representative.

Within a given sector of mutual funds (for example, money market, short-term bonds, and international stock), funds with low annual operating fees can more easily produce higher total returns for you. There's less of a drag on your returns.

A mutual fund's operating expenses are essentially invisible to you. That's because they're deducted before you're paid any return. The expenses are charged on a daily basis, so there's no need to worry about trying to get out of a fund before these fees are deducted.

Expenses matter on all funds but more on some and less on others. Expenses are critical on a money market mutual fund and very important on bond funds. Higher expenses lead to a lower yield to you. Fund managers that can beat the averages in these markets are few and far between.

With stock funds, expenses are a less important (but still important) factor in picking a fund. Don't forget that over time, stocks have averaged returns of about 10 percent per year. So if one stock fund charges 1 percent in operating expenses more than another, you're already giving up an extra 10 percent of your expected returns.

Some people argue that stock funds that charge high expenses may be justified in doing so if they are able to generate higher rates of return. There's no evidence that they do. In fact, funds with higher operating expenses tend to produce *lower* rates of return. This trend makes sense because operating expenses are deducted from the returns a fund generates.

Consistently high operating expenses at a mutual fund usually indicate two possible situations. Either the fund has little money under management and therefore cannot be managed as efficiently, or the fund owners are greedy. In either case, I don't think you want to be a shareholder at such a fund.

Stick with funds that maintain low total operating expenses and that don't charge sales loads (commissions). Both types of fees come out of your pocket and reduce your rate of return.

There's no reason to pay a lot for the best funds, as Table 11-2 shows.

Table 11-2	Mutual Fund Operating Expense Ratios	
Fund Type	*Expense Ratio Range*	*Who's Got a Lot of 'em*
Money market funds	0.2% – 0.4%	Vanguard, Fidelity (Spartan)
Bonds funds	0.2% – 0.5%	Vanguard, Fidelity (Spartan), PIMCO
Hybrid	0.2% – 1%	Vanguard, Fidelity
U.S. stock	0.2% – 1%	Fidelity, Vanguard, others
International stock	0.4% – 1.3%	Vanguard, T. Rowe Price, others
Index	0.2% – 0.5%	Vanguard, Schwab
Specialty	0.4% – 1.3%	Fidelity, Vanguard

Risk-adjusted rate of return

A fund's *performance,* or historic rate of return, is another important factor to weigh when selecting a mutual fund. As all mutual fund materials tell you, past performance is no guarantee of future results. Analysis of historic mutual fund performance proves that some of yesterday's stars turn into tomorrow's skid-row bums.

Many former high-return funds achieved their results by taking on high risk. Funds that assume higher risk should produce higher rates of return. But high-risk funds usually decline in price faster during major market declines. Thus, in order for a fund to be considered a *best* fund, it must consistently deliver a favorable rate of return given its risk. The only way that you can assess that factor is to look at a fund's *risk-adjusted return.*

You can't assess risk-adjusted performance on your own unless you have a computer (and a newer model at that) for a brain. You need to use one of the mutual fund information sources recommended later in this chapter.

Fund manager and fund family reputation

Much is made of who manages a specific mutual fund. While the individual fund manager is important, a manager is not an island unto herself. The resources and capabilities of the parent company are equally important.

For example, the departure of a portfolio manager with a good track record usually makes headlines. Peter Lynch's departure from the Fidelity Magellan fund is a good example. Some analysts said, "Dump the fund; the star is gone." Now, if you were managing Fidelity's mutual funds, wouldn't you put another capable manager at the helm of the Magellan fund? Of course you would — you're not in mourning and you're not stupid. And that's why Magellan has done just fine since Lynch's departure. Fidelity is an outstanding company in terms of its capability at managing money in U.S. stock funds. It has a pool of talented managers to draw upon when a manager leaves the firm or moves to another fund.

Different companies have different capabilities and levels of expertise in relation to different types of funds. Vanguard, for example, is terrific at money market, bond, and conservative stock funds, thanks to their low operating expenses.

Your needs and goals

Selecting the best funds for you also requires an understanding of your investment goals and desire to take risks. A good fund for your next-door neighbor is not necessarily a good fund for you. You have a unique risk profile and goals.

If you've determined your needs and goals already, terrific! Understanding yourself is a good part of the battle. But don't shortchange yourself by not being educated about the investment you're considering. If you do not understand what you are investing in and the risks entailed, then you should stay out of the game.

Prospectus and annual reports

Mutual fund companies produce information that can help you make decisions about mutual fund investments. All funds are required to issue a *prospectus*. This legal document is reviewed and audited by the U.S. Securities & Exchange Commission. Most of what's written isn't worth the time it takes to slog through it.

The most valuable information — the fund's investment objectives, costs, and performance history — is summarized in the first few pages of the prospectus. This part you should read. The rest is comprised mostly of tedious details about the mechanics of how the fund is run.

Funds also produce annual reports that discuss how their funds have been doing and provide details on the specific investments that a fund holds. If, for example, you want to know which countries an international fund invests in, ask for the most recent annual report. The mutual fund newsletters and directories recommended later in the chapter also report this type of information.

The Best Places to Invest in Mutual Funds

The mutual fund field has attracted a lot of new competitors tempted by the riches that early winners have accumulated. Banks, insurance companies, and even airlines have jumped on the bandwagon. Unfortunately, most of these companies sell load funds.

Consider using the following leading firms (chosen by using the criteria discussed in the "Selecting the Best Mutual Funds" section earlier in this chapter) for mutual funds investments.

Fidelity Investments

Fidelity Investments (800-544-6666), headquartered in Boston,, Massachusetts, is the nation's largest mutual fund company with more than $260 billion under management. Fidelity has about 80 local branch offices around the U.S. and offers 24-hour customer service.

Fidelity's roots trace back to the 1940s, when Edward C. Johnson II took over the then-fledgling Fidelity Fund from its president, who felt that he couldn't make enough money as the head of an investment fund! Johnson's son, Ned (Edward C. Johnson III), took over management of Fidelity in 1972.

Fidelity offers a number of excellent mutual funds, particularly those that invest in U.S. stocks. If you're the kind of person who likes to pick among 30 different brands of potato chips at the store, you'll love Fidelity. They offer more than 200 different funds, more than any other mutual fund company (specific Fidelity funds are recommended in Chapters 12 and 13).

Consider using Fidelity particularly for investments in retirement accounts. Non-retirement accounts in many of their best stock funds typically cost you 2 – 3 percent in sales fees (which you should avoid whenever possible).

Fidelity offers a higher-yielding (thanks to lower operating expenses) series of money market and bond funds known as Spartan funds. These funds carry higher minimums — usually $10,000 to $25,000.

Fidelity also offers discount brokerage services through which, if you're so inclined, you can trade individual securities or buy mutual funds from other fund companies (a service similar to that offered by Charles Schwab and other discount brokers). Using Fidelity for other mutual fund purchases is okay but not the best choice at this point. Other discount brokers offer a better fund selection and charge lower transaction fees, especially for smaller purchases. Fidelity has improved its service significantly since it started a year ago, so stay tuned.

The Vanguard Group

The Vanguard Group (800-662-7447), headquartered in Valley Forge, Pennsylvania, is the nation's largest exclusively commission-free mutual fund provider with over $130 billion under management. Vanguard is a solid base for safety-minded investors who want to invest in money market, bond, and conservative stock funds.

To understand and appreciate Vanguard, you need to know a bit about John Bogle, founder of the Vanguard Group of mutual funds. He's a little bit like the Ralph Nader of the mutual fund industry.

Bogle has long criticized other mutual fund companies for gouging investors. He believes (and I agree) that operating efficiencies in the mutual fund industry haven't been passed onto fund shareholders. Despite fund industry assets mushrooming twentyfold to $2 trillion from less than $100 billion in 1979, average fund operating expenses have gone up, not down.

Bogle came up with a unique ownership structure for Vanguard. He insisted that the management of individual funds be contracted out to the private money-management firms with whom Vanguard negotiates the best deal.

Vanguard mutual fund investors (now numbering around 5 million) own the company. Thus, Vanguard, the company, makes no profit. You can buy its funds at cost — that is, with no mark-up.

Mutual fund operating expenses, which are deducted from a fund's returns before shareholders are paid, are by far lower at Vanguard than at any other company in the industry. In comparison to 1.03 percent for the average mutual fund, Vanguard's fund operating expenses average just 0.30 percent. To put this difference in perspective, imagine if Ford could sell you a midsize car for $4,400 when Honda and GM equivalents cost $15,000.

Thus, Vanguard investors begin the investment performance race with a head start of about 0.7 percent per year in return. With money market and bond funds, the Vanguard expense advantage is significant. As discussed earlier in the chapter, these markets are highly efficient; even the best fund managers can add relatively little performance value.

In managing stock funds, where performance is supposed to be more closely tied to the genius of the fund manager, Vanguard's parsimony hasn't harmed performance. Vanguard offers many excellent stock funds. The number of top-performing Vanguard stock funds is all the more impressive given that competitors often merge a poor-performing fund into another to eliminate the lagging fund's record. Vanguard does not engage in this practice.

Vanguard is also the mutual fund innovator of index funds (discussed earlier in this chapter), which are unmanaged portfolios of the representative securities that comprise an index, such as the S&P 500. Vanguard offers the broadest selection of index funds and has the lowest operating expense average (0.18 percent) in the business.

Charles Schwab & Co.

Charles Schwab & Co. (800-526-8600), headquartered in San Francisco, California, is the nation's largest discount brokerage firm with assets of over $100 billion. It offers 24-hour customer service and has more than 200 local branch offices. Schwab was founded in 1974 by Charles R. Schwab, an innovator in the industry.

It's not really appropriate anymore to speak of Schwab as a discount broker, a term applied to firms that trade individual securities. The majority of customer assets at Schwab now are in mutual funds.

Schwab's "Mutual Fund Marketplace" service allows investment through a single account in more than 800 mutual funds from all the major no-load companies (including some not available to smaller investors). It's like going shopping in a giant mutual fund supermarket!

The advantage of using Schwab's service is that it greatly simplifies the paperwork and buying and selling of different fund companies' funds. There's no need to fill out applications from each mutual fund company you'd like to invest in. And instead of getting a separate statement from each company, you get one statement from Schwab that summarizes all of your mutual fund holdings.

Cost is the only drawback to using their mutual fund service rather than buying funds from fund companies on your own. You have to pay a little extra for the benefits.

With the exception of a handful of Schwab mutual funds, the funds in Schwab's Mutual Fund Marketplace are managed by other companies, such as Fidelity, Vanguard, T. Rowe Price, and so on. Because Schwab isn't actually managing the money, it charges you a transaction fee when you buy and sell mutual funds in their supermarket. Table 11-3 lists recent costs for some different-size trades:

Table 11-3	Schwab's Transaction Fees
Amount Invested	*Schwab's Transaction Fee**
Less than $5,000	$29
$ 5,000	$30
$10,000	$60
$30,000	$120

*If you place your mutual fund trade through Schwab's computer software packages, StreetSmart, Equalizer (see Chapter 22), or by touch-tone phone, you get a 10 percent discount on these fees. If, when you sell one fund, you place an order to invest that money in another fund, you pay the fee (see Table 11-3) on the sell order only and a reduced fee ($15) for the buy order.

When you buy and hold funds for the long-term (which is what you should be doing instead of trading a lot), the cost of Schwab's service is small.

You should also know that Schwab offers more than 200 funds without transaction fees (that is, at the same cost as through the mutual fund company itself). These are called *No Transaction Fee* funds. You shouldn't buy these funds just because they are available without a transaction fee. Some of them, particularly the bond funds, carry higher operating expenses.

Schwab and other discount brokers can afford to offer other companies' mutual funds without charging a transaction fee because the fund company shares a small percentage (usually 0.25 percent of its annual operating expense fee) with the discount broker for servicing the customer account.

Runner-up: Jack White & Company

Founded in 1975, Jack White & Company (800-323-3263) is a discount brokerage firm based in San Diego, California, with approximately $1 billion in customer account assets. Like Schwab and a handful of other discount brokers, it offers a mutual fund service, too.

White is known as a *deep discounter.* Its fees are discounted from a traditional discount broker's charges. Table 11-4 shows White's fee schedule for mutual fund transactions.

Table 11-4	Jack White & Co.'s Mutual Fund Fee Schedule
Amount Invested	*White's Transaction Fee**
Less than $5,000	$27
$5,000	$27
$10,000	$35
$30,000	$50

*If you consistently place larger mutual fund trades, White can save you money. But it is a no-frills broker. You won't find a local branch office in your area (unless you live in the San Diego area). And its representatives aren't available 24 hours a day, seven days a week (White's hours are 5 a.m. to 5 p.m. PST).

White also offers a nifty service, called Connect, that allows holders of load (commission-based) mutual funds to sell their shares to another buyer. The buyer pays a flat $200 fee instead of the normal 4 – 8.5 percent commission that an investment salesperson earns. For purchases of $5,000 or more of a mutual fund, this service can save a buyer hundreds or thousands of dollars. The seller benefits, too — getting paid $100 to sell a load fund through White's service.

An increasing number of discount brokers offer mutual funds from a variety of companies. Muriel Siebert & Co. offers significant numbers of funds as well as low transaction fees (although not as low as Jack White).

Mutual Fund Information Sources

Whether you're a novice or an experienced mutual fund investor, trying to get a handle on which funds are the best in various categories (such as international stocks and mortgage bonds) through mutual fund information and rating services can be overwhelming. Value Line and Morningstar, for example, track thousands of funds. These services are big, heavy, and awfully unwieldy for beginners to use.

Many publications track and recommend load mutual funds, which are sold through an investment salesperson. As discussed earlier in the chapter, sales commissions typically deduct 4 – 8.5 percent from your investment dollars with a load fund. Perhaps more dangerous is the possibility that you'll end up in the hands of a salesperson who will recommend investments and other financial products that are not in your best interests (see Chapters 3 and 10).

Chapters 12 and 13 recommend the best mutual funds using criteria discussed earlier in the chapter. I recommend the following for intelligent, insightful articles and information about the best mutual funds on an ongoing basis.

Beware the worst sources

With the popularity of mutual funds, more and more business, personal finance, and news magazines publish mutual fund information and rankings. Many purport to rank funds using their criteria. For a variety of reasons, much of this information isn't useful to folks trying to make informed decisions. In fact, making decisions based on some of these so-called mutual fund studies is downright dangerous.

One of the nation's largest business magazines committed a number of major errors in its recent "Top Funds" analysis. The most egregious error was the ranking of funds solely on the basis of rate of return over a three-year period.

What's wrong with that? The first problem is that the publication completely ignored the volatility of the different funds. Funds that took more risk and were able to generate higher rates of return were awarded higher rankings.

Three years is also a very short time to look at fund performance. This particular three-year period witnessed a nearly uninterrupted upward march in stock and bond prices. Imagine betting on an athlete to win the Olympic decathlon after the shot-put competition. Sure, a stocky, muscular type can shot-put further than his competitors, but he may be huffing and puffing his way around the track in the mile run.

Another example of the "garbage in, garbage out" phenomenon is data provided by Lipper Analytic Services, a primary mutual fund information source for many newspapers. This organization assigns letter grades to funds just like your junior high school teacher did, except your teacher's system was probably more sound. Lipper grades funds within broad categories based solely on total return. The performance rankings that wind up in some newspapers can be for periods as short as *one year.*

Lipper has also made other major errors in classifying many of the newfangled brokerage firm funds that attempt to hide sales charges as no-load (in case you forgot, *no-load* means that no sales commissions are charged or paid). Funds sold through commission-based brokers and planners, who receive a 4- to 5-percent commission from your investment money, are *never* no-load.

These funds are merely deferred-load funds. If you invest in them for five to seven years, for example, then there's a charge. But if you don't stay in that long, you pay a ton of ongoing expenses, which are deducted from your investment. Either way, the investment salesperson gets a commission that comes out of your money. Either way, these aren't no-load funds.

Another mistake that some magazines commit in published mutual fund studies is dumping a truckload of data on you. They then order the mutual funds alphabetically so that you sift through pages and pages of rows and columns of numbers. You have better things to do with your time.

Sadly, one of the reasons they do so is *advertising*. I got a call last year from a self-proclaimed reporter for a large personal finance magazine. Mr. Reporter had an outline for an article he wanted to write about mutual fund investing in which he would profile mutual fund investors that had specific fund companies' investments. The list included a number of load funds, all of which were heavy advertisers in the magazine.

The reporter had no experience either as a business writer or in working for a financial services firm. A few minutes into our conversation, he asked me to explain a couple of terms I had used. He didn't know the difference between a stock fund and a bond fund! To this day, I marvel about this experience. You should enjoy the fact that, having read this chapter, you know a lot more about mutual funds than this reporter did.

No-Load Fund Analyst

No-Load Fund Analyst is a high-quality mutual fund newsletter that you probably haven't heard of. What you'll like best about this publication is that the editors, Craig Litman and Ken Gregory, have done a lot of the work for you in screening funds. They only track funds that can be bought directly from mutual fund companies or through discount brokers, which saves you from paying unnecessary sales commissions. *No-Load Fund Analyst* tracks a universe of approximately 200 of the best funds — more than enough even for the choosiest of investors.

The editors' primary business has always been their investment management business. They manage money for affluent individuals and institutions in no-load (commission-free) mutual funds. Their minimum account size is $1 million.

No-Load Fund Analyst is not for everyone. Although it contains model portfolios with specific fund recommendations and allocations, a typical 24-page issue carries a lot of commentary and in-depth analysis of trends in the fund industry and fund manager interviews and profiles. Some of the information gets a bit technical at times. In an industry in which many publications claim that they can double your money in a snap if you become a subscriber, *No-Load Fund Analyst* is downright sedate and boring. It includes no hype or you-shoulda-listened-to-us-last-year propaganda.

Personal interviews and tracking of individual fund managers is one unique and valuable aspect of Litman and Gregory's publication. Because they pay attention to this type of information, they recommend few funds at the mutual fund giant Fidelity, where fund managers are notorious for frequent fund-hopping.

Litman and Gregory are good at identifying talented fund managers at some of the smaller and lesser-known funds. However, because they recommend funds in numerous fund families, as an investor you must be willing to deal with a blizzard of paperwork to establish and keep accounts at many companies.

Alternatively, investors can set up an account at a discount brokerage firm (Charles Schwab or Jack White, for example) and purchase all of Litman and Gregory's recommendations through a single account. In fact, doing so is necessary to access some of the funds that are not available to smaller investors or are closed to new investors if you try to purchase them directly from the company.

New or current mutual fund investors looking for solid ideas, thoughtful research and analysis, and specific mutual fund recommendations should look no further than *No-Load Fund Analyst.* And at $195 per year, half the cost of Morningstar's *Mutual Funds,* it's a good value. A sample issue can be obtained for $10 by calling 800-776-9555.

Morningstar and Value Line

Both Value Line and Morningstar publish behemoth publications that track thousands of mutual funds. They're reference publications, not newsletters or magazines. If you already have a large portfolio of funds that you've invested in and want to check out a large number of other funds, then these publications may be of use to you.

The services are more similar than they are different. Value Line is the new kid on the block, having launched its service in late 1993. Both use a similar format, devoting a single page packed with all sorts of details, numbers, and a bit of commentary to each fund. Funds are ranked on a scale of from one to five (Morningstar uses stars, Value Line uses numbers).

The most common mistake investors make in using these publications is focusing too much on the ranking of specific funds. Both publications' lengthy guidebooks (which most people don't read) warn against doing so, although they don't say it strongly enough for my taste.

Their ratings are good in that they look at *risk-adjusted performance* — the performance of a fund and the risk (or volatility) that it took to achieve it. There are, however, a number of limitations to the rankings. One fatal flaw with both services is that they lump funds into broad categories when, in fact, many funds within the category invest in different types of securities.

For example, in the various stock fund categories, you find funds that invest exclusively in stocks and others that invest some of their money in bonds or other high dividend-paying securities, such as preferred stocks. These types of securities tend to reduce the volatility of a portfolio and do well in times of declining interest rates (such as we've had in the past decade).

Funds that invest in U.S. securities as well as those overseas are another example. Mutual funds that call or classify themselves as worldwide are put in a *global* or *worldwide* category. The others end up scattered throughout the U.S. stock and balanced fund categories. These misclassified funds have a leg up on their U.S.-focused competitors in the ratings because international securities tend to reduce the volatility of a fund.

The rankings also ignore fund operating expenses. Because the past is at best a weak predictor of things to come, you're more likely to succeed with funds that keep expenses down. As I explained earlier, high expenses are a handicap to generating good future returns.

Brokers and financial planners love the rating system because it makes it easier for them to sell you funds with commissions (load funds). They push those with high ratings, saying, "Here's an independent rating service's assessment of the fund we talked about."

Few publications in this world should be called *independent*. Morningstar and Value Line are not among them. The vast majority of investment brokers and financial planners who subscribe to these publications are investment sales-people who sell load (commissionable) mutual funds. A contributing editor at Morningstar, who has since left, once told me, "We could never say to avoid load funds, otherwise we'd lose a large number of subscribers."

Both services are packed with too much information and too many funds for the nonexpert investor. These publications are not for you unless you're willing to spend a lot of time learning how to digest all the information they contain.

The services are also not cheap. Annual subscription rates are $395 for Morningstar and $295 for Value Line. Check your local library, where you can use them for free, or obtain the three-month trial subscription that they both offer — Value Line's costs $49, Morningstar's $55.

Making Sense of Fund Performance Numbers

When you look at a statement for your mutual fund holdings, odds are that you're not going to understand it. It's not you — it's the statement.

Why it's so complicated

The hardest part is getting a handle on how you're doing. Specifically, most people want to know and have a hard time discerning how much they've made or lost on their investment. *You cannot deduce a figure by comparing the share price of the fund today versus what you originally paid for the fund.*

The problem is that mutual funds make distributions. Well, it's actually not a problem — when a fund makes a distribution to you, you get more shares of the fund. But distributions create an accounting problem because they reduce the share price of a fund.

Therefore, over time, following just the share price of your fund doesn't tell you how much money you've made or lost.

Imagine that the share price of your mutual fund is like a balloon with a small rock tied to the end of a string attached to it. The balloon (representing fund share price) struggles to rise, but the rock (representing fund distributions) keeps pulling down on the balloon.

The only way to figure out exactly how much you've made or lost on your investment is to compare the total value of your holdings in a fund today versus the total dollar amount you originally invested. If you've invested chunks of money at various points in time, this exercise becomes much more complicated. Check out recommended investment software in Chapter 22 if you want your computer to help you crunch your own numbers.

Ultimately, you should really care about the total rate of return the fund has produced over prior time periods (one year, three years, and so on). You can call the fund company's 800 number to get these figures, or you can read the fund's annual report. (This is what I do — calculating yourself is a pain!)

Total return

The *total return* of a fund is the percentage change of your investment over a specified period. For example, a fund may tell you that in 1993 its total return was 10 percent. Therefore, if you had invested $10,000 in the fund on the last day of 1992, your investment would be worth $11,000 at the end of 1993.

The following three components make up your total return on a fund: dividends, capital gains, and share price changes.

Dividends

Dividends are income paid by investments. Both bonds and stocks can pay dividends. Bond dividends tend to be higher. When a dividend distribution is made, you can receive it as cash (which is good if you need money to live on) or as more shares in the fund. In either case, the share price of the fund drops by an amount to exactly offset the payout. So if you are hoping to strike it rich by buying into a bunch of funds just before their dividends are paid, don't bother.

If you hold your mutual fund outside a retirement account, the dividend distributions are taxable income (unless they come from a tax-free municipal bond fund). Dividends are taxable whether or not you reinvest them as additional shares in the fund. See Chapter 12 for fund recommendations that make sense for your tax situation.

Capital gains

When a mutual fund manager sells a security in the fund, any gain realized from that sale (the difference from the purchase price) must be distributed to you as a *capital gain*. Typically, funds make one annual capital gains distribution in December.

As with a dividend distribution, you can receive your capital gains distribution as cash or as more shares in the fund. In either case, the share price of the fund drops by an amount to offset the distribution exactly.

For funds held outside retirement accounts, your capital gains distribution is taxable. As with dividends, capital gains are taxable whether or not you reinvest them in additional shares in the fund.

As I discuss in more detail in the next chapter, you may want to check with a fund to determine when capital gains are distributed if you seek to avoid making an investment in a fund that is about to make a capital gains distribution. This increases your current-year tax liability for investments made outside of retirement accounts.

Share price changes

You also make money with a mutual fund when the share price increases. This occurrence is just like investing in a stock or piece of real estate. If it's worth more today than when you bought it, you have made a profit (on paper, at least). In order to realize or lock in this profit, you need to sell your shares in the fund.

There you have it — the components of a mutual fund's total return are the following:

Dividends + Capital Gains + Share Price Changes = Total Return

Following and Selling Your Funds

How closely to follow your funds is up to you, depending on what makes you happy and comfortable. I do not recommend tracking the share prices of your funds on a daily basis. It's time-consuming, nerve-racking, and will make you lose sight of the long term. You'll be more likely to panic when times get tough.

Weekly, monthly, or quarterly check-in is more than frequent enough to follow your funds. Many newspapers now carry total return numbers over varying periods, so you can determine the exact rate of return that you've been earning. Ignore the letter grades that many papers carry — the grades are meaningless and misleading (see the "The Worst Mutual Fund Information Sources" earlier in this chapter).

Trying to time and trade the markets to buy at lows and sell at highs rarely works. You should sell a fund when it no longer meets the criteria mentioned in the section, "Selecting the Best Mutual Funds," located earlier in this chapter. A good time to sell may be when the fund loses some of its luster or because other fund companies' offerings improve in comparison to your fund.

Increasing numbers of mutual funds are popping up that label themselves *socially responsible.* This term means different things to different people. In most cases, though, it implies that the fund avoids investing in companies, such as tobacco manufacturers, which are harming people or the world at large. Because cigarettes and other tobacco products kill hundreds of thousands of people and add billions of dollars to health care costs, most socially responsible funds shun tobacco companies.

Socially responsible investing presents a couple of problems. For example, your definition of social responsibility may not match the definition of the investment manager who's running a fund. Another problem is that even if you can agree on what's socially irresponsible (such as selling tobacco products), funds aren't always as clean as you would think or hope. Although a fund may avoid tobacco manufacturers, it may well invest in retailers that sell tobacco products.

If you want to consider socially responsible funds (some specific funds are listed in the next two chapters), call the investment company and ask them to send you a recent report that lists the specific investments that the fund owns.

Chapter 12

Investing Money
Outside Retirement Accounts

Note: In this chapter, I discuss investment options for money held outside retirement accounts and include specific mutual fund recommendations. Chapter 13 reviews investments for money inside retirement accounts. This distinction may seem somewhat odd — it's not one that is made in most financial books and articles — but I have my reasons.

*I*t's useful to think of the two pots of money differently. Investments held outside retirement accounts are subject to taxation. You have a whole range of different investment options to consider when taxes come into play. Then again, some retirement accounts, such as those you obtain through your employer, limit your investment options. And special rules govern transfer of your retirement account balances.

Suppose you've got some money sitting around that you want to invest more profitably. People in this situation often have their money in a money market or bank savings account. At the time of this writing, you're probably getting no more than 3 percent and possibly as little as 1.5 – 2 percent in interest.

Never forget two things about investing this type of money:

✔ **Earning 2 – 3 percent is better than losing 20 – 50 percent or more.** Just talk to anyone who was sold a limited partnership in the past decade. So, don't feel bad about "saving" (low, safe return) instead of "investing" (chasing a potentially higher return).

✔ **To earn a higher rate of return, you must be willing to take more risk** (unless you jump into a higher-yielding savings or money market account, discussed later in this chapter). Earning a better rate of return means considering investments that can fluctuate in value — and, of course, the value can drop as much as it can rise.

Two Overlooked, Easy Investments

It's tempting to jump into the vast sea of investment options and start paddling around to fish for attractive options. You hear stories of people cashing in big on stocks or real estate that they bought years ago. Even if you don't have delusions of grandeur, you'd at least like your money to grow faster than the cost of living.

But before you take the investment plunge, consider the following frequently overlooked ways to put your money to work and earn higher returns without taking as much risk. These options may not be as exciting as other options, but they're financially astute and should improve your financial health.

Pay off high-interest debt

Many folks have credit card or other consumer debt that costs more than 10 percent per year in interest. Paying off this debt with savings is like putting your money in an investment with a guaranteed return equal to the rate you are paying on the debt.

For example, if you have credit card debt outstanding at 14 percent interest, then paying off that loan is the same as putting your money to work in an investment with a certain 14-percent annual return. Remember that the interest on consumer debt is not tax-deductible, so you would actually need to earn *more* than 14 percent investing your money elsewhere in order to net 14 percent after paying taxes.

Paying off some or all of your mortgage may make sense, too. This financial move isn't as clear, because the interest rate is lower than that on consumer debt and is usually tax-deductible. (See Chapter 9 for more details on this decision.)

Contribute to retirement accounts

If you have a chunk of money, make sure that you take advantage of the *terrific* tax benefits offered by a retirement account. If you work for a company that offers a retirement savings plan such as a 401(k), you should try to fund it at the highest level you can manage. If you earn self-employment income, look into SEP-IRAs and Keoghs. (All retirement-plan options are discussed in Chapter 8.)

If you need to save money outside retirement accounts for other short-term purposes (for example, for buying a car or a home), then keep doing what you're doing. But if you're continuing to accumulate money outside retirement accounts with no particular purpose in mind (other than that you like seeing the balances with all those nice, fat numbers), why not get some tax breaks *too* by contributing and investing through retirement accounts?

Investing money outside retirement accounts requires greater thought and consideration because your investments can produce taxable distributions. This is another reason to shelter more of your money in retirement accounts.

Taxes and Your Investments

Lots of folks invest their money in a way that increases their tax burden. In many cases, they (and sometimes their advisors) don't consider the tax impact of their investment strategies.

You are far more likely to make tax mistakes investing assets held outside retirement accounts. Distributions, such as interest, dividends, and capital gains, produced by non-retirement account investments are all exposed to taxation. If you're not living off your investments' distributions, consider investing this non-tax-sheltered money to minimize taxable distributions.

Many people make the mistake of not considering the potential tax implications of their investments *before* they invest. For example, consider a moderate-income person in the combined 35 percent tax bracket (federal plus state taxes) who keeps extra cash in a taxable bank savings or money market account paying 2 percent interest. If he pays 35 percent of his interest earnings in taxes, he ends up keeping only about 1.3 percent, all because the money is held outside a retirement account.

With a tax-free money market fund from the major mutual fund providers (stay tuned for more on these), an investor can easily earn more than this amount, completely free of federal and/or state taxes.

Another mistake many people make is investing in securities that produce tax-free income even though they're not in a high enough tax bracket to benefit. Tax-free securities always yield less than equivalent taxable ones. The taxable investment may end up yielding less after taxes than what you would have earned on tax-free investments. So, you must be in a high enough tax bracket to benefit from tax-free investments. But how high is high enough?

- ✔ **31 percent or higher federal tax bracket.** If you're in this bracket, you should definitely avoid investments that produce taxable income. For tax year 1993, the 31 percent federal bracket started at $53,500 for singles and $89,150 for married couples filing jointly.

- ✔ **28 percent or higher federal bracket.** In most cases, you should be as well or better off in investments that do not produce taxable income when investing outside retirement accounts. This may not be the case, however, if you're in tax-free money market and bond funds whose yields are depressed due to high operating expenses (you won't find them recommended in this chapter!).

- ✔ **15 percent federal bracket.** Investments that produce taxable income are just fine for you. You may end up with *less* if you purchase investments that produce tax-free income.

In the sections that follow, I give specific advice about investing your money while keeping an eye on taxes.

Savings/Emergency Reserve

No one can predict the future. There is simply no reliable way to tell what may happen with your job, health, or family. Is there a Caribbean cruise in your future? Maybe, maybe not. What will number seven be on David Letterman's next "Top 10 List"? And so on.

Because you don't know what the future holds in store for you, it's financially wise to prepare for the unexpected. Even if you're the lucky sort who sometimes finds $5 bills on street corners or wins radio call-in contests, you can't control the sometimes chaotic world in which you find yourself.

Conventional wisdom says that you should have approximately six months of living expenses put away for an emergency. This particular amount may or may not be right for you because it depends, of course, on how expensive the emergency is. Why six months, anyway? And where should you put it? Unfortunately, there are no hard and fast rules. How much of an emergency stash you need depends on your situation.

How much?

Most people find it easier to think of the safety reserve in terms of monthly income rather than in terms of total spending (although, for many people, these are one and the same). It doesn't really matter which figure you use. If you save a large percentage of your income (you spend 80 percent or less of what you earn), then use your spending as a gauge.

I recommend the following amounts under differing circumstances:

- ✔ Three months' income if you have other accounts such as a 401(k) or family members and close friends that you could tap for a short-term loan. This minimalist approach makes sense when you're trying to maximize investments elsewhere (for example, in retirement accounts) or have very stable sources of income.

- ✔ Six months' income if you don't have other places to turn for a loan. This higher amount also makes sense if your income isn't very stable or secure.

- ✔ Up to one year's income if your income can fluctuate wildly from year to year. If your profession involves a high risk of job loss, and if it could take you a long while to find another, you also have a greater need for a significant cash reserve.

If you don't have enough of a reserve, you obviously need to save more. If you're having a hard time doing so because of debt, read Chapter 5 for strategies to pay off debts; if it's because of overall spending, read Chapter 6 for spending-reduction strategies.

Where?

You need two things from your savings or emergency reserve:

- ✔ **Accessibility.** When you need to get your hands on the money for an emergency, you want to be able to do so quickly and without penalty.

- ✔ **Highest possible return.** You want to get the highest rate of return possible on it without risking your principal. This doesn't mean that you should simply pick the money market or savings option with the highest yield, because taxes are a consideration. What good is earning a little higher yield if you pay a lot more in taxes?

Bank and credit union savings accounts

If you have a few thousand dollars or less, your best and easiest path is to keep this excess savings in a local bank or credit union. Look first to the institution where you keep your checking account.

Keeping this stash of money in your checking account makes financial sense if the extra money helps you avoid monthly service charges because your balance occasionally dips below the minimum. In fact, keeping money in a separate savings account instead of in your checking account may *not* make sense if service charges wipe out your interest earnings.

Money market mutual funds

Discussed in Chapter 11, these funds are just like bank savings accounts — but better, in most cases. The best money market funds pay higher yields and give you check-writing privileges. And if you're in a high tax bracket, you can select a tax-free money market fund, which pays interest that is free from federal and/or state tax. You cannot get this feature with a bank savings account.

The yield on a money market is an important consideration. The operating expenses deducted before payment of dividends is the single biggest determinant of yield. All other things being equal (which they usually are with different money market funds), lower operating expenses translate into higher yields for you.

Another factor that may be important to you is other investing you may plan to do at the fund company where you establish a money market fund. For example, if you decide to do other mutual fund investing in stock and bonds at Fidelity, then keeping a money market fund at a different firm that offers a slightly higher yield may not be worth the time and administrative hassle. On the other hand, there's no reason you can't invest in funds at multiple firms (as long as you don't mind the extra administrative work), using each for its relative strengths.

Most mutual fund companies don't have many local branch offices (Fidelity and Schwab are notable exceptions), so you'll probably open and maintain your money market mutual fund through the fund's toll-free 800 phone line and the mail. Don't worry — your money is still accessible via check-writing, and you can also have money wired to your local bank on any business day.

Distance has its advantages. Because you can conduct business by mail and phone, there's no need to go schleping into a local branch office to make deposits and withdrawals. I'm *happy* to report that I haven't visited a bank office more than once a year over the past decade. If you're worried about a deposit being lost in the mail, don't. It rarely happens, and no one can legally cash a check made payable to you, anyway.

Be sure to endorse the check with the notation "for deposit only" under your signature.

(For that matter, driving or walking to your local bank isn't 100 percent safe. Imagine all the things that could happen to you or your money en route to the bank. You could slip on a banana peel, drop your deposit down a sewer grate, get mugged, kidnapped, or run over by a bakery truck. Who knows — you could walk into a bank holdup and end up being taken hostage.)

Watch out for "sales"

Beware of mutual funds running specials. Some mutual funds aren't above resorting to some of the same marketing gimmicks that make retailers so endearing. The most common ploy is for funds to have a "sale." They do so by temporarily waiving (sometimes called *absorbing*) operating expenses, which results in a fund being able to boost its yield. When the fund managers get hungry for profits, the operating expenses charged to the fund deflate the too-good-to-be-true yield like a nail in a bike tire. New York-based Dreyfus mutual funds is notorious for such shenanigans with their money funds, the number of which grows ever larger — they always seem to be launching a new series of money funds and then having a sale on them.

Unlike an item bought from a retailer, the decision to invest in a money fund is usually a long-term proposition. Fund companies like Dreyfus run sales because they know that a good percentage of the fund buyers lured in won't bother leaving when they jack up the prices (operating expenses).

You're better off sticking with funds that maintain "everyday low prices" (for operating expenses) to get the highest long-term yield. If you want to move your money to companies having specials and then move it back out when the special's over, be my guest. If you have lots of money and don't mind paper-work, it may actually be worth the bother.

Recommended money market mutual funds

Note: Be watchful of changing data. A mutual fund's operating-expense percentages can change over time — keep this in mind if you call the fund companies in Table 12-1 for an update. Just to make things challenging for you when you do call, fund representatives don't always have up-to-date information.

Fidelity's fund expenses are more likely to change than Vanguard's. On most of the Fidelity Spartan money market funds listed, Fidelity can charge operating expense ratios of up to 0.5 percent or so. Historically, it hasn't charged this much (it's had an extended sale). Vanguard's operating expenses shift about as often as a statue — for this reason, I recommend that you choose one of its funds first if it meets your needs.

Recommended taxable money market funds

Money market funds that pay taxable dividends are appropriate when you're not in a high tax bracket (less than 28 percent federal). Recent yields of these funds are about 3 percent.

Fidelity: (800) 544-8888. Vanguard: (800) 662-7447. Schwab: (800) 526-8600.

Table 12-1	Taxable Money Market Funds	
Fund	*Operating Expense*	*Minimum to Open*
Vanguard Money Market Reserves Prime Portfolio	0.3%	$3,000
Fidelity Spartan Money Market	0.3%	$20,000
Schwab Value Advantage	0.4%	$25,000

Recommended U.S. Treasury money market funds

U.S. Treasury money market funds are appropriate if you prefer a money fund that invests in U.S. Treasuries, which have the safety of government backing, or if you're not in a high federal tax bracket (less than 28 percent) but *are* in a high state tax bracket (5 percent or higher). Table 12-2 lists a few that I recommend. Recent yields of these funds are a bit less than 3 percent.

Table 12-2	U.S. Treasury Money Market Funds	
Fund	*Operating Expense*	*Minimum to Open*
Vanguard Money Market Reserves U.S. Treasury	0.3%	$3,000
Vanguard Admiral U.S. Treasury Money Market	0.15%	$50,000
Fidelity Spartan U.S. Treasury Money Market	0.4%	$20,000

Recommended state and federally tax-free money market funds

The tax-free money market funds such as those in Table 12-3 are appropriate when you're in a high federal (28 percent and up) *and* state tax bracket (5 percent or higher). If none is listed for your state or you're only in a high federal tax bracket, skip over to Table 12-4 — federally tax-free money market funds. Recent yields for these funds are around 2 percent.

Fidelity: (800) 544-8888. Vanguard: (800) 662-7447.

Table 12-3	State and Federally Tax-Free Money Market Funds	
Fund	*Operating Expense*	*Minimum to Open*
Vanguard CA Tax-Free Money Market	0.2%	$3,000
Fidelity Spartan CA Muni Money Market	0.3%	$25,000
Fidelity Spartan CT Muni Money Market	0.3%	$25,000
Fidelity Spartan FL Muni Money Market	0.4%	$25,000
Fidelity Spartan MA Muni Money Market	0.3%	$25,000
Vanguard NJ Tax-Free Money Market	0.2%	$3,000
Fidelity Spartan NY Muni Money Market	0.5%	$25,000
Vanguard OH Tax-Free Money Market	0.3%	$3,000
Vanguard PA Tax-Free Money Market	0.2%	$3,000
Fidelity Spartan PA Muni Money Market	0.5%	$25,000

A number of states do not have money market fund options listed in Table 12-3 (and some that do may have minimums that are too high for you). In some cases, none exists. In other cases, the funds available (and not on the recommended list) for that state have such high annual operating expenses, and therefore such low yields, that you are better off in a more competitively run federally tax-free only fund listed in Table 12-4.

Federally tax-free only money market funds

Federally tax-free only money market funds (the dividends on these are state taxable) are appropriate when you're in a high federal (28 percent and up) but *not* state (less than 5 percent) bracket or if you live in a state that doesn't have competitive state and federally tax-free funds available (see Table 12-3 to make sure). Recent yields of these funds are a bit above 2 percent.

Table 12-4	Federally Tax-Free Only Money Market Funds	
Fund	*Operating Expense*	*Minimum to Open*
Vanguard Municipal Money Market	0.2%	$3,000
Fidelity Spartan Municipal Money Market	0.3%	$25,000

How Much Time Ya Got?

Note: This section (and the recommended investments) assumes that you have a sufficient emergency reserve stashed away and are taking advantage of tax-deductible retirement account contributions already.

Which investments you should consider depends on your comfort level with risk. But it should also depend heavily on how much time you have until you plan to use the money. I'm not talking about investments that you won't be able to sell on short notice if need be (most of them you can). It's just that it is riskier to invest money in a more volatile investment if you may need to liquidate it in the short-term.

For example, suppose that you're saving money for a down payment on a house and are about a year away from having enough to make your foray into the real estate market. If you had put this "home" money into the U.S. stock market in the spring of 1987 (or 1972 or 1968 for that matter), by autumn you'd have been a mighty unhappy camper. You could have seen 30 – 40 percent of your money *vanish* in short order and your home dreams put on hold.

So, you need to choose investments that are suited to the time frame that you have in which to invest.

Most of the following recommended investments are different types of no-load (commission-free) mutual funds. Mutual funds are very liquid — they can be sold on any business day with a simple phone call. Funds come with all different levels of risk, so you can choose funds that match your time frame and desire to take risk. (Chapter 11 discusses all the basics of mutual funds.)

The different investment options are organized by time frame. They are also organized by your tax situation. (If you don't know your current tax bracket, be sure to pay a visit to Chapter 7.) The following are summaries of the different time frames:

- ✔ **Short-term investments.** These investments are suitable for a period of a few years — perhaps you're saving money towards a home or some other major purchase in the near future. Stocks, real estate, and other volatile investments are not suited for a period of a few years. Recommended investments are shorter-term bond funds, which are higher-yielding alternatives to money market funds. If interest rates increase, these funds drop slightly in value — a couple of percent or so (unless rates rise tremendously).

- ✔ **Intermediate-term investments.** These investments are appropriate for more than a few but less than ten years. Investments that fit the bill are intermediate-term bonds and very low-risk, well-diversified hybrid funds that include some stocks.

- ✔ **Long-term investments.** If you have a decade or more, then you can consider potentially higher-return (and therefore riskier) investments. Stocks, real estate, and other growth-oriented investments can earn the most money if you're comfortable with the risk involved.

Recommended Investments

Note: This section presumes that you've read the preceding section "How Much Time Ya Got?".

All the recommended investments that follow assume that you have *at least* a several-year time frame. You should consider these investments *only* if you have an adequate safety net of cash and are taking advantage of tax-deductible retirement account contributions already.

Bond funds

Bond funds that pay taxable dividends are appropriate when you're not in a high tax bracket (less than 28 percent federal). Table 12-5 lists some bond funds I recommend. **Note:** The asterisks and other symbols are explained after Table 12-8.

Asset allocation

Asset allocation is the process of figuring out how much of your vast wealth you should invest in different types of investments. You frequently (and most appropriately) do asset allocation with retirement accounts.

Ideally, more of your saving and investing should be conducted through tax-sheltered retirement accounts. That's generally the best way to lower your long-term tax burden (see Chapter 8 for more details).

If you have sufficient assets that you plan to invest outside retirement accounts, specific recommendations follow this section. For that portion of your investments that you intend to hold for the long-term (ten or more years), you can allocate according to the "Suggested asset allocation" section in Chapter 13.

Table 12-5	Taxable Bond Funds		
Fund	*Investments*	*Operating Expense*	*Minimum to Open*
Short-term (recent yields around 4.5% – 5 percent)			
Benham Adjustable Rate Government Securities */**	Adjustable-rate mortgages	0.5%	$1,000
1 PIMCO Low Duration **	Mostly corporate and mortgage bonds	0.4%	$1,000
Vanguard Short-Term Corporate	Mostly corporate, some treasuries	0.3%	$3,000
Intermediate-term (recent yields around 5.5% – 6%)			
Benham GNMA */**	Mortgages	0.5%	$1,000
1 PIMCO Total Return **	Corporate and mortgage bonds; small % overseas	0.4%	$1,000
1S PIMCO Total Return III **	Corporate and mortgage bonds; small % overseas	0.5%	$1,000
Vanguard GNMA	Mortgages	0.3%	$3,000
Vanguard Total Bond Index	Corporate and mortgages; some treasuries	0.2%	$3,000
Fidelity Spartan GNMA	Mortgages	0.3%	$10,000
Long-term (recent yields 6.5% and more)			
Vanguard Long-Term Corporate	Corporate bonds; some treasuries	0.3%	$3,000
Vanguard High Yield Corporate	Lower-quality corporate bonds	0.3%	$3,000

* = Available through Schwab without transaction fees (see Chapter 11).

** = Available through Jack White without transaction fees (see Chapter 11).

1 = Purchase through Schwab or Jack White because of high minimum or unavailable elsewhere (see Chapter 11).

U.S. Treasury bond funds

U.S. Treasury bond funds are appropriate if you prefer a bond fund that invests in U.S. Treasuries (which have the safety of government backing) or when you're not in a high federal tax bracket (less than 28 percent) but *are* in a high state tax bracket (5 percent or higher). See Table 12-6.

Table 12-6	U.S. Treasury Bond Funds		
Fund	*Investments*	*Operating Expense*	*Minimum to Open*
Short-term (recent yields around 4.25 percent)			
Vanguard Short-Term U.S. Treasury	Treasuries	0.3%	$3,000
Vanguard Admiral Short-Term U.S. Treasury	Treasuries	0.15%	$50,000
Intermediate-term (recent yields around 5.25 percent)			
Vanguard Intermediate-Term U.S. Treasury	Treasuries	0.3%	$3,000
Vanguard Admiral Intermediate-Term U.S. Treasury	Treasuries	0.15%	$50,000
Long-term (recent yields around 6.25 percent)			
Vanguard Long-Term U.S. Treasury	Treasuries	0.3%	$3,000
Vanguard Admiral Long-Term U.S. Treasury	Treasuries	0.15%	$3,000

State and federally tax-free bond funds

The state and federally tax-free bond funds listed in Table 12-7 are appropriate when you're in high federal (28 percent and up) *and* state (5 percent or higher) tax brackets. (If one is not listed for your state or if you're only in a high federal tax bracket, check out Table 12-8 — federally tax-free bond funds.)

Table 12-7   State and Federally Tax-Free Bond Funds

Fund	Investments	Operating Expense	Minimum to Open
Intermediate-term (recent yields around 4 percent)			
Benham CA Tax-Free Intermediate-Term */**	CA Municipals	0.5%	$1,000
Schwab CA Short-Intermediate Tax-Free *	CA Municipals	0.5%	$1,000
Long-term (recent yields around 4.75 – 5.25 percent)			
Benham CA Tax-Free Long-Term */**	CA Municipals	0.5%	$1,000
Fidelity Spartan CA High-Yield	Lower-quality CA Municipals	0.5%	$10,000
Vanguard CA Tax-Free Insured Long-Term	Insured CA Municipals	0.2%	$3,000
Fidelity Spartan CT Muni High Yield	Lower-quality CT Municipals	0.5%	$10,000
Fidelity MA Tax-Free High Yield	Lower-quality MA Municipals	0.5%	$2,500
Fidelity MI Tax-Free High Yield	Lower-quality MI Municipals	0.6%	$2,500
Fidelity MN Tax-Free	MN Municipals	0.6%	$2,500
Vanguard NJ Tax-Free Insured Long-Term	Insured NJ Municipals	0.2%	$3,000
Vanguard NY Insured Tax-Free	Insured NY Municipals	0.2%	$3,000
Vanguard OH Tax-Free Insured Long-Term	Insured OH Municipals	0.2%	$3,000
Vanguard PA Tax-Free Insured Long-Term	Insured PA Municipals	0.2%	$3,000

* = Available through Schwab without transaction fees (see Chapter 11).
** = Available through Jack White without transaction fees (see Chapter 11).

A number of states do not have bond fund options listed above (some that do may have minimums that are too high for you). In some cases, none exists. In other cases, the funds that are available (and not on the recommended list) for that state have such high annual operating expenses, and therefore such low yields, that you would be better off in the more competitively run federally tax-free only funds listed in Table 12-8.

Federally tax-free only bond funds

Federally tax-free only bond funds (the dividends on them are state taxable) are appropriate when you're in a high federal bracket (28 percent and up) but lower state bracket (less than 5 percent) or when you live in a state that doesn't have state and federally tax-free funds available (see Table 12-7 to make sure).

Table 12-8	Federally Tax-Free Only Bond Funds		
Fund	*Investments*	*Operating Expense*	*Minimum to Open*
Short-term (recent yields around 3 – 3.5 percent)			
Vanguard Muni Short-Term	Municipals	0.2%	$3,000
Vanguard Muni Limited-Term	Municipals	0.2%	$3,000
Intermediate-term (recent yields around 4.5 percent)			
Vanguard Muni Intermediate-Term	Municipals	0.2%	$3,000
Long-term (recent yields around 5 – 5.5 percent)			
Vanguard Muni Insured Long-Term	Insured Municipals	0.2%	$3,000
Vanguard Muni Long-Term	Municipals	0.2%	$3,000
Vanguard Muni High-Yield	Lower-quality Municipals	0.2%	$3,000

Bank certificates of deposit (CDs)

For many decades, bank CDs have been the investment of choice for folks with some extra cash that is not needed in the near-term. The attraction is that you get a higher rate of return on a CD than on a bank savings account or money market fund. And unlike bond funds, your principal does not fluctuate in value.

CDs include a number of drawbacks in comparison to bonds. The first is that your money is not accessible unless you cough up a fairly big penalty — typically six months' interest. With a no-load (commission-free) bond fund, if you need some or all of your money next week, month, or year, you can access it without penalty.

Another and less often noted drawback of CDs is that they only come in one tax flavor — taxable. Bonds, on the other hand, come in tax-free (federal and/or state) and taxable flavors. So if you're a higher tax bracket investor, bonds offer you a tax-friendly option that CDs can't.

As of this writing, for example, banks are paying around 4 percent for a 3- to 5-year CD. On a short- to intermediate-term bond fund, the current yield is around 5 percent.

Much is made, particularly by bankers, of the FDIC insurance that comes with bank CDs. The lack of this insurance on high-quality bonds shouldn't be a big concern. High-quality bonds rarely default; even if a fund held a bond that defaulted, it would probably be a tiny fraction (less than 1 percent) of the value of the fund, so it would have little overall impact.

Besides, the FDIC itself is no Rock of Gibraltar. Banks have failed and will continue to fail. Yes, you are insured if you have less than $100,000 in a bank, but in reality, if the bank crashes, you may have to wait a long time and settle for less interest than you thought you were getting. You are not immune from harm, FDIC or no FDIC.

If the U.S. government backing through FDIC insurance allows you to sleep better, you can invest in treasuries, which are government-backed bonds.

In the long run, you earn more and have better access to your money in bond funds than in CDs. And they make particular sense when you're in a higher tax bracket and would benefit from tax-free income on your investments. If you're not in a high tax bracket (federal 15 percent), and you have a bad day whenever your bond fund takes a dip in value, then consider CDs. Just make sure that you shop around to get the best interest rate.

Stock funds

The stock funds that are appropriate if you're not in a high tax bracket (less than 28 percent federal) are the same as those recommended in Chapter 13 in the section "Great Investment Recipes." **Important Note:** Do not use the recommended "agressive portfolio" at Fidelity because those funds levy sales charges. Choose one of the other investment companies in that section.

Other stock funds are appropriate if you don't want current income or are in a high tax bracket (28 percent and up). Note that all the following listed funds in Table 12-9 are intended as long-term investments. That's because funds that avoid bonds and dividend-producing stocks focus on stocks, particularly those of more growth-oriented companies. If you want other investments that are long-term and tax friendly, try municipal bonds (listed earlier in the chapter).

Table 12-9	Relatively Tax-Friendly Stock Funds						
			Total Return = Distributions + Price Changes through December 1993				
Parent	*Fund*	*Operating Expense*	*1 year*	*3 year*	*5 year*	*10 year*	
U.S. funds							
Fidelity	Fidelity	0.7%	18.4%	16.8%	14.3%	13.6%	
Dodge & Cox	Stock	0.6%	18.4%	16.8%	13.9%	15.4%	
S Dreyfus*/**	Third Century	1.1%	5.3%	14.0%	12.5%	12.1%	
Schwab*	Schwab 1000	0.4%	9.6%	...	...	...	
Vanguard	Index 500	0.2%	9.9%	15.4%	14.3%	14.6%	
Vanguard	Total Stock Index	0.2%	10.6%	...	...	...	
20th Century*/**	Heritage	1.0%	20.4%	21.7%	17.2%	...	
International funds							
Warburg Pincus**	International Equity	1.3%	51.3%	20.4%	...	...	
Vanguard	International Growth	0.6%	44.7%	12.6%	9.4%	17.0%	

* = Available through Schwab without transaction fees
** = Available through Jack White without transaction fees
S = "Socially responsible" (see end of Chapter 11).

Taxes and Mutual Funds

Investors often overlook tax consequences when selecting mutual funds. An increasingly popular investment vehicle, mutual funds hold more than $2 trillion in assets under management. (See Chapter 11 to learn all about mutual funds.)

With more than 4,000 choices available, mutual fund investors face information overload. Avoiding funds with high sales commissions and management fees and poor relative performance is a prudent way to narrow the choices.

The tax implications of a mutual fund's returns are an important factor that should influence your choice of funds. Historically, however, many mutual fund investors and publications have not focused on the tax-friendliness of some mutual funds versus others.

Numerous mutual funds effectively reduce their shareholders' returns because of their tendency to produce more taxable distributions (capital gains and dividends are discussed in Chapter 11). Many mutual fund investors are affected by taxable distributions because more than half the money in mutual funds resides outside tax-sheltered retirement accounts.

"Ranking Mutual Funds on an After-Tax Basis," a pioneering study conducted by John B. Shoven and Joel M. Dickson at Stanford University, found that taxes have an important impact on the relative performance of mutual funds. In particular, the study demonstrated that mutual fund capital gains distributions have a significant impact on an investor's after-tax rate of return. The Shoven and Dickson study found large differences between the before-tax and after-tax rates of return generated by stock mutual funds.

The following example highlights the dangers of picking a stock mutual fund for investment outside retirement accounts simply on the basis of its reported rate of return. Over a recent five-year period, the Founders Special fund averaged a 20.6 percent annual rate of return, outpacing the 20th Century Heritage fund, which averaged 17.6 percent per annum. On the surface, it would seem that Founders is the better of the two funds, beating its rival by 3 percent per year.

But that's only part of the story. All mutual fund managers buy and sell stocks during the course of a year. Whenever a mutual fund manager sells securities, any gain or loss from those securities must be distributed to fund shareholders. Securities sold at a loss can offset those liquidated at a profit.

If a fund manager has a tendency to cash in more winners than losers, significant capital gains distributions can result. Over the past five years, the Founders Special fund has made capital gains distributions averaging a whopping 9.5 percent of shareholder principal per year. The 20th Century Heritage fund, on the other hand, has averaged just 3.3 percent in annual capital gains distributions.

Thus, more of the 20th Century funds gains showed up in an appreciating share price of its fund, which allows more of its gains to compound effectively without taxation over time. Nearly half of the Founders fund total return has been distributed as taxable gains to its shareholders, which reduces their returns.

Choosing mutual funds that minimize capital gains distributions helps fund investors to defer taxes on their profits. By allowing their capital to continue compounding as it would in an IRA or other retirement account, fund shareholders receive a higher total return.

In addition to capital gains distributions, mutual funds also produce dividends that may be subject to higher income tax rates for some investors due to 1993 tax law changes (both for high-income earners and social security recipients).

Long-term investors benefit most from choosing mutual funds that minimize capital gains distributions. The more years that appreciation can compound without being taxed, the greater the value to the fund investor.

Investors who purchase mutual funds outside tax-sheltered retirement accounts should also consider the time of year they purchase shares in funds. December is the most common month in which mutual funds make capital gains distributions. When making purchases late in the year, investors may want to find out if and when the fund may make a significant capital gains distribution.

Index mutual funds

Some funds have a greater tendency to produce capital gains distributions. Actively managed portfolios, in their attempts to increase their shareholders' returns, buy and sell individual securities more frequently. This process increases the chances of the fund needing to make significant capital gains distributions.

Index funds are mutual funds that invest in a relatively fixed portfolio of securities. They don't attempt to beat the market. Rather, they invest in the securities to mirror the performance of an underlying index.

In an actively managed fund, in contrast to an index fund, a portfolio management team tries to identify those issues likely to outperform its peers. They constantly make changes in the portfolio in an attempt to always hold the best available securities.

Although index funds cannot beat the market, they have several advantages over actively managed funds. First, because they trade less than an actively managed fund, index-fund investors benefit from lower brokerage commissions. Secondly, because significant ongoing research need not be conducted to identify companies to invest in, index funds can be run at far lower operating expenses. All things being equal, lower brokerage and operating costs translate into higher shareholder returns.

Finally, because index funds trade less, they tend to produce lower capital gains distributions. For mutual funds held outside tax-sheltered retirement accounts, this reduced trading effectively increases an investor's total rate of return.

A recent study in the *Journal of Portfolio Management* demonstrated that only 21 percent of stock mutual funds outperformed an index fund over a 10-year period before taxes were considered, and only 7 percent outperformed an index fund after factoring in taxes. In other words, over this decade, an index fund outperformed more than three-quarters of large stock funds before taxes and more than nine out of ten funds on an after-tax basis.

Vanguard index funds

The Vanguard Group (800-662-7447), headquartered in Valley Forge, Pennsylvania, is the largest mutual-fund provider of index funds with about $20 billion in index funds. The challenge is choosing among all the different index funds they offer.

- ✓ **Vanguard Total Bond Index** tracks the overall performance of the bond market.

- ✓ **Vanguard Index 500** tracks the 500 largest traded company stocks that comprise the S&P 500 index. These companies account for about 80 percent of the total market value of securities outstanding.

- ✓ **Vanguard Index Total Stock Market** tracks, just as its name suggests, the overall performance of all stocks (there are about 5,000 of them!) that trade on the U.S. stock exchanges.

I don't recommend Vanguard's International Index funds (Pacific Basin and European Index funds). These indexes are weighted by the total market value of stocks in the respective regions they cover. The Pacific Fund has more than 80 percent of its assets in Japan, for example, which defeats the purpose of diversifying among different countries in an international stock fund. It also causes the fund to be more heavily invested in higher-priced (and perhaps more overpriced) markets.

Schwab index funds

San Francisco-based Charles Schwab & Co. (800-526-8600) offers tax-friendly stock index funds. What makes the Schwab Index funds tax-friendly is that whenever its fund managers need to sell securities because of changes in the index or shareholder redemptions, they make sure to offset capital gains with losses. The fund can achieve this result by having the flexibility to temporarily deviate from index weightings by small amounts.

- ✔ **The Schwab 1000 Fund** tracks an index, like other index funds. The Schwab 1000 fund invests in 1,000 of America's largest publicly traded companies, comprising nearly 90 percent of the total U.S. stock market value.

- ✔ **The Schwab Small-Cap Index Fund** tracks the performance of an index of the second 1,000 largest publicly traded U.S. companies.

- ✔ **The Schwab International Equity Index** tracks an index of 350 large companies overseas (excluding South Africa).

(The last two came off the assembly line in 1993.)

Choosing between Vanguard and Schwab stock index funds is difficult. Schwab's funds are a bit more tax-friendly but charge slightly higher annual operating expenses. The funds track different indexes, so it's difficult to do an apples-to-apples comparison of Vanguard and Schwab offerings. Take your pick — they're both good options. (For investing within retirement accounts, which is discussed fully in the next chapter, Vanguard's lower-cost funds win out.)

Real estate

Real estate can be a financially and psychologically rewarding investment. It can also be a money pit and a real headache if you buy the wrong property or get a tenant from hell. (I discuss real estate as an investment in complete detail in Chapter 15.)

Annuities

Discussed in detail in Chapter 8, *annuities* are accounts that are partly insurance but mostly investment. You should only contribute to one after you've exhausted contributions to retirement accounts. Because annuities carry higher annual operating expenses than comparable mutual funds, you should only consider them if you plan to leave your money invested for at least ten years and preferably 15 or more years.

The best annuities can be purchased from no-load (commission-free) mutual fund companies — specifically Vanguard (800-662-7447) and Fidelity (800-544-8888). See Chapter 13 for asset allocation recommendations.

Small-business investments

Investing in your own business or someone else's established small business can be a high-risk but potentially high-return investment. The best options are those you understand well. If you hear of a great business idea or company from someone you know and trust, do your research and make your best judgment — it may well be a terrific investment vehicle. But keep in mind that people are always willing to take more risk with other people's money than with their own, and that many well-intentioned people fail at their businesses.

Before investing in a project, ask to see a copy of the business plan. Talk to others not involved with the investment about the idea and learn from their comments and concerns (but don't forget that many a wise person has rained on the parade of what turned out to be a terrific business idea).

Beyond Entrepreneurship by James C. Collins, one of the best books written on entrepreneurship, documents great business ideas that weren't recognized as such early on. Steve Jobs, who founded Apple Computer, was turned down by Atari when he approached them with his idea for a personal computer. Hewlett-Packard also spurned his overtures, reminding him that he hadn't got through college yet. Fred Smith, who founded the overnight delivery service company Federal Express, received a "C" as a grade on a paper he wrote about the idea while in a Yale School of Management course. His professor said, "The concept is interesting and well formed, but in order to earn better than a 'C,' the idea must be feasible."

Avoid limited partnerships and other small-company investments pitched by brokers, financial planners, and the like. They want you to buy these because they earn a hefty commission from them. These brokers and planners usually find you by cold calling. You're much better off with no-load mutual fund investments.

Note: A provision in the 1993 tax law allows investors to exclude half of their capital gains (profits) from investments held for five or more years in small businesses valued at less than $50 million. With the maximum federal capital gains rate at 28 percent, this new provision lowers the capital gains tax to 14 percent. So, if you have a knack for identifying up-and-coming entrepreneurs, you may be able to make rewarding investments that aren't too taxing.

Chapter 13

Investing Money
Inside Retirement Accounts

. . . .

In This Chapter

▶ Investments to avoid in retirement accounts

▶ Understanding asset allocation

▶ How to allocate money in employer-sponsored plans

▶ How to allocate in plans that you design

▶ How to transfer retirement accounts

▶ Some great investment combinations

. . . .

*T*his chapter explains how to make decisions about investing money you currently hold in retirement accounts or plan to contribute to a retirement account. It also includes specific mutual fund recommendations.

For two main reasons, it's generally easier to invest money that's *inside* tax-sheltered retirement accounts such as Individual Retirement Accounts (IRAs), 401(k)s, SEP-IRAs, and Keoghs:

✔ **Money inside retirement accounts compounds and grows without taxation.** You only pay taxes on these funds when you withdraw money from the account (direct transfers to another investment firm are not withdrawals, so they are not taxed). Therefore, you need not concern yourself about the taxability of distributions, such as dividends and capital gains, that retirement account investments may produce. All you have to worry about is selecting investments that meet your needs and comfort level with taking risks.

✔ **The range of possible retirement account investments is more limited.** You can ignore "tax-free" bonds, for example. Direct investments, such as real estate and investments in small, privately owned companies, are not available or accessible in most retirement accounts.

Nevertheless, there are a few areas in which you should be cautious of retirement investing.

Inappropriate Retirement Account Investments

Financial advisors and other "experts" typically have no shortage of opinions about what they consider to be good investments. Some say that you should invest more heavily in the stock market for long-term growth potential. Others suggest being more conservative and diversifying into bonds, real estate, and precious metals. These may be good guidelines for you, depending on your goals, your financial situation, and the reliability of your friendly advisor.

Some investments for retirement accounts are simply inappropriate. The basic problem stems from otherwise intelligent folks forgetting, ignoring, or simply not knowing that retirement accounts are sheltered from taxation.

You should *not* make the following investments in retirement accounts.

Tax-free bonds

Investments that produce income that is tax-free either at the federal or state level don't make much sense inside retirement accounts. Tax-free securities always yield less than their taxable counterparts, so you are essentially giving away free yield.

Treasuries — that is, treasury bills, notes, or bonds — are a good example of investments that are purchased too frequently inside retirement accounts. (I've never understood why investors think that lending their money to the U.S. government, an organization with more than $4 trillion in debt outstanding, is 100-percent safe.) When you buy treasuries, you get the safety net of a government guarantee, but you also get a bond that produces interest that is free of state tax.

Although treasuries can't be called in for redemption before maturity, their safety can easily be replicated in other bonds. As you've learned by now, those fully taxable bonds yield more than state tax-free treasuries.

Some diversified mutual funds invest a portion of their funds in treasuries. Holding such a fund is not a mistake as long as the portion in these tax-free holdings is less than about 20 – 30 percent of the portfolio. Avoid funds that have the majority or all of their assets in treasuries. A surprising number of company retirement plans offer treasury mutual funds (which are nearly all treasuries) as an investment option. If you are in this situation, buy a copy of this book for your company's benefits department!

An even bigger no-no (but, thankfully, a much less common mistake) is investing in municipal bonds inside a retirement account. Municipals are free from federal and/or state taxation. As such, they yield significantly less than an equivalent bond that pays fully taxable dividends. They definitely don't belong in a retirement account. The better investment firms don't let you make this mistake.

Annuities

Annuities, an oddball investment discussed in Chapters 8, should have no place inside of retirement accounts, either. Annuities allow your investment dollars to compound without taxation. In comparison to other investments that don't allow such tax deferral, annuities carry much higher annual operating expenses, which depress your returns.

Purchasing an annuity inside an IRA, 401(k), or other type of retirement account is like wearing a belt and suspenders together. Either you have a peculiar sense of style, or you are spending too much time worrying about your pants falling down. In my experience, people who make this investment mistake frequently have been misled into it by investment salespeople.

Annuities pay hefty commissions, sometimes as high as 10 percent or more of the amount invested. In some cases, I think, the salespeople aren't being conniving and unethical — they just don't know any better. The insurance companies behind these products, in their enthusiasm to pump up salespeople to peddle them, conveniently skip over the details about when it's inappropriate to invest in annuites.

If you work for a nonprofit organization, your employer may allow you to contribute some of your paycheck into tax-sheltered annuities (TSAs). Don't, if you have other options. TSAs are also inferior investment choices. Since 1986, the tax laws allow nonprofit employees to invest their retirement money in mutual funds. Well-managed no-load (commission-free) funds have lower operating expenses and other advantages over TSAs. I discuss nonprofit retirement plans, known as 403(b) plans, later in the chapter.

Limited partnerships

Limited partnerships, which are sold through investment salespeople, are treacherous, high-commission, and high-cost investments. Part of their supposed allure, however, are the tax benefits they generate. But when you buy and hold a limited partnership in a retirement account, you lose the ability to take advantage of many of the tax deductions. This is another one of the many reasons to avoid investing in limited partnerships.

Asset Allocation: Spreading It Around

In almost any type of retirement account, you have investment options. Most people get a big headache when they try to decide how to spread their money across those choices. (If you have to select the investment options yourself, such as in a self-employed SEP-IRA or Keogh plan, you've got other decisions to make as well. More on this aspect later in this chapter.)

The specific amounts that you decide to invest into the different options is known as *asset allocation*. This important buzzword is thrown around a lot in the financial pages. I explain it in more detail later in this chapter. (I don't mean to keep you in suspense, but I have my reasons — your patience will be rewarded.)

Suggested asset allocations

With good reason, people are concerned about placing their retirement account money in investments that can decline in value. You may feel that you're gambling with dollars intended for the security of your golden years.

Many working folks have time and need to make this money grow. You may have 15 – 20 years or more before you need to draw on the bulk of your retirement account assets. If some of your investments drop a bit over a year or two, what's the big deal as long as the value of your investments has time to recover?

Your current age and the number of years until you retire should be the biggest factors in your allocation decision. The younger you are and the more years you have before retirement, the more comfortable you should be with growth-oriented (and more volatile) investments, such as stock funds.

Table 13-1 lists some guidelines for allocating retirement account money. All you need to figure out is how old you are and the level of risk you're comfortable with.

Table 13-1	Allocating Retirement Account Money	
Your Investment Attitude	*Bond Allocation (%)*	*Stock Allocation (%)*
"Play it safe"	= Age	= 100 – age
"Middle of the road"	= Age – 10	= 110 – age
"Aggressive"	= Age – 20	= 120 – age

For example, if you're the conservative sort who doesn't like a lot of risk but recognize the value of striving for some growth to make your money work harder, you're a *middle-of-the-road* type. Using the preceding table, if you're 40 years old, you might consider putting 30 percent (40 – 10) in bonds and 70 percent (110 – 40) in stocks.

If your plan includes more than one stock mutual fund as an option, you may want to try discerning which options are best by using criteria outlined in Chapter 11. If it's safe to assume that all your retirement plan's stock fund options are good, you can simply divide your stock allocation equally among the choices.

If one or more of the choices is an international stock fund, consider allocating at least 20 percent (*play it safe*) of your stock fund money (not the total), 35 percent for *middle-of-the-road* to as much as 50 percent (*aggressive*) overseas.

If, in Table 13-1, the 40-year-old, middle-of-the-road type is investing 70 percent in stocks, then about 35 percent of the stock fund investments (which works out to be around 25 percent of the total) could be invested in international stock funds.

Historically, most employees haven't had to make their own investing decisions with retirement money. Pension plans, in which the company directs the investments, were more common in previous years. It's interesting to note that in a typical pension plan, companies choose to allocate the majority of money to stocks (about 50 percent), with a bit less in bonds (about 35 percent) and other investments.

Allocating money in plans where your employer selects the investment options

In some company-sponsored plans, such as 401(k)s, you are limited to the predetermined investment options your employer offers.

Plans differ in the specific options they offer, but the basic choices are the following:

Money market/savings accounts

These do not fluctuate in value and, at the time of this writing, yield around 2.5 – 3 percent. You have no risk of losing money because these accounts don't drop in value. However, there is the risk that your investment will not keep up with or stay ahead of inflation and taxes (which are due upon withdrawal of your money from the retirement account).

One reason you might utilize this option if you already have a large lump of money accumulated is that you're cautious about investing too quickly in riskier investments. For regular contributions coming out your paycheck, this choice makes little sense.

If you utilize the borrowing feature that some retirement plans allow, you may need to keep money in the money market investment option. You may want to utilize it also if you plan to leave soon and want your money safe and secure in preparation for its upcoming move.

Bond mutual funds

Bond mutual funds invest in a mixture of typically high-quality bonds (described in Chapter 11). Bonds pay a higher rate of interest or dividends than do money funds. Depending on whether your plan's option is a short-term, intermediate-term, or long-term fund, the current yield is probably in the neighborhood of 4.5 – 6.5 percent.

Bond funds carry higher yields than money funds, but they also carry greater risk because their value can fall if interest rates increase. However, bonds tend to be more stable in value than stocks. As I discussed in the last section, aggressive, younger investors should keep a minimum amount of money in these funds, whereas older folks who want to invest more conservatively may want to invest more money this way.

Guaranteed-investment contracts (GICs)

GICs are backed by an insurance company and typically quote you a rate of return projected one or a few years forward. The return is always positive and certain — thus there's none of the uncertainty that you would normally face with bond or stock investments (unless, of course, the insurance company fails).

The attraction of these investments is that your account value does not fluctuate (at least, not that you can see). The insurance company normally invests your money mostly in bonds and maybe a bit in stocks. The difference between what these investments generate for the insurer and what they pay you in interest is profit to the insurer. The yield is usually comparable to that of a bond fund.

For people who would hit the eject button the moment a bond fund slides a bit in value, GICs are soothing to the nerves. And they're certainly better than a money market or savings account in yield — usually 2 – 3 percent higher.

Like bonds, however, GICs don't give you the opportunity for long-term growth of your money. And over the long haul, you should earn a better return in a mixture of bond and stock investments. You pay for the peace of mind in the form of lower long-term returns by having a return guaranteed in advance. GICs also have the minor drawback: Insurance companies, unlike mutual funds, can and do fail, putting GIC investment dollars at risk.

Balanced mutual funds

Balanced mutual funds invest in a mixture primarily of stocks and bonds. This one-stop shopping concept makes investing easier and smoothes out fluctuations in the value of your investments — funds investing exclusively in stocks or in bonds make for a rougher ride.

These funds are solid options and, in fact, can be used for the majority of your retirement plan contributions.

Stock mutual funds

Stock mutual funds invest in stocks, which usually provide greater long-term growth potential but also wider fluctuations in value from year to year. Some companies offer a number of different stock funds, including those investing overseas. Unless you plan to borrow against your funds for a home purchase (if your plan allows), you probably should have a healthy helping of stock funds.

Stock in the company you work for

Some companies offer employees the option of investing in the company's stock. I generally advocate avoiding this option for the simple reason that your future income and other employee benefits are already riding on the success of the company. If the company hits the skids, you may lose your job and your benefits. You certainly don't want the value of your retirement account to be dependent on the same factors.

If you think that your company has its act together and the stock is a good buy, investing a portion of your retirement account is fine — but no more than 25 percent. Don't forget that lots of smart investors track companies' fortunes, so odds are that the value of your company's stock is pretty fair. If you can buy the stock at a discount as compared to its current market value, so much the better.

Allocating money in plans that you design

With self-employed plans (SEP-IRAs and Keoghs), certain 403(b) plans for nonprofit employees, and IRAs, you get to select the investment options as well as the allocation of money among them.

In the sections that follow, I discuss the best investment options for these plans, organized by which investment firm you use for your investments. (Profiles of the best investment firms and background information about understanding mutual funds is provided in Chapter 11.)

To determine the percentage allocations to be made among the different funds recommended in this section, read the preceding section "Suggested asset allocations." But before I get into specific investment recommendations, let me deal with some common questions that you may have regarding how many investment firms you should use and how, if the need arises, to transfer your accounts.

Transferring retirement accounts

With the exception of plans maintained by your employer that limit your investment options, such as 401(k)s, you can move your money held in SEP-IRAs, Keoghs, IRAs, and many 403(b) plans (also known as *tax-sheltered annuities*) to most any major investment firm you please. Moving the money is pretty simple. If you can dial an 800 number, fill out a couple of short forms, and send them back in a postage-paid envelope, you can transfer an account. The investment firm to which you are transferring your account does the rest.

Here's a step-by-step list of what you need to do to transfer a retirement account to another investment firm. Even if you're working with a financial advisor, you should be aware of this process to ensure that no hanky-panky takes place on the advisor's part:

1. **Decide where you want to move the account.**

   The best investment companies are profiled in Chapter 11, and specific investment options within those firms are recommended in the next section of this chapter.

2. **Obtain an account application and asset transfer form.** Call the 800 number of the firm you are transferring the money to and ask for an *account application and asset transfer form* for the type of account you are transferring — for example, SEP-IRA, Keogh, IRA, or 403(b).

   Note: It's important to ask for the form for the *same* type of account you currently have at the company from which you are transferring the money. You can determine the account type by looking at a recent account statement — it should say near the top of the form or in the section with your name and address. If you can't figure it out on a cryptic statement, call the firm where the account is currently held and ask a representative what type of account you have by referencing your account number.

3. **Complete the account application and asset transfer form.** Completing these for your new investment firm opens your new account and authorizes the transfer.

You shouldn't take possession of the money in your account yourself to get it over to the new firm. The tax authorities impose huge penalties if you do a transfer incorrectly. It's far easier and safer to let the company to which you're transferring the money do the transfer for you.

If you have questions or problems, the firm(s) to which you are transferring your account have armies of capable employees waiting to help you. Remember, these firms know that you are transferring your money to them, so they roll out the red carpet.

If you deal with a firm that has local branch offices, such as Fidelity or Schwab, a representative at the branch can help you prepare the paperwork for the transfer. Just remember to bring along a recent statement for the account you plan to transfer.

4. **Figure out what securities you'll transfer and which need to be liquidated.** Transferring existing investments in your account to a new investment firm can cause problems. If you're transferring cash (money market accounts) or securities that trade on any of the major stock exchanges, it's not a problem.

If you own publicly traded securities, it's often better to transfer them *as is* to your new investment firm, especially if it offers discount brokerage services. You can then sell your securities through that firm more cheaply.

If you own mutual funds unique to the institution you're leaving, check with your new firm to see if it can accept them. If not, you need to call the firm that currently holds them to sell them.

CDs are tricky to transfer. Ideally, you should send in the transfer forms a month or so before they mature — few people do this. If the CD matures soon, call the bank and instruct them that when the CD matures, you would like the funds to be invested in a savings or money market account that you can access without penalty when your transfer request lands in the mailbox.

5. **(Optional) Let the firm out of which you're transferring the money know that you are doing so.**

If the place you're transferring from doesn't assign a specific person to your account, definitely skip this step. If you're moving your investments from a brokerage firm where you've dealt with a particular broker, the decision is more difficult.

Most people feel obligated to let their representative know that they are moving their money. In my experience, calling the person with the bad news is usually a mistake. Brokers or others who have a direct financial stake in your decision to move your money will try to sell you on staying. Some may try to make you feel guilty for leaving, and some may even try to bully you.

It may seem the coward's way out to write a letter, but writing usually makes it easier on both sides. You can polish what you have to say, and you don't put the broker on the defensive. Or (although I don't mean to encourage lying) it *may* be better not to tell the *whole* truth. Excuses such as you think you have a family member in the investment business who will manage your money for free may help ease the pain in leaving.

Then again, telling an investment firm that its charges are too high or that it has sold you a bunch of lousy investments that it misrepresented may help the firm to improve in the future. Don't fret too much — do what's best for you and what you're comfortable with. Brokers are not your friends. Even though they may know your kids' names, your favorite hobbies, and your birthday, it is a *business* relationship.

6. **Mail the completed account application and transfer forms to your new investment company.**

Transferring your existing assets typically takes a month to complete.

Never, ever sign over assets such as checks and security certificates to a financial advisor, no matter how trustworthy and honest he or she may seem. The advisor could abscond with them quicker than you can say Bonnie and Clyde. Transfers should not be completed this way. It's much more of a hassle.

7. **If the transfer is not completed within a month, get in touch with your new investment firm to determine what the problem is.**

If your old company is not cooperating, a call to a manager there may help to get the ball rolling. The unfortunate reality is that investment firms will cheerfully set up a new account to *accept* your money on a moment's notice, but they will drag their feet, sometimes for months, when it comes time to relinquish your money. To light a fire under their behinds, tell a manager at the old firm that you're sending letters to the National Association of Securities Dealers (NASD) and the Securities and Exchange Commission (SEC) if they don't complete your transfer within the next week.

Transferring retirement accounts from an employer (lump sum distributions)

If you leave a job, you are confronted with a slightly different transfer challenge: moving money from an employer plan into one of your own retirement accounts. Typically, employer retirement plan money can be rolled over into your own IRA. Check with your employer's benefits department or a tax advisor for details.

Should I use one investment firm or more than one?

The recommended firms listed at the end of this chapter offer a large enough variety of investment options, managed by different fund managers, that you can feel comfortable concentrating your money at one firm. The advantages of a focused approach are less administrative hassles and the need to learn the nuances and choices of just one firm.

You may want to invest through a number of the different firms if you like the idea of spreading your money around. If you use a discount broker like Charles Schwab or Jack White, you can have your cake and eat it, too. You can diversify across different mutual fund companies through one brokerage firm, but you pay small transaction fees to do so on some of your purchases and sales of funds. (See Chapter 11 for more information about how the discount brokerage firms mutual fund services operate.)

A relatively new tax law requires employers to withhold 20 percent of your retirement account as a tax when you receive the money from your plan. So, if you intend to put your money into an IRA (a wise tax move), and you take possession of your retirement money, you must come up with the 20 percent that your employer withheld. You must wait to be reimbursed by the government for this 20 percent until you file your annual tax return.

Never take possession of money from your employer's retirement plan. To avoid the 20 percent tax withholding and a lot of other hassles, simply inform your employer where you want your money to be sent. Prior to doing so, you should establish an appropriate account (an IRA, for example) at the investment firm you intend to use. Then tell your employer's benefits department what investment firm you would like your retirement money transferred to. Ideally, you can send your employer a copy of your account statement, which contains the investment firm's mailing address, your account number, and so on.

When you leave a job, particularly if you are retiring or being laid off after many years of service, money-hungry brokers and financial planners probably will be on you like a pack of bears on a tree leaking sweet honey. It's fine to want to get help with your investments. (Just be sure to read Chapter 3 to avoid the pitfalls in hiring financial help.)

Great Investment Recipes

When you invest money in retirement accounts, you don't have to worry about taxes on the distributions that your investments may be producing. The distributions, as well as the growth on your investments, are tax-sheltered.

Therefore, the appropriate investments for you to consider are the same investments discussed in Chapter 12 that were okay to use if you didn't have to worry about taxable distributions. The only major change is that more Fidelity funds are included in the following list of stock funds. Because Fidelity Investments, the giant mutual fund company, waves sales commissions on many of their better stock funds when you invest in them in retirement accounts, more Fidelity funds are included in the following list of stock funds. You can use the list of taxable bond funds in Table 12-5 in Chapter 12.

You can create your own mix of mutual funds by using the guidelines in the "Suggested asset allocations" section earlier in this chapter. In the sections that follow, I give some specific recipes that you may find useful for investing at the premier investment companies I profile in Chapter 11.

Note: For each firm, I recommend a conservative and an aggressive portfolio. These terms are used in a relative sense. Because some of the recommended funds do not maintain fixed percentages of their different types of investments, the actual percentage of stocks and bonds that you'll end up with may vary slightly from the targeted percentages. Don't sweat it.

Where you have more than one fund choice, you can pick one or do them all and split the suggested percentage between them. If you don't have enough money today to divide it up as I suggest, you can achieve the desired split over time as you add more money to your retirement accounts.

Fidelity

The following two Fidelity (800-544-8888) recommendations are for a conservative mix and an aggressive mix.

A conservative portfolio with 50 percent stocks, 50 percent bonds

Fidelity Balanced — 1/3

Fidelity Puritan — 1/3

Fidelity Asset Manager — 1/3

An aggressive portfolio with 80 percent stocks, 20 percent bonds

Fidelity Balanced — 35 percent

Fidelity Contrafund — 20 percent

Fidelity OTC and/or Low-Priced Stock — 25 percent

Fidelity International Growth & Income — 20 percent

Vanguard

The following two Vanguard (800-662-7447) recommendations are for a conservative mix and an aggressive mix.

A conservative portfolio with 50 percent stocks, 50 percent bonds

Vanguard Total Bond Index — 25 percent

Vanguard Wellesley Income — 25 percent

Vanguard Asset Allocation — 30 percent

Vanguard International Growth — 20 percent

An aggressive portfolio with 80 percent stocks, 20 percent bonds

Vanguard Star — 50 percent

Vanguard Total Stock Market Index — 10 percent

Vanguard International Growth — 40 percent

Charles Schwab or Jack White

The following recommendations are for a conservative mix and an aggressive mix from either Charles Schwab or Jack White.

A conservative portfolio with 50 percent stocks, 50 percent bonds

Benham Adjustable Rate Government Securities — 20 percent

PIMCO Low Duration — 20 percent

Fidelity Balanced — 20 percent

Neuberger & Berman Partners and/or Fidelity Fund — 25 percent

T. Rowe Price International Stock and/or Warburg Pincus International Equity — 15 percent

An aggressive portfolio with 80 percent stocks, 20 percent bonds

PIMCO Total Return — 20 percent

Twentieth Century Heritage and/or Columbia Special — 40 percent

Warburg Pincus International Equity and/or Oakmark International and/or Vanguard International Growth — 40 percent

Issues Unique to 403 (b) Plans

Note: 403(b) plans are retirement savings plans available through nonprofit organizations. If you don't work for such an organization, you may as well skip this last part of the chapter.

Fidelity and Vanguard are terrific firms to invest in with 403(b) accounts (specific fund recommendations are given earlier in the chapter for investing at Fidelity and Vanguard). Schwab and other discount brokers don't offer 403(b)s. However, if you have a 403(b) or tax-sheltered annuity to which you are no longer contributing, you can roll over this money into an IRA account through one of these firms or another mutual fund company.

No-load (no sales charges) mutual funds are superior investment vehicles compared to insurance company annuities on several fronts:

- ✔ Mutual fund companies have a longer and more successful investment track record than do insurance companies, many of which have only recently entered the mutual fund arena.

- ✔ Insurance annuities charge higher annual operating expenses, often two to three times that of no-load mutual funds, which reduces your returns.

- ✔ Insurance company insolvency can risk the safety of your investment in an annuity, whereas the value of a mutual fund depends only on the value of the securities in the fund.

- ✔ Insurance annuities come with severe charges and fees for early surrender; 403(b) plans with mutual funds do not.

With some 403(b) plans, you may borrow against your fund balance without penalty. If this capability is important to you, check with your employer to see whether it allows you to borrow without penalty. Although many insurance annuities advertise borrowing as an advantage, it is also a drawback because it may encourage you to raid your retirement savings.

Chapter 14

Investing for Educational Expenses

● ●

In This Chapter
- ▶ The right and wrong ways to save
- ▶ How the financial aid system works
- ▶ How will you pay for college when the time comes?
- ▶ Determining how much Junior's education is going to run you
- ▶ Calculating how much to save
- ▶ Good and bad investments for educational costs

● ●

*I*f you're like most parents, just turning to this chapter makes you tense and anxious. That feeling is understandable. Much of what you read about educational expenses, particularly college expenses, says that if costs keep rising at the current rate, it's going to cost you several hundred thousand dollars to give your youngster a quality education.

It need not, and probably won't, cost you as much as these gargantuan projections suggest.

Whether you've already started saving or are about to begin a regular college investment plan, odds are quite high your emotions are leading you astray. The hype about educational costs may scare you into taking a path that is less financially beneficial than others that are available.

The Biggest Mistake Nonwealthy Parents Make when Saving for Their Kids' Education

If you're a parent, it's a given that you want what's best for your children. Not only do you want to be able to provide good learning opportunities for them when they are young, but you also want to give them choices. When little Homer and Gwendolyn are filling out their college applications, you don't want to have to say that you can't afford to send them to their dream school.

Being considerate and thoughtful parents, you may start investing money in a separate account for them, perhaps in their name or through some other financial product, such as a life insurance policy. Doing so is usually a financial mistake of major proportions in the short- and long-term.

I know you're going to think that my idea sounds selfish — I admit that on the surface it does seem that way. But you have to provide for your own financial security *before* saving for your child. Let me explain.

Think back to your most recent trip by airplane. Remember what the flight attendants instructed you to do in an emergency? In the event of a loss of air pressure that necessitates the use of oxygen masks, you are instructed to put your oxygen mask on *first*. Only then should you help your children with their oxygen masks.

Consider for a moment why they recommend this approach. Your instinct may be to ensure that your children are safe before taking care of yourself, but by taking care of yourself first, you are stronger and better able to help your children.

Similarly, in regard to your personal finances, you need to take care of yourself first. You should be saving and investing through retirement-type accounts that give you significant tax benefits. Your initial contributions to a 401(k), SEP-IRA, Keogh, or other retirement account (described in Chapter 8) are usually tax-deductible. An additional and substantial benefit is that once your money is placed in these accounts, it grows and compounds without taxation until you withdraw it.

The mistake many, particularly middle-class, parents make is saving for future educational expenses by putting money in accounts in their child's name (called *custodial accounts*) or saving outside retirement accounts in general. You receive no tax deduction on your contributions to these accounts. And as I discuss later, the more money you accumulate outside tax-sheltered retirement accounts, the less assistance you're likely to qualify for from federal and state sources.

Take care of your long-term financial needs (for example, saving through tax-advantaged retirement accounts) first. By doing so, you strengthen your financial health, which better enables you to help your kids with their educational expenses in the long run. (See Chapter 8 to learn how to save for retirement and reduce your taxes.)

How the Financial Aid System Works

Just as your child shouldn't choose a college based solely on whether she thinks she can get in, she shouldn't choose a college on the basis of whether you think you can afford it. Everyone should apply for financial aid. More than a few parents who don't think that they qualify for financial aid are pleasantly surprised to find that they have access to loans as well as grants (free money you don't pay back).

The first step in the financial aid process is to complete the Free Application for Federal Student Aid (FAFSA), which is available from any high school or college. As its name makes clear, you pay nothing for submitting this application other than the time it takes to complete the paperwork (it takes more time than watching a TV sitcom but probably less time than it takes to get a driver's license). Some private colleges also require that you complete the Financial Aid Form (FAF), which asks for more information than the FAFSA.

States have their own financial aid programs, so check with your local high school or college financial aid office to get the forms to apply to these as well. Some colleges also require submission of supplementary forms directly to them.

The data you supply through student aid forms is run through a *financial needs analysis,* a standard methodology approved by Congress. The needs analysis considers a number of factors, such as parents' income and assets, age and need for retirement income, number of dependents, number of family members in college, and unusual financial circumstances, which you explain on the application.

The needs analysis calculates how much money you, the parent(s), and your child, the student, can be expected to contribute toward educational expenses.

Even if the needs analysis determines that you don't qualify for "needs-based" financial aid, you will still have access to loans that are *not* based on need if you go through the financial aid application process. (The guidelines for who qualifies as needy are determined by Congress. You may feel needy, but if the folks back in Washington don't agree, you can't tap into some government loan programs' resources.)

Treatment of retirement accounts

Under the current needs analysis, the value of your retirement plans is *not* considered an asset. Money that you save *outside* retirement accounts, including money in the child's name, is counted as an asset and reduces your eligibility for financial aid.

Therefore, it does not make sense to forego contributions to your retirement savings plans in order to save money in a taxable account for Junior's college fund. When you do, you pay higher taxes both on your current income and on the interest and growth of this money. In addition to paying higher taxes, you are expected to contribute more to your child's educational expenses.

Comparing the plans of the Selfish family and the Good Intentions family

Imagine two families, the Selfish family and the Good Intentions family, both of whom live in identical neighborhoods. They own identical homes that they purchased at exactly the same cost. They have identical mortgages and identical jobs that pay the same salaries.

Both families give birth to twin children on the same day. The only financial difference between these two families is that the Good Intentions family starts saving $100 per month in a non-retirement account when their twins are born to help pay for the children's future college expenses. (Because they have to pay income tax on this money, the Good Intentions family is actually putting only about $63 per month per child to work.)

The Selfish family saves the same amount, $100 per child per month, in their retirement savings plans. Because they pay no federal and state tax

income tax on this money, all of their contributions go to work in the retirement savings plan.

Assuming that both families' investments average an 8-percent-per-year rate of return before taxes, the Good Intentions family ends up with about $22,100 per child when the kids turn 18. The Selfish family, on the other hand, has more than $48,500 per child when their twins celebrate their 18th birthdays.

Apart from deciding where to invest money for college, these two families continue to live parallel financial lives in every other way. When the children of the two families apply for financial aid, however, the Selfish family kids qualify for a good deal more aid. The Selfish family actually holds higher assets, but given the current financial aid criteria and regulations, the Good Intentions family looks wealthier on paper because they hold more money outside their retirement accounts.

Treatment of money in the kids' names

If you plan to apply for financial aid, it's a good idea to save money in your name rather than in your children's names (custodial accounts). Colleges expect a much greater percentage of money in your child's name (35 percent) to be used for college costs than money in your name (6 percent).

If you're affluent enough that you expect to pay for your kid's entire educational costs, investing through custodial accounts can save you on taxes. Prior to your child reaching age 14, the first $1,200 of interest and dividend income is taxed at your child's income tax rate rather than yours. After age 14, *all* income generated by investments in your child's name is taxed at your child's rate.

Treatment of home equity and other assets

Your family's assets also include equity in real estate and businesses you own. Although the federal financial aid analysis no longer counts equity in your primary residence as an asset, many private (independent) schools continue to ask parents for this information when making their own financial aid determinations. Thus, paying down your home mortgage more quickly instead of funding retirement accounts can harm you financially. You may end up with less financial aid and pay more in taxes.

The need to reform the financial aid system

The fact that the financial aid system treats assets differently when held outside rather than inside retirement accounts should encourage you to save for retirement. The more money you stash in retirement accounts, the greater your chances of qualifying for financial aid and the more money you qualify for. Saving inside retirement accounts is not selfish — it's financially responsible and beneficial to your children.

The federal government could support saving for retirement and education by revising the tax code to allow parents to take money out of tax-sheltered retirement accounts without penalty when used for paying educational expenses.

Another inequity in the current financial aid determination process is that it makes no allowance for differences in the cost of living across the country. If you live in a high-cost urban area, such as New York, Los Angeles, or San Francisco, the financial aid system makes the erroneous assumption that you are able to live on and contribute the same amount for college costs as someone with equivalent income who lives in a low-cost rural area. Some adjustment for differences in cost of living should be considered in the system.

How Will I Pay for Educational Expenses?

Now you're probably wondering how you'll come up with money to pay for education if you keep stashing away money in retirement accounts. Terrific question.

There isn't one correct answer, because it depends on your unique situation. But in most cases, even if you have some liquid cash that can be redirected to your child's college bill, you will, in all likelihood, have to borrow some money.

Some tips

If you're a homeowner, you can borrow against the equity (market value less the outstanding mortgage loan) in your property. Doing so is usually best because you can borrow against your home at a low interest rate, and the interest is tax deductible. Some company retirement plans — for example, 401(k) — allow borrowing as well.

A host of financial aid programs, including a number of loan programs, allow you to borrow at reasonable interest rates. As with some mortgage loans on real estate, federal government educational loan programs are variable interest rate programs — which means that the interest rate you're charged floats, or varies, with the overall level of interest rates. Most programs, for example, are tied to the interest rate (3.1 percent is generally added) on three-month to one-year treasury bills. Thus, current rates on these loans are in the vicinity of 6.5 percent. The rates are also capped so that the interest rate on your loan can never exceed 8.25 – 9 percent on loans originated at this writing.

A number of loan programs, such as Unsubsidized Stafford Loans and Parent Loans for Undergraduate Students (PLUS), are available even when your family is not deemed financially needy. Only Subsidized Stafford Loans, on which the federal government pays the interest that accumulates while the student is still in school, are limited to those students deemed financially needy.

Most loan programs limit the amount that you can borrow per year as well as in total throughout a student's undergraduate and graduate school education. If you need more money than allowed on loans that limit borrowings, PLUS loans can fill the gap: Parents can borrow the full amount needed after other financial aid is factored in. The only obstacle is that you must go through a credit qualification process. Unlike privately funded college loans, federal loans' main qualification stipulation is that you don't have negative credit (recent bankruptcy, more than three debts over three months past due, and so on). For more information from the federal government about these student loan programs, call the Federal Student Financial Aid Information Center at 800-433-3243.

In addition to loans, there are a number of grant programs available through schools and the government as well as through independent sources. You can apply for the federal government ones via the FAFSA. Grants available through state government programs may require a separate application. Specific colleges and other private organizations (including employers, banks, credit unions, and community groups) also offer grants and scholarships.

Many scholarships and grants don't require any work on your part — simply apply for financial aid through colleges. Other programs need seeking out — check directories and databases at your local library, your child's school counseling department, and college financial aid offices. Also try local organizations, churches, employers, and so on. You have a better chance of getting scholarship money through these avenues.

College scholarship search services are generally a waste of money; in some cases, they are actually scams. Some of these services charge up to $100 just to tell you about scholarships that either you will automatically be considered for or that you're not even eligible for. The "legitimate" services may tell you about scholarships for, say, $500 that require you to obtain and complete an application and essays. Most people who lack the initiative to use the free references that I described earlier in this chapter probably won't follow through on the recommendations of these services anyway.

Your child can work and save money during high school and college. In fact, if your child qualifies for financial aid, he or she is expected to contribute a certain amount to education costs from employment during the school year or summer breaks and from savings. Besides giving Junior a stake in his or her own future, this training encourages sound personal financial management down the road.

The borrowing versus saving debate

More than a few investment firms and financial planners argue that in the long run, it's far cheaper for you to save for your children's college expenses rather than borrow for them.

This claim is not true. If you are able to save in retirement accounts and then separately borrow the money needed for college costs later, you can come out far ahead, thanks to the tax benefits that retirement accounts provide and the increased financial aid you may receive by not accumulating so much outside retirement accounts.

The conflict of interest of these organizations and planners is that they can't sell you investments if you channel your savings into your employer's retirement plan. They have every reason to scare you into action (and into their hands).

What's college going to cost?

College can cost a lot. The total costs vary substantially from school to school. The average annual cost (including tuition, fees, books, supplies, room, board, and transportation) at private colleges is running around $18,000 per year and around $8,500 at public colleges and universities. The more expensive schools can cost up to 35 percent more.

Is all this expense worth it? While many critics of higher education claim that tuition should not be rising faster than inflation and that costs can, and should, be contained, it is hard to deny the value of going to college. Whether it is a local community college, your friendly state university, or a selective Ivy League school, investing in education is worth the effort and the risk.

The definition of an investment is an outlay of money for an expected profit. Unlike a car that depreciates in value each year that you drive it, an investment in education yields monetary, social, and intellectual profit. A car is more tangible in the short-term, but an investment in education (including borrowing money) gives you more bang for the buck in the long run.

Colleges are now finding themselves subject to the same types of competition that for-profit companies confront on a daily basis. As a result, schools are having to clamp down on rising costs. As with any other product or service purchase, it pays to shop around. You can find good values — schools that don't cost an arm and a leg and provide a quality education.

Setting realistic savings goals

If you have money left over *after* taking advantage of retirement accounts, by all means try to save for your children. As discussed earlier, you should ideally save in your name unless you know that you won't need or want to apply for financial aid, including those loans that are available regardless of your economic situation.

Be realistic about what you can afford given your other financial goals, especially saving for retirement (see Chapter 8). Being able to pay the full cost of a college education or anything approaching the full cost, especially at a four-year private college, is a luxury of the affluent.

If you're a modest income earner, consider trying to save enough to pay a third or at most half of the cost. You can easily make up the balance through loans, employment, and the like.

Filling out Table 14-1 can help you get a handle on how much you should be saving for a child.

Note: Don't worry about correcting for inflation. This worksheet takes care of that through the assumptions made on the returns of your investments as well as the amount that you save over time. If your child has expensive taste in schools, you may want to tack on 20 to 30 percent to the following average figures.

- Average cost of a four-year private college education today: $72,000.

- Average cost of a four-year public college education today: $34,000.

Table 14-1	How Much to Save for College
Figure Out This	*Write It Here*
1. Cost of school you think your child will attend.	$ _____
2. Percent of costs you'd like to pay (for example, 20% or 40%).	x _____ %
3. Line 1 times line 2 is amount you'll pay (in today's dollars).	= $ _____
4. Number of months until your child reaches college age.	_____ months
5. Amount to save per month (today's dollars). Line 3 answer divided by line 4 answer.	= $ _____ / month

This calculation works because you assume that the money you're saving will grow at the rate of college inflation. The amount you need to save (calculated in line 5) needs to be increased once per year by the increase in college inflation — 5 or 6 percent should do.

Good and Bad Investments for Educational Funds

Many financial companies pour millions of dollars into advertising for investment and insurance products that they claim are the best ways to make your money grow for your little gremlins — I mean, children.

What makes for good and bad investments in general applies to investments for educational expenses, too. Chapter 10 gives a thorough overview of what to look for and what to beware of. The following are considerations specific to college funding.

Good investments

As discussed in Chapter 11, the professional management and efficiency of no-load mutual funds makes them a tough investment to beat. Chapters 12 and 13 provide recommendations for investing money in funds both inside as well as outside tax-sheltered retirement accounts. The important issue is to gear the investments to the time frame involved until your children need to use the money. The closer your child gets to attending college and using the money saved, the more conservatively the money should be invested.

Bad investments

Life insurance policies that have cash values are some of the most oversold investments to fund college costs. The usual pitch is: Because you need life insurance to protect your family, why not buy a policy that you can borrow against to pay for college? Makes sense, doesn't it?

The reason you shouldn't is that you're better off contributing to retirement accounts. These investments give you an immediate tax deduction that saving through life insurance does not. Because life insurance that comes with a cash value is more expensive, parents are more likely to make a second mistake — not buying enough coverage. If you need and want life insurance, you're better off buying lower-cost term life insurance (see Chapter 17).

Another poor investment for college expenses is one that fails to keep you ahead of inflation, such as savings or money market accounts. You need your money to grow to afford educational costs down the road.

Prepaid tuition plans should generally be avoided. A few states have developed plans to allow you to pay college costs at a specific school (calculated for the age of your child). The allure of these plans is that by paying today, you eliminate the worry of not being able to afford rising costs in the future.

This logic doesn't work for several reasons. First, odds are quite high that you don't have the money today to pay in advance. If you have that kind of extra dough around, you're better off using it for other purposes (and you're unlikely to worry about rising costs, anyway). You can invest your own money — that's what the school's going to do with it anyway.

Besides, how do you know which college your child will want to attend and how long it might take Junior to get through? Coercing your child into the school you've already paid for is a sure ticket to long-term problems in your relationship with your teenager.

Overlooked investments

Too often I see parents knocking themselves out to make more money so that they can afford to send their kids to more expensive (and therefore supposedly better) private high schools and colleges. Sometimes families want to send younger children to costly elementary schools, too. Families stretch themselves with outrageous mortgages or complicated living arrangements to get into neighborhoods with top-rated public schools or to send their kids to expensive private elementary schools that they can barely afford.

The best school in the world for your child is you and your home. The reason many people I know, including me and my siblings, were able to attend some of the top educational institutions in this country is that concerned parents worked hard, not just at their jobs but at spending time with the kids while they were growing up. Rather than working to make more money (with the best of intentions to buy educational games or trips or to send the kids to better schools), in my humble opinion, some parents could do more for their kids by focusing more energy on the child.

I see parents scratching their heads about their child's lack of interest and achievement academically — they blame the school or TV or society at large. These factors may contribute, but education begins in the home. Schools can't do it alone.

This is another reason not to live up to your income (that is, to continually raise your spending and living standards to use your income fully). Living within your means not only allows you to save more of your income, but it also can free more of your time to raise and educate your children.

Chapter 15

Real Estate 101

● ●

In This Chapter

▶ To buy or not to buy

▶ Determining how much to spend and what to buy

▶ Ways around a lack of a down payment

▶ How to work with real estate agents

▶ How to find the right property and negotiate the best terms

▶ Understanding title insurance, escrow fees, and inspections

▶ Knowing when to sell and how to do it with or without an agent

▶ Real estate investment options

● ●

Note: This chapter does not cover mortgages. Chapter 9 contains everything you always wanted to know (but were afraid to ask) about selecting and saving big bucks on a mortgage. Throughout this chapter, "home" refers to a property you own, be it a condominium or single family residence.

*W*hen you put your money in a bank account or a mutual fund, all you have to show for it is a razor-thin piece of paper with microscopic type showing how much money you've got. But it doesn't look much like money, and you can't actually do anything with it immediately. Hard to get much satisfaction from that.

But real estate — well, that's another matter. Real estate is big, tangible, substantial, and virtually immovable. Doesn't look much like money, either, but it's very satisfying.

Buying a home or investing in real estate can be a financially and psychologically rewarding experience. On the other hand, owning real estate can be a real pain in the butt. Purchasing and maintaining property can be one of the most time-consuming, emotionally draining, and financially painful experiences in managing your personal finances.

Perhaps you want to know how, or whether, you can get out of the rental market and buy a home. Or maybe you're interested in cornering the local real estate market and making millions in investment property. In either case, you can learn many lessons from carefully observing those who have traveled before you to the frontiers of real estate exploration.

To Buy or Not to Buy

You may be tired of moving from rental to rental. Perhaps your landlord doesn't keep up the place as well as you'd like, and you have to ask permission every time you want to hang a picture on the wall. You may desire the financial security and rewards that seem to come with homeownership. Maybe you just want a place to call your own. On the other hand, maybe your mom or dad keeps asking when you're going to grow up and settle down, and you just can't seem to commit.

Ultimately, the reason you're thinking about buying a home doesn't really matter. People's decisions about housing usually involve much more than financial motivations. Whether you're tired of hauling your stuff from apartment to apartment or just don't want to live with pink and black wallpaper anymore, in my book that's a good enough reason to buy a home.

Many people debate endlessly, in some cases for years, about whether to buy a home or continue renting. Some financial considerations may help you decide.

From a financial standpoint, you really shouldn't buy a place unless you can anticipate being there for at least three years and preferably five or more. Buying and selling a property entails a lot of expenses, including the cost of getting a mortgage (points, application and credit report fees, and appraisal fees), inspection expenses, moving costs, real estate agents' commissions, and title insurance. To cover these transaction costs plus the additional costs of ownership, a property needs to appreciate a fair amount before you can be as well off financially as if you had continued renting. A property needs to appreciate about 15 percent just to offset these expenses.

If you may need or want to move in a couple of years, it's risky to count on that kind of appreciation. If you're lucky (that is, if you happen to buy before a sharp upturn in housing prices), you may get it. If you're not, you will probably lose money on the deal.

Some people are willing to invest in real estate even when they don't expect to live in it for long and would consider turning their home into a rental. Doing so can work well financially in the long haul, but don't underestimate the responsibilities that come with rental property. (Think of the horror movies based on the premise of tenants from hell. Or talk to friends and colleagues who've been landlords.)

Some financially successful long-term renters I've seen include people who pay low rent — either because they've made housing sacrifices or live in a rent-controlled building. If you're consistently able to save a good percentage of your earnings (10 percent or more), you're probably well on your way to achieving your future financial goals.

One problem you won't have in renting over the long haul is having a lot of your money tied up in your home. Many people enter their retirement years with a substantial portion of their wealth in their homes. As a renter, you have all your money in financial assets that you can probably tap into more easily.

Some happy renters are tempted to buy a property elsewhere as an investment and rent it out or use it when they like. Be sure to read the sections later in this chapter dealing with investment property and second homes. This decision is neither straightforward nor simple.

The costs of owning versus renting

An important financial consideration for many renters is the cost of owning a home. Some people assume that owning costs more. In fact, owning a place doesn't have to cost a truckload of money. It can even cost less than renting.

On the surface, buying a place seems a lot more expensive than renting. You're probably comparing your monthly rent (a couple hundred dollars to over $1,000, depending on where you live) to the purchase price of a property, which is usually a number with a whole lot more digits — $100,000, $200,000, or more. When you consider a home purchase, you're forced to think about your housing expenses in one huge chunk rather than in small monthly installments like a rent check.

Tallying up the costs of owning a place can be a useful and not-too-complicated exercise. To make the comparison fair, you need to figure out what it would cost on a *monthly basis* to buy a place *comparable* to what you're renting. If you want to purchase a place nicer than what you're currently renting — and no one ever seems to want to buy a place that's worse than what they're renting — then you need to determine what it would cost you to rent the nicer place. Hint: Be realistic!

The worksheet in Table 15-1 enables you to compare the costs of owning to renting. **Note:** In the interest of reducing the number of variables, all this "figuring" assumes a fixed-rate mortgage, *not* an adjustable (see Chapter 9 for more on mortgages).

Table 15-1   Monthly Expenses: Renting versus Owning

Figure Out This	Write It Here ($ per month)
1. Monthly mortgage payment (see "Mortgage" below)	$ _____
2. Plus monthly property taxes (see "Property tax" below)	+ $ _____
3. Equals total monthly mortgage plus property taxes	= $ _____
4. Your income tax rate (see Table 15-3)	% _____
5. Times Line 3	x $ _____
6. Equals tax benefits	= $ _____
7. Subtract Line 6 from Line 3	− $ _____
8. Equals after-tax cost of mortgage and property taxes	= $ _____
9. Plus insurance ($30–$75/mo., depending on property value)	+ $ _____
10. Plus maintenance (1% of property cost divided by 12 months)	+ $ _____
11. Equals total costs of owning (add lines 8, 9, and 10)	= $ _____

Now, compare Line 11 in Table 15-1 with the monthly rent on a comparable place to see which comes out (roughly) ahead, owning or renting.

Mortgage

To determine the monthly payment on your mortgage, simply multiply the relevant number from Table 15-2 by the size of your mortgage expressed in (divided by) thousands of dollars. For example, if you will be taking out a 30-year, $100,000 mortgage at 7 percent, then multiply 100 by 6.65 for a $665 monthly payment.

Table 15-2   Your Monthly Mortgage Payment

Interest Rate	15-Year Mortgage	30-Year Mortgage
4.0%	7.40	4.77
4.5%	7.65	5.07
5.0%	7.91	5.37
5.5%	8.17	5.68

Interest Rate	15-Year Mortgage	30-Year Mortgage
6.0%	8.44	6.00
6.5%	8.71	6.32
7.0%	8.99	6.65
7.5%	9.27	6.99
8.0%	9.56	7.34
8.5%	9.85	7.69
9.0%	10.14	8.05
9.5%	10.44	8.41
10.0%	10.75	8.78

Property tax

Ask a real estate person, mortgage lender, or your local assessor's office what your annual property tax bill would be for a house of similar value to the one you are considering buying (the average is 1.5 percent of your property's value). Divide this amount by 12 to arrive at your monthly property tax bill.

Tax savings in homeownership

The following shortcut works quite well in determining your tax savings in homeownership: Multiply your federal tax rate (see Table 15-3) by the total amount of your property taxes and mortgage. Technically speaking, not all of your mortgage payment is tax deductible — only the portion of the mortgage payment that goes to interest is tax deductible. In the early years of your mortgage, the portion that goes toward interest is nearly all of it. On the other hand, your property taxes will probably rise over time.

Table 15-3	1993 Federal Income Tax Brackets and Rates	
Singles Taxable Income	**Married-Filing-Jointly Taxable Income**	**Federal Tax Rate**
Less than $22,100	Less than $36,900	15%
$22,100 to $53,500	$36,900 to $89,150	28%
$53,500 to $115,000	$89,150 to $140,000	31%
$115,000 to $250,000	$140,000 to $250,000	36%
Over $250,000	Over $250,000	39.6%

You may earn state tax benefits as well from your deductible mortgage interest and property taxes. On the other hand, you probably won't capture its full value due to the intricacies of claiming itemized deductions in the income tax system.

If you want to know more precisely how homeownership may affect your tax situation, get out your tax return and try plugging in some reasonable numbers to "guesstimate" how your taxes will change. You can also speak with a tax advisor.

The long-term cost of renting

When you crunch the numbers to see what it may cost you on a monthly basis to own rather than rent a comparable place, you may discover that owning isn't quite as expensive as you thought. Or you may find that owning costs somewhat more than renting. This discovery may tempt you to think that, financially speaking, renting is cheaper than owning.

Be careful not to jump to conclusions. Remember that you're looking at the cost of owning versus renting *today*. What about five, ten, or 30 years from now? As an owner, your biggest monthly expense — the mortgage payment — does not increase (assuming that you buy your home with a fixed-rate mortgage). Your property taxes, homeowner's insurance, and maintenance expenses — which are generally far less than your mortgage payment — are the items that increase with the cost of living.

As a renter, however, your entire monthly rent is subject to the vagaries of inflation. The exception to this rule is when you live in a rent-controlled unit, where the annual increase allowed in your rent is capped. Rent control does not eliminate price hikes; it just limits them.

Suppose you are comparing the costs of owning a home that costs $160,000 to renting that home for $800 a month. Table 15-4 compares the cost of owning the home per month (after factoring in tax benefits) to your rental costs over 30 years. (This assumes that you take out a mortgage loan equal to 80 percent of the cost of the property at a fixed rate of 7 percent and that the rate of inflation of your homeowner's insurance, property taxes, maintenance, and rent is 4 percent per year.) What happens to the value of the property is ignored in these calculations.

Table 15-4 Cost of Owning versus Renting over 30 Years

Year	Ownership Cost per Month	Rental Cost per Month
1	$ 920	$800
5	$ 980	$940
10	$1080	$1140
20	$1360	$1690
30	$1800	$2500

As you can see in Table 15-4, it costs a little bit more in the first few years to own the home than to rent it. In the long run, however, owning is a bit less expensive. This is because more of your rental expenses increase with inflation.

If you've been paying attention, you may be thinking that if inflation doesn't rise 4 percent per year, renting could end up being cheaper. This is not necessarily so. Suppose that there is no inflation at all. Your rent shouldn't escalate, but homeownership expenses (property taxes, maintenance, and insurance) shouldn't, either. And with no inflation, you can probably refinance your mortgage at a rate lower than 7 percent. If you do the math, you find that owning should still cost less in the long run with lower inflation, but the advantage compared to renting is less than during periods of higher inflation.

So, You've Decided to Buy a House

Buying and owning your own home can be a wise financial move. It's exciting to go bopping around to check out homes on the market (looking in other people's closets) and think about where your beer can collection will go. For most people, some of that excitement wears off once they get a sense of how much homes cost!

Buying a home is a long-term commitment. You will probably take out a 15- to 30-year mortgage to finance your purchase. The home you buy will need all sorts of maintenance over the years. Owning a home is a bit like running a marathon over 15 or 30 years — you're paying for something or other all the time (or so it seems!).

Before you make a commitment to buy, it's important to take stock of your overall financial health.

How much should you spend?

Lenders tell you the maximum that you are qualified to borrow (see Chapter 9 for details). But that doesn't mean that you should borrow the maximum. What about your other financial options and goals? The most common mistake made in buying a home is not considering your overall financial situation.

If you fall in love with a home and buy it without looking at your monthly expenditures and long-term goals, you may end up with a home that dictates much of your future spending. For example, how much should you be saving monthly to reach your retirement goals? How much do you spend (and want to continue spending) on fun stuff like travel and entertainment? If you want to continue your current lifestyle (and the expenditures inherent in it), you have to be honest with yourself about how much you can really afford to spend as a homeowner.

First-time home buyers in particular run into financial trouble because they don't know their spending needs and priorities and don't know how to budget for them. As much as buying a home can be a wise decision, it can also be a huge burden. Some people have trouble curtailing their spending despite the large amount of debt they just incurred and, in fact, spend even more because there are all sorts of nifty things to buy for a home. Many people prop up their spending habits with credit. For this reason, a surprisingly large percentage — some studies say about half — who borrow additional money against their home equity use the funds to pay other debts.

Don't let your home control your financial future. Take stock of your overall financial health (see Chapter 2), especially where you stand in terms of retirement planning if you hope to retire before age 70 or so (see Chapter 8), *before* you buy property or agree to a particular mortgage.

Why retirement savings should affect how much you spend on a home

Suppose two different home buyers with identical incomes are considering buying the same home. Buyer A is 30 years old and has already put away $40,000 in her retirement accounts. Buyer B, on the other hand, is 10 years older (he's 40), yet doesn't have any money stashed in retirement accounts.

Because she has a head start, Buyer A is in a much better position overall to afford the home purchase because she doesn't need to save as much toward retirement as Buyer B.

Should I buy a condo, townhouse, or co-op?

Most people's image of a house is a single-family home — a stand-alone house (with a lawn and white picket fence). In some areas, however, particularly in higher-cost neighborhoods, non-single-family housing is more common. *Condominiums* (you own the unit and a share of everything else), *townhomes* (attached or row houses), and *cooperatives* (you own a share of the entire building), are higher-density housing units. The allure is obvious — these types of homes are generally less expensive. In some cases, as an owner, you don't have to worry about some of the general maintenance because the owner's association (which you pay for, directly or indirectly) takes care of it.

If you don't have the time, energy, or desire to keep up a property, these types of shared housing can make sense. They may also provide you with better security than a stand-alone home.

As investments, single-family homes generally do better in the long run. That said, you should remember that a rising tide raises all boats. In a good real estate market, single-family as well as other types of housing appreciate, although single-family homes tend to do better. The reason is that the principle of supply and demand drives real estate prices. Shared housing is easier to build (and to overbuild). It's harder to put up houses because more land is required. In areas where available land is scarce, single-family homes tend to be more attractive to potential buyers. Most people, when they can afford it, still prefer a stand-alone home. These factors tend to put a damper on the appreciation of shared-housing units.

If you can afford a smaller single-family home instead of a larger shared-housing unit, buy the single-family home. Shared-housing prices tend to hold up better in already developed urban environments. If possible, avoid them in suburban areas where more building may still take place.

How do I buy when I don't have a down payment?

Many people don't have the equivalent of 20 percent or more of the purchase price in savings to buy a home without private mortgage insurance. Here are a number of solutions for the down payment blues:

- ✔ **Go on a spending diet.** One sure way to come up with a down payment is to raise your savings rate by slashing your spending. Take a tour through Chapter 6 to learn strategies for doing so.

- ✔ **Consider lower-priced properties.** Some buyers want their first home to be a palace. Smaller properties and ones that need some work can help to keep the purchase price, and therefore the required down payment, down.

- ✔ **Find partners.** You can usually get more home for your money when you buy a building in partnership with one, two, or a few partners. Make sure to write up a legal contract to specify what will happen if a partner wants out.

- ✔ **Seek reduced down payment financing.** Some property owners or developers may be willing to finance your purchase with as little as 5 to 10 percent down. You can't be as picky about properties because not as many are available under these terms — and many that are need work or haven't yet sold for other reasons.

- ✔ **Get assistance from family.** If your parents, grandparents, or other relatives have money dozing away in a savings or CD account at 4 percent interest or less, they may be willing to lend (or even gift) you the down payment. You can pay them a higher rate of interest and thus be able to buy a home — a win/win situation.

- ✔ **Obtain private mortgage insurance (PMI).** Some lenders may offer you a mortgage even though you may only be able to put down 5–10 percent of the purchase price. The insurance generally costs a few hundred dollars per year and pays the lender off if you default and they lose money on the property. Once the property rises enough in value or you pay down the mortgage enough to have 20 percent equity in the property, you can deep-six the PMI.

Working with real estate agents

Odds are that when you buy or sell a home, you'll work with a real estate agent. Real estate agents, like many financial planners, earn their living on commission. As such, their incentives are different from yours and can sometimes be at odds with what's best for you.

Unlike commission-based financial planners, property buyers and sellers usually understand the real estate commission system. They know that agents get a cut of the deal — that fact is not hidden.

A top-notch real estate agent can be of significant help in your purchase or sale of property. On the other hand, a mediocre, incompetent, or greedy agent can be a real liability. Real estate agents don't have as bad a reputation as used car salespeople, but it's not great, either. The following quotations capture some fundamental problems among real estate agents:

> ". . . Commissions are overpriced, quality of service bears no relation to commission levels, agents face serious conflicts of interest, most buyers are inadequately represented by agents, and agents dominate most state regulatory bodies. The residential real estate industry functions as a cartel that overcharges home buyers and sellers over $10 billion a year."
>
> — Consumer Federation of America (a nonprofit consumer advocacy group)

> "For the most part agents look out for themselves. The problem. . . is the commission. The only way you're going to get someone to really look out for your interests is to pay him an hourly fee. If he gets a commission, his overwhelming motivation is to see that the deal closes with a minimum of effort on his part."
>
> — John T. Reed, *Residential Property Acquisition Handbook*

Ten conflicts of interest that real estate agents can have

Working on commission tends to bring out the worst human behaviors and traits. It's not that bad people work on commission. It's just that the compensation system skews a real estate agent's recommendations. In many cases, biases or inappropriate ways of doing business accumulate and harden over the years. Some agents honestly may not recognize the conflicts in what they're doing.

Here are the most common conflicts of interest to watch out for:

Buy now, sell now

"If you're gonna buy, now's the time to buy."

"Prices and interest rates are low now, but they could rise any day."

"If you're gonna sell, now's a good time."

"The market could worsen before it gets better — prices are up."

Because agents work on commission, it costs them money when they spend time with you and you don't buy or sell. They want you to complete a deal, and they want that deal as soon as possible — otherwise, they don't get paid. Don't expect an agent to give you objective advice about what you should do given your overall financial situation. Speak with a tax or financial advisor who works on a fee-for-service basis and provides advice after examining your overall financial situation.

Spend more (and take an adjustable mortgage)

Because real estate agents get a percentage of the sales price of a property, they have a built-in incentive to encourage you to spend more. Adjustable-rate mortgages (discussed in Chapter 9) allow you to spend more because the interest rate starts at a lower level than on a fixed-rate mortgage. Thus, real estate agents are far more likely to encourage you to take an adjustable. But adjustables are a lot riskier — you must understand these drawbacks before signing up for one.

Buy my company's listings

Agents also have a built-in incentive (higher commission) to sell their own listings. Especially problematic are cases in which one agent represents both the property seller and the buyer in the transaction. Agents holding open houses sometimes try to sell to an unrepresented buyer who likes their open house. There's no way one person can represent the best interests of both sides. Agents also often receive a higher commission selling listings belonging to other agents in their office. Beware.

I don't waste my time working with small fries like you

Because agents work on commission and get paid a percentage of the sales price of the property, many are not interested in working with you if you can't or simply don't want to spend a lot. Some agents may reluctantly take you on as a customer but then give you little attention and time.

Buy in my area

Real estate agents typically work a specific territory. As a result, they usually can't objectively tell you the pros and cons of the surrounding region. Most won't admit that you may better meet your needs by looking in another town (or some other part of town) where they don't normally work. Before you settle on an agent (or an area), spend time in different territories to learn about the pros and cons of the areas.

Get your loan from a higher-cost lender

If you don't get approved for a loan, the entire real estate deal will unravel. So, it's a good thing that real estate agents want you to get approval for a loan. But it may cause them to refer you to a more expensive lender who has the virtue of high approval rates. Be sure to shop around — you can probably get a loan and get it more cheaply.

Also, beware of your agent referring you to mortgage lenders and brokers, because your agent may be getting a referral fee. Such payments should be disclosed but frequently aren't.

Use this inspector — he's easy

Inspectors are supposed to be objective third parties who are hired by the potential buyer to evaluate the condition of a prospective property. Their job is to uncover problems that your novice eye can't see. I've heard of tougher (nit-picky) inspectors referred to as "deal killers" by disgruntled real estate agents. Some inspectors get more referrals from agents because they aren't tough. But you'll be the one who's sorry if your newly acquired home has undiscovered problems due to an inadequate inspection.

I'm helping the seller cover up problems

Some agents, under pressure to sign up a seller, agree to be criminal accomplices. Not disclosing known defects or problems is a civil violation. In most cases, it seems, the seller may not explicitly ask an agent to help cover up a problem, but the agent may look the other way or not tell the whole truth.

I'd rather credit back than reduce the purchase price

After an initial agreement on a sales price, negotiations in real estate deals can begin again if circumstances change or new information surfaces. For example, your inspections may uncover problems you weren't previously aware of. The purchase price you agreed to before was based on what you knew at that time. You may feel justified in asking for a price reduction.

Agents involved in your deal are far more likely to suggest and favor a *credit back,* wherein the seller credits money to you at closing instead of reducing the sales price. This technique benefits agents because it does not reduce their commission, which is based on the sales price. But a price reduction may benefit both the buyer and seller — besides the agent's commission, other items such as property taxes may be based on the sales price. Some agents are willing to go along with an overall price reduction if their commission is based on the previously agreed upon (higher) price.

They scratch my back and I scratch theirs

Some agents (as employees do in other occupations) refer you to lenders, inspectors, and title insurance companies that have referred them business. A referral, of course, should first and foremost be based on the competence of the person to whom you're being referred. Too often in referrals, this criterion is minor or, in some cases, nonexistent. Some agents also solicit and receive referral fees (or bribes) from mortgage lenders, inspectors, and contractors to whom they refer business.

Qualities to look for in real estate agents

Whether you're hiring an agent to work with you as a buyer or seller, you want someone who is competent and with whom you can get along. Working with an agent costs you a lot of money — make sure that you get your money's worth.

Interview several agents. Check references. Ask each agent for the names and phone numbers of at least three clients with whom they've worked in the past six months in the geographical area in which you are looking.

You should look for these traits in any agent you work with, whether as a buyer or seller:

- **Full-time employment.** Some agents work in real estate as a second or even third job. Information in this field changes constantly — keeping track of it is hard enough on a full-time basis. It's hard to imagine a really good agent being able to stay on top of the market and moonlight elsewhere.

- **Experience.** When you're establishing a new checking account, working with an employee straight out of school, first week on the job, isn't going to harm you financially — it may just take a little longer to get the job done. With a real estate deal, you've got a lot at stake financially and emotionally. You want to do the best that you can. Hiring someone with experience doesn't necessarily mean looking for an agent who's been kicking around for decades. Many of the best agents come into the field from other occupations, such as business and teaching. Some sales, marketing, negotiation, and communication skills can certainly be learned in other fields, but experience in this field does count.

- **Honesty and integrity.** You're trusting your agent with a lot. If they don't level with you about what a neighborhood or particular property is really like, you suffer the consequences.

- **Interpersonal skills.** An agent has to be able to get along not only with you but also with a whole host of other people involved in a typical real estate deal: other agents, property sellers, inspectors, mortgage lenders, and so on. An agent doesn't have to be Mr. or Ms. Congeniality, but he or she should know how to put your interests first without upsetting others.

✔ **Negotiation skills.** Putting a real estate deal together involves negotiation. Is your agent going to exhaust all avenues to get you the best deal possible? Most people don't like the sometimes aggravating process of negotiation, so they hire someone else to do it for them. Be sure to ask the agent's references how the agent negotiated for them.

✔ **High quality standards.** Sloppy work can lead to big legal or logistical problems down the road. If an agent neglects to recommend an inspection, for example, you may be stuck with undiscovered problems after the deal is done.

Buying and selling require somewhat different skills. Some rare agents can do both outstandingly well. There's no law or rule that says that you must use the same agent when you sell a property as when you buy. Don't feel obliged to sell through the agent who worked with you as a buyer just because he sends you holiday cards every year asking how the garden is growing. Remember, he works on commission.

Agents sometimes market themselves as *top producers,* which means that they sell a relatively larger volume of real estate. This title doesn't count for much for you, the buyer. It may be a red flag of an agent that focuses on completing as many deals as possible. When you're buying a home, you need an agent who has the following particular skills and knowledge:

✔ **Patience (not a hard-sell).** When you're buying a home, the last thing you need or want is an agent who tries to push you into making a deal. You need an agent who is patient and willing to allow you the necessary time to get educated and help you make the best decision for you.

✔ **Local market and community knowledge.** If you're looking to buy a home in an area in which you're not currently living, an informed agent can have a big impact on your decision.

✔ **Financing knowledge.** As a buyer, especially a first-time buyer or someone with credit problems, you should look for an agent who can refer you to lenders who can handle your type of situation, which can save you a lot of legwork.

Should I buy without a real estate agent?

A competent and ethical real estate agent can add enough value to your purchase to warrant the commission you pay. The claim that it doesn't cost you anything as a buyer to buy through an agent is a falsehood. If you're not working with an agent, a seller may be willing to accept a lower offer because he or she needs to pay just one agent's commission instead of two.

Buyer's brokers

Increasing numbers of agents are marketing themselves as *buyer's brokers.* Supposedly, they represent your interests as a property buyer exclusively.

Legally speaking, buyer's brokers may sign a contract saying that they represent your — and only your — interests. Before this enlightened era, all agents contractually worked for the property seller.

The title, buyer's broker, is one of those things that sounds better than it really is. Agents representing you as buyer's brokers still get paid only when you buy. And they still get paid on commission as a percentage of the purchase price. So they still have an incentive to sell you a piece of real estate, and the more expensive it is, the more commission they make.

You can purchase on your own if you're willing to do some additional legwork. You need to do the things that a good real estate agent does, such as searching for properties, scheduling appointments to see them, and coordinating inspections.

If you don't work with an agent, you should consider having an attorney review the contracts, unless you're a legal expert yourself. Besides, in most cases, real estate agents are not legal experts, anyway. In some states, you need to hire an attorney in addition to the real estate agent.

One drawback to working without an agent is that you have to do the negotiations yourself. If you're a good negotiator, doing so can work to your advantage. But if you get too caught up emotionally in the situation, negotiating for yourself can backfire.

If you're experienced or savvy about real estate and have found a property on your own, there's no reason you can't put a deal together yourself. Go ahead — it's been done before. And you'll probably come out ahead financially. Most people, however, are better off hiring a good agent.

Finding the right property and location

Shopping for a home can be fun. You get to peek inside other people's refrigerators and drawers. For most people, finding the right house at the right price can take a lot of time. It can also entail a lot of compromise when you're buying with partners or a spouse (or children, if you choose to share the decision making with them).

A good agent (or several in different areas) can help with the legwork. Here are the main things to consider:

- ✔ **Cast a broad net.** Before you start your search, you may have an idea about the type of property and location you are interested in or think you can afford. You may think, for example, that you can afford only a condominium in the neighborhood you want. But if you take the time to check out other communities, you may be surprised to find one that meets most of your needs and has affordable single-family homes. You'd never know that, though, if you narrowed your search too quickly. Even if you've lived in an area for a while and think that you know it well, look at different types of properties in a number of different areas before you start to narrow your search. Be open minded and be sure to know which of your many criteria for a home you *really* care about. You may have to be flexible on some of your preferences.

  If you're working with an agent, make sure you don't overlook homes that are for sale by owner (that is, not listed with real estate agents). Otherwise, you may miss out on some good properties.

- ✔ **Find out actual sales prices.** Don't look at just a few homes listed at a particular price and get depressed because they're all dogs or you can't afford what you really want. Before you decide to renew your lease on your apartment, remember that properties often sell for less than the price at which they are listed. Find out how much some of the places you look at end up selling for. Doing so gives you a better sense of what you can really afford as well as what some places seem to be really worth.

- ✔ **Spend time in the neighborhood.** Even (and especially) if you fall in love with a house at first sight, go back to the neighborhood at different times of day and on different days of the week. Knock on a few doors and meet your potential neighbors. You may discover, for example, a flock of chickens in the backyard next door or that the street and basement flood every other winter. Once you buy a home, you're stuck with it. Make sure that you know what you're getting yourself into.

- ✔ **Research the area.** What are the schools like? Go visit them. Don't rely on statistics about test scores. Talk to parents and teachers — what's really going on at the school? Even if you don't have kids, the quality of the local school has direct bearing on the value of your property. Is crime a problem? Call the local police department. Will future development be allowed? If so, what type? Talk to the planning department. What will your property taxes be? Is the property located in an area susceptible to major risks, such as floods, mud slides, fires, or earthquakes? Consider these issues even if they are not important to you, because they can affect the resale value of your property.

Negotiating the best terms

When you work with an agent, the agent usually carries the burden of the negotiation process. But you need to have a plan and strategy in mind — otherwise, you might overpay for your home. Here are some recommendations for getting a good deal:

✔ **Never fall in love with a property.** If you've got money to burn and you can't imagine life without the home you've just discovered, then pay what you will. Otherwise, always keep in the back of your mind that other good properties are out there.

✔ **Have a back-up property.** Even if you're about to make an offer, don't get emotionally committed to the house yet. Maybe you saw another home that would meet your needs just as well. Or maybe you can conceive of a home that would be slightly better than the one on which you're making an offer. Keeping these things in mind is part of the process of not letting yourself fall in love with a house before it's actually yours.

✔ **Learn about the property and owner before you make your offer.** How long has the property been on the market? What are its flaws? Why is the owner selling it? (For example, if the seller is moving because she got a job in another town where she's about to close on a home purchase, she may be eager to get her money out and may be willing to reduce the price. Or if the house has been on the market for a while, the seller may be tired and more willing to negotiate than after just a week on the market.) The more you understand about the property you want to buy and the seller's motivations, the better you will be able to draft an offer that meets both parties' needs.

✔ **Get comparable sales data to support your price.** Too often, home buyers and their agents pick a number out of the air when making an offer. If you were the seller, would you be persuaded to lower your asking price? Pointing to recent and comparable home sales to justify your offer price strengthens your case.

✔ **Remember that price is only one of several negotiable items.** Sometimes sellers get fixated on selling their homes for a certain amount. Perhaps they want to get at least what they paid for it themselves several years ago. You may be able to get a seller to pay for certain repairs or improvements or to offer you an attractive loan without all the extra loan fees that a bank would charge. Likewise, the real estate agent's commission is negotiable, too.

To learn how to be a better negotiator in real estate (and other aspects of your life), consider picking up a copy of *Getting to Yes: Negotiating Agreement Without Giving In* by Roger Fisher and William Ury (Penguin).

Negotiating a real estate agent's commission as a buyer

Conventional wisdom says that the seller pays the agent's commission, so it doesn't concern or cost you as a buyer. Wrong! If the agents involved in your real estate deal are amenable to reducing their commissions, all things being equal, the seller may be willing to accept less money for the property.

If you, as the buyer, and the property seller aren't that far apart on price, there's no reason not to suggest that the agents lower their commissions. To get a deal done, you may be surprised at what agents are willing to do. Read the section later in this chapter about negotiating real estate agents' commissions.

Games real estate agents play to get a deal done

The thirst for a commission brings out the worst in agents. They'll tell you numerous fibs to motivate you to buy on the seller's terms. One common one is to say that there are other offers coming in on the property you're interested in to get you to not take time to think about your offer. Or they'll say that the seller already turned down an offer for x dollars to get you to make a higher offer that a seller would be more likely to accept. Another is to say that the seller may be willing to come down to y dollars to get you to offer more.

Another tactic is the car dealer trick — blaming the office manager for not allowing them to reduce their commission. The bottom line is that if it's not in writing, be skeptical.

Saving strategies

Here are some ideas on how to reduce your costs when buying a home.

Saving on your mortgage

In the long haul, your mortgage may cost you more than you're paying for the house. Be sure to check out Chapter 9 to learn all about getting the right mortgage at the best rate.

Saving on title insurance and escrow fees

Many people don't seem to know that title insurance and escrow fees vary from company to company. As a result, they don't bother to shop around and simply use the company that their real estate agent or mortgage lender suggests.

Mortgage lenders require title insurance to protect against someone else claiming legal title to your property. This can happen, for example, when a husband and wife split up and the one who remains in the home decides to sell and take off with the money. If both spouses were listed as owners on the title, the spouse who sold the property (possibly by forging the other's signature) had no legal right to do so. The other spouse could come back and reclaim rights to the home even after it has been sold. In this event, both you and the lender could get stuck holding the bag. (If you're in the enviable position of paying cash for a property, you should still buy title insurance even though a mortgage lender won't prod you to do so. You need to protect your investment.)

Escrow charges pay for neutral third-party services to ensure that the instructions of the purchase contract or refinance are fulfilled and that everyone gets paid.

When you call around for title insurance and escrow fee quotes, make sure that you understand all the fees. Many companies tack on all sorts of charges for things such as courier fees and express mail. If you find a company with lower prices and want to use it, it doesn't hurt to ask for an itemization in writing so that there are no surprises.

Real estate agents and mortgage lenders can be a good starting point for referrals, as they usually have a broader perspective on cost and service quality of different companies. Call other companies as well — agents and lenders may be biased toward certain companies simply because they are in the habit of using them or have referred clients to them before.

An insurance company's ability to pay claims is always important. Most state insurance departments monitor and regulate title insurance companies. You can check with them if you're concerned. You can also ask the insurer for copies of its ratings from insurance-rating agencies (see Chapter 16 for more details). Title insurers rarely fail, and most state departments of insurers do a good job in shutting down financially unstable ones.

Inspect, inspect, inspect

When you buy a home, you're probably making one of the biggest (if not *the* biggest) financial purchases and commitments of your life. Unless you've built homes and done contracting work yourself, you probably have no idea what you're getting yourself into when it comes to furnaces and termites.

Spend the money and time to hire inspectors and other experts to evaluate the major systems and potential problem areas of the home. Areas that you want to check include

- ✔ Overall condition of the property
- ✔ Electrical, heating, and plumbing systems
- ✔ Foundation
- ✔ Roof
- ✔ Pest control and dry rot
- ✔ Seismic/slide risk

Inspection fees often pay for themselves. If you uncover problems that you weren't aware of, the inspection reports give you the information you need to go back and ask the property seller to fix the problems or reduce the purchase price of the property to compensate you for correcting the deficiencies yourself.

Never accept a seller's inspection report as your only source of information. When a seller hires an inspector, he or she may hire someone who won't be as diligent and critical of the property. For example, what if the inspector is buddies with the seller or agent selling the property? By all means, review the seller's inspection reports if available, but get your own as well.

As discussed earlier, beware of inspectors who are popular with real estate agents. They may be popular because they are soft touches and don't rock the boat by bothering to document all the property's problems.

As with other professionals whose services you retain, interview a few inspection companies. Ask which systems they inspect and how detailed a report they will prepare for you. Consider asking the company you're thinking of hiring for customer references. Ask them for names and phone numbers of three people who used their service about six months ago.

The day before you close on the purchase of your home, do a brief walk-through of the property to make sure that everything is still in the condition it was before and that all the fixtures, appliances, curtains, and other items that were to be left as per the contract are still there. Sometimes, sellers (and their movers) "forget" what's to be left or try to test your powers of observation.

Selling Your Home

As discussed in the section "Qualities to look for in real estate agents," selling and buying a home demand agents with different strengths. When you're selling a property, you want an agent who can get the job done efficiently and for as high a price as possible.

As a seller, you should seek agents who have marketing and sales expertise and are willing to put in the time and money necessary to get your home sold. Don't necessarily be impressed by an agent who works for a large company. What matters more is what the agent is going to do to market your property.

Negotiating real estate agent commissions and listings

When you list your home for sale, the contract that you sign with the listing agent includes specification of the commission to be paid if the agent is successful in selling your home. In most areas of the country, agents usually ask for a 6 percent commission. In an area that has lower-cost housing, they may ask for 7 percent.

Regardless of the commission an agent says is "typical," "standard," or "what my manager requires," *always* remember that commissions are negotiable.

Because the commission is a percentage, you have much greater ability to get a lower commission on a higher-priced home. If an agent makes 6 percent selling both a $200,000 home and a $100,000 home, the agent makes twice as much on the $200,000 home. Yet selling the higher-priced home does not take twice as much work. (Selling a $400,000 home certainly doesn't take four times the effort of a $100,000 home sale.)

If you live an area with higher-priced homes (above $200,000), there's no reason not to ask for 5 percent commission on your listing. For expensive properties ($400,000 and up), a 4 percent commission is reasonable.

Agents argue that they do a lot of work to sell property. And they sometimes put many hours into deals that never come to fruition. Agents who work for a company say that they share a good portion of the commission with the owners of their real estate company. I've even heard agents argue that they need the higher commission because of all the income taxes they have to pay on their earnings!

Commission follies

It's a myth, largely perpetuated by real estate agents, that the seller pays the commission. Both buyer *and* seller pay. If agents weren't involved in the deal, the seller could afford to sell for less and still come out ahead. Selling for less, of course, saves the buyer money. So, home buyers as well as sellers should care about the commission the agents involved in the deal get. Buyers should feel free to make it a negotiable item when making an offer on a property.

It's often easier to negotiate an agent's commission when an offer is on the table and the agent wants to get a signed deal. Don't let them try to snow you in saying that because the seller signed a contract that included the commission percentage, it can't be changed. Everything is negotiable when an offer is in play.

If you are committed to buying or selling, you have every right to pay a reasonable fee for the time that an agent puts into your transaction. The commission levels I recommend above are more than fair.

In terms of the length of the listing agreement, three months is reasonable. If you give an agent too long a listing (6–12 months), they may simply toss your listing into the multiple listing book and not expend much effort to get your property sold. Practically speaking, you can fire your agent whenever you want, regardless of the length of the listing agreement. But a shorter listing (for example, three months) may be more motivating for your agent.

Should I sell without a real estate agent?

The temptation to sell without an agent is usually to save the commission that an agent deducts from your home's sale price. If you have the time, energy, and marketing experience, you can sell your home and possibly save some money.

MLS

The major problem with attempting to sell your home on your own is that you can't list it in the *multiple listing service (MLS),* which only real estate agents can access. Some people have said, and I concur, that the MLS functions as an effective near monopoly over the selling of homes. And if you're not listed in the MLS, many potential buyers will never know that your home is for sale. Agents working with buyers don't generally look for or show their clients homes that are for sale by owner.

Legalities

Besides saving you time, a good agent can help ensure that you're not sued for failing to disclose known defects of your property. If you decide to sell your home yourself, make sure that you have access to a legal advisor who can review the contracts.

Discount brokers

Discount brokers charge less than traditional real estate agents to help you sell your home. They may help you develop advertisements, prepare contracts, and negotiate with potential buyers. You may be responsible for showing the home to prospective buyers.

Discounters usually charge a fixed fee or a percentage of the sales price. The cost should be much less than a traditional agent would charge. Try contacting Help-U-Sell (800-366-1177), a discounter that has 350 offices nationwide. They can tell you whether they have an office in your area.

A good resource to learn more about selling real estate with or without a real estate agent is *How to Sell Your House, Condo or Co-op,* by Amy Sprecher Bly, Robert W. Bly, and the editors of Consumer Reports Books (Consumer Reports Books; 800-272-0722).

Should I keep my home until prices go up?

No. Many homeowners are tempted to hold onto their properties when they need to move if the property is worth less than when they bought it or if the real estate market is soft. It's probably not worth the hassle of renting out your property or staying or the financial gamble to hold the property.

You may reason that in a few years, the real estate storm clouds will clear and you can sell your property at a much higher price. Here are three risks associated with this way of thinking:

- ✔ First, you can't know what's going to happen to property prices in the next few years. They might rebound, but they could stay the same or drop even further. A property needs to appreciate at least a few percent per year just to make up for all the costs of holding and maintaining it.

- ✔ If you haven't been a landlord, don't underestimate the hassle and headaches associated with this job.

- ✔ Once you convert your home into a rental property, you need to pay capital gains tax on your profit when you sell it if it does appreciate (talk to your friendly neighborhood tax advisor for more details). This tax wipes out much of the advantage of having held onto the property until prices recovered. (If you want to be a long-term rental property owner, you can do a "tax-free exchange" into another rental property once you sell.)

Should I keep my home as long-term investment property if I move?

Possibly. Don't consider doing so unless it really is a long-term proposition (ten or more years). As discussed in the preceding section, selling rental property can have tax consequences.

One advantage to keeping your current home as an investment property after you move is that you already own it. Locating and buying a property takes time and money. You also know what you have with your current home. If you go out and purchase a property to rent, you're starting from scratch. (Be sure to read the next section to help you evaluate real estate as an investment opportunity.)

Real Estate as an Investment

If you own your own home already (and even if you don't), you may be interested in real estate as an investment. Over the long term, real estate, like stocks, has been a good investment, returning investors an average of 8–10 percent per year.

Real estate is not a gravy train or a simple way to get wealthy. Like stocks, real estate goes through good and bad performance periods. Most people who make money investing in real estate do so because they invest over many years.

Besides providing solid rates of return, real estate is quite different from most other investments. In the following sections, I talk about what makes real estate a unique and really pretty neat investment.

You can use it

You can't live in a stock, bond, or mutual fund (although I suppose you could build yourself a pretty substantial fortress with all the paper these companies fill your mailbox with each year).

Real estate is the only investment that you can use (live in) or rent out to produce income. Pretty nifty! As I discuss later, you need to be careful converting rental to home or home to rental property, because it can have nasty implications if you sell the property.

They ain't makin' any more

There's only so much buildable land on this here Earth. (Although it's entirely possible that someday someone will figure out a way to colonize outer space, it's just as possible that life out there could have the same idea about landing *here* — making life even more crowded for us!)

Land is in finite supply. And because humans (being life-forms) like to reproduce, the demand for land and housing continues to grow. Consider the areas that have the most expensive real estate prices in the world — Hong Kong, Tokyo, Hawaii, San Francisco, and Manhattan. In these densely populated cities, there is virtually no new land upon which to build.

Zoning regulates usage

Local government regulates the zoning of property, and zoning determines what a property can be used for. If you were allowed to tear down a small single-family home and replace it with a ten-story apartment building, for example, the value of your land would be worth much more than it currently is. (Maybe you can do this — it never hurts to find out zoning details!)

What you can use a piece of land for is, well, a privilege. Kind of like when you were made to go to bed at a certain hour when you were a kid. Under special circumstances, you could ask for and be granted more privileges.

Leverage

Real estate is also different from other investments in that you can borrow a lot of money — up to 80–90 percent or more of the value of the property. So just because a property costs $100,000 doesn't mean that you and your modest savings balance can't buy it.

The word *leverage* is used to describe that your relatively small investment of 10–20 percent down can be used to purchase, own, and control a much larger investment. So the advantage of leverage is that if the value of your real estate goes up, you make money on your investment and all the money that you borrowed.

For example, suppose you plunk down $20,000 to purchase a property for $100,000. If the property appreciates to $120,000, on paper you've made a profit of $20,000 on an investment of just $20,000. In other words, you've made a 100 percent return on your investment. That's the good news.

But leverage works both ways. If your $100,000 property decreases in value to $80,000, even though it's only dropped 20 percent in value, you've actually lost (on paper) 100 percent of your original $20,000 investment.

It's possible to get a good buy

Economists and other financial observers use the term *efficient markets* to describe that the price at which many investments sell accurately reflects their true worth. Some investment markets are more efficient than others because of the large number of transactions and easily accessible information.

Real estate markets can be inefficient at times. Information is not always easy to come by, and you may find an ultramotivated or uninformed seller. The good news is that if you are willing to do some homework, you may be able to purchase a property below, perhaps by as much as 10–20 percent, its fair market value.

Real Estate Investment Options

You can invest in real estate in a number of different ways. Some rarely make sense because they're near certain money losers. Others may work for you depending on what you're looking for.

Investment property

Real estate is like other types of investments: Prices are driven by supply and demand. You can invest in homes or small apartment buildings and rent them out. In the long run, investment-property buyers hope that their rents and the value of the property will increase faster than their expenses. (Chapter 10 teaches you the basics of investments in general.)

Real estate is like stocks in that you have an ownership position in an asset. That means greater potential for profit, but it also means greater risk. I'm often asked, "What's a better investment, stocks or real estate?"

This is a little bit like asking whether strawberry or vanilla ice cream is better. Over the long haul, diversified stock and real estate portfolios both have been good investments, rewarding investors with an average annual return of about 8–10 percent per year (exceptions can be found, and don't forget that the past does not predict or guarantee the future).

And a little place in the country

A sometimes romantic notion and extended part of the so-called American dream is the weekend getaway — a place you can escape to a couple of times a month. When it's not in use, you may be able to rent it out and earn some income to help defray part of the expenses of keeping it up.

If you can realistically afford the additional costs of a second, or vacation, home, I'm not going to tell you how to spend your extra cash. But please don't make the all-too-common mistake of viewing a second home as an investment. The way most people use them, they're not.

Investment real estate is property that you rent out 90 percent or more of the time. Most second-home owners I know rent their property out very little — 10 percent or less of the time. As a result, second homes are usually money drains.

Part of the allure of a second home is the supposed tax benefits. Even when you qualify for some or all of them, tax benefits only partially reduce the cost of owning a property. I've seen more than a few cases in which the second home is such a cash drain that it prevents its owners from contributing to and taking advantage of tax-deductible retirement savings plans.

If you don't rent out a second home property most of the time, ask yourself whether you can afford such a luxury. Can you accomplish your other financial goals — saving for retirement, paying for the home in which you live, and so on — with this added expense? Keeping a second home is more of a consumption than an investment decision.

Whether you should invest in real estate or stocks depends partly on what appeals to you. Some financial considerations that are unique to your situation may tip the scales in one direction or the other.

Consider the following major issues in deciding which investment may be better for you:

- **Time and patience.** The first and most important question to ask yourself is whether you're cut out to handle the responsibilities that come with being a landlord. Real estate is a time-intensive investment. Investing in stocks can be time-intensive as well, but it doesn't have to be if you use professionally managed mutual funds. You can hire a property manager with real estate to reduce the workload.

- **Access to retirement accounts.** An often-overlooked drawback to investing in real estate is that you earn no tax benefits while you're accumulating your down payment. Retirement accounts such as 401(k)s, SEP-IRAs, Keoghs, and so on (discussed in Chapter 8) give you an immediate tax deduction as you contribute money to them. If you haven't exhausted contributing to these accounts, consider doing so first.

- **Which investments you know more about.** Some folks feel uncomfortable with stocks and mutual funds because they don't understand them. If you have a better handle on what makes real estate tick, you have a good reason to consider investing in it.

- **What makes you happy.** Some people enjoy the challenge that comes with managing and improving rental property. It's a bit like running a small business. If you're good at it and have some good luck, you can make money and derive endless hours of enjoyment.

- Although few will admit it, some real estate investors get an ego rush from a tangible display of their wealth. Sufferers of this "edifice complex" can't obtain similar pleasure from a stock portfolio that is detailed on a piece of paper (although others have been known to boast of their stock market prowess and wealth).

Real estate investment trusts

Real estate investment trusts (REITs) are like a mutual fund of real estate investments. A typical REIT invests in different types of property, such as shopping centers, apartments, and other rental buildings.

REITs trade as securities on the major stock exchanges. You can research and purchase individual REITs. Even better is to buy a mutual fund that invests in a diversified mixture of REITs. Both Fidelity and Cohen & Steers offer no-load (commission-free) funds that invest mostly in REITs. Fidelity's is called the Fidelity Real Estate Investment fund. Cohen & Steers' is called Cohen & Steers Realty and must be bought through discount brokers like Charles Schwab and Jack White (see Chapter 11 for more information about these firms).

Some real estate writers have criticized REITs, saying that they aren't "real" real estate investments, whatever that means. REITs are a good alternative for people who want to invest in real estate without all the hassles and headaches that come with directly owning and managing rental property. Fidelity's fund has returned an average of 14.2 percent per year over the past five years. You can easily buy REITs as a retirement account investment (you can't do so with rental property) and you can buy them with borrowed money as well. If you buy the previously mentioned funds through a discount broker, you need pay only 50 percent down (although doing so is riskier, and I don't recommend it).

Limited partnerships

In Chapter 10, I give good reasons to avoid these investments. Limited partnerships that are sold through stock brokers and financial planners who work on commission are burdened by high sales commissions and ongoing management fees. Real estate investment trusts, discussed in the preceding section, are much better alternatives. REITs also have the virtue of being completely liquid.

Time shares

Time shares are another nearly certain money loser. With a time share, what you buy is a week or two of ownership, or usage, of a particular unit, usually a condominium in a resort location. If you pay $8,000 for a week (in addition to ongoing maintenance fees), you're paying the equivalent of $400,000 for the whole unit, but a comparable unit may sell for only $150,000. All the extra mark-up pays the salespeople's commissions, administrative expenses, and profits for the time-share development company.

People usually get hoodwinked into buying a time-share when they're enjoying a vacation someplace. They're easy prey for salespeople who want to sell them a souvenir of the trip. The cheese in the mousetrap is an offer of something free (for example, a free night's stay in a unit) for going through the sales presentation.

If you can't live without a time-share, consider buying a used one. Many previous buyers, who almost always have lost a good hunk of money, are trying to dump their shares (which should tell you something). You may be able to buy a time-share at a fair price. But why commit yourself to taking a vacation in the same location and building at the same time each year? Many time-shares let you trade your weeks; however, doing so is a hassle, and you're limited by what you can trade for, which are typically time slots that other people don't want — that's why they're trading them!

Part IV
Protecting What You've Got

The 5th Wave   By Rich Tennant

"The first thing we should do is get you two some good insurance. Let me get the 'Magic 8-Ball' and we'll run some options."

In this part . . .

You discover that just because insurance is boring doesn't mean you can ignore it. Therefore, I show you how to obtain the right kind of insurance to shield you from the brunt of unexpected major expenses and protect your future earnings and your assets. I reveal which types of insurance you do and do not need, what you should avoid, what to include and what not to include in your policies, and how much of which things you should insure. Plus, you finally face other creepy but important stuff such as wills, probate, and inheritance taxes.

Chapter 16
Insurance Basics

●●

In This Chapter

▶ How the insurance industry works

▶ The three laws of buying insurance

▶ How to save thousands of dollars and get the insurance coverage you need

▶ What to do if you are denied coverage

▶ How to get 'em to cough up your claim money

●●

*U*nless you work in the industry (by choice), insurance is, for most people, a dreadfully boring topic. Most people associate insurance with disease, death, and disaster and would rather do just about anything other than review their insurance coverage. But because you don't want to deal with money hassles when you are coping with catastrophes — illness, disability, death, fires, floods, earthquakes — you should take care of insurance well before you need it.

Insurance is probably the least understood and least monitored area of personal finance. Studies by the nonprofit National Insurance Consumer Organization show that more than nine in ten Americans purchase and carry the wrong types and amounts of insurance coverage. My own experience as a financial counselor confirms this statistic. Most people are overwhelmed by all the exclusions and limitations on policies, not to mention the jargon in sales and policy statements. As a result, people get insurance from the wrong companies, pay more than is necessary for some policies, or get insured through companies with poor reputations for servicing customers with claims on their policies.

Insurance: A Big, Inefficient Business

Consider these tantalizing tidbits about the insurance industry: More than 35,000 insurance companies employ more than 1.5 million people, half of whom are the agents and brokers who sell the stuff. Nearly 1 in every 12 dollars spent in our economy goes to pay for insurance.

In *The Invisible Bankers,* an insightful book on the insurance industry, author Andrew Tobias makes the observation that the insurance industry, like the IRS and postal service, interacts with all Americans; however, to accomplish their goals, the insurance companies need twenty times more employees than the IRS and three times more employees than the U. S. Postal Service.

Unlike mutual funds or mortgages, which are often available directly from the companies that issue them, virtually all insurance is sold through insurance agents who work on commission. Because of the commission structure, it is difficult to shop around for the best deal and to figure out — and buy — policies and features that are in your best interests.

One of the primary reasons the insurance industry is so inefficient is that it enjoys a unique (and unfair) exemption from federal antitrust regulations. The McCarran-Ferguson Act of 1945, a little-known piece of legislation, allows insurance companies to dictate a fixed price for a specific policy that they sell through their commission-based agents. Unlike shopping for a Sony 19-inch color television set or a Ford Taurus GL, there is no difference in price among the various sellers of a given insurance policy. You can't see which seller offers the best prices or bargain for a better deal. (The commission varies — true — and I'll get to that soon.)

Equally problematic is the fact that insurers exert tremendous control and influence, through lobbying and representation on state insurance regulatory boards, over the entities that are supposed to oversee them — state governments.

Why all these details about insurance industry? Because understanding the industry will help you comprehend the weird stuff on policies, the high costs of most policies, and the inefficiency of most insurers. And, hopefully, you will also become informed enough to make your voice heard when you speak to insurers and government regulators about ways to improve insurance for consumers.

The Three Laws of Buying Insurance

I know your patience and interest in learning about insurance may be limited, so I've boiled it down to three fairly simple but powerful concepts that can easily save you thousands of dollars over the rest of your insurance-buying years. And while you're saving money, you can still get the coverage you need to avoid a financial catastrophe.

Law 1: Insure for the big stuff, don't sweat the small stuff

Imagine, for a moment, that you are offered the chance to buy insurance that reimburses you for the cost of a magazine subscription in the event the magazine folds and you don't get all the issues you paid for. Because a magazine subscription doesn't cost that much, I don't think you would buy that insurance.

What if you could buy insurance that pays for the cost of a restaurant meal if you get food poisoning? Even if you're splurging at a fancy restaurant, there's not a lot of money at stake, so you would probably decline that coverage, as well.

The point of insurance is to protect against losses that would be financially catastrophic to you. The examples above are silly, but they illustrate the mistake that many people make of buying insurance that covers small potential dollar losses. Sure, you want the satisfaction (the revenge?) of being "reimbursed" for the hassle of something being lost or going wrong. But you would probably get more satisfaction out of putting the money in a punching bag in your basement (and letting loose on it when things go wrong!) rather than throwing the money away on insurance.

Avoiding small potato policies

A good insurance policy can seem expensive. A policy that doesn't cost much can fool you into thinking you're getting something for next to nothing. Policies that cost little also cover little — they are priced low because they aren't covering large potential losses. The following are examples of common insurance policies that are generally a waste of your hard-earned dollars.

Extended warranty and repair plans

Isn't it ironic that right after the salesperson persuades you to buy a television, computer, or car — in part by saying how reliable the goods are — they try to convince you to spend more money to insure against the failure of the item? If the stuff is so good, why do you need insurance? Product manufacturers' warranties typically cover problems in the first three months to a year. If you need to pay for a repair out of your own pocket, it won't be a financial catastrophe.

Home warranty plans

If your real estate agent or the seller of the home wants to pay the cost of a home warranty plan for you, it would be ungracious to turn it down (as grandma would say, you shouldn't look a gift horse in the mouth). But don't buy this type of plan for yourself. In addition to requiring some sort of fee (around $30 to $50) if you need a contractor to come out and look at a problem, home warranty plans limit how much they'll pay for major problems. Your money is much better spent on hiring a competent inspector to uncover problems and have them fixed *before* you buy the home. Everyone buying a house should expect to spend money on repairs and maintenance — that's just being realistic! To buy insurance for the smaller repairs and maintenance is a waste of money.

Dental insurance

If your employer pays for dental insurance, take advantage of it. But you shouldn't pay for this coverage on your own. Dental insurance generally covers a couple of teeth cleanings each year and limits payments for more-expensive work.

Credit life and credit disability policies

Many direct mail firms try to sell policies that pay a small benefit in case you die with an outstanding loan (a credit life policy) or a small monthly income in the event of a disability (a credit disability policy). These policies are usually sold by credit card companies such as VISA, MasterCard, Discover, and American Express. Some companies even sell you insurance to pay off your credit card bill in the event of your death or disability. The cost of this insurance seems low, but that's because the potential benefits are small. In fact, these policies are extraordinarily expensive, given how little insurance you're buying. If you need life or disability insurance, purchase it. But get enough coverage and buy it in a separate, cost-effective policy (see Chapter 17 for more details).

One exception to avoiding the credit life and disability insurace rule is if you are in poor health and you can buy these insurance policies without a medical evaluation. In that case, these policies may be the only ones you have access to. This is another reason that these policies are expensive. If you're in good health, you are paying for the people with poor health who can enroll without a medical examination and who undoubtedly make more claims.

Daily hospitalization insurance

Insurance policies that pay a certain amount per day, usually $75 – $100, are often sold to older people. These policies operate on the idea that you need income if you're in the hospital. Of course, what you really need is comprehensive (major medical) health insurance. One day in the hospital can rack up a bill of several thousand dollars, so $100 can be gone in an hour or less! These policies don't offer coverage for the big ticket expenses. If you don't have a comprehensive health insurance policy, get it! But skip this loser of an insurance plan if you are in good health.

Insuring packages in the mail

You buy a $40 gift for a friend, and when you go to the post office to ship it, the friendly postal clerk asks if you want to insure it. For a couple of bucks, you think, why not? The U.S. Postal Service may have a bad reputation for many reasons, but it rarely loses or damages things. Go spend your money on another gift instead!

Contact lens insurance

The things this country comes up with to waste money on just astound me. There really is contact lens insurance! The money goes to replace your contacts if you lose or tear them. Lenses are cheap. Don't waste your money on this kind of insurance.

Little stuff riders

Many policies that are worth buying, such as auto and disability insurance, have all sorts of add-on riders. These are extra bells and whistles that insurance agents like to sell because of the high profit margin. On auto insurance policies, for example, you can buy a rider for a few bucks per year that pays you $25 each time your car needs to be towed. Having your vehicle towed isn't going to bankrupt you, so it isn't worth insuring against. (Besides, what are you doing that your car is constantly being towed?)

Likewise, small insurance policies that are sold as add-ons to bigger insurance policies are usually not necessary and are overpriced. For example, you can buy some disability insurance policies with a small amount of life insurance added on. If you need life insurance, it's less costly to purchase a sufficient amount in a separate policy.

I can hear you saying, "But I collected on that policy you're telling me not to buy!" Of course you'll collect on some of the preceding policies because damages and losses do happen. But over the course of many years, these policies aren't worth the cost relative to the small protential benefit. On the average, insurance companies pay out just 60 cents in benefits on every dollar collected. Most of the preceding policies pay you back just 20 cents in benefits (claims) for every dollar you invest.

Taking the highest deductible you can afford

Most insurance policies have deductibles — the maximum amount you must pay in the event of a loss before your insurance coverage kicks in. On many policies, such as auto and homeowner's/renter's coverage, most folks opt for a $100 to $250 deductible.

There are two benefits to taking a higher deductible:

- **You save premium dollars.** Year in and year out, you can enjoy the lower cost of an insurance policy with high deductibles. You may be able to shave 15 – 20 percent off the cost of your policy. Suppose, for example, that you can reduce the cost of your policy by $100 per year by raising your deductible from $250 to $1000. That $750 worth of coverage is costing you

$100 per year. You would need to have a claim of $1,000 or more every eight years — highly unlikely — to come out ahead.

- ✔ **You don't have the hassles of filing small claims.** If you have a $300 loss on a policy with a $100 deductible, you need to file a claim to get your $200 (the amount you're covered for after your deductible). Filing an insurance claim can take hours of time and can be an aggravating experience. In some cases, you may even have your claim denied after jumping through all the necessary hoops.

If you have low deductibles, you may file more claims (although this doesn't necessarily mean you'll get more money). If you file more claims, you may be rewarded with jacked-up premiums — in addition to the headache of preparing those blasted forms! If you file too many claims, you may even have your coverage canceled!

Buy insurance to cover all possible financial catastrophes

The beauty of insurance is that it spreads all risks over millions of other people. You should insure against what could be a huge financial loss for you. The price of insurance isn't cheap, but it is relatively small in comparison to the potential total loss. Many people make the mistake of not insuring against what could be a financial catastrophe.

Think for a moment about what your most valuable assets are. (No, it's not your dry wit or your elegant nose.) If you're still in your working years, it's probably your future earnings. If you were disabled and unable to work, what would you live on? That's why long-term disability insurance exists. If you have a family that is financially dependent on your earnings, how would your family manage financially if you died? Life insurance can fill the financial void left by your death.

If you're a business owner, what would happen if you were sued for $1,000,000 for negligence in some work that you messed up? Liability insurance can bail you out.

In this age of soaring medical costs, you can easily rack up a $100,000 hospital bill in short order. That's why you need major medical health insurance coverage. And, yet, a surprising number of people don't carry any, particularly those who work in small businesses.

Many people make the mistake of buying insurance based on their perceived likelihood of making a claim, so they don't insure against potentially devastating but less likely losses. "What are the odds", I hear people say, "that I'll suffer a long-term disability or that I'll be sued for $1,000,000?" I agree that the odds are quite low. But the odds aren't as low as zero. The risk is there. The problem is that you just don't know what bad luck will befall you or when.

Besides, don't think you can figure the odds any better than the insurance companies can. The probability of your making a claim, large or small, is predicted with a great deal of accuracy by the insurance companies. That's why they employ armies of actuaries to calculate the odds of bad things happening and the frequency of current policyholders making particular types of claims. The companies price their policies accordingly.

So buying or not buying insurance based on your perception of the likelihood of needing the coverage is just plain dumb. Insurance companies aren't stupid; in fact, they are ruthlessly smart! When insurance companies price policies, they look at a number of factors to determine the risk or likelihood of your filing a claim. Take the example of auto insurance. If you're a single male, age 20, living the fast life in a high-crime city, driving a macho, turbo-sports car, and having two speeding tickets in the past year, you're gonna pay a whole lot more than a couple in their 40s, living in a low-crime area, driving a four-door sedan, and having a clean driving record.

Psychologically, it's tempting to buy insurance coverage for many of the little things that are more likely to occur. You don't want to feel like you're wasting your insurance dollars. You want to get some of your money back, darn it! You are more likely to get into a fender bender with your car or have a package lost in the mail than you are to lose your home to fire or suffer a long-term disability. But if the fender bender costs $500 (which you end up paying out of your pocket because you took my advice to take a high deductible), it isn't going to be a financial disaster. You probably won't be happy about having to pay for it, but you can and will. If you lost your entire home in a fire or you lost your ability to earn an income because of a disability, that would be a financial loss that could cause you major harm. You can't afford that major loss, and that's what you want to insure against.

Law II: Buy the broadest coverage possible

Another major mistake people make when buying insurance is purchasing coverage that is too narrow. For example, rather than buying life insurance, some folks buy "flight insurance" at an airport self-service kiosk. They seem to worry more about their mortality when getting on an airplane than they do when getting into a car. If they die on the flight, their beneficiaries collect. But if they died the next day in an auto accident or if they get some dreaded disease, the beneficiaries don't collect anything.

Thinking about a premature death is not fun, but you can't possibly know, in advance, what the cause of your death may be. If you want those people who are financially dependent on you to receive money to replace your lost income, you need coverage that pays them, regardless of how you meet your untimely demise. It doesn't matter how you feel about the safety of airplanes compared to New York City taxis or whether your fortune teller says you'll live a long life.

The medical equivalent of flight insurance is cancer insurance. Older people, fearful of having their life savings depleted by a long battle with this deadly disease, are easy prey for unscrupulous insurance salespeople pitching this insurance. If you get cancer, cancer insurance pays the bills. But what if you get heart disease, diabetes, AIDS, or some other disease? The cancer insurance doesn't pay the costs. Major medical insurance that covers your medical bills regardless of their cause is the proper solution.

A major attraction of the narrow coverage policies is the cost. Because the insurers are on the hook for claims under a limited set of circumstances, they can afford to sell coverage at what seems to be a lower price.

Another reason people buy these narrow-coverage policies is based on misperception and irrational or uncontrollable emotions. For example, some folks fear flying and think that they are at the greatest risk when they are in a plane. Statistically, however, flying is far safer than driving. But those whose knees shake and palms sweat on flights buy flight insurance because of their fear of flying. That's the same reason the elderly can be hoodwinked into buying cancer insurance — they are fearful of the disease.

You want to get the broadest possible coverage that you can. Buy life insurance, not flight insurance. Buy major medical coverage, not cancer insurance.

Law III: Shop around and buy direct

The cost of insurance varies tremendously from company to company. Whether you're looking at auto, home, life, disability, or other types of coverage, some companies may be charging double or triple for the same coverage as other companies. The companies charging the higher rates may not be better about paying claims, however. You may end up with the worst of both possible worlds — high prices and lousy service. Happily, there are companies that have both low costs and great service.

Most insurance is sold through agents and brokers who earn commissions based on what they sell. This, of course, tends to bias what they recommend that you buy. I see this bias in action all the time. A study done by Cummins and Weisbart and cited in Andrew Tobias's book *Invisible Bankers* confirms this bias, ". . . 48% of the time, an agent's decision on where to place a customer's business was based on which insurer paid the highest commission."

Not surprisingly, policies that pay agents the biggest commissions also tend to be more costly. In fact, insurance companies compete for the attention of agents by offering bigger commissions than other insurers. If you browse through magazines and other publications targeted to insurance agents (I'm sure you're anxious to do this), you'll see ads in which the very largest text is the commission percentage offered to agents who sell the advertiser's products.

Besides the attraction of policies that pay higher commissions, agents also get hooked, financially speaking, to companies whose policies they sell frequently. Once an agent has sold a certain amount of a company's insurance policies, he is rewarded with higher commission percentages on any future sales. Just as airlines bribe frequent fliers with mileage bonuses, insurers bribe agents with fatter commissions for their loyalty.

It is a challenge to shop around not only because most insurance is sold by agents working on commission but also because insurers set their rates in mysterious ways. Because they price their policies based on an analysis of how much of a risk you are, one company may offer low rates to me but not to you and vice versa.

Despite the obstacles, there are several strategies for obtaining low-cost, high-quality policies. Chapters 17 and 18 recommend how and where to get the best deals on specific types of policies. The following tips offer smart ways to shop for insurance.

No-load insurance

Your best bet for getting a good insurance value is to buy policies from the increasing number of companies that are selling their policies directly to the public and are cutting the insurance agent and the accompanying commission out of the picture. Just as you can purchase no-load mutual funds directly from an investment company without paying any sales commission, you also can buy no-load insurance.

Annuities, which are more investment than insurance products (described in Chapter 8), are backed by insurers and are usually sold through insurance agents. In recent years, however, annuities have been increasingly sold directly to the customer, without sales commission, through such no-load mutual fund companies as Vanguard and Fidelity. (See Chapter 12.)

Discount insurance agents

Just as discount brokers, such as Charles Schwab and Quick & Reilly, allow you to buy and sell securities at substantially reduced commissions, two states (California and Florida) now permit discount insurance agents. Agents can't simply reduce the price of the policies they sell (because insurers forbid this), so discount insurance agents typically rebate back to you a portion of the commission that they earn, which effectively lowers your cost of buying coverage.

The largest and best discount insurance firms are California-based Direct Insurance Services (800-622-3699) and Florida-based Fee-For-Service (800-874-5602). These firms mainly sell life and disability insurance coverage. Direct Insurance Services rebates 50 percent of commissions back to you. Fee-For-

Service is paid a marketing fee (commission) by the insurers, so it doesn't rebate commission; however, its policies' prices are among the lowest available. Be sure to read Chapter 17 for more specifics about how to buy personal insurance coverage.

There is currently legislation before Congress that would repeal the insurance industry's federal antitrust exemption and allow agents in all 50 states to compete on the pricing of the policies that they sell and to allow agents to rebate commissions to consumers. Don't hold your breath on this getting through any time soon — insurance companies and agents are a powerful lobbying force. Most people don't even know that the legislation is pending or how it would benefit them, but you can bet the insurance companies and agents do and are maneuvering stealthily to defeat it.

If you would like to see the insurance industry opened up to the same competitive forces as other industries (which would save us all big bucks), write a letter to your state insurance commissioner, congressperson, senator, or the president today.

Employer and other group plans

When you buy insurance as part of a larger group, you generally get a lower price because of the purchasing power or clout of the group. Most health and disability policies that you can access through your employer (if it's a reasonably large one) are less costly than equivalent policies that you can buy on your own.

Likewise, many occupations have professional associations through which you may be able to obtain lower cost policies. Not all associations offer better deals on insurance, so make sure to compare what they offer with other options available to you.

Insurance agents who want to sell you an individual policy can come up with 101 reasons why buying from them is preferable to buying through your employer or some other group. Agents can't sell you a policy and make a commission if you buy your policy through a group plan. So in most cases, agents' arguments for buying a policy from them include a lot of self-serving marketing hype. In some cases, agents tell outright lies (which are hard to detect if you're not insurance-savvy).

In the chapters that follow, you'll learn exactly what you need in the policies that you buy so that you can determine whether a group plan meets your needs. In almost all cases, group plans, especially through an employer, offer the necessary benefits. So as long as it's cheaper than an identical policy you could buy as an individual, you'll save money buying through the group plan.

One exception to the group plan rule is life insurance. Group life insurance plans usually aren't cheaper than the best life insurance policies you can buy individually. If the policies are competitively priced, however, group policies may have the attraction of convenience (ease of enrollment and avoiding the long-winded sales pitches from life insurance salespeople). Group life insurance policies that allow your enrollment without a medical evaluation will probably be more expensive. If you're in good health, you should definitely shop around.

If you know you'll be leaving your job to become self-employed, it may make sense for you to secure an individual disability policy before you leave your job. Your employer's health insurer may allow you to convert your health insurance policy into an individual one when you leave.

The straight poop on commissions and how insurance is sold

The commission paid to an insurance agent is never disclosed through any of the documents or materials that you receive in the process of buying insurance. (This information ought to be disclosed by insurers and agents, just as sales charges on mutual funds are disclosed through a prospectus.) The only way you can know what the commission is on a policy and how it compares with other policies is to ask the agent. There's nothing wrong or impolite about asking. It's your money, after all, that pays the commission. You need to know whether a particular policy is being pitched harder because of its commission.

Commissions are typically paid as a percentage of the first year's premium on the insurance policy. (Many policies pay smaller commissions on subsequent premiums.) On life and disability insurance policies, for example, a 50 percent commission on the first year's premium is not unusual. On life insurance policies that have a cash value, commissions of 80 to 100 percent of your first year's premium are possible. Commissions on health insurance are lower, but generally not as low as commissions on auto and homeowner's insurance.

The Financial Health of Your Insurers

In addition to the price of a policy and the insurer's reputation and track record with claims, an insurer's financial health is an important consideration when you choose a company. If you faithfully pay your premium dollars year after year, you'll be more than a little bummed out if the insurer goes bankrupt right before you have a major claim.

Insurance companies can fail just like any other companies, and dozens do in a typical year. There are a number of organizations that evaluate and rate, with some sort of letter grade, the financial viability and stability of insurance companies. The following list includes the major rating agencies:

- ✔ A. M. Best
- ✔ Moody's
- ✔ Standard & Poor's
- ✔ Duff & Phelps
- ✔ Weiss Research

Letter grades work just the way they do in high school: A is better than B or C. Each company uses a different scale. Some companies have as their highest rating AAA, and then AA, A, BBB, BB, and so on. Others use A, A-, B+, B, B-, and so on. Just as some teachers grade more easily, some firms, such as A. M. Best, have a reputation for giving out a greater number of high grades. Others, such as Weiss Research, are tough graders. Unlike school, however, you want the tough critics when researching where to put your money and future security.

Just as it is a good idea to get more than one medical opinion, two or three credit ratings can give you a better sense of the safety of an insurance company. Stick with companies that are in the top two — or, at worst, three — levels on the different rating scales. The insurance companies recommended in the following chapters meet this criterion.

You can obtain current rating information about insurance companies, free of charge, by asking your agent for a listing of the current ratings. Ask the insurer itself if you are interested in a direct-sales policy.

While the financial health of an insurance company is important, it's not as big a deal as some insurers (usually those with the highest ratings) and agents make it out to be. Just as financially unhealthy banks are taken over and merged into viable ones, sickly insurers usually follow a similar path under the direction of state insurance regulators. In most failures, claims are paid. The people who usually lose out are those who had money invested in life insurance or annuities with the failed insurer. Even then, you'll typically get back 80 or 90 cents on the dollar of your account value with the insurer, but you may have to wait years to get it.

Help! I've Been Denied Insurance Coverage!

Just as you can be turned down when you apply for a loan, you can also be turned down when applying for insurance. For personal insurance, you can be turned down when you are found to have an existing medical problem (a preexisting condition). If you're applying for medical, life, or disability insurance, an insurance company will be less excited about selling you a policy if it sees a reason that you may be more likely than a person in good health to have medical problems that can lead to a claim.

Here are some strategies to employ if you are ever denied coverage:

- **Ask the insurer why you were denied.** Perhaps the company made a mistake or misinterpreted some information you provided in your application. If you are being denied coverage because of a medical condition, see what information the company has on you and whether the information is accurate.

- **Request a copy of your medical information file.** Many people don't know that just as you have a credit report file that details your use (and misuse) of credit, you also have a medical information report. You can request a current copy by writing the Medical Information Bureau at P.O. Box 105, Essex Station, Boston, MA 02112. You can also call them at (617) 426-3660. If there's a mistake on your report, you have the right to request that it be fixed. As with changing your credit report, the burden is on you to prove that the information in your file is incorrect. This can be a major hassle — you may even need to contact physicians you've seen in the past because their medical records could be the source of the incorrect information.

- **Shop other companies.** Just because one company denies you coverage doesn't mean that all insurance companies will. Some insurers better understand certain medical conditions and are more comfortable approving applicants with those conditions. Most insurers, however, charge a person with a blemished medical history a higher rate than a person with a perfect health record, but some companies penalize you less than others. That's why you must shop around even harder if you have a medical condition. An agent that sells policies from multiple insurers, a so-called "independent agent," can be helpful because they can shop among a number of different companies.

How to Get Your Insurer to Pay Your Claims

In the event you suffer a loss and file an insurance claim, it would be nice to believe that your insurance company will cheerfully and expeditiously pay your claims. Given all the money you've shelled out for coverage and all the hoops you jumped through to be approved for coverage in the first place, that's a reasonable expectation.

There are many reasons that insurance companies make your life miserable when you try to collect from them, however. In some cases, they may actually be right — your claim may not be covered under the terms of the policy. At a minimum, the insurer wants documentation and proof of your loss. Other people who have come before you have been known to cheat, so insurers aren't about to take your word for anything.

In other cases, though, you're right, and the insurers are just jerking you around. Some companies view paying claims as an adversarial situation and take a "negotiate tough" stance. It's a mistake to think that all insurance companies are going to pay you a fair and reasonable amount unless you make your voice heard.

The following tips tell you how to ensure that you get paid everything your policy entitles you to.

Document your case

When you're insuring assets, such as your home and its contents, it helps your case to have a record of what you own. A videotape is the most efficient record, but a handwritten list detailing your possessions works, too. Just remember to keep this record away from your home (if your home burns to the ground, you'll lose your documentation too!).

If you are robbed or are the victim of an accident, get the names, addresses, and phone numbers of witnesses. File police reports, too, if for no other reason than to document the problem for filing an insurance claim.

Prepare your case

Filing a claim should be viewed the same way as preparing for a court trial or an IRS audit. Any information you provide verbally or in writing can and will be used against you to deny your claim. First, you should understand whether the policy you bought covers your claim (this is why it helps to get the broadest coverage possible). Unfortunately, the only way to find this out is by getting out the policy and reading it. Policies are hard to read because they use legal language in non-user-friendly ways.

A possible alternative is to call the claims department and, *without* providing your name, ask a representative whether a particular loss (such as the one that you just suffered) is covered under its policy. There's no need to lie to the company, but there's no need to tell the representative who you are and that you're about to file a claim, either. You're call is informational so that you can understand what your policy covers. Some companies are not willing to provide very specific information, however, unless a specific case is cited.

After you initiate the claims process, keep records of all conversations and all copies of documents that you have provided the claims department. If you have problems down the road, this "evidence" can bail you out.

Enlist support

The agent who sold you the policy may be helpful in preparing and filing the claim. A good agent can help increase your chances of getting paid and getting paid sooner. If you're having difficulty with a claim for a policy obtained through your employer or other group, speak with the benefits department or a person responsible for interacting with the insurer. These folks have a lot of clout because of the potential threat to the agent and/or insurer of losing the entire account.

For policies that you buy on your own, try contacting the state department of insurance. You can find their phone number in the state government white pages of your phone book or possibly in your insurance policy.

If all else fails and you have a major claim at stake, try contacting an attorney who specializes in insurance matters. You can find these specialists in the yellow pages of your phone directory under "Attorneys — Insurance Law." Your state department of insurance, local bar association, or other legal, accounting, or financial practitioners also may be able to refer you to someone.

Chapter 17

Insurance on You

● ●

In This Chapter

▶ Life insurance

▶ Disability insurance

▶ Health insurance

▶ What you need and what you don't

▶ The most overlooked personal insurance.

● ●

*Y*our family and friends know how "valuable" you are. But your great personality doesn't have financial value — unless you're Jerry Seinfeld and you've parlayed it into a television show and bestselling book. If you're not financially independent yet, you need some insurance to safeguard one of your most valuable assets: your ability to earn an income. Multiply your current income by the number of years you plan to work — you'll come up with a pretty big number (unless you're not currently employed, in which case you should go back to your family and friends for a little ego boost).

In addition to protecting your income, you also need to insure against catastrophic expenses. I can't protect you against a spending spree, but I can tell you how to insure for payment of extraordinary expenses, such as those incurred during an illness or accident.

Life Insurance

If others are financially dependent on you, you may need some life insurance. If no one is financially dependent on you — if you're single or financially independent — rejoice that you don't need to waste any of your hard earned dollars on life insurance.

In a household with two income earners, you can forego life insurance if your household could still maintain an acceptable lifestyle if one of the incomes were gone. On the other hand, if you are dependent on each other's incomes, each of you should buy life insurance to provide a financial supplement in case one of you passes away.

Life insurance makes sense if you have major financial commitments and obligations, such as children and significant household expenses, including a mortgage or rent. It also makes sense to consider life insurance if an extended family member is currently or likely to be dependent on your future income. (Alternatively, if you have a will, you can leave assets to specific people to ensure they are taken care of when you're gone.)

How much do you need?

If you need life insurance, deciding how much to buy is as much a subjective thing as it is a data issue. I've seen some worksheets that are incredibly long and tedious (some are worse than your tax returns). There's no need to get fancy. If you're like me, your eyes start to glaze over if there are more than 20 lines of calculations to complete. It doesn't have to be that complicated.

The main purpose of life insurance is to provide a lump sum payment that replaces the deceased person's income. The question you need to ask yourself is how many years of that person's income do you want to replace? Table 17-1 provides a simple way to calculate how much life insurance you should consider purchasing. To replace a certain number of years of income, multiply the appropriate number in the table by the person's annual after-tax income.

Table 17-1	Life Insurance Need Calculation
Years of Income to Replace	*Multiply Annual After-Tax Income* by*
5	4.5
10	8.5
20	15
30	20

*You can roughly determine your annual after-tax income in one of two ways. You can get out last year's tax return (and form W-2) and calculate it by subtracting the federal, state, and social security taxes you paid from your gross employment income. Or you can estimate it by multiplying your gross income by 80 percent if you're a low-income earner, 70 percent if you're a moderate-income earner, or 60 percent if you're a high-income earner. (You need to replace only after-tax, not pre-tax, income because life insurance policy payouts are not taxed.)

Another way to determine the amount of life insurance to buy is to think about how much you will need to pay for major debts or expenditures, such as your mortgage, other loans, and college for your children. If, for example, you'd like your spouse to have enough of a life insurance death benefit to be able to pay off half of your mortgage and pay for half of your children's college education, then simply add half of your mortgage amount to half of their estimated college costs (see Chapter 14 for approximate numbers) and buy that amount of life insurance.

Social security, if you're covered, can provide so-called *survivors* benefits to your spouse and children. However, if your surviving spouse earns more than about $20,000 per year, he or she is not going to get any coverage (so you can skip the rest of this section). If either you or your spouse anticipates earning less than $20,000 per year, however, you may want to factor this into how much life insurance to buy. Contact the Social Security Administration at (800) 772-1213 and ask for form 7004, which allows you to receive an estimate of your social security benefits.

The Social Security Administration can tell you how much your survivors will receive per month in the event of your death. Suppose that this benefit amounts to 40 percent of your current income. The shortcut to factor this in the calculations you just did is to reduce the amount of insurance that you estimated you will need to replace your income (see Table 17-1). If social security survivor benefits will replace 40 percent of your income, you need to purchase only 60 percent (100 percent minus 40 percent) of the amount you calculated earlier.

Term versus cash value life insurance

In the next ten seconds, I'm going to tell you how you can save hours of time and thousands of dollars. Ready? *Buy term life insurance.* (The only exception is if you have a high net worth — a couple million bucks or more — in which case, you may want to consider other options. See the estate-planning section in Chapter 18.) If you've already figured out how much life insurance to purchase and this is all the advice you need to go ahead and buy it, you can skip the rest of this section (and go to the head of the class!).

The following information is for the rest of you who want all the details behind my recommendation for term insurance. Or maybe you've heard (and have already fallen prey to) the sales pitches from life insurance salespeople, most of whom love selling cash value life insurance because of the huge commissions it pays.

Cash value life insurance is the most oversold insurance and financial product in the history of the industry. As you'll soon discover, there is only a very small percentage of people for whom cash value life insurance makes sense. You would think that the vast majority of life insurance that is bought by people like you — and therefore sold by agents — is term. Wrong! The last numbers I saw showed that about 80 percent of life insurance that is sold is cash value because many people don't know any better. Don't make the same mistake.

Let's start with some background. Despite the variety of names that life insurance marketing departments have cooked up for policies, life insurance comes basically in two flavors:

- **Term insurance** is pure life insurance: You pay an annual premium for which you receive a predetermined amount of life insurance protection. If the insured person passes away, the beneficiaries collect; otherwise, the premium is gone. In this way, term life insurance is similar to auto or homeowner's insurance.

- **Cash value insurance.** All other life insurance policies (whole, universal, variable, and so on) combine life insurance with a supposed savings feature. Your premiums not only pay for life insurance, but some of your dollars are also credited to an account that grows in value over time, assuming you keep paying your premiums. On the surface, this sounds potentially attractive. People don't like to feel that all their premium dollars are getting tossed away.

  But there's a very big catch. For the same amount of coverage (for example, for $100,000 of life insurance benefits), cash value policies cost you about 8 times (800 percent) more than comparable term policies.

Agents know the buttons to push to get you interested in buying the wrong kind of life insurance. Here are typical arguments they'll make for purchasing cash value polices, followed by the real truth.

"It's all paid up after x number of years. You don't want to be paying life insurance premiums for the rest of life, do you?"

Agents show you all sorts of projections that imply that after the first 10 or 20 years of paying your premiums, you'll have such a large cash value in your policy that you won't need to pay more premiums to keep the life insurance in force.

The only reason that you may be able to stop paying premiums is that you've poured too much extra money into the policy in the early years of payment. Remember that cash value life insurance costs eight times as much as term. Imagine that you're currently paying $500 a year for auto insurance and an insurance company comes along and offers you a policy for $4,000 per year. They tell you that after 10 years, you can stop paying and still keep your same coverage. I'm sure you wouldn't fall for this sales tactic, but many people do when they buy cash value life insurance. You need to recognize that only by overcharging today can the insurer afford to continue your coverage in later years without a premium payment.

"You won't be able to afford term insurance when you are older or retired."

As you get older, the cost of term insurance increases because the probability of your dying rises. But life insurance is not something you need all your life! It's typically bought in a person's younger years when financial commitments and obligations outweigh financial assets. Twenty or thirty years later, the reverse should be true.

If you retire twenty or thirty years from now, you probably won't need life insurance to protect your employment income because there won't be any to protect! In the meantime, term insurance saves you a tremendous amount of money. For most people, it takes 20 – 30 years for the premium they are paying on a term insurance policy to finally catch up to (equal) the premium they've been paying all along on a comparable amount of cash value life insurance purchased today.

One exception to the preceding comment is the case of a small business owner who owns a business worth more than, say, one or two million dollars and who would not want his heirs to be forced to sell the business to pay estate taxes in the event of death. (See "Cash value life insurance" later in this chapter.)

"You can borrow against the cash value at a low rate of interest."

Such a deal! It's your money in the policy, remember? If you deposited money in a savings or money market account, do you think it would be much of a benefit to pay for the privilege of borrowing your own money back? If you borrow on the policy, you increase the chances of the policy exploding on you — leaving you with nothing to show for all the premiums to pay.

"Your cash value grows at a tax-deferred rate."

Ah, a glimmer of truth at last. It's true that the cash value portion of your policy grows without taxation until you withdraw it. But if you want tax-deferred retirement savings, you should first be taking advantage of such retirement savings plans as 401(k)s, 403(b)s, SEP-IRAs, and Keoghs (see Chapter 8) that give you an immediate tax deduction for your current contributions in addition to growth without taxation until withdrawal.

Money paid into a cash value life policy gives no up-front tax breaks to you. If you've exhausted the tax-deductible plans, then variable annuities or a nondeductible individual retirement account (IRA) can provide tax-deferred compounding of your investment dollars (see Chapter 8).

Life insurance tends to be a mediocre investment anyway. The insurance company quotes you an interest rate for the first year only. After that, it's up to the company's discretion for what it pays you. If you don't like the future interest rates, you can be penalized for quitting the policy (see "Cash value life insurance," later in this chapter). Would you ever invest your money in a bank account that quoted an interest rate for the first year only and then penalized you for moving your money in the next seven to ten years?

"It's forced savings."

Many agents argue that a cash value plan is better than nothing — at least it's forcing you to save. This is silly reasoning because so many people drop out of cash value life insurance policies after just a few years of paying into them.

If you like the idea of forced savings, there are many better ways of accomplishing it without using life insurance. Any of the retirement savings accounts mentioned in the preceding sales pitch can be set up for automatic monthly transfers. If your employer offers such a plan, it can deduct your contributions right out of your paycheck — and it doesn't shave a commission off the top!

"Life insurance is not part of your taxable estate."

This part of the sales pitch is about the only sound reason that exists for buying cash value life insurance. Under current federal laws, a single person can pass on $600,000 free of inheritance taxes; a couple can pass on $1,200,000. Even if you're one of the lucky, elite minority who can expect to pass away with such an estate, there are numerous other ways to reduce your taxable estate (see Chapter 18 for other estate planning options that reduce inheritance taxes).

Cash value policies are aggressively pushed by insurance salespeople because of the high commissions that insurance companies pay them. Commissions on cash value life insurance range from 50 – 100 percent of the first year's premium paid by you. An insurance salesperson, therefore, can typically make *ten times* (yes, you read that right) the commission by selling you a cash value policy rather than term insurance.

You are ultimately paying the high commissions that are built into these policies when you purchase cash value life insurance. As you can see in a policy's cash value table, you won't get back any of the money you dump in the policy if you quit the policy in the first two to three years. The insurance company can't afford to give you any of your money back in those first few years because so much of it has been paid to the selling agent as commission. That's why these policies penalize you in the first seven to ten years for withdrawing your cash balance.

In addition to the restrictive features of the "savings" portion of the cash value policies, these policies are expensive ways to purchase life insurance. Because of the high cost of these policies (about eight times the cost of term), you are more likely to buy less life insurance coverage than you need. — that's the sad part of the insurance industry's pushing of this stuff. The vast majority of life insurance buyers need more protection than they can afford to buy with cash value coverage.

Purchase low-cost term insurance, and do your retirement investing separately. Life insurance is rarely a permanent need, and over time, you can gradually reduce the amount of term insurance that you carry as you accumulate more assets and savings.

Term insurance features

Term insurance policies have several features to choose from. So that you can make an informed decision about purchasing term insurance, I'll briefly go over these features.

How often your premium adjusts

Term insurance can be purchased such that your premium adjusts (goes up) annually or every 5, 10, 15 or 20 years. The less frequently your premium adjusts, the higher the initial premium and its incremental increases will be. As you get older, the risk of dying increases, so the cost of your insurance goes up. The advantage of a premium that locks in for, say, 15 years is that you have the security of knowing how much you'll be paying. You also need not go through medical evaluations as frequently to qualify for the lowest rate possible The disadvantage is that you'll be paying more in the earlier years than you would on a policy that adjusts more frequently. In addition, you may want to change the amount of insurance you carry as your circumstances change, but would be throwing money away if you dump a policy in a long-term premium guarantee.

Policies that adjust the premium every five to ten years offer a happy medium between price and predictability.

Guaranteed renewability

This feature guarantees that the policy cannot be canceled because of poor health and is standard practice on better policies.

Insurer's financial stability

As discussed in Chapter 16, you should opt for insurers that will be here tomorrow to pay your claim. Don't get too hung up on the reliability of insurance companies, however, because term life settlements usually get paid, even if the insurer fails, because the state or another insurer almost always bails out the companies.

I do not recommend any additional riders or add-on features on life insurance policies because they are generally unnecessary, and they provide high profit margins for insurance companies and agents.

Where to buy term insurance

A number of sound ways are available to obtain high-quality, low-cost term insurance. If you choose to buy through a local agent — because you know her or because you'd prefer to buy from someone close to home — you should invest a few minutes of your time to get quotes from one or two of the following sources to get a sense of what's available in the insurance market. If nothing else, your familiarity with the market will prevent an agent from selling you an overpriced, high-commission policy.

Here are four places you can get high-quality, low-cost term insurance:

- ✔ **USAA** sells low-cost term insurance direct to the public (800-531-8000).

- ✔ **Fee-For-Service** is another good source for low-cost term insurance (800-874-5602). It is paid a marketing fee, which is basically a commission, from the companies whose insurance it sells.

- ✔ **Insurance agency quotation services** send you a handful of relatively user-friendly proposals from the highest-rated, lowest-cost companies available. Like other agencies, the services receive a commission if you buy a policy from them, which you're under no obligation to do. Unlike local insurance agents, they don't hound you (don't give them your phone number if you don't want to be called, however). They'll ask you your date of birth, whether you smoke, and how much coverage you'd like. The best quotation service in terms of customer service, pricing, and presentation of information is SelectQuote (800-343-1985).

- ✔ **Discount Brokers.** If you live in California you can buy term life insurance inexpensively from a discount broker. Direct Insurance Services (800-622-3699) is a big discounter. It sells mainly life and disability insurance coverage. Direct Insurance Services rebates typically 50 percent of commissions back to you.

How to get rid of cash value life insurance

If you were snookered into buying a cash value life insurance policy and want to get rid of it, go for it. *But don't cancel the coverage until you first secure new term coverage.* If you need life insurance, you don't want to have a period when you're not covered (Murphy's Law says *that's* when disaster would strike).

Cashing in a cash value life insurance policy has tax consequences. For most of these policies, you must pay tax on the amount you receive that is in excess of the premiums you paid over the life of the policy. Because some life insurance policies feature tax-deferred retirement savings, you may incur a 10-percent penalty on earnings withdrawn before age 59½, just the way you would with an IRA.

You can avoid early withdrawal penalties and taxation on accumulated interest in a life insurance policy you'd like to terminate by doing a tax-free exchange into a no-load (commission-free) *variable annuity policy.* The no-load mutual fund company through which you buy the annuity takes care of transferring your existing balance. If you want to withdraw the cash balance in your life insurance policy, check with the IRS or a tax advisor to clarify what the tax consequences may be. (See Chapter 8 for more information about annuities.)

If you need cash value life insurance

As discussed earlier in the chapter, purchasing cash value life insurance may make sense if you expect to have an inheritance tax problem (owing a lot of taxes). Read the section in Chapter 18 on estate planning before making any decisions.

Cash value life insurance is just one of numerous ways to reduce your inheritance taxes. Don't expect to get objective information on this important decision from anyone who sells cash value life insurance. Beware of insurance salespeople masquerading under the guise of self-anointed titles, such as estate planning specialists or financial planner.

Among the best places to shop for the best cash value life insurance policies are:

- ✔ **USAA** (800-531-8000)
- ✔ **Ameritas** (800-552-3553)
- ✔ **Fee-For-Service** (800-874-5602)

Note: Residents of California can also consider the discount insurance broker, Direct Insurance Services (800-622-3699), which rebates 50 percent of its commission to consumers.

If you want to obtain some cash value life insurance proposals, avoid local insurance agents at all costs, especially while you're in the learning stage (you're at a tender, vulnerable place). Agents aren't as interested in education as they are in selling (big surprise). Besides, the best cash value policies can be obtained free of most (or all) sales commissions if you buy from the preceding sources. The money saved on commissions is reflected in a much higher cash value for you — up to several thousand dollars worth.

Disability Insurance

As with life insurance, the purpose of disability insurance is to protect your income. The only difference is that you're protecting the income for yourself. If you're completely disabled, you still have living expenses, but you probably can't earn an income. If you throw out your back while reliving your athletic glory days with your aging adult body and wind up in bed for a couple of weeks, that won't be as much of a disaster to your finances as it is to your ego! What would be a financial disaster, however, is if you're disabled in such a way that you can't earn an income for several years.

Most large employers offer disability insurance to their employees. Many smaller employers and all self-employed people are left to fend for themselves. As a result, many people don't have disability coverage. Being without disability insurance is a risky proposition, especially if, like most working people, you need your employment income to live on. If you're married and your spouse earns a large enough income that you can make do without yours, then you may consider skipping disability coverage. (Keep in mind, though, that your expenses may go up if you are disabled and require special care or medical attention.) The same is true if you've already got enough money accumulated for your future years (you're financially independent).

It's easy for most people to dismiss the need for disability coverage. The odds of suffering a long-term disability seem so remote — and they are. But if you meet up with bad luck, disability coverage can alleviate you (and possibly your family) of a major financial burden.

Most disabilities are caused by medical problems, such as arthritis, heart conditions, hypertension, and back/spine or hip/leg impairments. Some of these ailments are caused by advancing age, but more than a third of disabilities are suffered by people under age 45. The vast majority of these medical problems cannot be predicted in advance, particularly those caused by accidents, which happen at random.

Social security pays long-term benefits only if you are not able to perform any substantial, gainful activity for more than a year or if your disability is expected to result in death. In fact, 70 percent of all applicants for social security disability benefits coverage are turned down. Furthermore, social security disability payments are quite low because they are intended to provide only for basic, subsistence-level living expenses.

Worker's compensation, if you have coverage through your employer, does not pay benefits at all if you get disabled away from your job. This compensation is too narrow a form of disability insurance — you need coverage that kicks in regardless of where and how you are disabled.

A few states have gotten into the disability insurance business, but the coverage is typically not extensive enough because benefits are paid over too short a period of time (rarely more than a year). State programs are also generally not good values because of the cost for the small amount of coverage they provide.

How much disability insurance do you need?

You need enough disability coverage to provide you with sufficient income to live on until other financial resources are available. If you don't have much saved in the way of financial assets and you would want to continue with the lifestyle supported by your current income, get enough disability coverage to replace your entire take-home (after-tax) monthly income. The benefits you purchase on a disability policy are quoted as dollars per month that you receive if disabled. So if your job provides you with a $2,000-per-month income after payment of taxes, then you ask for a policy that provides a $2,000-per-month benefit.

If you pay for your disability insurance, the benefits are tax-free (but hopefully you won't ever have to collect them). If your employer picks up the tab, your benefits are taxable, so you need a higher amount of benefits.

In addition to the monthly coverage amount, you also need to select the duration of time you want a policy to pay you benefits. You need a policy that pays benefits until an age at which you become financially self-sufficient. For most people, that's age 65 or so. If you've crunched some numbers (see Chapter 8) and see that you expect to be financially independent by age 55, you can usually get a policy that pays benefits that long — it'll cost you less than one that pays benefits to you until age 65. On the other hand, if you anticipate continuing to be dependent on your employment income past your mid-60s, you may want to obtain disability coverage that pays you until a later age.

If you're within five years of retiring or need benefits only for a few years because you're sure that someone (probably a family member) can support you financially over the long-term, you can buy a policy that pays benefits for just five years. These policies can save you a lot of money.

Other features you need in disability insurance

Disability insurance policies have many features that may be confusing to you. So that you can make an informed decision about purchasing disability insurance, I'll briefly go over these features.

- **Definition of disability.** An *own occupation* disability policy provides benefit payments if you cannot perform the work you normally do. Some policies pay you only if you're unable to perform a job for which you are *reasonably trained* (some policies revert to this definition after a few years of being own occupation). Own-occupation policies are the most expensive because there's a greater chance the insurer will have to pay you. It may not be worth the extra cost for you unless you're in a high income, specialized occupation, and you'd have to take a big pay cut to do something else (and you wouldn't be happy — apart from whatever the disability — about a reduced income and the required lifestyle changes).

- **Noncancelable and guaranteed renewable.** These features guarantee that your policy cannot be canceled because of poor health conditions. If you purchase a policy that requires periodic physical exams, you can lose your coverage just when you are most likely to need it.

✔ **Insurer's financial stability.** As discussed in Chapter 16, you should choose insurers that will be here tomorrow to pay your claim. But don't get too hung up on the safety of the company, because benefits are paid even if the insurer fails because the state or another insurer almost always bails them out.

✔ **Waiting period.** This feature is the "deductible" on disability insurance — the lag time between the onset of your disability and the time you begin collecting benefits. As with other types of insurance, you should take the highest deductible (longest waiting period) that your financial circumstances allow. This lag time significantly reduces the cost of the insurance and eliminates the hassle of filing a claim for a short-term disability. The minimum waiting period on most policies is 30 days, and the maximum can be up to 1 to 2 years. Consider a waiting period of 90 days or 6 months, if you can get along without income for that period of time.

✔ **Residual benefits.** This option pays you a partial benefit if you have a disability that prevents you from working full-time.

✔ **Cost-of-living adjustments (COLAs).** This feature automatically increases your benefit payment by a set percentage or in accordance with changes in inflation. The advantage is that it retains the purchasing power of your benefits. A modest COLA, such as 4 percent, is worth having.

✔ **Future insurability.** This is a clause that many agents will encourage you to add. Future insurability allows you, regardless of health, to buy additional coverage. For most people, it's not worth paying for the privilege of buying more coverage later because your income that you earn today fairly reflects your likely long-term earnings (except for cost-of-living increases). Because disability insurance is sold only as a proportion of your income, the only people for whom this feature might make sense are those whose income is artificially low now and who are not only confident of its rising significantly in the future, but also need to protect it. (For example, you just got out of medical school and are earning a low salary while working as a resident.)

✔ I do not recommend any additional riders or add-on features because they are generally unnecessary, insure small items, and are high profit items for insurance companies and agencies.

Where to buy disability insurance

The best place to check for buying disability insurance is through your employer or professional association. Unless these groups have done a lousy job shopping for coverage, group plans offer better value than you can purchase on your own. Just make sure that the plan that's offered meets the specifications discussed in the preceding section.

Don't trust an insurance agent to be honest about the quality of a disability policy your employer or other group is offering. Agents have a huge conflict of interest when they criticize these options because the group insurance cuts them out of the picture. If you opt to purchase disability insurance through a local agent, tread carefully. Some agents try to load down a policy with all sorts of extra bells and whistles to pump up the premium and their own commission.

If you need to purchase disability insurance on your own, check with Fee-For-Service (800-874-5602) and USAA (800-531-8000) for competitively priced policies. If you live in California, discount insurance broker Direct Insurance Services (800-622-3699) can sell you a policy at substantially reduced commissions.

If you buy disability insurance through an agent, use a process called *list billing*. With list billing, you sign up with several others for coverage at the same time and are invoiced together for your coverage. It can knock up to 15 percent off an insurer's standard prices. Ask your insurance agent how this works.

Other "Insurance" to Protect Your Income

Life insurance and disability insurance replace your income if you die or suffer a disability. But you could also see your income reduced or completely eliminated if you lose your job. There is no formal insurance policy to buy to protect you against the forces that can cause this to happen, but there are a few things you can do to reduce your risk.

Make sure that you have an emergency reserve of money that you can tap into if you lose your job. (Chapter 12 offers specific guidelines for deciding how much money is right for you.)

Another form of "insurance" is to continually attend to your skills and professional development. Not only does upgrading your education and skills ensure that you are employable if you have to hit the streets to look for a new job, it may also help you keep your old one.

Health Insurance

Everyone needs health insurance, but not everyone has it. Some people who can afford it choose not to buy it, believing that they're healthy and are not going to need it. Others who opt not to buy health insurance figure that if they ever really need it, they'll get care even if they can't pay. To a large extent, they're right, and the care is usually a lot more expensive by the time they seek it (due to advanced illness, emergency room visits, and so on). This is one reason for some of the millions of uninsured people.

Choosing the best plan for you

Before Medicare, the government-run insurance program for the elderly, kicks in at age 65, odds are you will obtain your health insurance through your employer. Be thankful if you do. Employer-provided coverage eliminates the headache of shopping for your own coverage and is usually cheaper than coverage bought on your own.

If you have options through your employer or need to hunt for a plan on your own, here are the major issues to consider when selecting among the health insurance offerings in the marketplace.

Major medical coverage

You need a plan that covers the *big* potential expenses: hospitalization, physician, and ancillary charges, such as X-ray and laboratory work. For women, if you're entering or already in your child-bearing years and may want to have children, make sure that your plan has maternity benefits.

Choice of physicians, hospitals, and other health care providers

Increasing numbers of health insurance plans contract with specific health care providers, which restricts your choices. Health maintenance organizations (HMOs) and preferred provider organizations (PPOs) are the main plans that restrict your choices. They keep the cost of the plan down because they negotiate lower rates with providers.

HMOs and PPOs are more similar than they are different. The main difference is that PPOs pay the majority of your expenses if you use a provider outside their approved list. If you do this with an HMO, you typically won't be covered at all.

Plans that allow you to use any health care provider you want are becoming less common and more expensive in most areas. If there is a particular physician or hospital that you have your heart set on using, check which health

Health insurers: bigger is usually better

With health insurance plans, you should give preference to plans that insure large numbers of people and that have been around longer. Many insurers operate in a bunch of different insurance businesses. You want those that are the biggest in the health insurance arena. Larger plans can negotiate better rates from providers, and older plans are more likely to be here tomorrow. The problem of your plan going under is not so much a risk that you might not get paid benefits — states usually bail out failed insurers — but that you might have to search for coverage with an existing medical problem. Nationally, Kaiser, Blue Cross, Blue Shield are the older and larger health insurers.

insurance plans they accept as payment. If you can't use their services in the restricted choice plans, ask yourself if the extra cost of the open-choice plan is worth being able to use their services. If you're interested in being able to use alternative types of medical professionals — that is, chiropractors, acupuncturists, and so on — check to see if the plans you're considering cover these services.

Don't be deterred from lower-cost HMO and PPO plans by stories of how hard it is to get an appointment with a doctor or other logistical hassles. This can happen in plans with open choice too — doctors are always running late or are overbooked. It is also a myth that doctors who can't get patients on their own are the only ones who sign up with restricted-choice plans.

Lifetime maximum

Health insurance plans specify the maximum total benefits that they'll pay over the course of your life. Although a million dollars may be more money than you could imagine having, that's the minimally acceptable level of total benefits. With the cost of health care today, you can blow through that in short order if you develop major health problems. Ideally, choose a plan that has no maximum or that has a maximum of at least two or three million dollars.

Deductibles and copayments

As with other insurance policies, if you pay the first chunk of money on claims, you'll save significant money on your premiums. Many policies have annual deductible options, such as $250, $500, $1,000, and so on, as well as copayments, typically 20 percent or so. Don't worry if you have a $100,000 claim — you won't have to pay $20,000 in the copayment. Plans with copayments almost always have maximum out-of-pocket limits (usually $1,000) that cap the total cost to you under the copayment. Most HMO plans (discussed earlier in this chapter) don't have deductible and copayment options. Most just charge a nominal amount — around $5 — for a physician's office visit.

To reduce your health insurance premiums, choose the plan with the highest deductibles and copayments that you can afford. In plans provided by your employer, give preference to plans with low out-of-pocket expenses if you know you have health problems since you'll be more likely to file claims.

Guaranteed renewable

You want a health insurance plan that will keep renewing your coverage without your needing to take more physical examinations to prove your continued good health.

Buying health insurance through agents

You can buy many plans through agents and some directly from the insurer. If it's sold both ways, it doesn't cost you anymore to go through an agent.

Health insurance agents have a conflict of interest common to all financial salespeople working on commission: The higher the premium plan they sell you, the bigger the commission they earn. So, an agent may try to steer you into higher-cost plans and not suggest some of the strategies discussed in the previous section to reduce your cost of coverage.

If you're denied coverage

When you try to enroll with a particular health insurance plan, you may be turned down because of health problems you currently have or previously had. It's possible that your *medical information file* (the medical equivalent of a credit report) contains information explaining why you were turned down. (Read the section in Chapter 16 to learn about what to do if you're denied coverage.)

If you have a so-called *preexisting condition* (current or prior medical problems), you have several options to pursue the secure health insurance:

- **Try health insurance plans that don't discriminate.** A few plans, typically Blue Cross, Blue Shield and some HMO plans such as Kaiser, will sometimes take you regardless of your condition.

- **Find a job with an employer whose health insurer doesn't require a medical exam.** Of course, this shouldn't be your only reason for seeking new employment, but it can be an important factor. Likewise, if you're married, you may be able to get into a group plan if your spouse takes a new job.

- **Check to see if your state offers a plan.** An increasing number of states (*more* than half, at last count), maintain pools that insure people with preexisting conditions who are unable to find coverage elsewhere. Try contacting your state's insurance department to see if your state offers such plans — you can find the phone number in the state government section of your phone book. I suppose, in a really drastic situation, if your state doesn't offer one of these plans, you could move to a nearby state that does.

Long-term care insurance

Long-term care insurance is meant to cover medical costs that Medicare doesn't. Medicare, the government-run health insurance plan for the elderly, is a comprehensive major medical plan. Enrollment in Part A (hospital expenses) is automatic. Part B, which covers physician and other charges including home health care coverage, is optional. If you have coverage under both parts you will be covered for most major expenses.

Medigap insurance

Medigap generally pays the deductibles and copayments that Medicare charges. Because the total Medicare deductibles and copayments for even the longest hospitalizations tend not to exceed several thousand dollars and are often less than $1,000, Medigap insurance isn't worth it for most people. If you are unable to pay for the deductibles and copayments because your income is low and you require repeated physician and hospital services, Medicaid, the state-run medical insurance program for low-income people, may help pay your bills.

Medicare often pays only 80 percent of the physician charges that the program allows on its fee schedule. Some physicians charge higher fees than allowed by Medicare, other don't. Check with your physician(s) to see that they do not charge a fee higher than that listed on Medicare's fee schedule. If they do, you should consider going to another physician if you can't afford the fee or want to save yourself some money.

The biggest fear and reason that elderly people consider extra health insurance is that Medicare pays only for the first 100 days in a skilled nursing facility. Anything over that is your responsibility. Medigap policies don't address this issue.

Nursing-home insurance

Insurance agents, eager to earn a hefty commission from selling you a policy, will tell you that *nursing-home insurance* is the solution to your concerns about an extended stay in a nursing home. Don't get your hopes up. This insurance is extremely difficult to shop for and unnecessary for most people. Policies are complicated and filled with all sorts of exclusions and limitations. On top of all that, they're expensive, too.

The decision to purchase nursing-home insurance is a tradeoff. Do you want to pay thousands of dollars annually from age 60 onward to guard against the possibility of a long-term nursing-home stay? If you live into or past your mid-80s, you could pay more than $50,000 to $100,000+ in a nursing-home policy. If you end up in a nursing home for years on end, you'll come out ahead financially if you bought nursing-home insurance. The majority of people are in homes less than a year, though, because they either pass away or move out.

If you have relatives or a spouse who would probably care for you in the event of a major illness, you should definitely *not* waste your money on nursing-home insurance. If it gives you peace of mind to know that a long-term nursing-home stay were covered, consider buying the insurance. Remember, though, that unlike other potential catastrophic expenses, you have a back-up already — *Medicaid* (state-provided medical insurance) can pick up the cost if you can't.

If you're concerned about having your stash of money wiped out by an extended nursing home stay and you've always dreamed of passing money onto family or a favorite charity, you could start giving it away while you're still healthy. If you're already in poor health, there are legal experts that do Medic-aid planning, which is strategizing to preserve your assets and keep them away from the government.

Consumer Reports last conducted a thorough evaluation of the major nursing-home insurance policies in their June 1991 issue. Don't even think about buying coverage or getting in the clutches of an insurance salesperson until you've read this insightful piece (try the library).

The Most Overlooked Form of Insurance

You buy health insurance to cover large medical expenses, disability insurance to replace your income in the event of a long-term disability, and perhaps life insurance to provide money in the event of your death to those dependent on your income. Many people buy all the right kinds of personal insurance, spending a small fortune over the course of their lives in the process. Yet they overlook the obvious, virtually free, protection: taking care of themselves.

If you work hard and use many of life's modern conveniences, you could end up being the Great American Couch Potato. Odds are that you've heard of most of these forms of "life insurance," but if you're still on the couch, it apparently didn't sink in. So, I'll review them for you sofa spuds:

✔ Don't smoke.

✔ Drink alcohol in moderation.

✔ Get plenty of rest.

✔ Exercise regularly.

✔ Eat healthfully (see the sidebar "Think about going veggie" and surround-ing areas in Chapter 6 for diet tips that improve your health and save you money).

✔ Get regular health care check-ups for medical, dental, and vision.

✔ Take time to smell the roses.

Chapter 18

Insurance for Your Assets

• •

In This Chapter

▶ Including important features in your homeowner's/renter's policy

▶ Deciding what automobile policy options are necessary and what are unimportant

▶ Planning your estate

• •

*I*n Chapter 17, I discussed the importance of protecting your ability to earn a living and insuring against large, unexpected medical expenses. But you also need insurance on your other assets such as your home, related personal property, and car.

You need to insure some of these other assets for two reasons:

✓ **Your assets are valuable.** If you were to suffer a loss, it could be a financial catastrophe for you to have to replace the assets out of your own pocket.

✓ **For liability purposes.** This reason is less well-known. If someone were injured or killed in your home or because of your car, a lawsuit could be even more financially devastating than an outright loss of the offending asset.

Homeowner's/Renter's Insurance

When you buy a home, most lenders require that you purchase homeowner's insurance. But even if they don't, you are wise to do so, because your home and the personal property within it are worth a great deal and would cost a bundle to replace.

As a renter, damage to the building in which you live is not your financial concern, but you still have personal property that you may want to protect. And there's also the possibility, albeit remote, that you could be sued by someone who is injured in your apartment.

Features to get on a homeowner's/renter's policy

When shopping for a homeowner's or renter's policy, you should consider the following important features.

Dwelling coverage

The amount of *dwelling coverage* you need should be determined by the cost of replacing a home that you own (renters don't need this coverage). (Condominium owners should check whether the coverage that the condo association has bought for the entire building is sufficient.) Neither the purchase price nor the size of your mortgage has anything to do with how much dwelling coverage you need. Ask yourself how much it would cost to *rebuild* your home if you lost it completely in a fire, an attack of locusts, or whatever. The cost to rebuild should be based on the size (square footage) of your home.

Be sure that your policy includes a *guaranteed replacement cost* provision. This nifty little feature ensures that the insurance company will rebuild the home even if the cost of construction is more than the policy coverage. If the insurance company underestimates your dwelling coverage, then *they* have to make up the difference.

Just to make your life more complicated, insurers define guaranteed replacement cost differently. Some companies pay for the full replacement cost of the home, no matter how much it ends up costing. Other insurers set limits. For example, the company may only pay up to 25 percent more than the dwelling coverage on your policy.

Note: Ask your insurer how it defines guaranteed replacement cost if you're concerned about this issue.

If you have an older property that has many expensive items that do not meet building codes, consider buying a rider that pays for code upgrades. This covers the cost of rebuilding your home to comply with building codes that are more stringent today than when your home was built. Ask your insurance company what your basic policy covers and what it doesn't cover. Some companies include a certain amount (for example, 10 percent of your dwelling coverage) for code upgrades in the base policy.

Liability insurance

Liability insurance protects you against lawsuits arising from bad things that happen to others on your property. At a minimum, you want enough insurance to cover your financial assets — covering two times your assets is better.

Buying extra coverage is inexpensive and well worth the cost. The probabilities of being sued are low but if you *are* sued, you could owe big bucks. If you have substantial assets to protect, you might consider umbrella or excess liability coverage (discussed later in this chapter).

This coverage is one of the side benefits of purchasing coverage as a renter — you protect your personal property as well as insure against lawsuits. (But don't be reckless with your banana peels now that you have liability insurance!)

Personal property coverage

On a homeowner's policy, the amount of personal property coverage is derived from the amount of dwelling coverage you carry. Typically, you get personal property coverage of 50 – 75 percent of the dwelling coverage. This is usually more than enough.

As a renter or condominium owner, you need to choose a dollar amount of the personal property that you want covered. Make a list (or take pictures or videos) of your belongings with an estimate of what they're worth. Keep this updated; you'll need it if you have to file a claim.

Some policies come with *replacement cost guarantees,* which pay you for the cost to replace an item. This payment can be considerably more than what a used item is worth when it's damaged or stolen. If this feature is not part of the standard policy sold by your insurer, you may want to purchase it as a rider, if available.

When filing a claim, it also helps your case to be able to document what personal property you had. Probably the simplest and fastest way to do this is to make a videotape of your belongings. Alternatively, you can maintain a file folder of receipts for major purchases and make a written inventory of your belongings. No matter how you document your belongings, don't forget to keep the documentation somewhere besides your home — otherwise it could be destroyed along with the rest of your house in a fire or other disaster.

Flood and earthquake insurance

As discussed in Chapter 16, you want to purchase the broadest possible coverage when buying any type of insurance. The problem with homeowner's insurance is that it is not broad enough — it doesn't cover losses due to earthquakes and floods. Such disaster coverage must be purchased piecemeal.

Many people mistakenly believe that earthquakes occur only in California. I wish this were true for those of you who live in the other 49 states, but it's not. In fact, one of the strongest earthquakes in history happened in the Midwest in the last century, and known (though not very active) fault lines lie along the

East coast. Because the cost of earthquake coverage is based on insurance companies' assessment of the risk of your area and property type, you shouldn't decide whether to buy insurance based on your perception of how small a risk a major quake is. The risk is already built into the price.

Another common misconception for not getting quake insurance is the belief that the government will bail you out. The vast majority of government financial assistance is through low-interest loans. Loans, unfortunately, need to be repaid, and the money will come out of your pocket.

Some people believe that in a major quake, insurers would go bankrupt and wouldn't be able to pay claims. This is highly unlikely given the reserves that insurers are required to keep and the fact that the insurance companies *reinsure* — that is, they buy insurance to back up the policies they write.

To help keep the cost of earthquake insurance down, consider taking a 10 percent deductible. Most insurers offer deductibles of 5 or 10 percent of the cost to rebuild your home. Ten percent of the rebuilding cost is a good chunk of money. But what you want to insure against is losing the other 90 percent.

There are approximately 20,000 communities around the country that can be affected by floods. Like earthquakes, floods are not a covered risk in standard homeowner's policies, so you need to purchase a flood insurance rider. Check with your current homeowner's insurer or those recommended in this chapter. The federal government flood insurance program (800-638-6620) can provide background information on the types of policies made available through private insurance companies.

The only people who might consider not buying earthquake or flood coverage are people who have little equity in their property and who are willing to walk away from the property and the mortgage in the event of a major quake or flood. Keep in mind that doing so damages your credit report, because you will have essentially defaulted on your loan.

You may be able to pay for much of the cost of earthquake or flood insurance by raising the deductibles on the main part of your homeowner's/renter's insurance and other insurance policies, such as those for autos. You can more easily afford the smaller claims, not the big ones. If you think flood or earthquake insurance is too costly, compare those costs with what you will incur to completely replace your home and personal property. Buy this insurance if you live in an area that has a chance of being affected by these catastrophes.

Crime insurance

If you live in a high-crime area, you may find that you're unable to find an insurer willing to sell you a policy. The federal government offers a Crime Insurance Program to help if you find yourself in this predicament. Call 800-638-8780 for more information.

Deductibles

As I discussed in Chapter 16, you're better off with the highest deductibles you're comfortable with. You'll save on insurance premiums year after year and you won't have to go through the hassle of filing small claims. The point of insurance is to protect against losses that would be catastrophic, not the little losses.

You may qualify for special discounts. Companies and agents that sell homeowner's and renter's insurance don't always check to see if you're eligible for discounts. If your property has a security system, if you are older, or if you have other policies with the same insurer, you may qualify for a lower rate. Don't forget to ask.

Where to buy homeowner's and renter's insurance

Each insurance company prices its policies based on its own criteria. So the lowest-cost company for my property might not be so for yours. You have to shop around for the best rates at several companies. The following is a list of companies that historically offer lower-cost policies for most people and that have good track records with customer satisfaction and payment of claims (based on state insurance department filings and *Consumer Reports* surveys):

- ✓ **USAA.** Available to military officers and their family members. Call the company for specifics to see if you might qualify (800-531-8080).
- ✓ **State Farm.** Check your local phone directory for agents who sell.
- ✓ **Allstate.** Check your local phone directory for agents who sell.
- ✓ **Nationwide Mutual.** Check your local phone directory for agents who sell.
- ✓ **GEICO.** Call for specifics (800-841-3000).

> ✔ **Liberty Mutual.** Check your local phone directory for agents who sell.
>
> ✔ **Erie Insurance.** Does business primarily in states in the Midwest and Mid-Atlantic. Check your local phone directory for agents who sell.
>
> ✔ **20th Century.** Does business only in California (800-443-3100).

You may have access to more-specific information for your state. Many state insurance departments, which you can locate through the state government listings in your phone book, conduct surveys of insurers' prices and tabulate complaints received.

Don't worry that some of these companies require you to call an 800 number for a price quote. This doesn't mean they are unreachable. This process saves you money because these insurers don't have to pay local agents commissions to hawk their policies. These companies also have local claims representatives to help you if and when you do have a claim.

Avid readers of *Consumer Reports* will note that some of the preceding recommended companies didn't earn the highest customer satisfaction ratings from that publication. State department insurance complaints are a more valid and reliable measure because they reflect actual reported problems. Self-reported customer satisfaction ratings (as in *Consumer Reports*) are subject to much more bias. A common example is that consumers who pay a higher price are more likely to be effusive in their praise if they haven't had a claim — people have a need to justify their choices, especially if they're spending a great deal of money.

A number of the previous companies sell other types of insurance that are not as competitively priced. Life insurance is a good example. (Check out the recommendations in Chapter 17 for the best places to purchase this type of insurance coverage.)

Auto Insurance

Over the course of your life, you'll probably spend tens of thousands of dollars on auto insurance. Much of the money that people spend on auto insurance is wasted, because their insurance money is not spent where it is most needed.

Factor the cost of insuring a car into your decision as to which car you buy. Simply call your insurer and ask for price quotes for the different models you're considering. Also, you may be eligible for special discounts on auto insurance. Don't forget to tell your agent or insurer if your car has a security alarm, air bags, and anti-lock brakes. If you're older or have other policies or cars insured with the same insurer, you may also qualify for discounts.

Features to have on an auto insurance policy

You should look for the following important features when searching for an auto insurance policy.

Bodily injury liability

As with homeowner's insurance, liability insurance provides insurance against lawsuits. In the case of your car, accidents can and do happen. Make sure you have enough liability protection at least to cover your assets. (Coverage of double your assets is preferable.)

Property damage liability

This insurance covers damage done by your car to other people's cars and property. It is usually determined as a consequence of the bodily injury amount selected.

Uninsured or underinsured motorist liability

If you are in an accident with another motorist and he doesn't carry his own liability protection, this coverage allows you to collect for lost wages, medical expenses, and pain and suffering incurred in the accident. If you already have a comprehensive major medical plan and long-term disability insurance, then this coverage is redundant. To provide a death benefit to those financially dependent on you in the event of a fatal auto accident, buy term life insurance (see Chapter 17).

You give up the ability to collect for general pain and suffering if you drop this coverage. Uninsured or underinsured motorist liability also covers passengers in your car who may lack adequate medical and disability coverage.

Deductible

To keep your premiums down and eliminate the need to file small claims, take the highest deductibles you are comfortable with (most people should consider $500 to $1000). On an auto policy, there are two deductibles: *Collision* and *Comprehensive.* Collision (you guessed it) applies to claims arising from collisions. Comprehensive applies to "comprehensive" claims — other claims for damages not caused by collision (for example, a window broken by vandals).

As your car ages and is worth less, you can eventually eliminate your comprehensive and collision coverages altogether. The point at which you do this is up to you. Remember that the point of insurance is to compensate you for losses that are financially catastrophic to you. For some people, this amount may be as high as $5,000 or more, whereas others would choose $1,000 as their threshold point.

"Little stuff," or coverage to skip

Auto insurers have dreamed up all sorts of riders, such as towing and rental car reimbursement, that cover small-dollar items that aren't usually worth insuring. On the surface, these little riders appear to be inexpensive. But given the small amount of money you could likely collect plus the hassle factor of filing a claim, they're quite expensive.

Riders that waive the deductible under certain circumstances make no sense either. The point of the deductible is to reduce your policy cost and the hassle of filing small claims. *Medical payments coverage* typically pays a few thousand dollars for medical expenses. If you and your passengers carry major medical insurance coverage, this rider isn't really necessary. Besides, a few thousand dollars of medical coverage doesn't protect you against catastrophic expenses.

Where to buy auto insurance

You can use the same list presented earlier in this chapter for homeowner's insurers to look for specific auto insurers.

Umbrella Insurance

Umbrella or excess liability insurance is additional liability insurance that is added on top of the liability protection on your home and car(s). If you are fairly affluent and have, for example, $700,000 in assets, you can buy a one-million-dollar umbrella policy for $200 or less per year to add to the $300,000 you have on your home and car. This is a small cost for big protection. Each year, several thousand people suffer lawsuits of more than one million dollars related to their cars and homes.

It is usually necessary to purchase this insurance through your existing homeowner's or auto insurance company.

Investment Insurance

Don't forget to diversify your investments to reduce the risk of your portfolio being whipsawed by a particular type of economic environment or the performance of a few securities. Chapter 10 discusses the benefits of diversification and how to choose investments that do well under different conditions. Chapter 11 discusses how mutual funds are powerful investment vehicles that make diversification easy and cost-effective.

Estate Planning

Estate planning is the process of preparing what is to happen to your financial assets when you die. It may seem a bit odd to think of this in the context of insurance. But the time and cost of various estate-planning maneuvers is really nothing more than buying insurance. Thinking about it in this way can help you to better evaluate whether or not certain options make sense at particular points in your life.

Wills

If you have minor (dependent) children, a *will* is a necessity to name a guardian for them. In the event that you and your spouse should both die without a will, the state (courts and social-service agencies) decides who will raise your children. Therefore, even if you cannot decide at this time who would raise your children, you should *at least* appoint a trusted guardian who could decide for you.

Without a will, your heirs are powerless, and the state will appoint an administrator to supervise the distribution of your assets at a fee of around five percent of your estate. A bond must also be posted at a cost of several hundred dollars.

If you don't have kids, a will still makes good sense to state your wishes for how you would like all your worldly possessions to be handled and distributed. If you die without a will, your state decides how to distribute your money and other property, according to state law. Therefore your friends, more-distant relatives, and favorite charities will probably receive nothing.

Living wills and medical power of attorney

These are useful additions to a standard will. A living will tells your doctor what, if any, life-support measures you would accept or would not accept. A medical power of attorney grants authority to someone you trust to make decisions with a physician regarding your medical care options.

The simplest and least costly way to prepare a will, a living will, and a medical power of attorney, is to use one of the high-quality, user-friendly software packages developed by attorneys (see Chapter 22 for my recommendations).

You don't need an attorney to prepare a will

Most attorneys, in fact, have administrative staffs prepare wills using software packages! What makes a will *valid* is that it is witnessed by three people.

According to recent research conducted by *Forbes* magazine, computer-generated wills have not caused any unusual problems to date. Hiring an attorney becomes more valuable when the value of your estate exceeds $600,000, the level at which estate taxes begin.

If doing it all yourself seems overwhelming, another option (besides hiring an attorney) is to use a paralegal typing service to help you prepare the documents. The National Association for Independent Paralegals (707-935-7951) can provide you with some names of paralegals in your area. These services generally charge 50 percent or less of what an attorney charges.

Probate and living trusts

Because of our quirky legal system, even if you have a will, some or all of your assets must go through a court process known as *probate*. Probate is the legal process for administering and implementing the directions in a will.

Property and assets that are owned in joint tenancy or inside retirement accounts (such as IRAs or 401-Ks) that have designated beneficiaries generally pass to heirs without having to go through probate.

A *living trust* effectively transfers assets into a trust. You control those assets and can revoke the trust whenever you desire. The advantage of a living trust is that upon your death, assets can pass directly to your beneficiaries without going through probate. Probate is a lengthy, expensive hassle for your heirs. Attorney probate fees run around 5 – 7 percent of the value of the estate. In addition, your assets become a matter of public record as a result of probate.

Living trusts are likely to be of greatest value to people who meet the following criteria:

- ✔ Age 60 and older
- ✔ Single
- ✔ Assets worth more than $100,000 that must pass through probate (including real estate, nonretirement accounts, and business)

As with a will, you do *not* need an attorney to establish a legal and valid living trust. (See the software recommendations in Chapter 22 and consider paralegal services mentioned in the previous section on wills). Attorney fees to establish a living trust can range from $700 to $2,000. A competent attorney who charges reasonable fees is of greatest value to people with large estates (greater than $600,000) who do not have the time, desire, and expertise to maximize the value derived from estate planning.

Note: Living trusts keep assets out of probate but have nothing to do with minimizing inheritance taxes.

Estate planning to minimize inheritance taxes

Whether or not you will have an inheritance tax problem is dependent on several issues. Under current tax laws, an individual can pass $600,000 and a couple can pass $1,200,000 to beneficiaries without federal inheritance taxes.

How much is left?

First and most importantly is how much of your assets you will use up during your life. This depends on how your assets grow over time, as well as how rapidly you spend money. During retirement, you will (hopefully) be spending your money.

I've seen affluent individuals worrying about inheritance taxes on their money throughout their retirements. If your intention is to leave your money to your children, grandchildren, or a charity, why not start gifting while you're still with us so that you can enjoy the act of giving? You can gift $10,000 annually to each of your beneficiaries, *tax-free*. By gifting money, you reduce your estate and, therefore, the inheritance taxes owed on it.

If you have substantial assets, a variety of other strategies can reduce your beneficiaries' inheritance-tax burden. A number of different trusts can help, as well as purchasing *cash-value life insurance*. Cash-value life insurance benefits are free of inheritance taxes.

What about my business?

Small-business owners whose businesses are worth one million dollars or more may want to consider cash value life insurance under specialized circumstances. If you lack the necessary other assets to pay expected inheritance taxes and you don't want your beneficiaries to be forced to sell the business, you can buy cash value life insurance to pay expected inheritance taxes.

What about life insurance?

People who sell cash value insurance — that is, insurance salespeople and others masquerading as financial planners — too often advocate life insurance as the one and only way to reduce inheritance taxes. A number of other methods discussed in this section are superior in most cases because they don't require spending money on life insurance (which is not free).

Learning more

A couple of good books can educate you further about reducing your inheritance taxes with estate-planning options:

- *Price Waterhouse Retirement Planning Advisor* (Pocket Books). Contains an excellent overview of estate planning to minimize inheritance taxes.
- *Plan Your Estate* by attorney Denis Clifford (Nolo Press). Gives more detailed information and strategies.

You may eventually want or need to contact an attorney who specializes in estate-planning matters. It's worth a little bit of your time to educate yourself first about the different options. More than a few attorneys have their own agendas (increased fees) about what you should do, so be careful.

Part V
The Part of Tens

The 5th Wave · By Rich Tennant

IN A BIZARRE MIX-UP, KEN BALANCES A BUS SCHEDULE INSTEAD OF HIS CHECKBOOK, AND THEN CONTINUES BY BOOKING A SEAT FOR HIM AND LAVERNE IN THE LOCAL BANK'S SAFE DEPOSIT BOX.*

* From that time forward, Laverne handled their financial affairs.

In this part . . .

You encounter what might be called a diverse and valuable hodge-podge. Here you'll find the choicest information, ranging from the best financial software packages to a list of common mistakes people make in their finances to common tax mistakes. Here you'll also find the all-important "Ten Questions to Ask Financial Planners Before You Hire Them," which may save you a lot of heart-ache and money. Why "tens"? Why not?

Chapter 19

Ten Most Common Financial Mistakes

● ●

*M*aking financial mistakes can cost you a lot of money and time and is terrible on the ego. This book will help you avoid many days in the school of hard knocks.

If you avoid major mistakes, you've won at least half the battle in managing your money. As a financial counselor, I see the mistakes that people make. And whether you have an M.B.A., G.E.D., or a wooden head, you're just as likely to fall into these common financial traps.

Not planning

Human beings were born to procrastinate. That's why there are deadlines and extensions. The IRS says you must file by April 15th. But you can get an extension for a few more months. With your finances, there are no deadlines to force you to get it together. And there are virtually unlimited extensions!

Procrastination and ignorance about how to get the most from your money is costly. You end up paying higher taxes, having gaps in your retirement and insurance coverage, and overpaying for financial products. Of course planning your finances isn't as much fun as planning a vacation, but doing the former will help you take more of the latter.

Overspending

If you hope to someday retire, or start that business you've dreamed of, or buy a home, you have to learn to save a good portion of your monthly income. Most people don't. Because we get an A+ as spenders.

The average American saves less than 5 percent of after-tax income (in contrast with the average Canadian who saves about 9 percent, French at 12 percent, German at 14 percent, and Japanese at 15 percent). It's a simple arithmetic result that savings is the difference between what you earn minus what you spend. So to increase savings, you have to work more (yuck!) or learn how to spend less.

Buying on credit

Even with the benefit of today's lower interest rates, carrying a balance month-to-month on your credit card or buying a car on credit means that even more of your future earnings are earmarked for debt repayment. Buying on credit encourages you to spend more than you can really afford.

Talk to your grandparents or parents who lived through the Great Depression, and they'll tell you a terrific financial rule to live by. Never borrow money to buy something that depreciates in value (like a car, clothing, or vacation). It's okay to borrow money for investments that could appreciate, such as real estate or a business (or education).

Not saving (early) enough for retirement (and overpaying taxes)

Most people say they want to retire by the their mid-60s or sooner. In order to accomplish this financially, you need to save a reasonable chunk (around 10 percent) of your income starting sooner rather than later (unless you're banking on an inheritance). The longer you wait to start saving for retirement, the harder it will be to reach your goal. And you'll pay much more in taxes to boot.

Falling prey to financial sales pitches

You work hard for your money. The last thing you want to do is have it slip through your fingers. Great deals that can't wait for you to think about it or to obtain a second opinion are often disasters waiting to happen. You're especially prone to be taken advantage of or to make the wrong financial decision when a person with a vested interest is pitching you.

A sucker may be born every minute, but a slick salesperson is born every second!

Not doing your homework

Many firms offer comparable products. So to get the best deal, you need to shop around. To be thorough, read some reviews and get advice from disinterested, objective third parties. You need to check references and track records to minimize your chances of hiring someone who is incompetent, self-serving, or out to defraud you.

Making decisions based on emotion

You are most vulnerable to making the wrong moves financially after a major life change (that is, job loss, divorce) or when you feel the pressure. Maybe your investments have plunged in value. Or a recent divorce has you fearing that you won't be able to afford educational expenses, so you pour thousands of dollars into some newfangled financial product.

Not separating the wheat from the chaff

In any field in which you're not an expert, you run the danger of following the advice of someone who you think is an expert but really isn't. Just because someone has authored an article or calls himself a financial planner doesn't mean he knows anymore on a given topic than you do. On many financial topics or decisions, if you ask ten people, you may get half a dozen different opinions and answers. While this may be useful if you're on *Family Feud*, you often need to choose the one path that's best for you. This book teaches you to separate the financial fluff from the financial facts.

Exposure to catastrophic risk

No, I'm not talking about going on a camping trip with 100 eighth-graders. If you or your family were to suffer a loss that would be financially devastating and don't have insurance to pay for the loss, you're too vulnerable.

Many in the Midwest, for example, didn't have flood insurance to pay for the devastating losses caused by the 1993 floods. In California in recent years, more than a few earthquake and fire victims were uninsured or inadequately insured. People without a savings reserve and support network can end up homeless. Many people lack sufficient insurance coverage to replace their income. Don't wait for a tragedy to strike to learn whether or not you have the right kind of insurance coverages.

Focusing too much on money

Sound financial management includes keeping money in its proper perspective. Too much emphasis on making and saving money can warp your perspective on what's important in life. Money is not the first or even second priority in happy people's lives. Your health, relationships with family and friends, and having a fulfilling career and interests are more important.

Chapter 20

Ten Questions to Ask Financial Planners before You Hire Them

● ●

*W*hen you hire a financial planner, there's a lot at stake. Besides the cost of their services, you're placing a lot of trust in the planner's recommendations. These ten questions get at the core of how a planner earns income, potential conflicts of interest, and competence.

What percentage of your income comes from fees paid by your clients versus commissions from the products you sell?

Asking this question first may save you the trouble and time of asking the next nine. The right answer is, "100% of my income comes from fees paid by clients." Anything less than 100% means the person you're speaking with is a salesperson with a vested interest in recommending certain strategies and product purchases.

All advisors who provide investment advice must register with the U.S. Securities and Exchange Commission (SEC). They must file Form ADV otherwise know as the "Uniform Application for Investment Advisor Registration." This lengthy document asks for very specific information from investment advisors, such as:

- ✔ A breakdown of where their income comes from
- ✔ Relationships and affiliations with other companies
- ✔ Each advisor's educational and employment history
- ✔ The types of securities the firm recommends
- ✔ The firm's fee schedule

In short, Form ADV provides — in black and white — answers to all the above questions. In a pitch over the phone or marketing materials sent in the mail, a planner is much more likely to gloss over or avoid certain issues. Although it's possible an advisor can lie to the SEC on Form ADV (it has happened on numerous occasions), it's likely an advisor will be more truthful on this form than in her own marketing to you.

You can ask the advisor to send you a copy of her Form ADV, or call the SEC for a copy at (202) 272-7450.

What percentage of fees paid by your clients are for ongoing money management versus hourly financial planning?

The answer here will provide a big clue as to whether the planner has an agenda to convince you to hire him to manage your money. If what you want are objective and specific financial planning recommendations, you should seek advisors who derive their income from hourly fees. Many counselors and advisors call themselves "fee-based," which usually means they make their living managing money. If you want a money manager, you can hire the best quite inexpensively through a mutual fund or an established money manager if you have substantial assets (see Chapter 11).

What is your hourly fee?

Rates, as with legal and tax advisors, vary all over the map. I've seen and heard of fees as low as $50 per hour all the way to several hundred dollars per hour. If you do shop around, you can find terrific planners who charge around $100 per hour and who work faster than a snail's pace. Since good planners spend a reasonable portion of their time researching and running their business, don't assume they're getting rich at your expense at this rate. Running a business is costly, but there's no reason you should pay $200-$300 per hour unless you're wealthy and want an advisor who only works with people like you.

Do you perform tax or legal services?

Be wary of someone who claims to be an expert beyond one area. The tax, legal, and financial fields are vast in and of themselves and are difficult for even the best and brightest planner to cover simultaneously. One exception is the accountant who also performs some basic financial planning by the hour. Larger firms may have specialists available in different areas.

What work and educational experience qualifies you to be a financial planner?

There's no one right answer here. Ideally, a planner should have experience in the business or financial services field. Some say look for planners with at least five or ten years experience. I've always wondered how planners earn a living their first five or ten years if folks won't hire them until they reach these benchmarks?! A good planner should also be good with numbers, speak in plain English, and have good interpersonal skills.

Education is sort of like food. Too little leaves you hungry. Too much might leave you feeling stuffed and uncomfortable. And less of high quality is better than a lot of low quality. Don't place too much value on the CFP (Certified Financial Planning) degree. Most planners with this "credential," which can earned by taking a self-study course at home, sell products. (See Chapter 3).

Have you ever sold limited partnerships? Options? Futures? Commodities?

The correct answers here are *no, no, no, no*. If you don't know what these disasters are, see Chapter 10. Be cautious working with any planner who claims to have reformed and seen the light to avoid these commission-laden, sure-loser places to put your money. Professionals with poor judgment may not repeat the same mistakes, but they're more likely to make some new ones at your expense. My experience is that even advisors who have "reformed" are unlikely to be working by the hour. Most work on commission or want to manage your money for a hefty fee.

Do you carry liability insurance?

You wouldn't (or shouldn't) let a contractor into your home to do work without knowing they have insurance to cover any mistakes they make if they make your home look like the one in the movie *Money Pit*. Likewise, you should insist on hiring a planner who carries protection in case a major mistake is made for which he is liable. Make sure he carries enough coverage given what he'll be helping you with.

Some counselors may be surprised by this question or may think you're a problem customer looking for a lawsuit. On the other hand, accidents happen and that's why insurance exists. So if the planner doesn't have liability insurance, she missed one of the fundamental concepts of planning: insure against risk. Don't you make the same mistake by hiring her.

Can you provide references of clients with needs similar to mine?

Take the time to ask other people what the planner did for them. Inquire what the advisor's greatest strengths and weaknesses were. You'll also learn a bit about the planner's track record as well as style. And because one of your goals should be to have as productive a relationship as possible with your planner, the more you learn about the planner, the easier it will be for you to hit the ground running if you hire her. Some advisors have even been known to lighten their fees for clients they get along with well.

Some financial advisors offer a "free" introductory consultation. If this is offered to allow you to check out the advisor, and you feel comfortable with hiring that planner, fair enough. My experience has been that most planners who do this work on commission or will try to sell you on a money management service. So the "free" consultation ends up being a big sales pitch for why you should buy certain products or services through them.

The fact that a planner doesn't offer a "free" consultation may be a good sign. Counselors who work strictly by the hour and are busy can't afford to burn an hour of their time for an in-person "free" session. They also need to be careful of folks seeking "free" advice. Such advisors usually are willing to spend 15-20 minutes on the phone answering background questions. They should also be able to send background materials by mail and provide references if you ask.

Will you provide me with written strategies and product recommendations that I can implement on my own if I choose?

This is an important question. Some advisors may indicate that you can hire them by the hour. But then they only provide generic advice without much specifics. Even worse is the troubling trend among planners who "double dip" — they charge an hourly fee to make you feel like you're not working with a salespeople. Then they try selling commission-based products. Also beware that some advisors say that you can choose to implement the plan on your own, but then they only recommend financial products with commissions.

How is implementation handled?

Ideally, find a planner who gives you a choice whether or not you can hire him to help with implementation once the recommendations have been presented to you. If you know that you will follow through on the advice and can do without further discussions and questions, don't buy the planner's time to implement. On the other hand, if you hired the counselor in the first place because you lack the time, desire, and/or expertise to manage your financial life, building implementation into the planning work makes good sense. If you're the type of person who needs to tie a string around a finger to remember to do something but then forget why it's there, pay for the necessary hand-holding.

Chapter 21

Ten Costly Financial Planning and Tax Mistakes

• •

*Y*our taxes should not be an island unto themselves. Your financial planning decisions should factor in your taxes. The tax system is hopelessly and unreasonably complicated, but there's no reason you can't learn from the mistakes of others. The following are the most typical tax-costly blunders.

Not saving and investing through retirement accounts

All the tax deductions and tax deferrals that come with accounts such as 401(k)s and IRAs were put in the tax code to encourage saving for retirement. So why not take advantage of the benefits? You probably have your reasons or excuses — that's why there's a list of reasons why people underfund retirement accounts in Chapter 8. Most reasons just don't make good financial sense. Read the list!

Even if you're not immediately motivated toward retirement, you can use retirement savings to achieve other financial goals. For example, some employer retirement plans allow you to borrow against your account balance. You can save for down payment on a home, for example, reduce your taxable income while you're saving, and then borrow from yourself when you need the money.

Not buying a home

In the long run, owning should cost you less than renting. And because mortgage interest and property taxes are deductible, the government in effect subsidizes the cost of homeownership. So treat yourself to your own abode. And don't let the lack of money for a down payment stand in your way — there are many ways to buy real estate with little money down. (See Chapter 15 for ideas.)

Ignoring the financial-aid tax system

Money that you save outside of tax-sheltered retirement accounts is assumed to be available to pay educational expenses by the college financial-aid system in this country. As a result, middle- and upper-income families qualify for far less financial aid than they otherwise would. So, in addition to normal income taxes, an extra financial-aid tax is effectively exacted. Be sure to read Chapter 14, which talks about the right and wrong ways to save and invest for educational costs.

Getting advice after a major decision

Too many people hire help *after* a disaster to clean up (or cover up). It is generally wiser and less costly to seek preventative help. Don't use a tax preparer just to fill in the numbers on your return. You may need help in making decisions during the year before it's time to file the tax return (when it's probably too late to change many of the previous year's activities).

Make sure to get advice before you make any major moves. The wrong move when selling a piece of real estate or taking a large sum from a retirement account could cost you thousands in taxes.

Not withholding the right amount of taxes

If you're self-employed or earn significant taxable income from investments outside of retirement accounts, you should be making quarterly tax payments. Likewise, if during the year you sell a major asset at a profit, you may need to make a quarterly tax payment.

Don't be a "should've" victim. People often don't discover that they should have paid more taxes during the year until they complete their return in the spring or get a penalty notice from the IRS and their state. Then they have to come up with a sizable sum all at once.

Some self-employed people dig themselves into a perpetual tax hole. They get behind during their first year of self-employment and are always playing catch-up.

Call the IRS at 800-TAX-FORM and ask for Form 1040-ES, *Estimated Tax for Individuals*. This form explains how to calculate quarterly tax payments and includes payment coupons and envelopes in which to send your checks. If you can't figure it out or hate forms, call a tax preparer — now.

Some people have too much tax withheld during the year. The overpayment may occur year after year. Although it's nice to get a hefty refund check every spring, why should you loan money to the government interest-free? If you know that you would otherwise spend the money, then this forced savings strategy may have some value. But there are other, better ways to force yourself to save. You can set up all sorts of investments funded by automatic contributions from your paycheck or from a bank or investment account. Of course, if you *prefer* to loan the IRS more money, go right ahead.

Being a Zöe Baird

Poor Zöe Baird. She was President Clinton's nominee for Attorney General who was nixed because she didn't pay social security taxes for her nanny. If you have household employees who are U.S. citizens, it's better to withhold social security taxes. You're supposed to do so for any household employee whose wages exceed $50 in a calendar quarter.

Each year, millions of other household employers make the same violations that Zöe Baird did. These folks aren't bad people. Yes, the tax laws in this area are a nightmare. Nevertheless, you should follow them.

Besides complying with the law, you benefit because you may be allowed to take advantage of tax breaks when the person helps with childcare. Employees benefit by building up social security credits that qualify them for monthly retirement income payments.

Call the IRS (800-TAX-FORM) and ask for Form 942, *Employer's Quarterly Tax Return for Household Employees.* This form is supposed to be filed quarterly — you have a full month after the end of each quarter to file (for example, until the end of April for the January-to-March quarter). Once a year, you also need to pay unemployment tax for household employees whom you pay $1,000 or more per calendar quarter. Request Form 940, *Employer's Annual Federal Unemployment Tax Return,* from the IRS. Some states have similar requirements — contact your state's employment tax office for information.

Not taking legal deductions

In most cases, folks miss out on perfectly legal deductions because they don't know that they can take them. Ignorance is costly. So, if you're not going to take the time to learn about the tax system, spring for the cost of a competent tax preparer at least once. If you have a computer, try one of the user-friendly software packages or preparation guides.

Fearing an audit, some taxpayers (and even some tax preparers) avoid taking deductions that they have every right to take. Unless you have something to hide, this oversight is expensive and silly. Remember that a certain number of returns are randomly audited every year, so you may do nothing wrong or inappropriate and get audited anyway!

Ignoring tax considerations when investing money

Suppose that you have some stock that you want to unload so that you can buy a sexy new car. You figure out which of your stocks has the poorest future prospects but is riding high, sell it at a significant capital gain, and generally feel pretty good about yourself. Come tax time, you may feel differently. The taxes due from the sale of investments (except those in retirement accounts) should factor into all your decisions about what you sell and when.

What you invest in (outside of retirement accounts) should also be driven by your tax situation. If you're in a relatively high tax bracket, you probably don't want investments that pay much in taxable distributions, which only add to your tax burden (see Chapter 12 for more info).

Ignoring timing of events you can control

The amount of tax you pay on certain transactions can vary, depending on the timing. If you're nearing retirement, for example, you may soon be in a lower tax bracket. To the extent possible, you should delay investment income until your taxable income drops and take as many deductions or losses as you can now.

Not using tax advisors properly

If your situation is at all complicated, it's usually a mistake to go it alone and rely only on IRS guides. They're certainly not going to highlight opportunities for tax reduction and are sometimes hopelessly complicated. Try a preparation or advice book or software package.

If you're not willing to make that effort, don't make the mistake of not hiring a tax advisor or preparer. You'll probably more than save the tax preparer's fee if you try to go it alone but don't know what you're doing.

It's most beneficial to use a tax advisor when you're faced with new tax questions or problems. If your situation remains complicated or you would do a worse job on your own, by all means keep using a preparer. But don't pay a big fee year after year to a tax advisor who simply fills in the blanks. If your situation is unchanging or not that complicated, go ahead and try it yourself.

Chapter 22

Ten Great Financial Software Packages

● ●

*A*s with other components of the information superhighway, the number and quality of personal finance software packages is growing rapidly. Good software can guide you to better organization and management of your personal finances, it can help you complete mundane tasks or complex calculations more quickly and easily, and it can provide basic advice in unfamiliar territory.

Good software can make you feel in control of your life. Mediocre and bad software can make you feel like a dummy — or at the very least, make you want to tear your hair out. Mediocre and bad packages usually end up in the software graveyard.

Having reviewed many of the packages available, I can assure you that it's not your fault if you can't use some of this stuff. Too many packages assume that you already know things such as your tax rate, what your mortgage options are, and the difference between stock and bond mutual funds. Much of what's out there isn't user-friendly and is too technically oriented. Some of it is even flawed in its financial accuracy.

A good software package, like a good tax or financial advisor, should be your partner in helping you better manage your finances. It should simply and concisely explain financial terminology and provide a road map to help you make decisions by offering choices and recommendations so that you can "play" with alternatives before following a particular course of action.

With increasing regularity, financial software packages are being designed to do more than one task or to address more than a single area of personal finances. But there are no packages that cover the whole range of issues in your financial life. Here are my recommendations by category for the best of what's outthere:

Note: My recommendations for the *best* personal finance software packages appear in **bold** type. I mention the runners-up if they make sense for certain types of situations, but they are not highlighted in bold. Unless otherwise stated, you can purchase the recommended software packages through most software sellers.

Checkbook and bill payment software

Every month, you write out by hand a bunch of checks, many of which go to the same organizations you paid in prior months. Besides being a repetitive, time-consuming chore, hand-writing those checks doesn't help you figure out how much you spent on different areas of your budget during the past six or twelve months.

Checkbook software automates the process of paying your bills and prepares the reports that detail your spending by category — so that you can get a handle on where the fat is in your budget. In addition, when you have to make your monthly payment to the phone company, for example, your monthly check, already made payable to the phone company, pops up on-screen at your command. All you have to do is fill in the new amount that you have to pay. And your checks get printed on your computer's printer, completely eliminating the process of writing and mailing in checks. (For a small monthly fee, you can even pay your bills electronically.)

Quicken (available in Windows, DOS, and Macintosh versions) is the best and easiest to use checkbook software. A big reason for this usability is that Intuit, the company that produces Quicken, has an unusually strong commitment to soliciting feedback from real people who use the product. In addition to offering the printed checks and electronic bill-payment features, Quicken is a great financial organizer. The program also allows you to track your investments and other assets and your loans and other financial liabilities.

Over time, Intuit has added a number of enhancements to the program that allow you to do some nifty things besides paying your bills with computerized checks:

- A financial calendar can remind you when it's time to pay particular bills.

- Quicken's Intellicharge system offers a solution to the problem of untracked spending via credit card transactions. If you use a Quicken VISA credit card and pay a small fee, the Intellicharge feature allows you to receive your monthly transactions by modem or on diskette. Quicken can then track both your credit and check spending.

- Quicken Companion (available in the Windows version only) is a small add-on package that enables you to estimate and analyze the tax consequences of various financial maneuvers and to track and obtain current prices for your investments.

Although many small-business owners have used Quicken for their accounting needs, **QuickBooks** (available in the Windows and DOS versions) is a nifty, straightforward software package specifically designed for keeping track of the finances for a small business.

Retirement planning software

Retirement planning software helps you to plan for retirement by crunching the numbers for you. But it can also teach you how particular changes — such as your investment returns, rate of inflation, your savings rate — can affect when, and in what style, you can retire.

The most user-friendly and educational retirement planning package is the **Fidelity Retirement Planning Thinkware** (DOS version only). The program advises you on the importance of saving for retirement and, through various modules, leads you step-by-step through the calculations of how much you need to save for retirement.

Not only does the package help you with the calculations based on straightforward assumptions, it lets you get fancy and play with the assumptions. The software also gives you advice on how to allocate your investment dollars to different types of investments and presents background information on Fidelity's mutual funds, which are among the best in the country. This package is only available through Fidelity (800-457-1768) and costs $15.

A solid retirement-planning program is Vanguard's Retirement Planner (available in a DOS version that you can run under Windows as well). This program is not as user-friendly or graphically appealing as Fidelity's. One of its major drawbacks is that it is designed to run numbers for only one individual. Two-income couples have to run the program for each person individually.

What I like best about Vanguard's software is the investment history lesson it offers. You can take an historical tour through the years to gain an understanding how stocks, bonds, and savings-type investments have performed during different time periods. "Worst" performance years are also highlighted to show you the risk inherent in certain types of investments. A separate module can help educate you about the different mutual funds available through Vanguard, one of the nation's largest and best mutual fund companies. This software can only be purchased through Vanguard (800-876-1840) and sells for $15.

Quicken and some of the other checkbook packages have retirement-planning calculators that do a decent job in giving you a sense of where you stand with saving and planning for retirement. If you're a Macintosh user, Quicken for Macintosh is a good option.

Tax preparation software

Tax preparation software can save you lots of time and money. Unlike most other personal finance software, this type of software is relatively easy to learn because you just have to enter data that the program specifically asks for. The program then plugs the data into the appropriate tax form. Good tax preparation software contains virtually every form you may need to file your return. This feature virtually eliminates any chance that you have to run to the post office for specialized forms you didn't realize you'd need until April 14th.

The best tax preparation programs are **TurboTax** (Windows and DOS versions) and **MacInTax** (Macintosh version). These programs are easy to use. They "interview" you to gather the necessary information and select the appropriate forms based on your responses. More experienced taxpayers can bypass the interview and jump directly to the forms they know they need to complete. Both programs do a superb job of flagging overlooked deductions and identifying strategies for specific situations.

In addition to the federal tax packages, tax preparation programs are available for state income taxes too. TurboTax for DOS is available for all states, and the Windows version is available for 19 states and the District of Columbia. If you want a state tax program and live in a state for which TurboTax is not available, Personal Tax Edge is an alternate selection for Windows and is available for all states that have an income tax except Hawaii and Washington DC. Many state tax forms are fairly easy to complete because they are based on information from your federal form. If that's your situation, you may just skip buying the state income tax preparation packages and prepare the state return by hand.

Investment software

There are two major types of investment software. The first type of package allows you, through data that you enter, to track and create reports on your investments. For beginning investors or those who just want a simple, easy-to-understand system for tracking the value and performance of their investments, **Quicken** (in DOS, Windows, and Mac versions) is your best bet. Quicken Companion allows you to obtain current price quotes for your mutual fund and other security investments (so that you can monitor your investments every night, if you'd like).

If you want a more extensive analysis that comes with advice, one of the oldest packages on the market is Managing Your Money (available in DOS and MacIntosh versions; Windows version rumored to appear soon). While I can recommend this program for those who want a sophisticated investment tracking and management package, I do so with qualifications. Software reviewers, who tend to be impressed with technical gizmos, love it, but I think this package is the most overrated in the field because it is not very user-friendly. In addition to investment management, Managing Your Money contains checkbook features and electronic bill-payment features. However, Quicken is easier to use — and less expensive — for these purposes.

The second type of investment software allows you to actually invest and trade, as well as do investment research, through your computer. These packages allow investments through a specific investment company. Your choice of the investment company is the major difference among the recommended packages. (For more information on deciding which investment firms you'd like to work with, see Chapter 11.) An added benefit of investing through this type of software is the 10 percent discount on transaction fees for trades placed through your computer.

StreetSmart is a relatively new package introduced in 1993. Developed by Charles Schwab & Company, StreetSmart allows you to access current information from your Schwab investment accounts and to analyze your portfolio. This feature eliminates the cumbersome process of manually entering all the information into your computer. (If you have other investments you want to track, you can manually enter them with this software.)

StreetSmart also gives you a financial library at your fingertips. For a small fee, you can access research reports from independent analysts and other financial data about thousands of companies. You can also obtain financial news and current securities prices. This software can only be purchased through Charles Schwab, either by calling (800) 334-4455 or at one of their branch offices. StreetSmart costs $59.

If you're a DOS user, your two choices are the **Fidelity On-line Xpress**, for investing through Fidelity, and The Equalizer, for investing through Schwab. Like StreetSmart, both of these packages allow you to trade on-line, access research reports and account information, and create summaries of your investments. These packages are more similar than they are different. Fidelity's software has a few more bells and whistles, but you should make your choice based on which investment firm you'd rather use. The Equalizer is available from Schwab (800-334-4455) and costs $59. On-line Xpress can be purchased through Fidelity (800-544-0246) or Egghead Software stores for $50.

Investment tracking and trading software can be helpful, but it can also encourage people to trade more than they should. Following investments on a daily basis (which some people do through newspapers) encourages you to think short term. Remember that the best investments are bought and held for the long haul (see Chapters 10 and 11 for more information).

If you are attracted to using the software for the 10 percent trading discount, you can have your cake and eat it too: Place your trades through Fidelity or Schwab by using a touch-tone telephone and get your 10 percent discount without spending your time and money on software.

Legal software

Just as you can prepare a tax return with the advice of a software program, you can also prepare common legal documents. This type of software may save you from the often difficult task of finding a competent and affordable attorney. Preparing documents with software can also save you money.

Using legal software is generally preferable to using fill-in-the-blank documents. Software has the built-in virtues of directing and limiting your choices and keeping you from making common mistakes. Quality software also incorporates the knowledge and insights of the legal eagles who developed the software.

If your situation isn't unusual, legal software may work well for you. As to the legality of documents that you create with legal software, remember that a will, for example, is made legal and valid by your witnesses; the fact that an attorney prepares the document is *not* what makes it legal.

The hands-down best package available to prepare your own will is **WillMaker** (available in Windows, DOS, and MacIntosh versions). This package is published by Nolo Press, a name synonymous with high quality and user friendliness in the legal publishing world. In addition to allowing you to prepare wills (in every state except Louisiana), WillMaker can help you prepare a *living will* and medical power of attorney (see Chapter 18).

Nolo's Living Trust software (available only for the Macintosh; Windows version reportedly in the works) allows you to create a living trust that serves to keep property out of probate in the event of your death (see Chapter 18). Like wills, living trusts are fairly standard legal documents that you can properly create with the guidance of a top-notch software package. The Living Trust package also advises you to seek professional guidance for your situation, if necessary.

The 5th Wave   By Rich Tennant

"I THINK 'FUZZY LOGIC' IS AN IMPORTANT TECHNOLOGY TOO. I'M JUST NOT SURE WE SHOULD FEATURE IT AS PART OF OUR TAX PREPARATION SOFTWARE."

Index